What those who have read the

When I read the devotions, I am definitely feasting on something rich, deeply spiritual, satisfying. But they don't stop with just spiritual food; each one contains a tasty recipe to satisfy our physical hunger. I highly recommend this book to every person who has a soul and family to feed.

—MARIE ARMENIA
AUTHOR, SONGWRITER, SINGER, SPEAKER
MEMPHIS, TENNESSEE

Karen's approach in responding to our God-given mandate to disciple others is creative, relevant, and enjoyable. Her meaningful selection of Scriptures and insightful applications for our daily lives reminds us that we do not "live on bread alone." *Food for the Hungry Soul* is a model for a "home mentoring" experience. The recipes, coupled with the written word, will satisfy a hunger to see radical change in lives as we set the table and engage in meaningful relationships with family and others. This is truly a recipe for living life intentionally with a touch of nostalgia from a proven kitchen! God's anointing rests on the home, and I believe this book to be God-inspired and encouraging.

—ANNE BLANCHARD
LICENSED ASSEMBLIES OF GOD MINISTER
CARLINVILLE, ILLINOIS

I love the devotions because they guide me spiritually in my daily life. It is so good to know that God's message goes all around the world, and I am blessed to be a part of this wonderful chain of prayer. What a great God we worship! I love the physical nourishment too— our Lord cares for all aspects of our lives.

—MILDRED BLUETT, CHURCH STEWARD
CINDERFORD, GLOUCESTERSHIRE, UNITED KINGDOM

God has blessed me with these daily inspirations so I might experience His grace and peace and in turn share His love with others. I especially like the prayers that help me explore my own weaknesses and refine my way of communicating with the Lord. How blessed we are to learn His words and walk His path together, even though we are in different corners of the world.

—NOREEN MAK, MARKETING AGENT
HONG KONG

The devotions reach down to where we live and make the Word alive in our spirit. They speak to life's issues with clear direction from God's Word and bring hope and encouragement for the journey.

—DANIEL SINACORI, GOSPEL SINGER, COMPOSER
NORTH PORT, FLORIDA

Karen's urgency for those who don't have a personal relationship with Jesus is depicted in her articulate devotional with passionate honesty. Her sincere desire for all to spend eternity in heaven praising God is evident as she deciphers the Bible and presents it in an understandable manner. Her love for Christ radiates from the page and is an example to everyone.

—MINDY TOUTANT, TEACHER
BLOOMSBURG, PENNSYLVANIA

FOOD for the HUNGRY SOUL

Taste and see that the Lord is good.
Psalm 34:8

Love,
Karen

Daily devotions and recipes for God's hurried people

FOOD
for the HUNGRY
SOUL

KAREN DOUGHTY

CREATION
HOUSE

Food for the Hungry Soul by Karen Doughty
Published by Creation House
A Charisma Media Company
600 Rinehart Road
Lake Mary, Florida 32746
www.charismamedia.com

Unless otherwise noted, all Scripture quotations are from the Holy Bible, New International Version. Copyright © 1973, 1978, 1984, International Bible Society. Used by permission.

Scripture quotations marked KJV are from the King James Version of the Bible.

Design Director: Bill Johnson
Cover design by Terry Clifton

Visit the author's website: foodforthehungrysoul.wordpress.com

Library of Congress Cataloging-in-Publication Data: 2012931525
International Standard Book Number: 978-1-61638-935-2
E-book International Standard Book Number: 978-1-61638-936-9

First edition

12 13 14 15 16 — 9 8 7 6 5 4 3 2 1
Printed in the United States of America/Canada

DEDICATION

To my four daughters, whom I love with all my heart:

Debbie,

Tami,

Cindy,

and

Tracy

I have no greater joy than to hear that my children are walking in the truth.

—3 John 4

ACKNOWLEDGMENTS

IN 2005, GOD inspired me to begin writing short daily devotionals to send to my four daughters via e-mail. Because they are all very busy moms, I wanted to make the devotions short yet soul-nurturing. With them, I included an easy yet delicious recipe, many of which they knew from their childhood days back home. *Thank You, God!*

Later on in the year, my husband was called to be the pastor of Glad Tidings Assembly of God Church in East Peoria, Illinois, where the secretary, Saundra Watkins, asked me if I had anything I'd like to contribute to the weekly bulletin. After telling her about my devotions, she encouraged me to include them each week. I agreed, and because of that, many prompted me to publish the devotions. *Thank you, Saundra, and all those who encouraged me!*

Though many have been an inspiration to see these devotions and recipes put into book form, there is one dear friend who has exceeded and succeeded to see this come to fruition. Her name is Carol Kamp, and she has used her God-given talents to design the artwork throughout this book. Carol believed in me and insisted, "There are a lot of people out there who need to read what God has inspired you to write." *Thank you, Carol!*

My beloved mother went to be with Jesus on February 11, 2011, when she was ninety-one years young. She taught me about Jesus and how to cook and also supplied many of these delicious recipes. *Thank you, Mom! I miss you, but I will see you again one day.*

For the many recipes contributed by friends, family, and my three sisters, Linda, Janice, and Donna, and sister-in-law, Arlene (all fantastic cooks): *Thank you!*

To Debbie, Tami, Cindy, and Tracy—my four wonderful daughters: You gave me purpose and fervency in assisting your busy lifestyles with a source of spiritual and physical sustenance. Is this not every mother's purpose? *Thank you, Lord, for allowing me to nurture these priceless gifts.*

Last but not least, I thank my wonderful husband, Fred, who so patiently and lovingly allows me to pursue my passions.

INTRODUCTION

FOOD FOR THE *Hungry Soul* is more than just another devotional book. Starting at the beginning of the Bible, with Genesis 1:1, and concluding at the end, with Revelation 22:21, it covers 366 messages from all 66 books of the Bible. For the novice, it's a haven of informal expositions, and for the scholar, it is a reinforcement of truth from God's holy Word. Though each devotion can be ingested in just one to two minutes, its effects are eternal. The scriptures used throughout the book proclaim the power, holiness, and sovereignty of God, while the prayers bring repentance and restoration through Jesus Christ. Also included each day is a quick and easy recipe, possibly to be used for that particular day. Most of them are main courses and some are sides. They are great comfort food recipes that most kids will like. Unlike any other book available, *Food for the Hungry Soul* is great for every man or woman who hungers after God yet struggles with the busyness of life.

TABLE OF CONTENTS

January

New Beginnings

Photo by David Kamp

January 1

In the beginning God created the heaven and the earth.

—Genesis 1:1, KJV

*I*N THE BEGINNING... That was such a long time ago, our minds can't even comprehend its measure. *In the beginning God*...God was; God is; and God shall forever be. *In the beginning God created*...How incredible can it be that in His divine and infinite power, God created this magnificent universe while it was yet dark, empty, and without form? With His mere breath, the heavens and earth were created as God spoke purpose, meaning, and direction into existence. While creating His masterpiece, God had Jesus in mind as the Savior of His wonderful work. God also had each one of us on His mind. He allowed His masterpiece to become broken through sin so He could enter His creation Himself, as a man, to restore it in such a way that it would never again be broken. That's what is meant by the words of Jesus as He hung humbly on the cross: "It is finished." God created this world, knowing His remarkable craftsmanship would be marred by sin and injustice, yet He did it because of His great love for you and me. What an awesome God He is!

Dear God and Creator of this marvelous universe: How awesome You are to have performed such an incredible miracle, and with me in mind. Forgive me for my sin and create in me a clean, pure heart. Help me today, in this new year, to begin a new life in You, one that bears witness to what a true Christian really is. In Jesus' name, Amen.

PORK AND SAUERKRAUT

1 pork loin roast (3–4 pounds)
1 teaspoon garlic powder
1 teaspoon salt
1 teaspoon pepper
1 large bag or can of sauerkraut
1 cup water + 1 beef bouillon cube dissolved

Put pork loin in a roasting pan. Sprinkle with garlic powder, salt, and pepper. Place sauerkraut and its juice over and around meat. Add water with bouillon to pan and cover with lid or foil. Bake at 350 degrees for 2–3 hours or until meat thermometer reads 155 degrees. Remove meat and sauerkraut, leaving as much juice as possible in pan if gravy is desired. To thicken, put ¼ cup flour in ½ cup cold water; stir until no lumps. Pour slowly into broth, stirring constantly over medium heat, until thickened. Serve with mashed potatoes.

January 2

And on the seventh day God ended his work which he had made; and he rested on the seventh day from all his work which he had made.

—GENESIS 2:2–3, KJV

GOD HAD JUST finished creating the heavens and the earth in their vast array of beauty. Six days He took to bring them into existence, and He wanted to rest. Was God tired, or did He take this time off as an example for us to rest? Perhaps God took off that seventh day for us to honor Him. God is God and has the strength and power to do anything He desires, but because He called this day to be one of rest and honor to Him, we must obey. God made us in His image, but He knew we would need to take a pause from work to restore our bodies physically, mentally, spiritually, and even socially. God thought it was so important, He made it one of the Ten Commandments: "Remember the sabbath day, to keep it holy" (Exod. 20:8, KJV). It wasn't just a suggestion or an option but a command. The Sabbath day is a holy day, a day we should respect and give honor to our Lord. Many are forced to work this day, but it's pertinent they take another day off to rest. If resting on the Sabbath was something God did, shouldn't we?

Dear God: Thank you for creating this universe where you have chosen me to live. Forgive me when I don't respect Your commands and instead do my own thing. The Sabbath is meant to honor You and also provide the rest I need after a busy week. Help me to pattern my life after You. In Jesus' name, Amen.

CHICKEN STROGANOFF

1½ pounds boneless, skinless chicken breasts
2 tablespoons flour
1 teaspoon salt
¼ teaspoon pepper
¼ cup butter
½ small onion, chopped
1 clove of garlic
1 can cream of chicken soup
1 cup sliced mushrooms *or* 1 can mushrooms, drained
1 cup sour cream
Rice or egg noodles

Cut chicken in large strips. In bowl, combine flour, salt, and pepper; coat chicken with mixture. In large frying pan, melt butter; add chicken and brown on all sides. Add onion and garlic; cook until onions tender. Add soup and mushrooms; cover. Simmer until chicken is cooked, about 15 minutes. Add sour cream just before serving. Thoroughly heat; serve over rice or noodles.

January 3

And God said, This is the token of the covenant which I make between me and you and every living creature that is with you, for perpetual generations: I do set my bow in the cloud, and it shall be for a token of a covenant between me and the earth.

—GENESIS 9:12–13, KJV

AFTER GOD DESTROYED the world with the waters of the Flood because of His universal judgment on an ungodly and unrepentant world, He promised Noah He would never do so again. As a perpetual reminder of that covenant, God set a rainbow in the sky. It is a continuing symbol of His mercy and grace to a sinful people. This beautiful spectrum of the seven colors of light, like the seven notes of music, speaks to us of the perfection of God. It was sin that brought the Flood and it is sin that blots the sunshine out of God's love and grace. But behind the clouds, the sun is still shining. The very water droplets of the clouds diffuse the light of God's presence into the glorious rainbow of His grace to sinners. The rainbow is a promise of the coming of Christ and the symbol of God's mercy and love toward all mankind.

Precious Lord: What a gracious and loving Father You are. Even when we sin, Your love remains unconditional and real. Thank You for the rainbow You sent to portray Your covenant with Your children and for Your Son, a symbol of Your love and mercy to this world. In Jesus' name, Amen.

BISQUICK PIZZA

2 (7.5-ounce) pouches Complete Buttermilk Biscuit Mix (suck as Bisquick)
1 cup water
1 (14-ounce) jar pizza sauce
1 (8-ounce) package sliced pepperoni
2 cups shredded mozzarella cheese

In bowl, stir biscuit mix and water until soft dough forms. Drop half of dough by spoonfuls evenly in bottom of greased baking dish (dough will not completely cover bottom of dish). Drizzle 1 cup sauce over dough; arrange ½ of pepperoni over sauce. Top with 1 cup cheese. Repeat layers with remaining dough, pizza sauce, pepperoni, and cheese. Bake at 375 degrees for 20–25 minutes or until golden brown. Cut into squares to serve.

January 4

I will sing unto the LORD, for he hath triumphed gloriously…

—EXODUS 15:1, KJV

OSES COMPOSED THIS song and sang it with the children of Israel after their deliverance from captivity in Egypt. It is the most ancient of all known songs. Holy and celebratory, it's sung to honor and exalt God. Do you find it easier to praise the Lord when things are going well or when life is a bit more challenging? Most would say when things are going well. But God is worthy of our praise all the time, no matter what the circumstances may be. He doesn't owe us anything but gives freely to us because of His great love. God made the ultimate sacrifice to purchase our redemption and bring us from spiritual death to spiritual life. This was the greatest of all miracles. God deserves our unconditional sacrifice of praise, even when things aren't going well or we don't feel like it. Let us sing unto the Lord, for He is highly exalted in our lives.

Dear Lord: Thank You for sacrificing Your Son on the cross so I might have eternal life. Forgive me for the times I don't praise You because I just don't feel like it. You deserve my sacrifice of praise, and when I praise You, You lift me up above those things that are trying to pull me down. I want to sing Your praise, as You are the most Holy God. You have triumphed gloriously in my life, and today and forever I will sing and exalt Your name. In Jesus' name, Amen.

LINGUINE WITH ASPARAGUS AND BACON

3 cups fresh asparagus (about 1 pound
1 (9-ounce) package refrigerated linguine
4 bacon slices (uncooked)
1 cup chopped onion
2 teaspoons minced garlic
1 teaspoon dried oregano
2 cups grape or cherry tomatoes
¾ cup water with 1 dissolved bouillon cube
1 tablespoon butter
¼ teaspoon salt
¼ teaspoon black pepper
2 tablespoons fresh lemon juice
½ cup (2 ounces) shredded Parmesan cheese
Parmesan cheese (extra for later, if desired)

Cut asparagus in 1-inch pieces; cook with pasta according to pasta package directions. Drain; set aside. Cook bacon in large skillet until crisp; remove from pan and crumble. Discard all but 1 tablespoon drippings. Add onion, garlic, and oregano to pan; sauté 4 minutes until onion lightly browned. Add tomatoes; cook 2 minutes. Add broth; bring to boil. Stir in butter, salt, and pepper; remove from heat. Put noodles in large bowl; add tomato mixture and juice; toss. Top with bacon and shredded cheese.

January 5

The LORD is my strength and my song; he has become my salvation. He is my God, and I will praise him, my father's God and I will exalt him.

—EXODUS 15:2

THESE ARE WORDS in a song that Moses and the Israelites sang to the Lord after He had delivered them from the Egyptians via parting the Red Sea. God had saved them, and they joyfully praised Him. We also were rescued from our enemy (Satan) when Christ went to the cross and gave His life for us. Just as the Israelites were saved as they walked on dry ground and the two sides of surging waters stood firm like a wall, we also must walk in victory on the path that God opened before us. If we choose to not walk with Him, the sea of life will swallow us up, as it did the Egyptians, and death will consume us.

Have you had a "Red Sea" experience? Have you made the decision to walk with God by accepting His Son into your heart? Is Christ your strength and song? If not, ask God to forgive you of your sins and come and dwell in your heart. Just as the Israelites put their trust in the Lord as they saw His great power, we must do the same. Then we will be able to sing and praise God, for He is our strength, our song, and our salvation.

Dear Lord: Thank You for parting the Red Sea for Moses and his followers. What an awesome manifestation of Your marvelous power that was! You have also rescued me from my enemy many times, and I praise You. Thank You also for sending Your Son Jesus to die for me so I might walk in victory and experience strength and salvation. In Jesus' name, Amen.

SCALLOPED CHICKEN

3 tablespoons butter
2 tablespoons flour
2 cups water + 2 chicken bouillon cubes
1 cup milk
½ teaspoon salt
½ teaspoon pepper
3 cups cooked rice
3 cups cooked chicken
8-ounce package mushrooms, sliced
½ cup slivered almonds
1 (4-ounce) jar pimientos, drained
1 cup buttered bread crumbs

Melt butter over low heat; add flour; blend well. Add chicken broth, milk, salt, and pepper. Stir constantly over medium heat until thickened. Butter a 2-quart baking dish; spread half of rice on bottom. Top with half of chicken, mushrooms, almonds, and pimientos. Pour half of sauce over top. Repeat layers; top with buttered breadcrumbs. Bake at 350 degrees for 45 minutes.

January 6

Sanctify yourselves therefore, and be ye holy: for I am the LORD your God. And ye shall keep my statutes, and do them: I am the LORD which sanctify you.

—LEVITICUS 20:7–8, KJV

THE BOOK OF Leviticus contains instructions for holy living. The laws were written to help the Israelites worship and live as God's holy people. The Bible is our book of instructions and was written so we, too, might know what it means to be a believer and follow God's commands.

Moses had just led the people out of Egypt into safety. Even though they were alive and free, they still weren't happy and didn't honor God with holy lifestyles. Are we not the same way today? We live in America, the land of the free, and have every opportunity to worship and praise God, but we grumble and complain and find every reason not to serve Him. Life without God is a life without purpose or worth. Unless we have repented from our sins and truly believe in our hearts that Jesus is the only way to find eternal peace and victory, we are unholy and unfit for the kingdom. The laws of the Scriptures were written for a purpose, and we need them to know how to live. Holiness comes only after we consecrate ourselves to God, repent of our sins, ask Jesus to live in our hearts, and continue to obey His Word.

O Lord: What a marvelous example of holiness You are. Your Word instructs us how to live, and we have a choice to keep Your decrees and serve Christ or ignore them and pay the penalty. Search my heart and reveal to me all that is unclean and unholy and remove it from my life. Help me to live a holy lifestyle and never again go back to my old ways. In Jesus' name, Amen.

MAC AND FOUR CHEESES

16-ounce package uncooked macaroni
4 cups milk
16 ounces cheddar cheese, shredded
16 ounces American cheese, shredded
8 ounces Muenster cheese, grated
8 ounces mozzarella cheese, grated
½ cup breadcrumbs

Cook macaroni according to package directions; drain, set aside, and keep warm. In large saucepan over medium heat, heat milk to almost boiling. Reduce heat to low; gradually add cheeses, stirring constantly. Cook and stir until all cheese has melted (about 5 minutes). Place macaroni in 4-quart greased baking dish. Pour cheese sauce over pasta; stir until well combined. Cover with breadcrumbs. Bake at 350 degrees for 40–60 minutes or until browned and bubbly.

January 7

The secret things belong unto the Lord our God: but those things which are revealed belong unto us and to our children forever, that we may do all the words of this law.

—Deuteronomy 29:29, KJV

DON'T YOU HATE when someone says they have a secret but can't tell you what it is? Or maybe you have told a secret to someone and that person betrayed you and told someone else, or vice versa? A secret is a hidden truth, and in this verse the *secret things* are divinely revealed hidden truths. There are many mysteries in the Bible; even scholars are unable to completely understand them. Why? Because *they aren't meant to be understood* by anyone but God. One example is that Jesus doesn't know when He will be sent by the Father to rapture the church, something known only by God (Matthew 24:36). God reveals the things He wants us to know so we might know His perfect law and will for our lives. We are always in the best interest of God, and He has reason for revealing some things and not others. Our responsibility is to merely trust His plan and judgment, knowing that He has all things in control.

Lord God: Thank You for caring enough about me to share only those things in Your wonderful plan that I am meant to know. I exalt You for revealing the words of Your law so I might study them and be obedient. Forgive me when I don't put my trust in Your plan for my life and try to do things on my own. Help me always to put my faith in You. In Jesus' name, Amen.

BAKED MOSTACCIOLI

1 pound ground beef
2 (24-ounce) jars spaghetti sauce
1 (16-ounce) container ricotta cheese
2 eggs
¼ cup grated Parmesan cheese
1 teaspoon garlic powder
½ teaspoon pepper
2 teaspoons Italian seasoning
1 (16-ounce) package mostaccioli, cooked/drained
1½ cups (8 ounces) shredded mozzarella cheese

Cook ground beef in large pan until done; drain. Add spaghetti sauce and cook on low 20 minutes. In bowl, combine ricotta and Parmesan cheeses with eggs. Add garlic powder, pepper, and Italian seasoning; mix well. Place half of pasta in greased baking dish. Spread ricotta mixture evenly over pasta. Spoon remaining pasta over ricotta mixture. Top with spaghetti sauce and mozzarella cheese. Bake at 350 degrees for 30 minutes or until hot and bubbly.

January 8

And if it seem evil unto you to serve the Lord, choose you this day whom ye will serve; whether the gods which your fathers served that were on the other side of the flood, or the gods of the Amorites, in whose land ye dwell: but as for me and my house, we will serve the Lord.

—Joshua 24:15, KJV

Before Moses died, an aide of his named Joshua was commissioned as the leader of Israel. God told Joshua to obey what Moses instructed him: to know the Book of the Law by meditating on it day and night, to not turn from it to the right or to the left, to be strong and courageous, and to not be terrified or discouraged. God told Joshua that if he followed these instructions, he would be successful in leading the Israelites across the Jordan River into the land of their inheritance.

Joshua obeyed, but not all of his people did. Even though God protected and blessed them, they still grumbled, worshiped idols, rebelled, and intermarried with non-believers. Joshua was angry with the people and told them they needed to fear the Lord and serve Him faithfully.

Just as Joshua warned the people to make a choice of whom they would serve, we need to do the same. God has blessed us in so many ways, yet we ignore His Word and worship idols of food, money, television, computers, clothing, sports, parties, jobs, and so on. We must abandon worldly lifestyles and strive for holiness. Choose today whom you will serve—*but as for me and my house, we will serve the Lord.*

Dear Lord: I praise and thank You for choosing me. Just as Joshua chose You, I also desire to serve You all the days of my life. Forgive me for my sin and help me to be strong and courageous as I face each new day. In Jesus' name, Amen.

BARBECUE CHICKEN PACKETS (for 6)

3 boneless, skinless chicken breasts, halved
6 pineapple rings + 6 tablespoons juice
1 green pepper (sliced into 6 rings)
1 sweet onion (sliced into 6 slices)
6 tablespoons barbecue sauce
6 teaspoons brown sugar

Place chicken in center of 6 large sheets of heavy-duty foil; top with remaining ingredients. Bring up foil sides. Double-fold top and ends to seal packet, leaving room for heat circulation inside. Grill 15 minutes or until chicken is done, or bake in 375 degree oven for 40 minutes. Cut slits in foil to release steam before opening packet. Serve with potatoes, noodles, or rice.

January 9

"So may all your enemies perish, O LORD! But may they who love you be like the sun when it rises in its strength." Then the land had peace forty years.

—JUDGES 5:31

THE BOOK OF Judges covers many years where the Israelites went from living in peace and obedience to God to living in sin and turmoil. After their leader Joshua died, many different national heroes ruled the nation; they were called judges. The people continued to waver in their relationship with God, and their disobedience and idolatry caused many problems, including civil war. At one point, the prophetess Deborah was leading Israel and saw the defiance of the people. A war she led had just ended when she cried out to the Lord—*and then the land had peace for forty years.*

Why did the people behave as they did, and how could they serve God one day and live in sin the next? It is because of the sinful nature we all have, that though we want to serve God with one hand, the other wants to hold on to the world. It's a battle, and whichever side we feed the most will become stronger and eventually win. Are we enemies of God, fighting against Him, or do we love Him and let His Son shine through us, as Deborah spoke? It's a decision we all have to make, and once we make it, we choose our destiny.

O Lord: Your Word is true and tells me exactly how to live if I want the sun to shine in my life. When I weaken and begin to sin, You come with Your Holy Spirit, touch my heart, and renew me with Your strength. Forgive me of my sins and help me to stay strong and revived in You. In Jesus' name, Amen.

NORTHWOODS WILD RICE SOUP

½ cup butter
1 onion, chopped
1 pound fresh mushrooms, chopped
1 cup chopped carrots
½ cup flour
½ teaspoon salt
½ teaspoon pepper
4 cups chicken broth
2 (12-ounce) cans evaporated milk
2 cups cooked wild rice
2 cups cooked chicken
1 (8-ounce) package cream cheese

In Dutch oven or large pot, melt butter; add onion, mushrooms, and carrots. Cook and stir over medium heat until carrots are tender. Stir in flour, salt, and pepper. Add broth; cook and stir until bubbly. Stir in milk, rice, chicken, and cream cheese. Cook and stir until cheese is melted. Serve.

January 10

May the LORD repay you for what you have done. May you be richly rewarded by the LORD, the God of Israel, under whose wings you have come to take refuge.

—RUTH 2:12

THESE ARE THE words spoken to Ruth by Boaz, a relative of her deceased husband who later became her husband. Ruth was a very tenderhearted woman who chose to follow God though it meant abandoning her own family and homeland. Ruth and her mother-in-law Naomi were both widows when they relocated to Bethlehem, the home of Naomi. Ruth could have returned to her native home, but she loved her mother-in-law so much, she wanted to go with her and serve her God.

There, she humbly worked in the fields of Boaz many long hours to provide food for Naomi and herself. Ruth was so humble she was willing to walk behind the other servant girls, picking up the grain they dropped or missed. Boaz saw Ruth's godly character and admired her for her loyalty to Naomi and God. He was touched by Ruth's life and blessed her with abundant grain.

We can learn much from Ruth's life. She was humble, loving, faithful, a diligent and very hard worker, a provider, obedient, and devoted. Ruth could have chosen the easy life by staying in her homeland, but God had a plan for her, and she followed Him, doing what she believed was the right thing. As we go about our busy lives, it's important that we remain in God's will. If we are obedient and keep God first in everything we do, Boaz's prayer for Ruth may also apply to us: *May the Lord repay you for what you have done. May you be richly rewarded by the Lord, the God of Israel, under whose wings you have come to take refuge.*

Dear God of Israel: Thank You for the plan You have for my life and for the inspiring story of Ruth's life. Help me to do as she did and put You and others first, even if it means hard work and fewer material things for myself. Keep me humble, O Lord! In Jesus' name, Amen.

PARMESAN BAKED SALMON

¼ cup mayonnaise
2 tablespoons Parmesan cheese
⅛ teaspoon pepper
4 salmon fillets, skin removed (about 1 pound)
2 teaspoons lemon juice
10 Ritz crackers, crushed (½ cup crumbs)

Mix mayonnaise, cheese, and pepper. Place salmon on foil-lined shallow baking pan. Drizzle with lemon juice. Top with cheese mixture; spread evenly over salmon. Sprinkle with cracker crumbs. Bake at 400 degrees for 12–15 minutes, until fish flakes easily.

January 11

In bitterness of soul Hannah wept much and prayed to the LORD. And she made a vow, saying, "O LORD Almighty, if you will only look upon your servant's misery and remember me, and not forget your servant but give her a son, then I will give him to the LORD for all the days of his life..."

—1 SAMUEL 1:10–11

HANNAH, WIFE OF Elkanah, a man who loved God and her very much, had been barren for many years. She was very distraught, often wept, and would not eat because she wanted a child so badly. One day while Hannah was visiting the temple, a priest named Eli saw her praying so intensely that he thought she was drunk. When Hannah convinced Eli she was praying and not drinking, he said to her, "Go in peace, and may the God of Israel grant you what you have asked of Him" (1 Sam. 1:17). Hannah left the temple that day no longer sad, and she ate. She conceived and gave birth to a son, whom she called Samuel, which means "because I asked the Lord for him." When he was three years old she took him back to the same temple and gave him over to the same priest, Eli, to raise.

This is an inspiring act of faithfulness, dedication, and integrity by Hannah. We have all made promises to God and not kept them. "If only You will get me out of this mess," we say, or, "If only You will give me..." or "I promise I'll serve You and go to church if...." But Hannah kept her word and did exactly as she promised God, and the Lord was with Samuel as he grew, and he became a great man of God.

Almighty Lord: You know my heart even before I speak, and You hear all my prayers. I have made promises to You and not kept my word; please forgive me. Show me those things in my life I need to give back to You, knowing it might mean getting rid of something, relocating, or selling something so I might give the proceeds to the needy. In Jesus' name, Amen.

HAM AND LINGUINE TOSS

1 (16-ounce) package fettuccine pasta
2 cups frozen peas, thawed
½ cup butter
¼ teaspoon garlic powder (optional)
2 cups cooked ham, small cubes
½ to 1 cup grated Parmesan cheese

Cook pasta according to package instructions, adding peas during the last 3 minutes of cooking. Drain and return to pan. Add butter and garlic powder; stir until dissolved. Add ham and Parmesan cheese; mix well and briefly heat.

January 12

The Lord came and stood there, calling as at the other times, "Samuel! Samuel!" Then Samuel said, "Speak, for your servant is listening."

—1 Samuel 3:10

Samuel was being raised by Eli, the priest of the temple where Samuel's mother, Hannah, had often gone to worship and pray. It was there she told the Lord that if He gave her a son, she would give him back to Him. God granted her prayer, and when Samuel was weaned, Hannah took him to Eli to raise as a servant of the Lord.

One night when Samuel was a young boy sleeping in the temple, he was awakened by what he thought to be Eli calling his name. Three times Samuel heard his name being called, and each time he ran to Eli to see what he wanted. Eli told Samuel to go back to bed, for he didn't call his name, so Samuel did. After the third time, Eli realized it was the Lord calling Samuel. Eli told Samuel to lie down, and if he heard his name being called again to answer the Lord by saying, "Speak, for your servant is listening."

Samuel obeyed Eli, and again the Lord called his name. Samuel answered with the words Eli had told him, and the Lord spoke to him, sharing with him a vision. Because of his obedience to Eli and his dedication to God, the Lord continued to appear and reveal Himself to Samuel through His word. And Samuel's word went throughout all of Israel.

Just as God spoke to Samuel, He also speaks to us. At that time, God spoke audibly, but today He speaks to us with His Holy Spirit. The important thing is that we stop and listen when He does speak. If we hear that inner voice tug at our hearts, do we also say as Samuel did, "Speak Lord, for Your servant is listening"?

Dear Lord: Thank You for sending Your Holy Spirit and Your Holy Word to speak to my heart. Please forgive me for the times I have ignored Your voice. Help me to be strong enough to stop what I am doing and take time to listen when You speak. In Jesus' name, Amen.

EGG AND SAUSAGE BISQUICK CASSEROLE

1 pound bulk sausage
6 eggs
1 cup Bisquick
1 cup shredded cheddar cheese
2 cups milk
1 teaspoon dry mustard (or regular mustard)

Fry sausage in pan until done; drain. Beat eggs well with mixer. Mix all ingredients together and pour into greased baking dish. Bake uncovered at 350 degrees for 1 hour or until done. Great for breakfast, brunch, lunch, or dinner. Serve with a salad, dish of fruit, or favorite vegetable.

January 13

Only fear the LORD, and serve him in truth with all your heart: for consider how great things he hath done for you.

—1 SAMUEL 12:24, KJV

SAMUEL, A GODLY servant and judge over Israel, was getting old so he appointed his two sons as judges. Because they were not godly like their father and lived dishonest lives, the people didn't want them; they wanted a king to lead them instead. Even though they should have been satisfied serving God as their king, they were not and insisted on having their own way. They refused to listen to Samuel and said they wanted a king over them like all the other nations. So Saul became their king, even though Samuel warned the people that their dishonor to God and persistence in having a king would bring them turmoil and grief.

Samuel felt rejected that the people no longer wanted him to serve them because he was old. The Lord assured Samuel that it was not him they were rejecting, but God. God reminded Samuel that even though He rescued the people out of Egypt and blessed them in so many ways, the people continued to forsake Him and serve other gods.

At one point, after Saul was king and things were not going well, the people were sorry for insisting on having a king. They asked Samuel to pray for them, that their lives would be spared. Samuel told the people to not be afraid. Even though they had done evil, they still could change and begin to faithfully serve God with their whole heart. God, through Samuel, gave the people another chance to make things right. God is a God of forgiveness and love and is ready and willing to receive us back again unto Himself. But He knows our hearts and if we are truly repentant. Let's consider all the wonderful things God has done, ask Him to forgive us of our sins, and begin to serve Him more faithfully.

Dear Lord: You have been so good to me, even when I didn't deserve it. I am sorry for the times I did not fear You enough to obey. Thank You for Your patience with me and for loving me, even when I am unlovable. In Jesus' name, Amen.

CHILI PHILLY CHEESE DIP

8 ounces Philadelphia cream cheese
1 (10.5-ounce) can chili
½ cup cheddar cheese
2 tablespoons chopped cilantro (optional)

Mix both cheeses and chili in a bowl. Microwave 40–60 seconds until cheese is melted. Stir every 20 seconds while cooking. Mix well; sprinkle with cilantro. Serve with chips or crackers.

January 14

Behold, to obey is better than sacrifice...

—1 Samuel 15:22, KJV

...for the LORD seeth not as man seeth; for man looketh on the outward appearance, but the LORD looketh on the heart.

—1 Samuel 16:7, KJV

SAUL CONTINUED TO do his own thing and disobey God's commands. He never entirely followed them with his whole heart. Saul thought a little obedience was better than none. But all of God's Word is to be obeyed; it is not a pick and choose option.

God no longer wanted Saul to be king because of his arrogance and rebellion, so He told Samuel to go to Bethlehem to find a man named Jesse, a father of eight sons. There, God would tell him which son to choose as king. Samuel obeyed, and when he met with Jesse, one of the sons, Eliab, caught his eye. He was tall and good-looking, and Samuel was sure this must be God's man. The Lord told Samuel that Eliab was not the one and that although man looks at the outward appearance, God looks at the heart.

Finally, the last son, David, a sheepherder and harpist, was brought to Samuel, and God told Samuel this was the one to be king. So Samuel took the oil and anointed David, and from that day on, the Spirit of the Lord was upon David in power.

Obedience! Obedience! Every decision we make should be done out of obedience to God's Word. But we have to study it to know exactly what it is God wants us to do. God already knows our hearts, and just like He blessed David, He will also bless us if we are obedient to His Word.

Righteous Lord: I praise and thank You for accepting my obedience as true worship and love for You. If I had nothing else to give, You would be honored by my trust and desire to do Your will. I repent of my disobedience to Your Word. Help me to become stronger in my walk with Christ. In Jesus' name, Amen.

STUFFED BAKED PORK CHOPS

4–6 thick pork chops
1 box Stove Top pork stuffing mix
1 can cream of mushroom soup
½ can water

Cut pork chops down center to make deep pocket, but do not cut all way through. Prepare stuffing according to package; stuff each pork chop. Place in greased shallow dish; cover with soup. Add ½ can water; cover with foil. Bake 40–45 minutes at 350 degrees. Remove foil; bake another 15 minutes, or until pork is done.

January 15

The LORD that delivered me out of the paw of the lion, and out of the paw of the bear, he will deliver me out of the hand of this Philistine.

—1 SAMUEL 17:37, KJV

DAVID, A YOUNG shepherd boy who became king, was full of the Lord's Spirit and power. Appointed by Saul to be his armor-bearer, they went out to fight the Philistine army. Goliath, a nine-foot-tall Philistine, dared the Israelites to send one of their men to fight him. Everyone feared Goliath, but David told Saul he would fight the giant. Saul said he was young and inexperienced, while the larger and stronger Goliath had been fighting wars for many years. David told Saul that while tending his father's sheep he rescued them from a lion and a bear. David said it was the Lord who delivered him, and he knew God would also deliver him from the hand of Goliath. So David took his sling and five stones and met Goliath face to face.

David told Goliath, "You come against me with sword and spear and javelin, but I come against you in the Name of the Lord Almighty, the God of the armies of Israel, whom you have defied" (verse 45). David continued to tell Goliath, "All those gathered here will know that it is not by sword or spear that the Lord saves; for the battle is the Lord's, and He will give all of you into our hands" (verse 47). As they walked closer to one another, David put a stone in his sling and with a whirl sank it deep into the giant's forehead, and Goliath fell dead. David triumphed over the giant that day.

We are able to triumph over the giants in our lives as well. They may not come in the form of nine-feet-tall men, but they are anything that stand before us trying to destroy our lives and faith in God. We must stand in the name of the Lord before our giant and let it know that no longer will it try to destroy us because the battle is the Lord's and He has already defeated the enemy for us.

My Lord and Deliverer: Thank You for the times You protect and deliver me from the enemy's snare. You provide strength for me to stand up and face my giant because it is not my battle, but Yours. With You, I am able to face every giant head-on and experience victory. In Jesus' name, Amen.

BAKED POTATOES (crockpot)

6 baking potatoes (1 potato per person)
Vegetable spray, butter, or oil

Prick potatoes with fork; spray or rub with butter or oil; wrap in foil. Place in crockpot; cook on low 6–8 hours. Rotate after 4 hours, if possible.

January 16

I will celebrate before the LORD.

—2 SAMUEL 6:21

KING DAVID WAS reigning over Israel and knew that to be blessed by the Lord, he would need to bring the ark of God back to his city. He went rejoicing and returned it to Israel. On the trip back, David stopped and sacrificed animals to show his thankfulness and joy to the Lord. The people of Israel also celebrated by shouting, singing, and blowing their trumpets. It was an exuberant time of commemoration to God.

David was so overcome in his worship, he danced and leaped with all his might, not even realizing that perhaps some of what he did was not appealing to his role as king. But he didn't care and only had praise and worship to the Lord on his mind. Though David was ridiculed for his behavior, he refused to be deterred by the criticism because the Lord was the only one he wanted to please.

This is where we all need to be in our worship to God. Just as David was exuberant in his freedom to worship, so should we also be. It starts with totally surrendering our will and focusing on the one true God. If some types of worship seem foolish, then consider this: David was selected by the Lord to be king of Israel, His chosen people. Because of his joy, he made the choice to act foolish and undignified before God. If it were okay for a king, then shouldn't it be okay for us? Was God honored by David's style of worship? Indeed He was, and He also is honored when we make the choice to worship Him, no matter how foolish it may seem.

Dear Lord: You are full of mercy and grace and awesome in power and holiness. You are my joy, my strength, my hope, and the only one worthy of all praise, glory, and honor. Thank You for the privilege of knowing You personally through Jesus. Please help me to celebrate You, no matter how foolish it may seem. In Jesus' name, Amen.

ALMOND BACON CHICKEN

4 bacon strips
4 skinless chicken breasts halves
¼ teaspoon pepper
1 can cream of onion soup
¼ cup chicken broth
¼ cup sliced almonds, toasted

Partially cook bacon, 3–4 minutes. Wrap bacon strips around chicken; sprinkle with pepper. Arrange in 8-inch baking dish. Mix soup and broth; pour over chicken. Bake at 350 degrees for 45–55 minutes, or until chicken is done. Sprinkle with almonds; serve.

January 17

And David said unto Nathan, I have sinned against the LORD.

—2 SAMUEL 12:13, KJV

WAR HAD BROKEN out. King David should have been with his men, but he remained in Jerusalem. One night, while on the roof of his palace, he saw a beautiful lady bathing. After inquiring, he was told she, Bathsheba, was married to Uriah, who was off at war. Even knowing this, David sent for her. He slept with her, and she became pregnant. Immediately, David made plans to conceal his sin, which eventually resulted in the death of Uriah. After Bathsheba mourned for her late husband, she and David were married. Soon after, their son was born.

Because David sinned by having an adulteress affair and having Uriah killed, the Lord was very unhappy with him. What David did was evil, though he thought no one knew. He forgot that although he had skillfully hidden his sin from men, he could not hide from God. The prophet Nathan gave David a word from the Lord that brought him to repentance. This was a defining moment for David as he confessed his sin and prepared to face the punishment of death. Instead, God showed David grace and forgave him, allowing him to live. David totally changed and developed a relationship with God like never before.

The same grace that set David free from his sin can also do the same for us. We must admit our guilt and confess it to God. He already knows what we have done, so He won't be surprised. We can pray as David prayed in Psalm 51 and be forgiven, healed, and restored and know God like we've never known Him before.

"Have mercy on me, O God, according to Your unfailing love; according to Your great compassion blot out my transgressions. Wash away all my iniquity and cleanse me from my sin. For I know my transgression and my sin is always before me. Against You, You only, have I sinned and done what is evil in Your sight, so that You are proved right when You speak and justified when You judge. Surely I have been a sinner from birth, sinful from the time my mother conceived me. Surely You desire truth in the inner parts; You teach me wisdom in the inmost place. Cleanse me with hyssop and I will be clean; wash me and I will be whiter than snow. Let me hear joy and gladness; let the bones You have crushed rejoice. Hide Your face from my sins and blot out all my iniquity. Create in me a pure heart, O God, and renew a right spirit within me. Do not cast me from Your presence or take Your Holy Spirit from me. Restore to me the joy of Your salvation and grant me a willing spirit to sustain me" (Ps. 51:1–12). In Jesus' name, Amen.

Today's recipe found on page 382 LASAGNA RECIPE

January 18

The LORD is my rock, and my fortress, and my deliverer; the God of my rock; in him will I trust: he is my shield, and the horn of my salvation, my high tower, and my refuge.

—2 SAMUEL 22:2–3, KJV

DAVID SANG THESE words, along with the rest of the fifty-one verses of 2 Samuel 22. He was praising God for delivering him from all his enemies and from the hand of Saul. It is a song of praise and can also be found in Psalm 18, except for a few changes. It's obvious that David was a man after God's own heart but not men's hearts. Though many hated David, including Saul, who wanted to kill him, David did not hate in return. Because of David's obedience and worship, God protected and blessed him throughout his whole life. It wasn't until his sin with Bathsheba that David displeased God by his sin. With a very repentant heart, David came to the realization of what he had done and began a relationship with God that was greater than ever.

David's adoration for the Lord and his passionate desire to express his love can be felt throughout the entire song. It came from deep within his soul and was real and uninhibited. We too can find hope and deliverance in David's song. It gives us the strength we need to go on, even in times of adversity and pain. God truly is our rock, our fortress, our deliverer, our shield, our horn of salvation, our stronghold, our refuge, and so much more. As we think about all that He is and all that He has done, let's be sure to take time to praise and thank Him, just as David did in this song.

Father God: "To the faithful You show Yourself faithful; to the blameless You show Yourself blameless; to the pure You show Yourself pure; but to the crooked You show Yourself shrewd. You save the humble, but Your eyes are on the haughty to bring them low. You are my Lamp, O Lord; the Lord turns my darkness into light. With Your help I can advance against a troop; with my God I can scale a wall" (2 Sam. 22:26–30). I love You, Lord. Thank You for first loving me. In Jesus' name, Amen.

CHEESY FLOUNDER

2 pounds flounder
½ cup mayonnaise
⅓ cup Parmesan cheese
Scant amount dill weed (optional)

Put fish in greased baking dish. Mix mayonnaise and cheese; spread over the top. Sprinkle with dill. Bake at 400 degrees for 15–20 minutes.

January 19

And he said, LORD God of Israel, there is no God like thee, in heaven above, or on earth beneath, who keepest covenant and mercy with thy servants that walk before thee with all their heart.

—1 KINGS 8:23, KJV

AFTER KING DAVID died, his son Solomon took his throne and ruled Israel. He was young and inexperienced, so he asked God for wisdom and discernment to know right from wrong and to rule his people. The Lord was so pleased with Solomon's request and the sincerity of his heart that He indeed granted it. Because Solomon didn't ask for wealth or a long life, God gave him wisdom and insight and made him the wisest man in all the nations. Solomon wrote 3,000 proverbs and 1,005 songs. He described plant life and taught about animals, birds, reptiles, and fish. News spread everywhere about him, and men from all the nations came to get advice and listen to him speak.

Solomon's father, King David, wanted so badly to build a temple for the Lord but was never able to because of continuous wars. So God used Solomon to build a magnificent structure. It took seven years to build, and then the ark of the Lord's covenant was brought to dwell in the temple. It consisted of two stone tablets that Moses placed in it with the commandments of God written on them. Solomon then stood before the altar of the Lord with his hands outstretched toward heaven and dedicated the temple to God with the words of 1 Kings 8:23–53. When he was finished, he blessed the people and reminded them to fully commit their hearts to God, live by His decrees, and obey His commands.

We are told throughout the Bible how we should obey God and commit ourselves wholly to Him. There is none like our Lord, not in heaven or on earth, and He deserves our faithful obedience.

O Lord: You are magnificent in power and awesome in strength. You keep Your covenant of love with Your children, and Your Word is the source of life that brings us hope. Help me follow Your way and share Your love with the world. In Jesus' name, Amen.

PARMESAN GARLIC BUTTER GREEN BEANS

1 (14-ounce) package frozen whole green beans
2 tablespoons butter
1 garlic clove, minced
1 tablespoon grated Parmesan cheese

Cook green beans per package directions; drain. Cook garlic 2–3 minutes in butter on medium-low heat. Pour over beans; sprinkle with cheese; gently toss.

January 20

If you do whatever I command you and walk in my ways and do what is right in my eyes by keeping my statutes and commands, as David my servant did, I will be with you.

—1 KINGS 11:38

GOD SPOKE THESE words to Jeroboam through the prophet Shijah concerning his future reign over Israel. Solomon, son of King David, reigned in Jerusalem over Israel for forty years. God blessed him greatly, and he was the wisest and wealthiest man in the world. But Solomon began to mingle and intermarry with foreign women, even though he already had a wife. These women did not serve God but worshiped other gods.

Soon Solomon left the God of his father and began to worship the gods of the women. The Lord warned him of His judgment if he continued to do evil. God gave him every opportunity to return, but Solomon's attitude wasn't right and his heart was cold. Because of his unwillingness to follow God's commands, Solomon's kingdom would be taken away; but because his father (King David) loved and obeyed God, the Lord spared a portion of it so he and his family still could remain in Jerusalem. God also waited until Solomon's son took over to carry out His judgment and separate the kingdoms.

Solomon's turning away from the Lord shows that mere knowledge of God and His Word is not enough to warrant a personal relationship and eternal life with Him. Sin comes from the heart and can be resisted if our heart is true to faith and love toward God. Solomon once lived a godly life and preached the Word to others, but he fell into blatant sin and immorality, defiled Israel, and dishonored the one true God. How could that happen to one who had so much and served God with his whole life? Just as Solomon took his eyes off God and put them on the lust of his flesh, it can happen to anyone. We must be cautious to always walk in the ways of the Lord.

Father: I love You and want to serve only You. Forgive me when I take my eyes off You and put them on people and things of this world. Guide me with Your Spirit to do what is right and abstain from anything that might cause me to fall away from Your will. In Jesus' name, Amen.

SWEET AND SOUR CHICKEN (crockpot)

4–6 boneless, skinless chicken breasts
1 (8-ounce) bottle Catalina salad dressing
1 packet dry onion soup mix
1 (10-ounce) jar apricot preserves

Put everything in crockpot; cook on high 4–5 hours. Serve with rice.

January 21

The ravens brought him [Elijah] bread and flesh in the morning, and bread and flesh in the evening; and he drank of the brook.

—1 Kings 17:6, kjv

THERE WAS A prophet from the northern kingdom of Israel during the reigns of Ahab and his son Ahaziah whose name was Elijah, which means "the Lord is my God." He was a righteous man who was unshakable in his convictions toward God. Elijah's life centered on the conflict the Israelites had between the worship of the Lord and the worship of Baal. His mission was to show them that they had fallen away from God and that He wanted to restore, reform, and reestablish their covenant with Him.

Because of their sin and disobedience, God brought judgment on Israel by withholding rain for three and a half years. This type of judgment mocked Baal because Baal worshipers believed Baal controlled rain and was responsible for abundant crops. During the drought, God told Elijah where to find food and water for himself. He told him to drink from a certain brook and receive food that ravens would bring to him. Because Elijah stood with God against the people of Israel's apostasy, God sustained him. He loved God and served Him. God, in turn, met Elijah's needs and provided for him. It isn't always easy to serve God and follow His commands; but if we will, He will care for us and meet our needs, just as He did for Elijah.

Dear Lord: You are such a wonderful, caring Father. You provide and sustain us in our time of need. Pardon me when I disobey Your commands and do my own thing. Help me to stay on track and always follow after You. In Jesus' name, Amen.

BAKED ZITI

1 pound lean ground beef or Italian sausage
2 (24-ounce) jars favorite spaghetti sauce (or homemade sauce)
4 cups shredded mozzarella cheese (divided)
16 ounces ricotta cheese
16 ounces tube-shaped pasta (ziti), cooked until slightly firm and drained
8 ounces grated Parmesan cheese

In large skillet, brown ground meat; drain. Stir in spaghetti sauce. Mix with ziti, 2 cups mozzarella, and all ricotta cheese. Pour into large greased baking dish. Cover and bake at 350 degrees for 40 minutes. Uncover; sprinkle with remaining mozzarella and Parmesan. Bake 5–10 minutes, until cheese is melted.

January 22

The LORD said, "Go out and stand on the mountain in the presence of the Lord, for the Lord is about to pass by."

—1 KINGS 19:11

THE LORD SPOKE this to the prophet Elijah when he had retreated to a cave after a long and wearisome journey. He was spiritually and physically drained from the many years of trying to get the Israelites to abandon their worship of Baal and return solely to the one true God. The labor and struggles of this battle appeared to be ending in failure. Instead of the people being thankful that Elijah cared about their souls, they were angry and wanted to kill him. He had poured out his whole life for the sake of truth and righteousness, but his efforts seemed hopeless.

At one point, Elijah begged God to take his life, but God's plan for his life was not over, and He visited Elijah in the cave where he slept. God assured Elijah that if he would go out and stand on the mountain, he would see the Lord.

Are we not also like Elijah and become exhausted and discouraged at times while working to do God's will? We may pour our lives into the work of the Lord and labor to see souls saved. Many missionaries go years without seeing a single convert, yet they press on for God. Parents and grandparents strive to see their children abandon their sinful ways to come to know Christ but become weary when they don't see the fruit of their labor. Elijah was faithful to God, and God took care of him, and He will do the same for us. When we are at our lowest, God in His mercy and grace invites us to join Him on the mountaintop. But...we must go and not miss the opportunity to see the Lord as He passes by.

Wonderful Lord: You are my fortress and shield. You care for my life and bring me to places of safety and shelter. When I am weary and discouraged and feel I cannot go on, You are there, inviting me to join You on the mountaintop. I am sorry when I give up too soon and become discouraged, for I know You will never leave me nor forsake me. In Jesus' name, Amen.

REUBEN SANDWICHES

4 slices rye or Italian bread
2 tablespoons Thousand Island dressing
4 ounces corned beef
2 slices Swiss cheese
½ cup sauerkraut, drained
2 tablespoons butter

Spread two slices of bread with Thousand Island dressing. Top each with corned beef, Swiss cheese, sauerkraut, and bread. Melt butter in skillet; grill sandwiches on both sides until brown.

January 23

And he said, Go forth, and stand upon the mount before the LORD. And, behold, the LORD passed by, and a great and strong wind rent the mountains, and brake in pieces the rocks before the LORD; but the LORD was not in the wind: and after the wind an earthquake; but the LORD was not in the earthquake: And after the earthquake a fire; but the LORD was not in the fire: and after the fire a still small voice.

—1 KINGS 19:11–12, KJV

THE PROPHET ELIJAH was in a cave, depressed and distraught because he felt defeated. He spent his whole life trying to persuade the Israelites to not worship idols but to worship God. At his lowest time there in the cave, God visited him. He told Elijah to go out of the cave and stand on the mountain and there he would see the Lord.

A powerful wind, an earthquake, and then a fire came, but Elijah did not see the Lord in any of these. Instead, God revealed Himself in the form of a gentle whisper. The voice asked Elijah what he was doing there. Elijah proceeded to speak of how hard he had worked to restore the Israelites' covenant with God, and now they were trying to kill him. Then God told Elijah what to do next. God was not done with him, though Elijah felt his life was over. God came to him, not in the wind, not in an earthquake, and not in the fire; but He came to him in a soft, gentle whisper.

We too become weary just as Elijah did trying to win souls for the kingdom. Discouragement comes when our loved ones reject our offers to go to church or listen to our pleas for their souls. But God knows our hearts and the labor of our love, and He will give us direction on what to do next. God is there, not in the wind, not in the earthquakes, but in that still, small voice. Listen, and you will hear Him.

Dear Lord: Your power is greater than the wind, earthquakes, and fire, even when it comes in just a whisper. Forgive me when I look for it in all the wrong places and disregard those soft gentle words You whisper to me. Help me know Your voice so I might follow the path You have paved for me. May You be glorified in all I say and do. In Jesus' name, Amen.

CORN PUDDING

1 box Jiffy cornbread mix
1 can cream-style corn
8 ounces sour cream
1 stick butter, melted
2 eggs
1 can whole kernel corn

Mix all ingredients; pour into greased dish. Bake at 350 degrees for 45 minutes.

January 24

And it came to pass, as they still went on, and talked, that, behold, there appeared a chariot of fire, and horses of fire, and parted them both asunder; and Elijah went up by a whirlwind into heaven.

—2 Kings 2:11, kjv

Elijah, a Tishbite prophet of God, had lived his life teaching, preaching, and leading others to serve God. He endured much hardship but also saw many great miracles. A man named Elisha was working in his fields when Elijah went and placed his mantle (cloak) over his shoulders, anointing him to be his son and successor. Elisha accepted and became an attendant and disciple of Elijah. They respected and loved one another, though they knew their time together would one day end.

One day while out walking, they came upon the Jordan River. Elijah took off his cloak and struck the water with it. The water divided, and the men crossed over on dry ground. Elijah asked Elisha what he would like him to do for him before they parted. Elisha asked for a double portion of Elijah's spirit.

As they walked on, Elijah was taken up in a whirlwind right before Elisha's eyes. Elisha was amazed and yet grief-stricken that his friend and mentor was gone. He thought the power of God also would be gone. As Elijah was taken up, his cloak fell from him. Elisha tore away his own clothing and picked up the fallen cloak of Elijah's. Thinking the power of God had left with Elijah, he stood on the bank of the river and struck the river with the cloak, just as Elijah had done. The Jordan River immediately parted, and Elisha crossed over, once again on dry ground.

Though Elisha was a God-fearing man, he also was human. He had trusted Elijah's wisdom and prophetic ministry so much, he wondered if God's power would be taken with him when he parted. But when Elisha tested God by striking the coat against the water, he witnessed the same power that was with Elijah.

We have times in our lives when we put our trust in others more than in God. We depend on their faith, wisdom, and power to carry us. It's important that we strive to grow spiritually in our faith so our relationship with God is personal and everlasting. Then, if God should call us to be separated from that one who has mentored or discipled us, our strength in the Lord will be evident and real.

Father: Thank You for Your mercy, grace, and awesome power in my life. Without You I can do nothing; with You I am able to do wonderful things in Your name. Help me to grow in my faith so I might live abundantly and victoriously until the day You call me home. In Jesus' name, Amen.

Today's recipe found on page 382 SEAFOOD ANGEL HAIR PASTA

January 25

When the body touched Elisha's bones, the man came to life and stood up on his feet.

—2 KINGS 13:21

ELISHA, THE DISCIPLE, attendant, and successor of Elijah, was a very gentle and affectionate man of God. He and Elijah were together for seven years before God took Elijah to heaven in a chariot of fire. After that happened, Elisha became the leading prophet in the Northern Kingdom of Israel and a consultant for Israel's kings.

During his fifty years of ministry, he witnessed many miracles because of the power of God in his life that was passed down from Elijah. They were mostly acts of mercy, which included healing a bitter spring, dividing the Jordan River, obtaining water for people and livestock to drink, multiplying a widow's oil, raising a boy from the dead, curing Naaman of leprosy, healing a poisonous stew, causing an iron ax to float, and striking the Syrians with blindness.

Though Elisha had performed many great miracles, he ironically acquired a fatal illness and died. But even after his death, the power of God was still evident when a dead man's body was thrown into Elisha's grave. When the body touched Elisha's bones, the man came to life and stood to his feet.

This miracle shows us that a godly person's influence does not end at death but can yet be a source of spiritual life for others even after they are gone. It also causes us to reflect on our own lives and the impact we have on others day by day. Are people revived and renewed by our words and compassion? Do we bring fresh hope, life, and enthusiasm to the discouraged and downtrodden? No person's actions stop with himself. What we say or do, whether for good or evil, affects the lives of those who have crossed our path one way or another, even after we are gone.

Father: Thank You for my heritage and for allowing me to be born into a godly family. Though many are gone, I still have the testimony of their lives to bring me strength and hope. Help me to pass on to my family a godly character and the blessing of being a child of the King. In Jesus' name, Amen.

SAUCY BEEF TIPS (crockpot)

1 - 1½ pounds lean stew meat, cut into 1-inch cubes
1 can cream of mushroom soup
1 can or jar of mushrooms
1 can French onion soup

Put everything in crockpot; cook 8 hours on low. Serve over rice, potatoes, or noodles.

January 26

The LORD warned Israel and Judah through all his prophets and seers: "Turn from your evil ways. Observe my commands and decrees, in accordance with the entire Law that I commanded your fathers to obey and that I delivered to you through my servants the prophets."

—2 KINGS 17:13

THE ISRAELITES HAD sinned against God for over two hundred years when finally God had enough. They rejected the messages from the prophets about righteousness and holy living, and they served the gods of the pagan world by adopting their customs and lifestyles. God's only option for Israel was a judgment to dissolve the nation, leaving only a small portion of faithful believers to experience the fulfillment of His promises. God warned them with the words of this verse, but they would not listen. Because of their repeated sin and unwillingness to obey God's Word, He removed His presence from them.

After all God had done for the Israelites, they would not listen. Many prophets tried to lead them to follow God, but their hearts were hard and they wanted to do their own thing. Is this not what we see today in our society? Preachers, prophets, teachers, and ministers of God all over the world are doing as Elijah, Elisha, Amos, Hosea, and other prophets did in trying to lead people to repentance and salvation. Just as the Israelites worshiped idols they believed would lead them to greater pleasure and prosperity, many of us are guilty of the same. It's time to get serious about serving God and repent of our greed and fleshly desires. He loves us so much, but if we are not careful, we too might find ourselves empty, lost, and without God's presence in our lives. Let's turn today from our sin and be broken before Him. As we do, God will fill us with His Spirit, His love, and a desire for righteousness and holy living.

Thank You, Lord, for sending prophets and ministers into my life to teach me how to serve You. I repent for wanting to do my own thing, even when Your Word tells me it's wrong. Guide me with Your Spirit to forever follow after You. In Jesus' name, Amen.

CHEESY CORN AND MAC (crockpot)

2 pounds Velveeta, cubed
16 ounces bowtie pasta
2 cups milk
2 cans whole kernel corn
2 cans creamed corn
2 sticks butter

Put all ingredients in crockpot on low for 3–4 hours, until pasta is tender.

January 27

Jabez cried out to the God of Israel, "Oh, that You would bless me and enlarge my territory! Let your hand be with me, and keep me from harm so that I will be free from pain." And God granted his request.

—1 CHRONICLES 4:10

L ITTLE IS KNOWN about Jabez, except that he was more honorable than his brothers and that his mother gave him his name because she bore him in sorrow—Jabez means "sorrow" or "pain." By this verse, we can see that Jabez was a man of prayer, and he prayed with a deep passion for God. Though Jabez was born into sorrow, God had a plan for his life. It is assumed that Jabez was born in poverty, and in this prayer he asks God to give him an increase and keep him from harm.

How many of us have gone through times of desperation and feelings of hopelessness in our lifetime, perhaps having been born into a poor family or with only one parent? Just as Jabez cried out to God for help, we too must do the same. God heard him, and He will hear us. God granted Jabez's request, and He will grant ours. As we cry out to God and tell Him what our needs are, He is listening and eager to grant our requests.

God of Israel: Thank You for loving me and hearing my prayers. You care about me, especially when I am sorrowful and in pain. Increase my territory so I might serve You better. Help me to use my resources to honor You. As You bless me, I promise to use it for Your glory. Bring lost souls into my life so I may tell them of Your saving grace. In Jesus' name, Amen.

CHICKEN AND DUMPLINGS

2 pounds boneless, skinless chicken breasts
5 cups water with 5 chicken bouillon cubes
1 teaspoon salt
½ teaspoon pepper
3–4 carrots, sliced
2 stalks celery, chopped
1 small onion, chopped
1 can evaporated milk
1 can buttermilk biscuits

Cut chicken into chunks. Put all ingredients, except evaporated milk and biscuits, in large pot; simmer 1 hour or until meat is done and vegetables are tender. Add evaporated milk; bring to rolling boil. Cut each biscuit into 5 pieces; drop each piece into boiling liquid. Put lid on, turn heat down, and cook 10 minutes or until dumplings have formed. Do not overcook or they will fall apart.

January 28

And David said unto God, I have sinned greatly, because I have done this thing: but now, I beseech thee, do away the iniquity of thy servant; for I have done very foolishly.

—1 CHRONICLES 21:8, KJV

THE LORD GAVE King David victory everywhere he went because he did what was just and right in God's eyes. But when God lifted His Spirit from Israel because of their continuous sin and rebellion, Satan rose up and tempted David to take his eyes off God and put them onto himself. He did so by having David take a census of Israel for the purpose of taxing the people so they might pay for the building of the temple. By doing the count, David was trying to exalt himself and no longer lived in humility to God. Satan led David to believe that God would endorse this prideful act, but this was evil in His sight, so God punished Israel.

David realized his sin and was sorry. He begged God to forgive him and lift the judgment off the people of Israel and punish only him. Though David was remorseful for his sin, God's judgment was still carried out upon Israel and him.

Throughout the Bible, we see recurring instances of divine punishment being carried out, even after confession, repentance, and forgiveness. By causing us to endure the consequences of sin, God honors His own law and shows Himself to be a righteous ruler. There may be times in our lives when we, too, are sorry for our sin and beg God to forgive us, but the consequences may still come. God owes us nothing. Forgiveness and the temporal punishment we might endure is merely the carrying out of His law. God loves us, and it is His choice whether a punishment is shortened, cancelled, or carried out to the fullest. He is a righteous and compassionate God, full of love and mercy, and will do what is just in His eyes.

Dear God: You are my righteousness, my Redeemer, and my Friend. You judge justly and right, according to Your law. I repent of the foolish things I do that are not honorable to You. Help me to follow after Your law and live according to Your will and way. In Jesus' name, Amen.

CROCKPOT ROAST

2–4 pounds rump roast
1 package onion soup mix
1–2 cans cream of mushroom soup
1 can water

Put everything in crockpot. Cook on high for 6 hours. Slice; return to crockpot until desired tenderness.

January 29

And you, my son Solomon, acknowledge the God of your father, and serve him with whole-hearted devotion and with a willing mind, for the LORD searches every heart and understands every motive behind the thoughts. If you seek him, he will be found by you; but if you forsake him, he will reject you forever.

—1 CHRONICLES 28:9

KING DAVID SPOKE these words to his son Solomon when he charged him to follow all the commands of the Lord and build a temple for the ark of God. To acknowledge God means knowing Him by learning about Him. It means living for Him and having close fellowship with Him by reading His Word and praying. Serving God means being obedient to His Holy Word and desiring His grace, kingdom, power, presence, will, and righteousness in our lives. It is recognizing the needs of others and then complying with the commands of the law in performing the duties to serve them. This is what it means to hunger and thirst for righteousness. In doing all of this, our attitudes must be right or it will mean nothing. God already knows if our hearts are sincere, humble, and pure. If they are, we will be a part of God's eternal purpose. If they are not, we choose His eternal rejection and punishment. The decision is ours; let's be careful to make the right choice.

Righteous Father: I acknowledge You as my Lord and King today and forever. My mind is fixed on Your law and Your love, and I choose to serve You as I serve others. Search my heart and see if there are any wrong motives in me. If there are, forgive me and make me pure and clean. You are the one I seek, and it's Your authority I want to follow. Help me walk in the straight and narrow and not fall when temptation comes. May I be found faithful when judgment day comes. In Jesus' name, Amen.

PARTY POTATOES

1 (2-pound) package frozen hash browns
1 can cream of celery soup
8 ounces shredded sharp cheddar cheese
1 small onion, chopped
1 (8-ounce) container sour cream
1 stick butter, melted
1 sleeve Ritz crackers, crushed

Mix all ingredients except butter and crackers. Pour into a 9x13-inch dish. Mix together melted butter and Ritz crackers and spread over the top. Bake uncovered at 350 degrees for 1 hour.

January 30

But who am I, and what is my people, that we should be able to offer so willingly after this sort? For all things come of thee, and of thine own have we given thee.

—1 Chronicles 29:14, KJV

KING DAVID HAD repented of his sin of pride and was once again serving and honoring God. He had become old and knew he was not going to build the temple of God, but it was something his son Solomon would do. God had given David the details for its construction and now he would share them with his son.

David instructed Solomon to be strong and courageous and not be afraid of the task before him. He assured him that God would be with him all the way, until the temple was completed. David gave of his own personal resources that were needed to build the temple. He provided gold, silver, bronze, iron, wood, onyx, turquoise, and all kinds of fine stone and marble. Then his leaders, officers, officials, and families consecrated themselves to the Lord and willingly gave everything they had toward the work. David was pleased with the results and rejoiced greatly in the Lord. In the words of this verse, David humbly admitted to God that though he and the others gave so very generously, it all belonged to God and came from Him in the first place.

Sometimes, we grudgingly give our resources to God, such as our tithes and offerings, but it all belongs to Him. God merely gives it to us to use. David prayed that God would give his son wholehearted devotion to keep His requirements, commands, and decrees and to do everything he could to build the temple of God. Shouldn't this be our prayer for ourselves and for our children?

Father: I praise You for everything You have given me. All I have has come from You. Help me to part with my personal resources and give back to You what is rightfully Yours. Forgive me when I withhold my finances from You, when I don't trust You to meet my needs. Help me to be obedient to Your Word. In Jesus' name, Amen.

RAMEN EGG DROP CHICKEN NOODLE SOUP

8 cups water
1–2 cups cooked, diced chicken (leftovers great)
2 packages Ramen noodles
2 eggs, beaten
4–6 green onions, chopped

Boil water; add chicken, noodles, and seasoning packets. Turn down to simmer; slowly pour in beaten eggs while gently stirring. Add chopped green onions; serve.

January 31

Give me wisdom and knowledge, that I lead this people, for who is able to govern this great people of yours?

—2 CHRONICLES 1:10

THIS WAS THE statement made by Solomon when God asked him what he would like to receive from Him. Solomon had served God and pleased Him more than any other king, and God wanted to bless him for it. Solomon humbly asked God for wisdom and knowledge to lead his people. He truly wanted to know God's heart, mind, and will for his life. Because of Solomon's humble request, God also gave him wealth, riches, and honor.

God is the giver of life to His children. He gives us grace, mercy, and salvation, along with our necessities and desires. God also gives us wisdom and knowledge if we truly want it, but that comes only through prayer and Bible study.

Even though we may acquire wisdom and knowledge, it doesn't guarantee us a place in heaven. Just as God warned Solomon to be careful to walk in His ways and obey His commands, we must do the same. Solomon was the wisest man in the world, yet he fell away from God because of disobedience and rebellion against what he knew was right. As we study God's Word and pray, it is absolutely necessary to apply what we know to our lives and obey the commands of God. Then we will be guaranteed a home in heaven.

Father: You are the giver of life and provider of great gifts. Thank You for everything You have given me and for Your gifts of mercy, grace, and salvation. I praise You for giving me wisdom to know Your heart by reading Your Word and having fellowship with You. In Jesus' name, Amen.

CHILI

1–2 pounds ground beef
1 large onion, chopped
3 cloves garlic, minced
1 (16-ounce) can mild chili beans
1 can Mexican stewed tomatoes
1 (14.5-ounce) can diced tomatoes
2 cups water
2 beef bouillon cubes
1 package mild chili seasoning
1 tablespoon chili powder (or to taste)
2 teaspoons cumin
1 teaspoon cocoa

In large pot, brown ground meat; drain. Add onion; cook until tender. Add all remaining ingredients; simmer 1–2 hours.

February

The
Greatest is Love

February 1

When the heavens are shut up and there is no rain because your people have sinned against you, and when they pray toward this place and confess your name and turn from their sin because you have afflicted them, then hear from heaven and forgive the sin of Your servants, your people Israel. Teach them the right way to live, and send rain on the land you gave your people for an inheritance.

—2 CHRONICLES 6:26–27

THIS WAS A portion of Solomon's prayer to God on behalf of the people of Israel. The temple of the Lord was completed, and Solomon stood before it and dedicated it to God. He was sorry for Israel's rebellion and sin and pleaded for their forgiveness. Solomon wanted God to deal with each person's heart that once knew Him so they would again walk in His ways. He also asked God to hear the prayers of those who once knew Him and wanted to serve Him again. Solomon's desire was that the whole earth would fear (love) God and know His name.

This prayer is one that we should all pray concerning the sin and rebellion of the world. It shows us that unrepentant sin can separate us from God, even though we once knew and served Him. We must be serious about the lost and feel the same burden for their souls as Solomon did.

Dear Lord: "When they sin against you—for there is no one who does not sin—and you become angry with them and give them over to the enemy, who takes them captive to a land far away or near; and if they have a change of heart in the land where they are held captive, and repent and plead with you in the land of their captivity and say, 'We have sinned, we have done wrong and acted wickedly'; and if they turn back to you with all their heart and soul in the land of their captivity where they were taken, and pray toward the land you gave their fathers, toward the city you have chosen and toward the temple I have built for your name; then from heaven, your dwelling place, hear their prayer and their pleas, and uphold their cause. And forgive your people, who have sinned against you" (2 Chron. 6:36–39).

Forgive me, Lord. Forgive me as a part of a nation that has turned its back on You and beheld sin and unrighteousness. Help me to be bold, strong, and live my life to honor You as my Lord and Savior. Draw the lost with Your Holy Spirit and cause them to seek salvation in You. In Jesus' name, Amen.

Today's recipe found on page 383 SWEET AND SOUR CHICKEN

February 2

If my people, which are called by my name, shall humble themselves, and pray, and seek my face, and turn from their wicked ways; then will I hear from heaven, and will forgive their sin and will heal their land.

—2 CHRONICLES 7:14, KJV

THE LORD ANSWERED Solomon with these words after he completed the temple of the Lord and had dedicated it to Him. Solomon prayed fervently for the people who once knew the Lord and those who never knew Him to be saved from their sin. God told Solomon He did hear his prayer and would forgive the people if they met certain criteria.

They would need to do four things. First, they would need to humble themselves. The people had shown such moral decline, spiritual apathy, and worldly compromise, and God wanted to know they were truly sorry and wanted to change. Second, they needed to pray. If they were serious about returning to God, their prayers would show sorrow and remorse. They would need to cry out earnestly in desperation for God's mercy and grace. Third, the people would need to seek God's face diligently and long for His presence in their lives. And fourth, they would need to turn from their wicked ways, genuinely repent of all their sin and idolatry, renounce conformity to the world, and strive to become closer to God than ever before.

If the people would do this, God promised to hear their prayers, forgive their sins, and heal their land.

The same is true for all of us today. Whether we once knew God and fell away or never knew Him at all, we have the assurance that if we do as He told the Israelites to do, we too will have forgiveness, peace, cleansing, restoration, and all the blessings of heaven.

Father: Forgive me when I fail to pray as I should. I repent of my complacency and neglect in doing what Your Word says I should do. Help me to do my part in this world to see You once again have the respect and honor You deserve. In Jesus' name, Amen.

CREAMY CORN (crockpot)

3 pounds frozen corn
½ cup butter
1 (8-ounce) package cream cheese
2 tablespoons sugar
¼ cup milk
6 slices American or Velveeta cheese

Put all ingredients in crockpot and cook on low for 4 hours; stir occasionally.

February 3

The king had granted him all his request, according to the hand of the LORD his God upon him.

—EZRA 7:6, KJV

And on the first day of the fifth month came he to Jerusalem, according to the good hand of his God upon him.

—EZRA 7:9, KJV

And I was strengthened as the hand of the LORD my God was upon me, and I gathered together out of Israel chief men to go up with me.

—EZRA 7:28, KJV

EZRA WAS A teacher who knew the Law of Moses very well. Since the God of Israel gave the Word to Moses, Ezra believed it (the Word) should be studied, obeyed, and taught by everyone.

Ezra is a model for us today because he was devoted to teaching and living God's Word so that truth, righteousness, and purity among God's people might be preserved. God was pleased with Ezra because of his dedication to Him. In just one chapter, it is mentioned three times that "the hand of the Lord his God was on him [Ezra]."

God honors obedience to His Word, and those who serve Him wholeheartedly reap His blessings. If we are loyal to our Lord and strive to live as close to His will as possible, we too will have the privilege and honor of knowing that the gracious hand of our God is on us.

Dear Lord: What an awesome God You are! It is such an honor to be Your child, and I am so blessed knowing Your gracious hand is on me. I give You glory for watching over me at all times and for guiding me with Your Holy Spirit where I should go and what I should do. Forgive me when I don't listen and take a different path. Help me to study, obey, live, and teach Your Word so others might know You and be saved. In Jesus' name, Amen.

BAKED CHEESE NOODLES

1 cup cottage cheese
1 cup sour cream
1 (6-ounce) package fine-cut noodles
2 tablespoons grated onion
1 teaspoon Worcestershire sauce
½–¾ teaspoon garlic salt
3 tablespoons butter
½ cup grated Parmesan cheese

Stir together cottage cheese and sour cream. Cook noodles according to package; drain and add to cottage cheese mixture. Add onion, Worcestershire sauce, garlic salt, and butter. Pour into greased baking dish. Sprinkle with Parmesan cheese and bake at 350 degrees for 40 minutes.

February 4

When I heard this, I tore my tunic and cloak, pulled hair from my head and beard and sat down appalled.

—Ezra 9:3

THIS WAS EZRA's reaction when he heard the Israelites had intermarried with non-believers. The Jewish people failed to separate themselves from those around them who were involved in immorality, idolatry, and all sorts of sinful lifestyles. Though God had warned them numerous times and gave them many opportunities to repent and turn back to Him, they refused and continued to live in sin. When Ezra heard the news that they had disobeyed the law again and were involved with those who followed detestable and impure pagan practices, he was grief-stricken and appalled. Ezra loved his people and he loved God, but he knew that unless they repented and turned from their sin, they would not inherit the kingdom of God. That Ezra would rip his clothes and pull out his hair and beard showed extravagant remorse on his part.

How do we react when someone we love turns their back on God and commits sin? Are we so grieved that we react in some extravagant way, or do we merely turn our heads and act as though it doesn't affect us? Ezra went to God in prayer, ashamed and disgraced on behalf of his people, and wept before the Lord for their souls. Is this not what we should also do when our loved ones fall into sin and turn their backs on the One who gave His life for them?

Dear God: You are holy, and You also want Your children to be holy. When we are not, You are displeased. Forgive me when I forsake being with people who love and obey You and begin to compromise my beliefs by spending too much time with others who don't honor You. Help me to keep my eyes on You and hunger after Your Word and the righteousness about which it speaks. I want to live my life so it will not be mistaken whom I serve; may I always represent You. In Jesus' name, Amen.

SIMPLE SIDE SALAD

½ cup canola or extra light olive oil
⅓ cup vinegar or wine vinegar
3–5 cloves garlic, minced
½ teaspoon salt
¼ teaspoon pepper
1 head lettuce, chopped

Mix together oil, vinegar, garlic, salt, and pepper. Refrigerate until ready to use. Chop or tear lettuce into bite-sized pieces. Toss with dressing before serving.

February 5

O LORD, God of heaven, the great and awesome God, who keeps his covenant of love with those who love him and obey his commands.

—NEHEMIAH 1:5

Then I prayed to the God of heaven, and I answered the king.

—NEHEMIAH 2:4–5

NEHEMIAH WAS A man of ability, courage, perseverance, and prayer. He was sent by the king of Persia to rebuild the wall of Jerusalem that had been damaged severely and also to bring spiritual renewal to the city. Because of the opposition Nehemiah knew would come, he fasted and prayed for four months. He poured out his heart to God and wept for the people he was so deeply burdened for and loved. Nehemiah loved the Lord and realized that really knowing Him and having His heart would happen only with prayer.

Though Nehemiah was not timid of long periods of fasting and prayer, there were also those times when he needed an answer from God rather quickly. One day, before the king sent him to restore the damaged wall, he asked Nehemiah why he was so sad. Nehemiah responded that his heart was heavy for the people of Israel because of their sin and disobedience to God, but also because of the damaged wall in Jerusalem where his forefathers were buried. The king then asked Nehemiah what it was that he wanted. Nehemiah didn't have time to fast and pray but merely paused in his thoughts and prayed to God for direction. Because Nehemiah fervently prayed daily and often fasted, he was able to answer the king promptly with the assurance that his brief prayer also was heard and answered by God.

We don't always have time to fast and pray for a decision or concern because we need a quick answer. If our prayer lives are "up to par" and we are daily having fellowship with the Lord, then He will hear our brief prayers, too, in that time of need.

O great and awesome God: Thank You for always being there for me. You hear me every time I mention Your name, and You are ready and willing to meet my requests. I'm sorry for the times I neglect having fellowship with You. Please help me to organize my time so being with You receives priority. In Jesus' name, Amen.

OVEN-ROASTED POTATOES

1 envelope onion soup mix
⅓ cup vegetable oil
6 potatoes, quartered

Put all ingredients in a shallow baking dish. Bake at 350 degrees for 1 hour, or until potatoes are tender and golden brown. Stir potatoes every 15 minutes while baking.

February 6

Do not grieve, for the joy of the LORD is your strength.

—NEHEMIAH 8:10

THE REBUILDING OF the wall of Jerusalem was completed. It was repaired in just fifty-two days, which everyone knew was an act of God because there was serious opposition from outside and inside the city. Nehemiah, the governor of Jerusalem, Ezra, the priest and scribe, and the Levite instructors gathered together with the Israelite people for a time of worship and praise to God. Ezra stood high and read the Book of the Law of Moses and explained to the people in words they could understand how they should live. As he read, the people became convicted of their sin and wept before the Lord. Because the Word was read with such clarity, power, and conviction, they understood the depth of their sin and feelings of guilt. They were sorry for the way they had lived and felt great remorse. Nehemiah instructed the people not to grieve but that because they were so deeply moved after understanding the Word, they would find their strength in the joy of the Lord.

God's Word, along with a sincere desire to obey its instruction, will produce true, heartfelt joy. This type of joy is found only after God's Word is revealed and through true repentance, reconciliation with God, and the presence of the Holy Spirit working daily in our lives. Though we may face various trials and temptations, the fellowship we have in Christ gives us the power and motivation to persevere in faith until the end.

Dear Lord: I love to gather with others and praise Your name. Because of my relationship with You, I am able to persevere though the trials and temptations that face me daily. In You, I find joy and strength. Your Word assures me that I am victorious when I put my trust in You. I'll praise Your name forever. In Jesus' name, Amen.

IMPOSSIBLE CHEESEBURGER PIE

1 pound ground beef
1 cup chopped onion
½ teaspoon salt
1 cup shredded cheddar cheese
1 cup milk
½ cup Bisquick baking mix
2 eggs

Cook ground beef until done; drain. Add chopped onion and salt; cook 5 minutes. Spread into greased 9-inch pie dish; sprinkle with cheese. Mix together milk, Bisquick, and eggs. Pour on top of beef mix. Bake at 400 degrees for 25 minutes, until knife inserted in center comes out clean.

February 7

Remember me for this, O my God, and do not blot out what I have so faithfully done for the house of my God and its services.

—Nehemiah 13:14

THIS IS WHAT Nehemiah prayed to God after he finished the wall around Jerusalem and was restoring worship in the temple. The Levite teachers and singers were doing their ministry, and the people were once again being blessed. They were now more faithful and willing to bring their tithes into God's house.

There were times, though, that Nehemiah had to rebuke those who were lax in their moral and spiritual commitment to God. He wanted to show no compromise for God's Word and His house. Nehemiah realized that as a leader he must have a holy anger toward unrighteousness and even take drastic measures to correct evil situations. He knew there would be a time for gentleness and meekness, but blatant disregard of God's will within the church must be dealt with seriously. Nehemiah took God's work passionately and with great zeal, exhorting the people to always do the same. We must do the same and strive to bring holiness and righteousness back into our churches and communities. If we don't do our part, who will?

O my God: You are magnificent and righteous, and there is none like You. I love and honor You as my King and Lord. Living a godly life isn't always easy, but You always refresh me when I am obedient to Your Word. Help me to look to You for strength to face the trials and temptations of life. Bring those into my life who need to know You, and may I have the zeal and compassion to lead them to a saving knowledge of You. In Jesus' name, Amen.

SHRIMP AND CHEESE CASSEROLE

3 eggs, beaten
1 can cheddar cheese soup
1 ½ cans milk
6 slices buttered bread
8 ounces sharp cheese, sliced
10–14 ounces pre-cooked medium shrimp
Dash of salt and pepper

In large bowl, mix together eggs, soup, and milk. Place 2 buttered slices of bread on bottom of buttered 2-quart baking dish. Lay slice of cheese on each, then half the shrimp. Add dash of salt and pepper. Make another layer, ending with bread and cheese. Pour soup mixture over everything. Bake at 350 degrees for 40 minutes, until brown and puffy. Tuna or chicken may be used in place of shrimp.

February 8

The Jews struck down all their enemies with the sword, killing and destroying them, and they did what they pleased to those who hated them.

—ESTHER 9:5

THE EVIL HAMAN, a high official to King Xerxes, had picked the thirteenth day of Adar for his plot to have all Jews killed. But with the help of Queen Esther and her uncle Mordecai, King Xerxes gave permission for the Jews to fight back against their enemies as an act of self-defense. Mordecai, a Jew, had become very prominent and was second in charge to the king. In his power with humility, he became well known and favored throughout the land.

As Mordecai's people fought back against their enemies, God blessed them with strength and power to kill thousands of men, including ten of Haman's sons. What Haman meant for Jewish genocide had been turned around and the opposite took place. Haman and his sons were dead and the Jews grew in number and were stronger in power. After the war was over, Mordecai called a two-day festival to celebrate God's deliverance of His people from Haman's evil plot to destroy them.

This should be a reminder to us that God can overrule any plot the enemy has to defeat us. We should never see ourselves as victims of fate or chance. God has a wonderful plan for each of us. It is never to see us harmed but to redeem us and give us hope.

Dear Lord: I love Your law and want to meditate on it all day long. It makes me wiser and gives me more understanding of who You are. Draw me close to You, and never depart from my side. May I be burdened for those whose enemies want to destroy them. Help me to lead them to safety by sharing the good news of the living Word with them. In Jesus' name, Amen.

MALAYSIAN PEANUT BUTTER CHICKEN

6–8 green onions or one small onion
1–2 cloves garlic, minced
¼ cup soy sauce
¼ cup peanut butter (smooth or chunky)
2 tablespoons brown sugar
3 tablespoons lemon juice
1 teaspoon coriander (optional)
¼ teaspoon cayenne pepper (optional)
2 ½ pounds chicken (dark, light, on or off bone)

Put all ingredients, except chicken, in food processor; pulse until blended. Pour into bowl; add chicken. Cover and refrigerate about 2 hours. Arrange chicken pieces in baking dish; pour sauce over it. Bake at 375 degrees for 45–55 minutes, basting occasionally. Serve with rice or noodles.

February 9

In the land of Uz there lived a man whose name was Job. This man was blameless and upright; he feared God and shunned evil.

—JOB 1:1

JOB HAD SEVEN sons, three daughters, seven thousand sheep, three thousand camels, five hundred yoke of oxen, five hundred donkeys, and a large number of servants. He was considered to be the greatest man among all the people of the East.

One day Satan came to the Lord and told Him that Job only loved and obeyed Him because He had blessed him so mightily. To prove Satan wrong, God gave him permission to test Job by killing and destroying all his family and earthly possessions. When everyone and everything had perished, Job fell to the ground and worshiped the Lord with these words (verse 21), "Naked I came from my mother's womb, and naked I will depart. The Lord gave and the Lord has taken away; may the Name of the Lord be praised." Job had passed his first test.

How do we react when something happens that causes us grief or loss? Do we get angry with God and curse Him or do we recognize that it is Satan, the author of all evil? Job had reacted with intense grief, yet he was submitted to God and worshiped Him in the midst of his calamity and loss. This is how we, as faithful believers, should respond when suffering and afflictions come upon us. We must humbly pray for God's grace and strength to see us through our circumstances and trials. As we do, our faith and trust will grow and God will be glorified in our lives.

Father God: You are my strength, my fortress, and my deliverer; in You is everything I need. When I cry to You for help, You are there. As Job faithfully worshiped You in his distress, may I do the same. Help me to seek You and not lose trust when trials come my way. May I look to You always in the times of great blessings and in the times of grief. In Jesus' name, Amen.

CHICKEN SALAD

3 boneless, skinless chicken breasts
½ cup celery, diced
½ small onion, diced (optional)
1 cup seedless grapes, halved
½ cup pecans or almonds, diced/slivered
½ cup mayonnaise
Dash salt and pepper
½ cup thawed Cool Whip

Cook chicken in small amount of water in pan until done; cool and dice. Mix all ingredients together. Serve with lettuce as a salad or on favorite bread as a sandwich.

February 10

So went Satan forth from the presence of the LORD, and smote Job with sore boils from the sole of his foot unto his crown.

—JOB 2:7, KJV

JOB ENDURED HIS first test and remained faithful to his Lord. Though Satan had killed all seven of his children and destroyed all his earthly possessions, Job still worshiped God. Now the second test was about to unfold, and the Lord once again gave Satan permission to attack Job.

This time, Satan afflicted him with painful sores all over his body. He was in pain day and night, and even Job's wife tempted him to abandon his integrity and curse God, but Job did not sin and remained loyal to his Lord.

Job exemplifies the patient endurance of a godly man, even though he suffered innocently. We are told in 2 Timothy 3:12 that everyone who wants to live a godly life in Christ Jesus will be persecuted, and this certainly holds true in Job's case. In 1 Peter 1:6–7, the apostle Peter says it this way: "In this you greatly rejoice, though now for a little while you may have had to suffer grief in all kinds of trials. These have come so that your faith—of greater worth than gold, which perishes even though refined by fire—may be proved genuine and may result in praise, glory and honor when Jesus Christ is revealed." What an encouragement it is to know that as we are tested with trials and circumstances, we are also being refined and made pure if we, like Job, remain loyal to our Lord.

Dear Lord: As the heavens declare Your glory, so do I praise and thank You for the awesome God You are. You watch me day and night and know everything about me. You know the trials and circumstances that face me daily, and You continue to bless and keep me. Thank You for allowing me to become refined by Your fire and for causing me to be made pure before Your eyes. Help me to remain loyal to You all the days of my life. In Jesus' name, Amen.

MACARONI AND CHEESE (crockpot)

1 (8-ounce) box macaroni
1 (12-ounce) can evaporated milk
1 ½ cups milk
2 eggs, beaten
¼ cup melted butter
1 teaspoon salt
3 cups sharp cheese

Cook macaroni according to box; drain. Combine all ingredients in greased crockpot, reserving some of cheese for topping. Cook on low 3–4 hours. Sprinkle cheese over the top and serve.

February 11

Then I would still have this consolation—my joy in unrelenting pain—that I had not denied the words of the Holy One.

—Job 6:10

JOB HAD LOST all seven of his children, all his earthly possessions, was being tormented continually from painful sores all over his body, and now faced the one thing that he dreaded: abandonment from God. Yet Job still was consoled by the fact that he did not turn from his Lord. He searched his heart thoroughly and was not conscious of any unrepentant sin. He faithfully served God and believed himself to be innocent of anything evil in God's eyes, but he wondered why God would allow these terrible things happen to him.

Through all the mental and physical anguish, Job still found joy in knowing he had not denied the Holy One whom he served. It is always easier to worship and serve God in the good times and harder when things are bad, but God wants our praise all the time. Philippians 4:4 tells us to rejoice in the Lord at all times. Life is a test, and how we respond to it determines our grade. Was it easy for Job to praise God in all he endured? No, but his faith in God was so strong that Job knew God surely must have some good reason for why He was allowing the enemy to tempt and test him so severely. As we face everyday trials, let's be careful to keep our attitudes in tune with God's and rejoice and praise Him for seeing us through the storms and trials of life.

Dear Lord: You are the One who lives in the sanctuary of my heart and the One who cares for me with an unfailing love. Thank You for loving me and for being with me through the storms of life. If it were not for Your power, I would have given up too soon; but You are always there when I need You. Keep me safe, O God, and be my refuge and shield. In Jesus' name, Amen.

ROLLED UP PANCAKES (English/Swedish)

1 cup flour
1 ¾ cups milk
2–3 eggs
¼ teaspoon salt
1 tablespoon sugar
1 tablespoon vegetable oil
Real lemon juice or fresh-squeezed
Sugar

Beat first 6 ingredients together with electric mixer until smooth. Pour 2–3 tablespoons into very hot 9-inch Teflon pan sprayed with cooking oil. Turn when top is dry, just until light brown. Sprinkle each crepe with sugar and lemon juice; roll and keep warm until ready to serve.

February 12

Though he slay me, yet will I trust in him: but I will maintain mine own ways before him.

—JOB 13:15, KJV

JOB CONTINUED TO trust and praise God though he was searching for reasons why God allowed him to be robbed of his health, wealth, and fellowship with Him. A few months had passed, and Job's body was deteriorating. The painful sores were festering, and his body was clothed in worms (Job 7:5). How much more could he take, and for how long would he have to endure? And what had he done wrong to deserve such punishment? These were Job's questions, and rightfully so. Job seemed to be delirious at times, probably from lack of sleep and infection. He even begged for death to come, but it didn't. But he pressed on in his faith and love for God. Job expressed that nothing or no one would ever change his mind regarding his relationship with God and that even if God chose to end his life, his hope would remain in Him.

The apostle Paul said it so well in Romans 8:36–39: "For your sake we face death all day long; we are considered as sheep to be slaughtered. No, in all these things we are more than conquerors through him who loved us. For I am convinced that neither death nor life, neither angels nor demons, neither the present nor the future, nor any powers, neither height nor depth, nor anything else in all creation, will be able to separate us from the love of God that is in Christ Jesus our Lord."

Father: You are my Rock and my Savior. When darkness is all around, the light of Your love shines down. Search my heart; see if there is any wicked way within me. Cleanse me and purify me so all is well with my soul. Teach me Your way, and lead me on a straight path forevermore. Help me to be strong when trouble comes and my faith is tested. In Jesus' name, Amen.

CHICKEN CHOWDER

4 slices bacon
3 tablespoons flour
½ teaspoon pepper
4 cups milk
2 cups frozen hash brown potatoes
1 (16-ounce) bag frozen corn
2 cups cooked chicken, diced
8 green onions, diced
8 ounces cheddar cheese, grated

Cook bacon until crisp; remove and crumble. Sprinkle flour over grease; cook until thickened on low. Add pepper, milk, potatoes, corn, chicken, and two-thirds of the green onions; bring to boil. Cook 10–15 minutes until potatoes are tender. Serve in bowls; top with the rest of onions, bacon, and cheese.

February 13

But he knoweth the way that I take: when he hath tried me, I shall come forth as gold. My foot hath held his steps, his way have I kept, and not declined.

—JOB 23:10-11, KJV

THIS SHOULD BE the testimony of every person, and especially every Christian. Job had lost everyone and everything—his family, his earthly possessions, his friends, his servants, and even God, who had turned from him. But Job wasn't bitter; instead, he tried to find God's purpose in the events and circumstances that had taken place in his life to try his faith.

How do we respond under tests and trials? Do we complain and become bitter toward God if something happens we think is unfair? Or do we do as Job did and remain close to the Lord? He followed in the steps of God, and we must do the same. When we go through trials in our lives that attack our strength and faith in God and are thinking of giving up and throwing in the towel, we must not do it! Just as Job pressed on, we too must closely follow God's steps and we will "come forth as gold."

Father: You are holy and just, and I love You with my whole heart. My eyes are fixed on You, and I will persevere, with Your help, until my life on earth is over. Forgive me when I feel persecuted by the world and then want to give up. Help me to walk in Your steps and not turn aside or look back. Thank You for the trials that have come to strengthen my faith, and thank You for the grace You have given me to win and come forth as gold. In Jesus' name, Amen.

FOIL-PACK TACO CHICKEN

4 boneless, skinless chicken breast halves (about 1 pound)
4 teaspoons taco seasoning mix
½ pound red potatoes, thinly sliced (about 2 cups)
½ cup thick and chunky salsa
¾ cup Mexican-style grated cheese
¼ cup sour cream

Sprinkle chicken with seasoning mix. Place potato slices on 4 large greased sheets of heavy-duty aluminum foil. Top with chicken, salsa, and cheese. Bring up foil sides; double-fold top and both ends to seal, leaving room for heat circulation inside. Place packets in baking pan. Bake at 350 degrees for 45 minutes or until chicken is thoroughly cooked and potatoes are tender. Allow packets to stand 5 minutes before opening. Cut slits to release steam before opening. Serve with sour cream.

February 14

After Job had prayed for his friends, the LORD made him prosperous again and gave him twice as much as he had before.

—JOB 42:10

JOB HAD THREE friends who, throughout his painful ordeal, would come and try to get him to curse God and relinquish his faith in Him, but Job would not. Yet as time went on, he became weary and less humble in his reasoning. Another friend and counselor, younger than the others, came to Job and scolded him for his self-righteous attitude. He made Job feel as though he did merit some of the pain due to sin he probably committed.

And then God spoke to Job. He told him of the complexity of the universe and that it was far too hard for him or any man to understand. God criticized Job for trying to comprehend the meaning of his suffering. He wanted Job to realize He created and ruled the world in wisdom and justice.

God instructed Job to pray for his friends. Job was obedient, and the Lord blessed him greater than before. He gave him back more than he ever had plus ten more children. His body was whole, and he lived many years to watch his children and grandchildren grow.

Job never did find the theological answer to why he suffered, but his story proved this: It isn't necessary to understand why we are faced with a handicap, affliction, or calamity of some sort. All we need to know is that God's divine presence is with us and all is well with our soul. Only when we are in true fellowship with the Lord is it possible to endure the circumstances and trials of life. With God, we are able to experience the joy and blessedness that comes by trusting in His mercy, compassion, and love, knowing that one day we will experience total healing and restoration for all eternity.

To You, O Lord, do I lift up my soul. Show me Your ways and teach me to love as You love and serve as You serve. When trials come, may I be found faithful and trust Your compassion, love, and grace to help me endure. My hope is in You, knowing that one day there will never again be pain and suffering. May my relationship with You be strengthened and refined as we walk together through every test and trial that comes. In Jesus' name, Amen.

CHEESY PIGS IN A BLANKET

1 can biscuits
4–5 slices cheese
8–10 hot dogs

Separate biscuits. Wrap ½ slice cheese and a hot dog into each one. Place on ungreased cookie sheet (seam side down); bake at 400 degrees for 10–15 minutes.

February 15

Blessed is the man who does not walk in the counsel of the wicked or stand in the way of sinners or sit in the seat of mockers. But his delight is in the law of the LORD, and on his law he meditates day and night.

—PSALM 1:1–2

WHAT WE DO with our time, what movies or television we watch, what magazines or books we read, what places we go, how we think, and how we act either honors or dishonors our Lord. Is the information we are feeding our minds wholesome and good, or would God be displeased by it? If we are to be Christlike, then a good way to test the things we do would be to ask ourselves if Jesus Himself would go there, do that, watch that, say that, or read that. And then, too, we should ask ourselves what things God's Word says we should do, watch, read, or go.

This is the law of the Lord. Laws tell us what we should and shouldn't do, and the one who thinks about the law and obeys it will be happy and blessed. Are you unhappy or feeling unblessed today? Read your Bible and obey the rules, and joy in Jesus will come.

Dear Lord: You are the delight and joy of my life; I yearn to know You in a greater way. I'm sorry for the things I do that are ungodly and contrary to Your will. Create in me a desire to meditate on Your Word and bring You honor as I walk in obedience to Your will. In Jesus' name, Amen.

CREAM OF BROCCOLI AND CAULIFLOWER SOUP

2 (10-ounce) packages frozen chopped broccoli *or* 1 bunch fresh broccoli, chopped
1 (10-ounce) package frozen cauliflower *or* ½ fresh cauliflower, chopped
2 cups chicken broth *or* 2 dissolved chicken bouillon cubes in 2 cups water
1 cup half-and-half (or whole milk)
1 teaspoon salt
¼ teaspoon pepper
2 cups grated Swiss or cheddar cheese

In saucepan, cook broccoli and cauliflower in broth until tender, about 15 minutes; let cool. Puree vegetables in food processor or blender, leaving a little chunky. Return to saucepan; add half-and-half, salt, and pepper. Heat on very low about 45 minutes; stir often. Mix in cheese right before serving.

February 16

Let the words of my mouth, and the meditation of my heart, be acceptable in thy sight, O LORD, my strength, and my redeemer.

—PSALM 19:14, KJV

GOD IS OUR strength, our hope, and the One who has saved us from sin and death. Our worship comes from our gratitude for what He has done and our recognition of who He is.

Worship is much more than what we do in church during the song service. It is also how we live our lives at home, work, school, places of employment, and communities. Worship involves every aspect of our lives; it is the condition of our hearts. At all times, we must be cautious of the words we speak, our actions, and our attitudes so others might see Jesus in us and also want to serve Him. The Lord is our Rock, as He is unmovable and unchangeable; and the Lord is our Redeemer, because He reached down into our pit of sin and rescued our souls from eternal death. He is a mighty God, and forever we shall rejoice and praise His name with the words of our mouths and the meditations of our hearts.

Dear Lord: You rescued me out of the wretched state of lostness I was in and planted me on solid ground. Now I am standing on You, my rock and Redeemer. Forgive me for my shortcomings and complacency in serving You. I want my heart to be pure so my life will illuminate the darkness of this world. May this day be a day of worship and honor to You, and may my life praise You not just in thought and words, but also in my actions. In Jesus' name, Amen.

STUFFED CABBAGE CASSEROLE

1 medium head cabbage
1 pound lean ground beef
1 medium onion, diced
½ cup uncooked rice
1 teaspoon garlic salt
1 teaspoon pepper
2 teaspoons Worcestershire Sauce
1 (32-ounce) can tomato juice, divided
1 tablespoon sugar
2 cans tomato soup

Cut cabbage into thin slices; use half to cover bottom of large greased baking dish. In bowl, mix ground beef, onion, rice, garlic salt, pepper, Worcestershire sauce, 2 cups of tomato juice, and sugar; spread mixture over cabbage. Cover with rest of cabbage. Mix soup with remaining tomato juice; pour over cabbage. Cover with foil. Bake at 325 degrees for 1½–2 hours, or until cabbage and rice are tender. Serve with mashed potatoes and sour cream, as desired.

February 17

The LORD is my shepherd; I shall not want.

—PSALM 23:1, KJV

M ANY NAMES FOR the Lord are found throughout the Bible, but one of the most meaningful is Shepherd. A shepherd is one who not only tends sheep but is a leader and companion to them. Unlike cattle, sheep cannot be driven; they must be led. The name pastor is a translation of the Greek word *poimen* that means "herdsman or shepherd." It's also used to describe the leadership and relationship of Jesus with mankind. In John 10:11 and 14, Jesus identifies Himself as "the good Shepherd." Peter describes Jesus as "the Shepherd and Overseer of our souls" (1 Pet. 2:25). Shepherds know their sheep, and the sheep know their shepherd's voice. A shepherd is gentle and loving with his sheep and protects them from danger. If a sheep should wander astray, the shepherd will leave his entire flock to find that one. If the sheep is injured, the shepherd will clean the wounds and rub ointment into them. Ezekiel 34:15–16 (KJV), says: "I will feed my flock, and I will cause them to lie down, saith the Lord God. I will seek that which was lost, and bring again that which was driven away." The Lord is our Shepherd, and He desires for us to know His voice, follow after Him, and not be in want.

Dear Lord: You are our good Shepherd. When we stray from Your presence, You come and find us, bringing us back to Your loving care. When we are hurt, You rub the oil of Your love into our wounds. The gentle way You lead gives us the desire to not wander far from Your voice. Thank You for Your tender care! In Jesus' name, Amen.

SHEPHERD'S PIE

1 pound ground beef
3 tablespoons flour
1 teaspoon garlic salt (divided)
½ teaspoon pepper
1 small onion, chopped
1 pound package frozen mixed vegetables
1 cup beef broth
2 cups hot mashed potatoes (instant okay)
4 ounces cream cheese
1 cup grated cheddar cheese, divided

Brown meat in large pan; drain. Add flour, ½ teaspoon garlic salt, pepper, onion, vegetables, and broth; cook until vegetables are slightly tender. Pour into greased baking dish. Mix mashed potatoes with ½ teaspoon garlic salt, cream cheese, and ½ of grated cheese; spread over meat. Sprinkle with remaining cheese. Bake at 375 degrees for 30 minutes until bubbly and lightly browned.

February 18

As the deer pants for streams of water, so my soul pants for you, O God. My soul thirsts for God, for the living God.

—PSALM 42:1–2

ONLY A TRUE believer is able to identify with the significance of this verse. Just as we physically crave water for our bodies to survive, so do we crave the things of God to survive spiritually. Water is essential for life, and without it we would die. The same is true for our souls; we cannot survive spiritually without partaking of the goodness of God. How do we know we are spiritually alive? The same way we know we are alive physically—we thirst. No one is able to survive without water, nor is any soul able to survive without drinking from the Well (Jesus) that will never run dry. It's obvious that water is the source from which we quench our physical thirst, but what about our souls? How do we quench our spirit's thirst? Mark 5:6 says: "Blessed are those who hunger and thirst for righteousness, for they will be filled." Thirsting for God means desiring His presence, power, holy Word, communion of Christ, fellowship of the Spirit, righteousness, and the return of Christ. It is essential that we be sensitive to the Holy Spirit's convicting work in our lives so we don't die a spiritual death. Just as the deer pants for his next drink of water, so should we for the living God.

Dear heavenly Father: Thank You for sending Your Holy Spirit to convict and guide me in the ways of righteousness. My soul thirsts for You each and every day, and as I seek You and have fellowship with You, my thirst is quenched. I long to know Your Word and look forward to Your return. Help me to share Your love with those around me so they, too, might come to a saving knowledge of Your grace. In Jesus' name, Amen.

PARMESAN ARTICHOKE DIP

1 (14-ounce) can artichoke hearts, finely chopped
½ cup mayonnaise
½ cup grated Parmesan cheese
2–3 drops Tabasco or Frank's hot sauce (optional)
Dash of garlic powder

Mix ingredients together; pour into small baking dish. Bake at 325 degrees for 20 minutes or until bubby and light golden brown. Serve with tortilla chips or crackers.

February 19

Restore to me the joy of your salvation and grant me a willing spirit, to sustain me.

—PSALM 51:12

PSALM 51 IS a song of repentance King David composed after his sins of adultery and murder were exposed. He threw himself on the Lord's mercy, admitting that all the evil he committed against others was really committed against God. He didn't try to justify what he did but simply asked God to forgive him. David cried out for God to create a new heart in him that would replace the old sinful one. His profound and remorseful confession that day was obviously real because David was called a man after God's own heart (1 Samuel 13:14). The joy of salvation is found only when we realize and accept the forgiveness, grace, and restoration that God gives when we choose to walk in obedience to His Word and truth.

Dear Lord: You have forgiven me, saved me, and restored to me the joy of my salvation. You reached down with Your upright hand, lifted me out of my sinful state, and gave me a new life. You are my Rock, and I will forever worship and praise Your holy name. In Jesus' name, Amen.

BLACK BEAN AND SAUSAGE STEW

1 tablespoon olive oil
1 small chopped onion
1 small chopped green bell pepper
8–12 ounces smoked sausage, sliced ¼ inch thick
2 cloves garlic, minced
1 (15-ounce) can black beans, drained and rinsed
1 (14.5-ounce) can beef or chicken broth
2 (14.5-ounce) cans stewed tomatoes, undrained
2 teaspoons cumin or chili powder or 1 of each
2 teaspoons dried oregano
¼ cup minced fresh parsley or cilantro (optional)
Hot pepper sauce, to taste (optional)

Put oil, onion, bell pepper, and sausage in pan; cook on medium heat until vegetables are tender, 4–5 minutes. Add everything else except cilantro and hot pepper sauce. Break tomatoes into small chunks. Bring to boil; reduce heat to low. Cover; simmer 20 minutes, stirring occasionally. Before serving, stir in cilantro and hot pepper sauce. Serve in bowls with a scoop of cooked rice.

February 20

Because thy lovingkindness is better than life, my lips shall praise thee.

—PSALM 63:3, KJV

DAVID WAS AT a low time in his life and he realized that without God, he was nothing. His heart longed to be satisfied by God, and Him only, as he poured out his feelings of despair and emptiness.

Just as David longed for the Father's love, God also longed for David's love. God created us to worship Him, and He yearns for fellowship with us, just as we yearn for Him. There is no worldly entertainment that will satisfy our need for a relationship with Christ. Reading God's Word, praying, and living in obedience to His will is the only answer to the longing we have in our spirits.

God's love is better than life, and when we truly believe that in our hearts, praising Him from the inside out will be easy. Our heavenly Father loves to hear our voices praise Him as we let Him know how much we love Him. God is love and God is life. Without Him, neither would be. Psalm 63 is a love song to the Father, and if we will pray or sing this aloud to Him, it will become our special love song to God. It is then that our spirits will be refreshed and our heavenly Father glorified.

Dear loving Father: You are better than life itself, and I glorify and praise Your holy name. You are my life, and You are my love. You are the reason for my being, and I will praise You all my days. Forgive me when my words are not glorifying to You. I need Your Holy Spirit to guide me and help me to seek You first in everything I do. Though I am inadequate in expressing my love for You, please know that I do honestly love and adore You. In Jesus' name, Amen.

AMAZING ASIAN SALAD

8 cups packed baby spinach leaves
1 red pepper, cut into thin strips
1 cup thin matchstick carrot sticks
3 green onions, thinly sliced
½ cup chow mein noodles
1 small can mandarin oranges
1 small can sliced water chestnuts, drained
¼ cup vegetable oil
2 tablespoons wine vinegar
1 tablespoon soy sauce
2 teaspoons sugar
⅓ cup favorite nuts, sliced (optional)

Drain juice from oranges; reserve. Combine first 7 ingredients in large bowl. Whisk together oil, wine vinegar, soy sauce, sugar, and reserved mandarin juice. Pour over salad; toss. If making salad ahead of time, refrigerate dressing; don't add noodles or dressing until ready to serve.

February 21

He that dwelleth in the secret place of the most High shall abide under the shadow of the Almighty.

—Psalm 91:1, KJV

This is an extremely comforting psalm about protection, victory, and eternal glory. It could be called the "Time of Trouble" Psalm because it refers mainly to the protection that God gives His people during troubling times. It is for now and also for the future. That being the case, every believer should prayerfully study it because it offers hope in an otherwise hopeless world. Psalm 91 is one of the key psalms in the Bible and should be read over and over again and memorized.

To dwell means to have absolute faith in our divine Father and to believe and live by the requirements of His eternal law. The secret place is the place where the Most Holy Father abides. It is a place of honor, respect, trust, faith, love, obedience, and so much more. It is a place where every believer should yearn to be, and it is the only place to be. To abide under the shadow of the Almighty is to live so close to the Master that wherever we are, the likeness (shadow) of God will be seen over us.

Most High and Almighty God: I praise You for Your love and compassion for me and for providing a place of refuge and shelter at all times. Thank You for allowing me the privilege of being so close to You that Your shadow is seen over me. I praise You for the peace You bring to me when the world around me is so troubling. Forgive me for my wicked ways and help me to obey Your holy Word so I might do my part in populating heaven. In Jesus' name, Amen.

RICE CASSEROLE

2 sticks butter
½ pound very fine noodles
2 cups instant rice
2 (10.5-ounce) cans French onion soup
2 (10.5-ounce) cans chicken broth
1 teaspoon soy sauce
1 cup water
1 (8-ounce) can sliced water chestnuts

Melt butter in a large skillet. Put in uncooked noodles and stir often, until golden brown. Using a 3-quart dish, transfer noodles and butter into dish. Add remaining ingredients and stir well. Bake at 325 degrees for 50–60 minutes. *Do not cover or stir during cooking.*

Hint: If using larger can of chicken broth, first measure for the 10.5-ounce cans, then use the extra broth as a substitute for the water. Add additional water if necessary to make 1 cup.

February 22

He shall cover thee with his feathers, and under his wings shalt thou trust: his truth shall be thy shield and buckler.

—Psalm 91:4, KJV

HAVE YOU EVER felt like crawling under the bed, wanting to hide from the whole world? Or maybe you feel like a dartboard and wonder if there are invisible circles on your body with numbers inside? You try so hard to do what is right and please everyone, but it seems to be of no avail. At times, we get overwhelmed with the responsibilities of life and just don't know which way to turn.

There is just one remedy to this malady, and that is to trust the Lord to see you through. We've all heard and said those words, but what do they really mean? A mother bird will spread her wings to protect her young from rain, storms, or other culprits trying to get to them. She will even die trying to protect them if it is required. This is what our Lord did for us. He spread out his arms and died so that we might live. He provided a way for us so we wouldn't have to pay the price of our penalties. Jesus faithfully and continually covers us with his love and gave us His Word to give us hope. When we feel like hiding from the world, we must quickly turn our thoughts to Jesus by reading or reciting a few passages, speaking our needs out to God, and then resting in the shield of His love.

Dear Lord: Thank You for shielding me with Your outstretched arms. You are my provider, and I take refuge under Your wings by trusting You as my guardian. I repent of the times I fail to rely on You and attempt to do things my own way. Help me to hide under Your wings when I need the armor of Your protection. In Jesus' name, Amen.

LINGUINE PARMESAN

1 tablespoon olive oil
1 tablespoon butter
1 teaspoon crushed red pepper flakes
3–5 cloves garlic, minced
½ cup regular or evaporated milk
1 tablespoon lemon juice
8 ounces linguine, cooked according to package
2 Roma tomatoes, diced
¼ teaspoon black pepper
½ cup grated Parmesan cheese

Heat oil and butter in large skillet. Remove from heat and add red pepper flakes and garlic; allow to sit 10 minutes. Add milk and lemon juice to skillet; simmer 10 minutes, stirring often. Add pasta and reheat. Before serving, add tomatoes, pepper, and cheese; toss and serve.

February 23

O Lord, you have searched me and you know me. You know when I sit and when I rise; you perceive my thoughts from afar.

—Psalm 139:1–3

GOD IS OMNIPRESENT and omniscient. He is everywhere, and He knows everything! He is our Creator, and He knows our thoughts, desires, fears, needs, cares, actions, motives, habits, flaws, and talents. There is nothing about us of which God is not aware. From the rising of the sun, He knows where we are and what we are doing. Because God doesn't sleep, He sees us as we sleep. Even in the dark or in our secret hiding place, it is as though a light were shining down upon us; we cannot hide from God. If we begin to speak, He knows the next word before it is even spoken. God saw us before we were formed, had a plan already made for us, and saw our lives mapped out before Him.

How precious it is to know that God has a purpose for each of us. Not one of us was created without His permission and intent. With this in mind, should we not stop each day and ask the Lord to search our hearts and see if there is anything there that would be offensive to Him? As we are repentant and willing to change, the sanctifying power of God will continue to unfold His perfect plan for our lives.

Dear Lord: I praise You for creating me in my mother's womb. Thank You for the plan and purpose You have intended, so unique and special, just for me. Search my heart and rid me of all the offensive ways You find. Help me live my life according to Your will so Your perfect plan would be fulfilled in my life. In Jesus' name, Amen.

CHICKEN SALAD CASSEROLE

4 boneless chicken breast halves
1 cup chopped celery
1 (8-ounce) can sliced water chestnuts
1 teaspoon lemon juice
1 cup mayonnaise
Dash salt and pepper
2 tablespoons grated onion
½ cup sliced almonds
1 cup shredded cheddar cheese
1 ½ cup crushed potato chips *or* 1 small can French fried onions

Cook chicken in greased pan with lid until done; dice. Mix chicken with remaining ingredients, except chips or onion rings. Pour into greased baking dish; cover with chips or onions rings. Bake in 350-degree oven for 30 minutes, until lightly browned.

February 24

The fear of the LORD is the beginning of knowledge: but fools despise wisdom and instruction.

—PROVERBS 1:7, KJV

THE BOOK OF Proverbs was written to instruct us how to live so we might avoid tragedies that result from sin. Though it was written by Solomon and others primarily for young people, we all should take heed to what is says and apply it to our lives.

To fear God is to love Him, which results in a desire to be obedient to His Word. Fearing (loving) God produces within us a reverence and respect of the Lord's majesty, power, and holiness. If we truly love God, we will not reject godly counsel but hunger and thirst after His righteousness, wisdom, and discipline. If the desire to know God's will isn't present in our hearts, we have not experienced a real personal relationship with Him. To remain in this state would only be for the foolish who care nothing about their souls and where they might spend eternity. Before seeking God's wisdom, we must first invite Jesus to come into our hearts and forgive us from all our sin. If we are sincere, a transformation will follow, and no longer will we desire the things of this world that are contrary to His Word, but our hearts will yearn to know more about God and what serving Him really means. This is where knowledge begins, just as the psalmist said.

Dear Lord: I praise You for loving me and taking me into Your family. Thank You for the hunger You have placed in my heart to know You more. I desire Your wisdom and knowledge and strive to receive instruction and discipline when it is needed and deserved. Help me to be strong in my faith and seek Your will over mine, each day that I live. In Jesus' name, Amen.

KEY WEST CITRUS CHICKEN

1–2 tablespoons oil
4 boneless, skinless chicken breasts
Salt and pepper to season
⅓ cup orange juice
3 cloves garlic, minced
¼ teaspoon ground ginger
⅛ teaspoon red pepper flakes
1 orange, thinly sliced

Season chicken; sauté in skillet with oil on medium heat until tender and no longer pink. Stir together orange juice, garlic, ginger, and red pepper flakes; pour into skillet with chicken. Bring to a boil; reduce heat; simmer, uncovered, 2 minutes. To serve, spoon pan juices over chicken; top with orange slices. Serve with rice.

February 25

Trust in the LORD with all thine heart; and lean not unto thine own understanding. In all thy ways acknowledge him, and he shall direct thy paths.

—PROVERBS 3:5–6, KJV

To TRUST GOD means to obey His Word. If we say we trust God but live contrary to what He teaches, then we don't really trust Him. The Bible is God's inspired Word of wisdom for us so we might live righteous and victorious lives and avoid the penalty of unconfessed sin. Trusting God is believing He loves us and cares deeply for our souls. Without God in our lives, we are limited to making decisions based only on what others tell us or what we think is the right thing to do. How much better it is to rely on the Holy Spirit to lead and guide our decisions! If we are careful to include Him in all our plans and put His will above ours, God promises to make straight the paths we travel. He will remove obstacles and break down barriers that have been placed there by the enemy to distract, confuse, or disable us from making right choices. As God's children, we can trust Him to faithfully meet our every need.

Dear Lord: You are a wise and faithful Father, and I love and praise You for all Your wonderful deeds. You care about Your children and want only the best for us. Your wisdom is what I long for, and I trust You to lead and guide me according to Your will. Forgive me for my failures and weaknesses; strengthen me as I seek to follow Your commands and ways. In Jesus' name, Amen.

ITALIAN CHICKEN AND RICE

1 tablespoon oil
1 pound boneless, skinless chicken breasts, cut into strips
3 cups cut-up fresh vegetables (broccoli, carrots, and red pepper)
1 (14.5-ounce) can chicken broth or 14 ounces water and 2 chicken bouillon cubes
2 cups minute white rice, uncooked
¼ cup Italian dressing

Heat oil in large skillet on medium heat. Add chicken; cook until lightly browned, stirring occasionally. Add vegetables; cook and stir 3–5 minutes or until crisp-tender. Stir in broth and bring to boil. Stir in rice and dressing; cover. Reduce heat to low; cook 5 minutes until liquid is absorbed and chicken is thoroughly cooked.

February 26

Above all else, guard your heart, for it is the wellspring [fountain] of life.

—Proverbs 4:23

W E MIGHT THINK of the head or brain being the organ of our body where actions are directed, but God's Word says it is the heart. In the Bible are many scriptures to support this truth. Deuteronomy 8:5 says we know things in our hearts. First Samuel 1:12–13 says we pray in our hearts. Psalm 19:14 says we meditate in our hearts. Psalm 119:11 says to hide God's Word in our hearts. Psalm 140:2 says we devise plans in our hearts. Proverbs 4:21 says we keep words in our hearts. Mark 2:8 says we think in our hearts. Mark 11:23 says we doubt in our hearts. Luke 2:19 says we ponder in our hearts. Romans 10:9 says we believe in our hearts. Ephesians 5:19 says we sing in our hearts.

The heart is the center of our emotions. Exodus 4:14 speaks about our glad hearts. Deuteronomy 6:5 speaks about the loving heart. Joshua 5:1 speaks about the fearful heart. Psalm 27:14 speaks about the courageous heart. Psalm 51:17 speaks about the repentant heart. Proverbs 12:25 speaks about the anxious heart. Proverbs 19:3 speaks about the angry heart. Isaiah 57:15 speaks about the revived heart. Jeremiah 4:19 speaks about the anguished heart. Jeremiah 15:16 speaks about the delighted heart. Lamentations 2:18 speaks about the grieving heart. Matthew 11:29 speaks about the humble heart. Luke 24:32 speaks about the excited or burning heart. John 14:1 speaks about the troubled heart. No wonder the psalmist warns us to guard our heart, for it truly is the fountain of life.

Dear God: Thank You for giving us hearts to love You and listen to Your Holy Spirit concerning the right way to live. Help me to not allow my heart to become hardened by ignoring Your voice and instruction. Fill my heart with love and compassion for lost hearts, and show me how to live my life so others would be drawn to You. In Jesus' name, Amen.

OYSTER STEW

1 pint oysters and liquid
4 tablespoons butter
4 cups milk
Salt and pepper to taste
Celery salt to taste
Dash paprika (optional)

In pan, simmer oysters and liquid with butter for 3–5 minutes, until edges begin to curl. In separate pan, slowly heat milk (do not boil); stir frequently. When milk is very hot, add oysters. Season with salt, pepper, celery salt, and paprika as desired. Serve in soup bowls.

February 27

My son, keep thy father's commandment, and forsake not the law of they mother.

—Proverbs 6:20, KJV

GOD IS THE creator of the family. He made Adam and Eve and gave them the ability to bear children; they were God's first family. Not every family has both parents at home raising the children together; not all married couples have children. But because God created the structure of the family, we should trust His workmanship and creativity enough to follow His plan for our lives. Ideally, it is best when both parents are serving the Lord and are in unity concerning the training of their children, but this isn't always the case. Each of us has had a time when we rebelled, were disrespectful, and disobeyed our parents' instructions. We thought they were trying to ruin all our fun, but the truth is, they were merely using the wisdom they received from their predecessors and wanted to see us spared of the consequences that come from making unwise decisions. Hopefully we will all use the wisdom of hindsight and remind our children and grandchildren of the importance of obeying God and those in authority over them.

Heavenly Father: Thank You for Your wondrous works and for the family You created for me. Show me ways I might be a blessing to them so they will see You in me. I'm sorry for the times I rebelled and didn't listen to my parents' commands and teachings. I was wrong in wanting to do my own thing, and yet they loved me in spite of myself. I desire to follow after You, even if it means receiving instruction from others. In Jesus' name, Amen.

PARMESAN CHICKEN AND RICE (crockpot)

1 can cream of mushroom soup
1 ½ cups milk
1 cup water
1 ½ ounce package onion soup mix
1 cup long-cooking rice, uncooked
4 boneless, skinless chicken breasts
4 tablespoons butter, sliced
½ teaspoon salt
½ teaspoon pepper
½ cup Parmesan cheese

Mix together soup, milk, water, onion soup mix, and rice; set aside. Sprinkle salt and pepper on chicken; place in greased crockpot. Place 1 tablespoon butter on top of each chicken breast. Pour soup mix over chicken; sprinkle with Parmesan cheese. Cover; cook on low 8–10 hours or on high 4–6 hours.

February 28

Her house is the way to hell, going down to the chambers of death.

—Proverbs 7:27, KJV

PROVERBS 7 IS a warning to all of us about the dangers of sexual immorality. It is the anatomy of a prostitute's evil desires to seduce vulnerable men who lack good moral judgment, and it is written as though it were taking place today. We are warned against the evil desires of an adulterer whose seductive ways are ruin to our souls.

But the Word gives us hope and a way to keep our bodies pure and free from sin. God instructs us to hold true to His commands and keep our minds pure and Christ-oriented. When evil or lustful thoughts come upon us, they must be immediately exterminated by changing our focus to something good or wholesome. Scripture memorization is extremely helpful when temptation strikes. By knowing that sin leads to sorrow, regret, and ultimately death, it is imperative that we strive for holiness in our own lives and then warn, train, teach, mentor, and pray for others so they won't be led down to the "chambers of death" created by the sexually immoral.

Father: Forgive me for the times I've entertained thoughts that were impure and unholy. Deliver me from the evil one so I might live according to Your Word. Help me to memorize scriptures so I am able to think on them when temptations come. I want to serve You with my whole heart and honor You in everything I do. Thank You for Your Holy Spirit who convicts, comforts, and leads me to a life that glorifies You and gives me hope and joy. In Jesus' name, Amen.

LASAGNA (using uncooked regular noodles)

1 pound lean ground meat
1 pound Italian sausage
2 (26-ounce) jars spaghetti sauce
1 cup water
15 ounces ricotta cheese
½ cup grated Parmesan cheese
2 eggs
6 cups mozzarella cheese
1 pound regular lasagna noodles, uncooked

Cook meat until done; drain. Add spaghetti sauce and water; heat through. Mix well the ricotta and Parmesan cheeses and eggs. Cover bottom of a greased 9x15-inch baking dish with sauce. Layer uncooked noodles, cheese mixture, sauce, and mozzarella. Repeat 2 more layers. Top with sauce and cheese. Cover tightly with greased or sprayed tin foil; bake at 350 degrees for 90 minutes. Remove foil for last 5–10 minutes. Let stand 10–15 minutes before cutting.

February 29

For wisdom is better than rubies; and all the things that may be desired are not to be compared to it.

—Proverbs 8:11, kjv

In 1 Kings 3:9, King Solomon prayed, asking God for a discerning heart to govern his people and distinguish between right and wrong. He could have asked for anything, but Solomon loved God and wanted only His wisdom. First Kings 4:29 (kjv) says, "And God gave Solomon wisdom and understanding exceeding much, and largeness of heart, even as the sand that is on the sea shore."

God's wisdom is available to everyone who knows Jesus as their Savior. We must not depend on our own or human wisdom; the Word tells us God looks at the wisdom of the world as foolishness (1 Corinthians 3:19). Unbelievers are limited to the wisdom they are able to obtain from their senses or others' opinions, while believers receive wonderful revelation knowledge from specific instructions and promises from the Word of God. James 1:5 assures us that if we lack wisdom but want it, all we need to do is ask for it and God will grant it. Praise God that Jesus died and rose again for sinners such as we are and then begins that transforming work of changing us from being fools to being wise men and women! Having God's wisdom is more precious than rubies, and nothing can be compared to it.

Dear God: Just as You granted King Solomon great measures of wisdom and understanding because he asked for it, so do You so faithfully give it to all of us who ask. I seek Your wisdom in my life so I might serve You more effectively. Forgive me for the times I relied on my own selfish thoughts and desires and called them Yours. Thank You for guiding me with Your Holy Spirit. It is when I am obedient that Your will becomes alive in my heart. In Jesus' name, Amen.

BREAKFAST BURRITOS

1 pound ground sausage
3–6 eggs
6–8 flour tortillas
4–8 ounces cheddar cheese, grated
Chopped onions (optional)
Chopped peppers (optional)
1 small can chopped green chiles (optional)
Salsa (optional)

Cook sausage until done; drain. Scramble eggs. Fill tortillas with ingredients as desired. Fold over bottom, sides, then top flap. Microwave for 10 seconds or wrap in aluminum foil and place in oven for 15 minutes on warm. May be frozen for later use.

Sowing the Seed

March

March 1

Instruct a wise man and he will be wiser still; teach a righteous man and he will add to his learning.

—PROVERBS 9:9

MANY OF US don't like criticism and become defensive and sometimes angry when it is directed toward us. But God's Word teaches that if we truly love Him and desire His wisdom, we will receive words of instruction from another source with an appreciative spirit. To love God means to fear Him and strive for holiness and righteousness in our lives. Sometimes the rebuking will come from a family member, a friend, a pastor, a teacher, or just an acquaintance, and our reaction will identify our true character. If we react negatively, our hearts are not right with Christ and our relationship with Him is in jeopardy.

Revelation 3:19 says, "Those whom I love I rebuke and discipline." Jesus tells us in John 16:8 that the Holy Spirit will convict us of our sin and judge us accordingly. Growing in our relationship with Christ is an ongoing process and sometimes comes in the form of rebuke and correction. The way we react confirms who we really are in Him.

Father: Thank You for sending Your Holy Spirit to counsel, comfort, and convict me of my sin. Without the Spirit working in my life, I would be lost and without hope. You orchestrated everything so well in Your plan and purpose for my life. Help me to accept godly criticism from others You have guided to help me when I am wrong or in sin. I want to grow in my love and relationship with You, and I know this is only done if my attitude and heart are right. Thank You for working in my life. In Jesus' name, Amen.

SANDWICH SOUFFLÉ

8 slices white bread, crusts removed
Soft butter
4 slices ham
2 slices American cheese
2 cups milk
2 eggs, beaten
Pinch of salt and pepper

Spread butter on both sides of bread. Make 4 sandwiches with ham and cheese. Place in buttered baking dish. Beat together milk, eggs, salt, and pepper. Pour over sandwiches and cover with plastic wrap. Refrigerate at least 2 hours. Bake at 375 degrees for 45–50 minutes. Serves 4.

March 2

Lazy hands make a man poor, but diligent hands bring wealth.

—Proverbs 10:4

King Solomon ruled over Israel for forty years and was known for his wealth, wisdom, and writings. During that time, he built the original temple of God that housed the ark of the covenant that contained the Ten Commandments. Though this was his greatest work, he engaged in numerous projects throughout Jerusalem and Israel. It could be rightfully said that he was one very motivated, hard-working man.

Because Solomon is the author of this proverb, he knew the true meaning behind the verse. He also knew that God created man to labor and provide for his family. In Proverbs 6:9–11, the lazy person is called a sluggard, which is another name for someone who is apathetic or immobile. He is warned to arise from his slothful state of mind and take some course of action so that poverty doesn't come. How selfish and shameful it is to be lazy when there is physical work to be done, but even greater than that is the lack of desire in working to harvest lost souls. Jesus said in Matthew 9:37 that the harvest is plentiful but the workers are few. We must strive to be more effective in our physical labors and also for the work that needs done in spreading the gospel.

Dear Lord: Thank You for this day You have made. I rejoice in knowing that You are in control and guiding me in the things I should do. My hands belong to You; help me to use them to honor and work for You. For the times I am slothful and waste precious time that could be used to help others so their load might be lightened, I am sorry. Use my hands to help spread the good news of Your love and salvation. In Jesus' name, Amen.

SWEET AND SOUR COLESLAW

Chop and Grate:

1 carrot
1 onion
1 green pepper
1 medium cabbage

Boil for one minute:

½ teaspoon salt
1 ¼ teaspoons celery seed
1 ¼ teaspoons mustard seed
⅔ cup sugar
1 ¼ cups vinegar
½ cup vegetable oil

Pour dressing over slaw and mix well. Refrigerate several hours before serving.

March 3

Whoever loves discipline loves knowledge, but he who hates correction is stupid.

—PROVERBS 12:1

MANY OF THE proverbs talk about wisdom, knowledge, discipline, and the foolishness of the way we live our lives. There are times when we all make unwise decisions and regret the consequences that come as a result. We look back and wish we had reacted differently or not done what we did. Perhaps it was that first social drink, cigarette, sexual sin, or a drug that eventually led to an addiction or downward spiral. Peer pressure made it seem so right at the time. A parent, family member, or friend may have tried to warn us, but we didn't listen. God's Word assures us that correction or discipline is a good thing and that if we welcome it, our lives will be enriched with knowledge. Accepting the advice or warning of that one who loves and cares for us is another way of saying we love God.

Father: I love You and praise Your holy name. Your Word is true and keeps me from destruction when I walk in obedience. Keep me on the right path, and bring others into my life to teach and train me in the way I should go. When I get off track, give me the fortitude to accept correction so I might be a loyal and faithful disciple. In Jesus' name, Amen.

CALICO BEAN SOUP

1 bag of 15-bean soup, rinsed, soaked for 8 hours or overnight, and drained
2 quarts water
1 ham bone with 1 pound meat trimmings *or* 1 ham steak trimmed of fat
1 (1-pound) can chopped tomatoes
1 onion, chopped
2 cloves garlic, minced, *or* 1 teaspoon garlic powder
Juice of 1 lemon
1 banana pepper or mild poblano pepper
1 teaspoon chili powder
1 carrot, finely chopped

Put drained beans, water, and ham in crockpot on high for 4 hours or simmer on stovetop for 3–3 ½ hours. Add rest of ingredients and simmer another 1–2 hours.

March 4

He who spares the rod hates his son, but he who loves him is careful to discipline him.

—Proverbs 13:24

GOD IS GENTLE and loving, and He wants us to be likewise. Why, then, are we told in His Word to discipline our children with the use of a rod if we love them? This may sound contradictory, but we are all born with a sinful nature that, left uncorrected, would lead to unpleasant consequences.

The rod was the other end of the shepherd's staff and was used to discipline a sheep that kept wandering away from the flock. Using a rod on children is just one way to discipline and should be used only when a child acts in willful disobedience, defiance, rebellion, or disrespect for what he has been instructed. It should be administered only in a wise, loving, and considerate manner. There are many other ways to discipline a child, such as time out, withholding privileges, performing certain duties, and so forth. The important thing is to be consistent and yet loving, always seeking God's wisdom in the type of discipline to use.

A child left undisciplined, according to this verse, is another way of saying he is hated, left to die, and ends up in hell. Proverbs 23:13–14 tells us that if we do not withhold punishment from a child, he will not die. Just as our heavenly Father loves us and yet administers discipline to us, we should do the same for our children because we love them (Hebrews 12:6–7; Revelation 3:19).

Dear God: Thank You for family and those You put in authority over me. Help me use godly discipline when needed and not act in anger or resentment as I correct my children or those under my authority. Forgive me when I react with emotions that are displeasing to You. May I be loving and wise in the decisions I make so You will be glorified in my life. In Jesus' name, Amen.

SAUSAGE GRAVY FOR BISCUITS

1 pound mild sausage
2 tablespoons butter
6 tablespoons flour
4 cups whole milk
½ teaspoon salt
½ teaspoon pepper

In large pan on medium-high heat, cook sausage until done; drain most of grease. Add butter and flour; mix well. Add milk, salt, and pepper. Simmer over medium-high heat, stirring constantly, until desired thickness. Serve over biscuits or toast.

March 5

There is a way which seemeth right unto a man, but the end thereof are the ways of death.
—PROVERBS 14:12, KJV

All we like sheep have gone astray; we have turned every one to his own way.
—ISAIAH 53:6, KJV

Therefore to him that knoweth to do good, and doeth it not, to him it is sin.
—JAMES 4:17, KJV

THERE ARE A lot of us walking in ways that seem right, but in many instances we have allowed our own feelings or the influence of others to lead us down the wrong path. We feel our ideas and the way we live are right or at least "okay" with God.

But let's examine our current path. Are we living mostly for ourselves? Do we value material possessions more than we should? Do we seek recognition, success, and power? Did we start on the right path, only to stray away on a yellow brick road that leads to danger? Are we depending on our own wisdom?

Our own ideas, our own convenience, and our own preferences are not necessarily the right way. Whether in our families, our workplaces, our church gatherings, or anywhere else, we can't do what we want to do, when and how we want to do it, and expect good outcomes. It must line up with the Word of God or the end will lead to death and destruction. If we are on the path that pleases God, when trials and temptations come, we can lean on the promises of God and stand firm in our conviction that: "For I know whom I have believed, and am persuaded that he is able to keep that which I have committed unto him against that day" (2 Tim. 1:12, KJV).

Father: You are the holy and majestic One, and I praise You today with all that is within me. You made a way for me that is right and leads to eternal life. Guide me with Your Holy Spirit to make right and holy decisions that honor You. When trials come, may I remember Your promises that are true and powerful so my life is guarded from death and destruction. In Jesus' name, Amen.

CROCKPOT PORK CHOPS

4–6 lean pork chops
12 ounces chili sauce
1 cup grape jelly
¼ cup barbecue sauce

Brown pork chops in pan with oil. Mix together remaining ingredients; cover bottom of crockpot with sauce. Layer pork chops, putting sauce between them. Cook on low 4–6 hours until done.

March 6

Wine is a mocker and beer a brawler; whoever is led astray by them is not wise.

—PROVERBS 20:1

A MOCKER IS ONE who scornfully ridicules, and a brawler is a troublemaker. The psalmist is describing the use of fermented drinks and their evil and dangerous effects. Many argue whether wine, drunk socially or in small quantities, is acceptable for the Christian. In the Old Testament, *yayin* (Hebrew for wine) referred to unfermented grape juice, which was not condemned; however, God forbade fermented wine, *shekar*. Priests of Israel in office had to abstain from all types of wine; not to comply meant the death penalty.

Why did God forbid it? The effects of intoxicating wine are never good. They lead to drunkenness, family tragedies, addiction, mockery of God, and all types of sin and immorality. The first mention of wine in the Bible is the drunkenness, sin, and shame of Noah. Because of the evil effects of fermented drink, God requires total abstinence as the high standard for His people. Leviticus 10:9, Numbers 6:3, Judges 13:4–7, Proverbs 23:31, Proverbs 31:4, Romans 14:21, 1 Thessalonians 5:6, 1 Timothy 3:3, and Titus 2:2 are just a few scriptures to support this.

In the New Testament, Jesus and His disciples drank unfermented wine and used it at the Last Supper. Fermented wine is not the product of the vine; only the pure fresh juice from the grape is (Matthew 26:29; Mark 14:25; Luke 22:18). Just as unleavened bread (uncorrupted with fermentation) had to be used, so did the wine (fruit of the vine) have to be unfermented, which represents the incorruptible blood of Christ. At the wedding of Cana, where Jesus performed His first miracle, the wine He miraculously made was unfermented, pure, sweet fruit of the vine. The wine of biblical times was either freshly squeezed grape juice, preserved grape juice, juice from dried grapes, or wine that was made from grape syrup and water. If it were fermented or even unfermented, it was stored diluted with water at a ratio up to twenty to one. If fermented wine were served, it was considered barbaric and defiling, and the rabbis were unable to bless it. Christians were even more cautious about the wine they drank, as they did not want to go against God's Word. Shouldn't we today want to avoid every possible trap set by the enemy to drag us into hell and comply fully with God's requirements for a higher standard of living?

Father: You are good, and only good things come from You. I praise and worship You for the mercy and love You pour out upon Your children. Thank You for giving me the strength and power I need to live a victorious life and not be led astray. In Jesus' name, Amen.

Today's recipe found on page 383 FRIED RICE

March 7

Train up a child in the way he should go: and when he is old, he will not depart from it.

—PROVERBS 22:6, KJV

THIS PROVERB HAS brought anxiety, guilt, encouragement, and hope to countless parents who face the blessing, dilemma, and bewilderment of child-rearing. The Hebrew word for train means "to dedicate," and the root of the same word can also mean "to give or cultivate a taste for."

When a child is born, Christian parents are encouraged to dedicate their little one to the Lord as a way of saying they will instruct him in the ways of the Lord. We are all born with a sin nature and must be taught godly principles and behavior. It is the responsibility of each parent to love their children enough to train them in the way they should go so that when they are at an appropriate age of understanding, they would seek God for themselves and accept Jesus as their personal Savior.

Dear Lord: You are the way, the truth, and the life. May every parent be drawn to You for strength and help as they raise their children to be godly in an ungodly world. I pray for children and parents all over this land, that together they would seek You, find You, and take the message of redemption into the highways and byways of their lives. May they hunger and thirst after righteousness and be strong in their faith as they go about each day with Your Holy Spirit as their Guide. In Jesus' name, Amen.

WHITE CHILI

1 pound boneless, skinless chicken breasts
1 medium onion
1 ½ teaspoons garlic powder
1 tablespoon vegetable oil
2 (15.5-ounce) cans great northern beans
1 (14.5-ounce) can chicken broth
1 (4.5-ounce) can chopped green chiles
1 teaspoon salt
1 teaspoon ground cumin
1 teaspoon dried oregano
½ teaspoon pepper
¼ teaspoon cayenne pepper
1 cup (8 ounces) sour cream
½ cup whipping cream

In large pan, sauté chicken, onion, and garlic powder in oil until chicken is no longer pink; dice. Add beans, broth, chiles, and seasonings; bring to boil. Reduce heat; simmer, uncovered, for 30 minutes. Remove from heat; stir in sour cream and cream. Serve immediately.

March 8

Rescue those being led away to death; hold back those staggering toward slaughter.

—PROVERBS 24:11

THIS IS A general statement concerning the command that as Christians we are instructed to intervene on behalf of innocent lives facing death. No specifics or illustrations are given. The reason for this is so we will not limit it to one group of humans and leave out another. We are not simply to rescue a certain color of people or the wealthy, healthy, intelligent, or strong; this command applies to all people. One such example is the heartbreaking tragedy of abortion. These innocent souls are incapable of representing themselves before a court of law. They face murder at the hands of those whose purpose was once only to practice medicine to restore health and life and not destroy it. The Bible teaches that life begins at conception, and to take an innocent life is the same as murder. Since the Roe v. Wade decision in 1973, at least 30 million babies have been aborted or murdered. This is astronomical and heartbreaking. If a group of innocent humans is being taken away to be slaughtered, then we who fear and love God ought to try to rescue them, based on God's command that we should not kill (Exodus 20:13). We must actively become involved in the rescue of innocent victims.

One way is to pray for those on the front lines of the battle. Pray for the politicians, the physicians, the ministers, and the pro-life leaders. Pray for expectant mothers to be willing and courageous to choose an alternative to abortion. We all must practice and model moral purity in our own lives and abstain from premarital and extramarital sexual involvement. There are many other ways to become involved; the important thing is to do something to back up what the psalmist is saying in this verse. If not us...then who?

Father: You are the giver of life and not the taker. It is sad how the world has chosen to kill innocent lives, and we need to become actively involved in changing this. Give us the desire to do our part in saving these ones so we aren't found guilty on Judgment Day. In Jesus' name, Amen.

CROCKPOT SMOTHERED CHICKEN

3–4 boneless, skinless chicken breasts
1 can cream of mushroom soup
1 envelope onion soup mix
16 ounces sour cream

Mix all ingredients; put in crockpot. Cook on low 8 hours. Serve with potatoes, noodles, or rice.

March 9

If thine enemy be hungry, give him bread to eat; and if he be thirsty, give him water to drink. For thou shalt heap coals of fire upon his head, and the LORD shall reward thee.

—PROVERBS 25:21–22, KJV

HUMAN NATURE WOULD tell us to pay back those who hurt us, while God's Word says to do the opposite. Why would we want to come to the aid of one who wronged us in some way? Maybe it was a simple thing like being cut off on the road or pushed back in line by a bully cutting in; or perhaps it was as serious as murder, kidnapping, or rape. Is there a level or degree of hurt for what we should forgive and show love?

Romans 12:14–21 says to bless and not curse those who persecute us. The apostle Paul encourages us to live in harmony with one another and not repay evil for evil. We are to do what is right in the eyes of everybody and not take revenge for anything anyone has done to us.

The second part of this verse tells us that doing good things to our enemies will cause their heads to burn or make them think about what they did and be convicted. It's not always easy to reward those who have hurt us, but God's Word says we should. Not only will it cause convicting effects on our offenders, but the Lord will reward us for being kind to them. And once again, God will be glorified!

Father: Because of Your forgiveness for those who crucified Your Son, I am able to forgive and do good for my enemies. Forgive me when I hold grudges and unforgiveness toward those who have hurt or offended me in some way. Help me to rely on Your strength to pardon their evil-doings. Because You have asked me to be kind and loving to them, victory will be mine. Thank You for teaching me to live and love as You do. In Jesus' name, Amen.

HASH BROWN CASSEROLE

1 (32-ounce) bag frozen hash browns
¼ teaspoon pepper
1 can cream of mushroom soup
1 (16-ounce) container French onion dip
1 (8-ounce) container sour cream
2 cups grated sharp cheddar cheese
½ cup melted butter
2 cups crushed corn flakes

Put potatoes in greased 9x13-inch baking dish. Mix pepper, soup, dip, sour cream, and cheese together in a bowl. Pour mixture over the top of the potatoes. Mix corn flake crumbs and melted butter; sprinkle on top. Bake at 350 degrees for 1 hour.

March 10

As a dog returns to his vomit, so a fool returneth to his folly.

—PROVERBS 26:11, KJV

EACH OF US is born with a sinful nature. We don't have to be taught how to sin; we must be taught how not to sin. Sometimes sin is subtle and creeps into our lives without our really recognizing it. Other times it is blatant and the direct result of a conscious desire to do evil. Either way, sin is sin and, left unrepentant, will lead to destruction and spiritual death.

It's always easier to recognize other's sins before we see our own, but we must be careful when pointing the finger and ignoring those downfalls to which we have become a slave. Second Peter 2:19 says, "For a man is a slave to whatever has mastered him" (those things in our lives that take precedence over serving God). Many of us have abandoned a life of corruption to come to a saving knowledge of Jesus Christ. But even though the gift of freedom is real and wonderful, we return to our old ways and once again become entangled in the sin of which we were once set free. This verse says it so well, for we all have seen a dog vomit and then lap it up. How foolish and disgusting this seems, but so is it the same when a Christian abandons his faith in God to return to the lifestyle of sin he once had. The next time we are tempted, we might envision this verse; it just might keep us from returning to a life of sin and shame.

Heavenly Father: Life with You is pure and wholesome, but living outside of Your will is destruction and evil. Forgive me when I act foolish and return to the sin from which You saved me. Guide me with Your Holy Spirit in the ways of righteousness so that my life brings glory and honor to Your name. In Jesus' name, Amen.

FOUR-CHEESE SPAGHETTI

8 ounces uncooked spaghetti
¼ cup butter
1 tablespoon flour
¼ teaspoon salt
¼ teaspoon pepper
1 ½ cups half and half cream
1 cup shredded mozzarella cheese
4 ounces Fontina cheese, shredded
½ cup shredded Provolone cheese
¼ cup shredded Parmesan cheese
2 tablespoons fresh parsley, minced

Cook spaghetti according to package. Melt butter in large pan on medium heat; stir in flour, salt, and pepper until smooth. Gradually stir in cream; bring to boil. Cook and stir 2 minutes or until thickened. Remove from heat; stir in cheese until melted. Toss with spaghetti and parsley.

March 11

If anyone turns a deaf ear to the law, even his prayers are detestable.

—PROVERBS 28:9

DOES GOD HEAR and answer every prayer? Psalm 66:18 tells us that those who take pleasure in unrighteousness have no hope of answered prayer when they call on God. Proverbs 14:29 says the Lord is far from the wicked, but He hears the prayer of the righteous. If we are the temples of the living God, He will live with us and walk among us; He will be our God, and we will be His people (2 Corinthians 6:16). It is our decision whether we want our prayers heard or not. If we obey God's Word, He will hear and answer our prayers according to His will. If we ignore God's commands and live according to our own will and way, coming to Him only on occasion when we want something, our prayers are detestable or disgusting to the Lord. To be sure our lines of communication are open to God, it is crucial that we search our hearts for any unconfessed sin, ask Him for forgiveness, invite Jesus to be our Savior and Lord, and then live as though He really is. It is then that we have the assurance that our prayers are being heard by God.

Dear God: Cleanse me of all my sin and unrighteousness. Show me those areas of my life that need readjusting so You are my ultimate priority and goal. When I am weak and tempted, come and be my strength. Help me to become the person of God You created me to be, and guide me with Your Holy Spirit to live according to Your Word. In Jesus' name, Amen.

PEPPER STEAK

1 ½ pounds sirloin steak, ½ inch thick
Dash salt and pepper
2–3 tablespoons oil
1 cup water + 1 beef bouillon cube
3 tablespoons soy sauce
1–3 cloves garlic, minced
2 onions, cut into eighths (about 1 cup)
2 green peppers, cut in strips
2 tablespoons cornstarch
¼ cup cold water
2 tomatoes, peeled, cut into eighths
3–4 cups hot cooked rice

Slice steak into thin strips across grain (easiest if meat is partially frozen); season with salt and pepper. In large pan, brown meat in oil over medium-high heat. Add water, bouillon, soy sauce, and garlic. Cover; simmer 20–30 minutes until meat is tender. Add onions and peppers. Cover; simmer 5 minutes. Blend cornstarch and water; stir slowly into meat mixture. Cook and stir until mixture thicken and boils; boil 1 minute. Remove from heat; add tomatoes. Serve over rice.

March 12

A man who remains stiff-necked after many rebukes will suddenly be destroyed—without remedy.

—Proverbs 29:1

THE BIBLE WARNS us about the deadly dangers of moral apostasy (abandoning or withdrawing from a former union with Christ). When this happens, one who has known Jesus as their personal Savior ceases to remain in Him and instead becomes enslaved, once again, to sin and immorality. How does this happen? It usually is a gradual decline in one's relationship and service to the Lord. The seriousness of God's Word begins to diminish while the desires for things of the world heighten. One becomes conditioned and tolerant to sin as the power of the Holy Spirit's convicting rebuke is ignored and rejected. Wickedness is no longer hated, and righteousness is looked at as only for the weak and frail. As this happens, hearts become hardened and that "still small voice" deep inside begins to fade. Each time it is ignored or pushed away, a heart grows harder and harder until eventually the Holy Spirit is so grieved He departs from the former believer. No longer is there any remedy for his soul.

But all who genuinely desire to come to God with repentant hearts have not reached the point of unpardonable apostasy. It is God's will that none would perish, and His mercy and grace are available for all who willfully come to Him.

Father: I repent for the times I was stiff-necked and reckless with my life. Reveal to me those things I do that might lead me into a dangerous mode of rejecting your Holy Spirit's conviction on my soul. Keep my heart soft and pliable, and help me to hate wickedness and love righteousness, as You desire. May I be an example of Your mercy and grace to those around me. In Jesus' name, Amen.

ROAST BEEF WITH MUSHROOM GRAVY

1 (3-pound) boneless chuck roast
3 tablespoons flour
3 tablespoons oil
1 onion, sliced
1 package onion soup mix
2 cloves garlic
1 can cream of mushroom soup
1 cup water
1 can mushrooms *or* 8 ounces fresh mushrooms (optional)

Rub flour on roast and brown on all sides in hot oil in skillet. Place roast in crockpot; add all other ingredients. Cook on high 4–6 hours, or until done.

March 13

Two things I ask of you, O Lord; do not refuse me before I die: Keep falsehood and lies far from me; give me neither poverty nor riches, but give me only my daily bread. Otherwise, I may have too much and disown You and say, "Who is the Lord?" Or I may become poor and steal, and so dishonor the name of my God.

—Proverbs 30:7–9

W HAT A HUMBLE request this was to the Creator of the universe who could grant wealth and fame to whomever whenever He desired. Agur, the author, could have asked God for anything he desired, but he knew nothing mattered outside of knowing Him. If he asked for material possessions and wealth, Agur realized he might be too busy or too self-centered to serve God. If he asked to be poor and needy, perhaps he would have to succumb to stealing to provide for his family, and thus dishonor the name of his God. Agur wanted only to have his needs met by trusting the Lord on a daily basis. This would keep him humble, reliant on God, and trusting Him only to supply his daily bread. Perhaps we all should be more like Agur and pray only to have enough income to adequately furnish our personal and family needs, to do God's work, and have enough to give to those in need.

Dear God: Thank You for all You have given me and for supplying my every need. You are so gracious, and You love and care about each one of Your children. Keep me humble, even if it means living one day at a time, trusting You for the income I need to meet the needs of my family. Help me to remember to serve my fellow man and give to those who are in need. In doing so, may they come to know You as Savior and Lord. In Jesus' name, Amen.

CHICKEN NUGGETS

2 cups crushed sour-cream-and-onion-flavored potato chips
1 egg
2 tablespoons milk
6 chicken breast fillets, cut into 1 ½-inch cubes
⅓ cup butter

Spread crushed chips in shallow dish. Beat egg and milk in a bowl. Dip chicken in egg mixture, then dredge in chips. Place on baking sheet; drizzle with melted butter. Bake at 350 degrees for 15–18 minutes, until golden brown. Serve with honey mustard, barbecue sauce, or ranch dressing.

March 14

Who can find a virtuous woman? For her price is far above rubies.

—Proverbs 31:10, KJV

Favor is deceitful, and beauty vain: but a woman that feareth the LORD, she shall be praised.

—Proverbs 31:30, KJV

WE ALL HAVE heard about and hopefully read the epilogue in Proverbs 31:10–31 describing the virtuous woman. It makes her not only sound virtuous but also perfect. Her whole life is centered on God, helping the poor and those in need, and loving and caring for her family. In the world we are living in today, is it even remotely possible for a woman to emulate the qualities of the woman spoken about here? The answer is yes. Even though many girls aren't taught by their mothers how to run a godly home and care for their families, God gives us guidelines in His Word about how we should live. There are also many books, Bible studies, and workbooks written on this subject. When the heart is right, the will is right; and when the will is right, we will prioritize our time and devotion to those areas most important to us. If we strive for excellence in our diverse roles as women through prayer and godly resources, we will become the women, wives, mothers, and businesswomen God truly wants us to be.

Dear Lord: I exalt You for this day and the family You have given me. Thank You for the wonderful instruction You provided in Your Word that teaches me how to live my life and care for my family. Forgive me when I am slothful and apathetic toward those things. May I turn to You for the strength I need to live a godly life in an ungodly world. In Jesus' name, Amen.

CRABBY CORN SOUP

¼ cup butter
¼ cup flour
1 quart whole milk
1 ¾ cups whole kernel corn (fresh, canned, or frozen)
1 cup chopped green onions
½ teaspoon pepper
½ teaspoon seasoning salt
1 tablespoon soy sauce
¼ cup chopped fresh parsley (optional)
1 (6–6 ½-ounce) can crabmeat, drained, flaked, and cartilage removed or meat from 1 ½ pounds cooked crab legs

Melt butter in heavy pot on medium heat. Add flour and gently stir; do not burn or let darken. Gradually add milk; stir constantly. Add corn and green onions; cook a few minutes, until tender. Add crabmeat, pepper, seasoning salt, and soy sauce; simmer until hot and bubbly; do not boil. Garnish with parsley.

March 15

"Meaningless! Meaningless!" says the Teacher. "Utterly meaningless! Everything is meaningless."

—ECCLESIASTES 1:2

KING SOLOMON WAS the wisest man in the world, and his kingdom was known for its affluent grandeur. Yet in spite of this, he believed life was empty and meaningless outside of knowing God and keeping His Word. There was a time in Solomon's life when he experienced great wealth, power, honor, fame, and sensual pleasures, but he remained disillusioned and empty.

Our lives aren't much different than his was. We are all born with a void that is in the shape of Jesus; nothing or no one is able to fit into that space except for Him. We will search high and low and deep and wide for things, people, places, entertainment, and so on to fill that void, but it doesn't happen and never will.

Before Solomon died, he looked back over his life and saw the spiritual decline that came from his sins of idolatry and self-indulgence. He was sorry for the futile attempt he made to find happiness in the ways he did. Perhaps in his writings he wanted to share his regrets and testimony with us so we would not make the same mistakes he did. Life is "meaningless, utterly meaningless," apart from the will of God. We must resolve to love God and obey His commands, for this truly is the only way to have life with meaning and purpose.

Dear God: Thank You for showing us Solomon's life and how sorry he was when he didn't live for You. Life without You is meaningless and empty, something I never want to experience. Forgive me when I take my eyes off You and place them on material things, looking for happiness and fulfillment. Help me to spread the good news of Your saving grace so others might also have purpose in their lives. In Jesus' name, Amen.

TRIPLE-BEAN BAKE

8 strips bacon
1 pound ground beef
1 small onion, diced
1 can baby lima beans, drained
1 can yellow beans, drained
¼ cup barbecue or chili sauce
1 can pork and beans
1 cup brown sugar

Cook bacon in pan until crisp; remove and crumble. Discard most of grease. Brown ground beef in same pan; drain. Add onion; cook until tender. Mix together all ingredients; pour into greased baking dish. Bake at 350 degrees for 60 minutes.

March 16

He brought me to the banqueting house, and his banner over me was love.

—SONG OF SONGS 2:4, KJV

CONTRARY TO THE Book of Ecclesiastes, which King Solomon wrote at the end of his life, the Book of Song of Songs was written early in his life when he was king of Israel. It's a wedding song he composed about his love and marriage to his bride, a lovely Shulammite maiden. The Holy Spirit inspired Solomon to write this book so we might recognize the joy and dignity of human love in marriage. God wants us to know that marriage should be kept pure, wholesome, and beautiful. The descriptive language used in Song of Songs is sensuous but demonstrates the pure and chaste emotion and romantic love that is sanctioned only between a bridegroom and his bride. Hebrews 13:4 tells us marriage should be honored by all and the marriage bed kept pure, for God will judge the adulterer and all the sexually immoral. The love spoken about in the Song of Songs is genuine and monogamous, saved only for one another and truly a gift from God. Just as the love of the bride and bridegroom is a beautiful example of a perfect union of a man and woman, so is the quality of love Christ has for His bride, the church: "And I saw a new heaven and a new earth: for the first heaven and the first earth were passed away; and there was no more sea. And I John saw the holy city, new Jerusalem, coming down from heaven, prepared as a bride adorned for her husband" (Rev. 21:1–2, KJV).

Father: Thank You for the sanctity of human life and for showing us the loveliness of a pure and wholesome relationship. I have hope knowing that one day You will return for me, Your church and bride. I want to be ready and adorned. Forgive me and cleanse me of all my sin so my heart and soul is beautifully enhanced and prepared to meet You. In Jesus' name, Amen.

ALFREDO SAUCE (for your favorite pasta)

½ cup butter
1 (8-ounce) package cream cheese
1 cup half-and-half
⅓ cup Parmesan cheese
1–2 teaspoons garlic powder, to taste
Pepper, to taste

In saucepan over medium heat, melt butter and cream cheese. Add half-and-half, Parmesan cheese, garlic powder, and pepper. Stir until well-mixed; remove from heat. Serve over hot pasta or with other recipes calling for Alfredo sauce.

March 17

When you spread out your hands in prayer, I will hide my eyes from you; even if you offer many prayers, I will not listen. Your hands are full of blood; wash and make yourselves clean. Take your evil deeds out of my sight! Stop doing wrong; learn to do right!

—ISAIAH 1:15–16

PRAYER IS CONVERSATION with God. It's beseeching the Lord or pouring out our souls and supplications in an effort to know, seek, or draw near to Him. Prayer must be sincere, humble, reverent, and offered with a sense of submission to the divine will of God. We pray in Christ's name when our mind is the mind of Christ. Our desires are the desires of Christ when His words abide in us (John 15:7). In prayer, we praise God for His goodness and righteousness and thank Him for blessings received.

But there are times when God doesn't hear our prayers. Psalm 66:18 says the Lord will not listen if we cherish sin in our hearts. Cherishing sin means there is something in our lives contradictory to God's will that we will not relinquish. But if we confess our sin (admit to God that what we are doing is wrong and against His will) and renounce it (abandon it), He will forgive us and hear our prayers (1 John 1:9). God instructs us to stop doing wrong and learn to do right; then He will listen. Second Chronicles 7:14 (KJV) says it so well: "If my people, which are called by my name, shall *humble* themselves, and *pray*, and *seek* my face, and *turn* from their wicked ways; then will I hear from heaven, and will forgive their sin, and will heal their land."

Dear Lord: Because of Your love and grace, I am able to have pardon for my sin. Thank You for the awesome God You are and for allowing me the privilege of being Your child. Strengthen my weak areas and show me how to turn from the wicked ways of the world and be a godly witness to others. In Jesus' name, Amen.

CHICKEN MAC CASSEROLE

3 boneless, skinless chicken breasts
8 ounces macaroni shells (any shape or size)
1 cup shredded cheddar cheese
1 small can sliced mushrooms, undrained
1 can cream of mushroom soup
1 cup milk
½ teaspoon salt
¼ teaspoon pepper

Cook chicken in small amount of water in pan, covered, until done; dice into small pieces. Boil macaroni until almost done (al dente); drain. Mix all ingredients together and pour into baking dish. Bake for 30–40 minutes at 350 degrees.

March 18

Come now, and let us reason together, saith the LORD: though your sins be as scarlet, they shall be as white as snow.

—ISAIAH 1:18, KJV

MANY TIMES THROUGHOUT His Word, God graciously invites us to come. Matthew 11:28 says all who are weary and heavy-burdened should come to Christ, and He will provide the needed rest. Mark 1:17 tells us to come and follow Christ and He will make us fishers of men (missionaries in our own world).

The invitation is made, but it is up to us whether or not we accept or reject it. God, in His infinite wisdom and knowledge, calls us to reason or carefully think about the condition of our hearts and lives.

When we sin, it leaves a stain on our souls that can only be removed by the cleansing power of Jesus, but that just doesn't automatically happen. We must recognize our sin and then come humbly to God, asking Him to forgive us through the shed blood of Jesus. When we do, our sin is not only forgiven, but the stain on our soul is totally removed. As we live our lives in total submission to God, we are able to walk in freedom of sin and celebrate His grace, forgiveness, love, and hope of one day being with Him.

Dear God: I praise You for convicting me of my sin. I have been rebellious and disobedient and want to change. Thank You for caring for me enough to remove my sins, blot out my transgressions, take on my pain, and forget the wrongs I committed. In Jesus' name, Amen.

STUFFED FRENCH TOAST

4 slices French or Italian bread, 1-inch thick
4 ounces cream cheese, softened
4 tablespoons strawberry preserves
¾ cup milk
2 eggs
2 teaspoons sugar
1 teaspoon vanilla
½ teaspoon cinnamon
2 tablespoons powdered sugar
2 cups sliced strawberries

Trim off crust from one side of bread. Cut a horizontal slit in each slice to make a pocket. In a bowl, combine cream cheese and preserves. Spread ⅛ of mixture inside each bread pocket. Pinch edges of bread together to hold in filling. In a bowl, whisk together milk, egg, sugar, vanilla, and cinnamon. Dip filled bread slices in egg mixture to coat. Melt butter in skillet and cook each slice until golden brown, turning once. Top with strawberries and sprinkle with powdered sugar.

March 19

And many people shall go and say, Come ye, and let us go up to the mountain of the LORD, to the house of the God of Jacob; and he will teach us of his ways, and we will walk in his paths.

—ISAIAH 2:3, KJV

ISAIAH IS REFLECTING here on the future glory of God's kingdom on earth, associating it with Mount Zion, a sacred mountain where the holy temple was located. Israel is portrayed as a light to all the nations that will gather there. The house is the temple of God and looked at as a place of refuge, strength, and peace.

Though this vision is prophesied for a time when God will rule and reign over all the earth, it is important that we who proclaim to be citizens of His kingdom respect these inspired scriptures for our lives today. Every believer should be overzealous about attending the house of worship so we might be taught the ways of the Lord. One day soon, all the nations of the world will desire to go up to the holy mountain of the Lord where Jesus Himself will teach us of His ways.

Dear Lord: What a day that will be when we will worship You together on Your holy mountain! You are hope to a hopeless world, lost in sin and depravity. Help me to do my part in teaching others about Your righteousness and grace. Forgive me when I complain about going to church when it's there I am taught about You and trained for Your service. In Jesus' name, Amen.

PINEAPPLE HAM LOAF

2 eggs
½ cup milk
1 cup finely crushed saltine crackers
¼ teaspoon pepper
1 ½ pounds (3 cups) ground cooked ham*
1 pound ground pork
1 small onion, finely chopped (optional)

Sauce:

1 cup brown sugar
1 teaspoon prepared mustard
⅓ cup vinegar
¼ cup water
1 (8-ounce) can crushed pineapple, undrained

In bowl, beat eggs; add milk, crackers, pepper, ham, pork, and onion; mix well. Shape into loaf; bake at 350 degrees for 45 minutes; drain grease if necessary. Mix sauce ingredients; pour over meat. Bake another 30 minutes, basting every 10 minutes.

*Use food processor to grind ham.

March 20

In the year that King Uzziah died I saw also the LORD sitting upon a throne, high and lifted up, and his train filled the temple.

—ISAIAH 6:1, KJV

K ING UZZIAH REIGNED for fifty-two years over the nation of Israel, and during that time there was peace and prosperity among the people. But because of that, there was also moral decay and a turning away from the Lord. In his early reign, Uzziah was humble and served God; but when he became strong and famous, he became proud and no longer served the Lord he once knew. When he died, around 740 B.C., fear and insecurity rose up within the people. Instead of turning to God, they rebelled even more and lived ungodly lives of sin and shame. It was during this time that the prophet Isaiah rose up and proclaimed a message of God's sovereignty, majesty, and holiness.

Throughout God's Word we are reminded over and over to pattern our lives after Him. Because God is holy, we are to be holy (1 Peter 1:15–17). Isaiah's vision is a reminder to us today that though the world around us exalts sin and depravity, we who have committed our lives to Christ exalt the Lord with our praise and submission to His Word. For He truly is high and lifted up and the holy and exalted One.

You, O Lord, are the holy and exalted One, and I praise You and lift You high. Thank You for loving me so I might in turn love You. Forgive my sins and help me to live my life holy and pleasing unto You. When You return for Your church, may I be found faithful and ready to go. In Jesus' name, Amen.

SPAGHETTI CARBONARA

1 (16-ounce package) spaghetti noodles
1–3 cloves garlic, minced
5–7 pieces bacon, cooked and crumbled
1 cup frozen peas
2 ½ cups heavy cream
1 cup Parmesan cheese, shredded
1 tablespoon Italian parsley, chopped
1 teaspoon black pepper

Prepare pasta according to package. In large frying pan over medium-high heat, heat garlic and cooked bacon pieces until they begin to sizzle. Add peas and cream. Bring sauce to boil; reduce heat slightly, and boil gently for 6–8 minutes. Sprinkle in Parmesan, stirring to blend and thicken sauce. Drain pasta thoroughly, and immediately toss with sauce in large bowl. Transfer to individual serving bowls; garnish with chopped parsley and black pepper to taste.

March 21

Also I heard the voice of the Lord, saying, Whom shall I send, and who will go for us? Then said I, Here am I; send me.

—ISAIAH 6:8, KJV

ISAIAH WAS IN the holy temple when he had a vision of God seated high on a throne while seraph angels worshiped Him from above. In the face of God's utmost holiness, Isaiah saw himself as an impure and sinful man. After he cried out to God for forgiveness, one of the seraph angels flew to him and touched his lips with a live coal from the altar, saying his guilt was gone and sin forgiven. It was after Isaiah was made clean that he was able to hear the voice of the Lord saying, "Who shall I send?" Isaiah answered the Lord, "Here am I. Send me!" It was then that he was commissioned as a prophet.

Just as Isaiah obeyed the call to tell the people about God and His redemptive power, so are we commanded to go into all the world and teach the people to be obedient to the Lord and become His disciples. If we don't go, who will?

Dear Lord: Thank You for Your glorious cleansing and redeeming power. I am willing to go and tell the world about Your love and grace. Give me the right words to speak to those with whom I come in contact so they would understand the meaning of salvation. Holy Spirit: Prepare their hearts to receive You and also say yes to Your call to take the message of salvation into the world. In Jesus' name, Amen.

FETTUCCINE ALFREDO

8 ounces cream cheese, cubed
¾ cup grated Parmesan cheese
½ cup milk
½ cup butter (1 stick)
¼ teaspoon pepper
⅛ teaspoon garlic powder (optional)
8 ounces fettuccine, cooked and drained
1 pound fresh chopped asparagus or broccoli (optional)
⅛ teaspoon ground nutmeg (optional)

Mix cream cheese, Parmesan cheese, milk, butter, pepper, and garlic powder in medium saucepan; cook on low until cream cheese melts and mixture is well blended. Cook noodles according to package. If using fresh asparagus or broccoli, add to boiling water about 8 minutes after noodles have been cooking. Cook about 4 minutes, or until tender. Drain noodles; mix with sauce. Sprinkle with nutmeg.

March 22

Therefore the Lord himself shall give you a sign; Behold, a virgin shall conceive and bear a son, and shall call his name Immanuel.

—Isaiah 7:14, KJV

THIS SCRIPTURE TURNS our hearts to the Christmas story and our Savior's birth, but God spoke this to Isaiah over seven hundred years before Jesus was even born. Ahaz, the king ruling Judah at the time of this prophecy, was a wicked and unbelieving man. During his reign, God permitted the kings of Israel and Syria to attack Ahaz and place his capital, Jerusalem, under siege. God wanted Ahaz to turn to Him for repentance and help; but instead, Ahaz formed an alliance with the king of Assyria. God sent Isaiah to encourage Ahaz to not place his hopes in man. If he refused to trust God, God would save His kingdom but Ahaz would still lose his throne. Isaiah even encouraged Ahaz to ask God for a sign to prove these things were so, but he stubbornly refused. It was under these circumstances that God, through Isaiah, said, "Therefore the Lord himself shall give you a sign." God knew believers in Judah were frightened and wondered what would become of them as they faced enemy attacks. God wanted them to trust Him in the midst of that most difficult situation. In the same way, God wants us to entrust ourselves to Him in the midst of our trials and troubles and not live in uncertainty and fear. He would rather have us proceed in life with the same confidence the apostle Paul had, who was able to say, "If God be for us, who can be against us?" (Rom. 8:31, KJV).

Dear Lord: You so graciously love us, in spite of our stubbornness and disobedience. I rejoice because You sent Your Son to represent love in action. Forgive me for my disbelief and sin. Help me to put my faith in You in all I do. In Jesus' name, Amen.

OVEN-FRIED CHICKEN (low-carb)

6–8 pieces chicken
2 eggs, slightly beaten
¼ cup sour cream
2 ½ cups crushed pork rinds (3 ounces)
1 teaspoon poultry seasoning
½ teaspoon pepper
5 tablespoons butter, melted

Mix eggs and sour cream in dish. Mix pork rind crumbs, poultry seasoning, and pepper in another dish. Dip chicken in egg mix, then into pork rind mix. Put chicken in baking dish. Drizzle with melted butter. Bake uncovered at 350 degrees for 1 hour, or until done.

March 23

For unto us a child is born, unto us a son is given: and the government shall be upon His shoulder: and his name shall be called Wonderful, Counselor, The mighty God, The everlasting Father, The Prince of Peace.

—Isaiah 9:6, KJV

L ONG BEFORE THE birth of Jesus, Isaiah prophesied about the Messiah who would come in a unique and marvelous way. These are the words Isaiah used to describe Him:

Surely this Wonderful Counselor, Mighty God, Everlasting Father, and Prince of Peace has come anointed by the Spirit of God to carry out the Father's will.

Mighty God: How do I thank You for such a priceless gift as You have given the world in Your Son, Jesus? Though He was sent for all, not all receive Him. I pray for Your Holy Spirit to speak to hearts today and draw them to repentance and restoration in Christ. In Jesus' name, Amen.

APPLE-CINNAMON BAKED FRENCH TOAST

1 loaf French bread, sliced 1 ½ inches thick
8 eggs, beaten
3 ½ cups milk
½ cup sugar
1 tablespoon vanilla
3 apples, peeled and sliced

Topping:

½ cup sugar
3 teaspoons cinnamon
½ teaspoon nutmeg (optional)
¼ cup melted butter

Place bread in greased or buttered 9x13-inch baking dish. Mix beaten eggs, milk, sugar, and vanilla. Pour half mixture over bread; put apples on bread. Pour remaining mixture over apples. Sprinkle with topping mixture. Pour melted butter over and refrigerate 6–8 hours or overnight. Bake at 350 degrees for 1 hour. Serve with maple syrup.

March 24

Thou wilt keep in perfect peace, whose mind is stayed on thee: because he trusteth in thee.

—Isaiah 26:3, KJV

DUE TO THE world's unbelief and compromise of God's Word, we are seeing an increase of unrest, confusion, and bewilderment. Those without Christ as Lord are searching in the wrong places to have their physical and spiritual needs met. Each of us is born with a sinful, selfish nature to please our fleshly desires, and without a total surrender of ourselves to God, we will never find true peace. When the courts removed the Word of God as the authority of this nation and humanism entered into the school system as God was ushered out, we began to see a continuous decline of peace and morality. Confusion, restlessness, and serving the god of self resulted.

True peace and freedom from anxiety can only be found when we die daily to our fleshly desires and live in total submission to Jesus Christ. To be kept in perfect peace does not mean circumstances may change, but it does mean we have hope, knowing the Lord is with us and will supply our every need. If we do our part and keep our minds focused on Him, God will do His part to grant us peace and calm in every storm.

Father: You are peace and assurance to my soul when I put my trust in You. As I believe in You, walk with You, talk with You, trust in You, and serve You, my faith grows and the gates of hell cannot prevail against me. You bring calm to every storm and hope for every situation that arises in my life. Forgive me when I don't keep my thoughts turned toward You and the result is fear and confusion. My hope and peace come when I trust in You. In Jesus' name, Amen.

TACO SALAD

1 pound ground meat
1 package taco seasoning mix
1 head lettuce, chopped
1 small onion, chopped
1 or 2 tomatoes, chopped
1 (10-ounce) bag corn chips (Fritos)
1 small can kidney beans, drained (optional)
1 cup cheddar cheese, grated
Taco sauce and sour cream (optional)
Red, French, or ranch dressing

Brown ground meat in pan; drain. Add seasoning packet and ¼ cup water; cook on medium-low 15 minutes. Prepare lettuce, onions, and tomatoes; set aside. On individual plates, put desired amount of taco chips, scoop of meat mixture, and other toppings and dressings as desired.

March 25

The grass withereth, the flower fadeth: but the word of our God shall stand forever.

—Isaiah 40:8, KJV

THE WORD OF God, Bible, Law, Truth, and Holy Scriptures are all names for the inspired and authoritative writings of the Old and New Testament. They are God's message to humanity and the only infallible witness to His saving power for all people. The purpose of God's Word is to teach, rebuke, correct, and train so we might be thoroughly equipped to do God's will here on earth. The Scriptures are to be viewed by us as the very breath and life of God, and we are to use them to conquer the power of sin, Satan, and the world in our lives. The Bible is absolutely true, without error, trustworthy, and infallible concerning all the issues of life. It is the expression of God's character and wisdom and gives us the only way of salvation in Jesus Christ. All forms of creation will become weak and eventually die, but God's Word will endure forever.

Heavenly Father: You are God, the mighty Creator, and the Rock of my salvation. I praise You for Your wonderful works and for loving me so much that You inspired others to write all those things You wanted me to know. Create in me a hunger for Your Word so I might know how to live my life. Help me to show Your love to others so they too might serve You. In Jesus' name, Amen.

CHICKEN BROCCOLI RICE CASSEROLE

3 cups cooked long grain rice
4 boneless, skinless chicken breasts, cooked and diced into bite-sized pieces
1 ½ pounds broccoli, cooked until tender and cut into bite-size pieces
2 cans cream of celery soup, undiluted
¾ cup mayonnaise
½ cup milk
1 teaspoon curry powder or other seasoning (optional)
3 cups (12 ounces) shredded sharp cheddar cheese

Place cooked rice evenly in greased 13x9-inch baking dish. Arrange chicken and broccoli on top. In bowl, mix soup, mayonnaise, milk, and curry powder; pour over chicken and broccoli; top with cheese. Cover loosely with foil; bake at 350 degrees for 45 minutes.

March 26

But they that wait upon the LORD shall renew their strength; they shall mount up with wings as eagles; they shall run, and not be weary; and they shall walk and not faint.

—ISAIAH 40:31, KJV

T O WAIT UPON the Lord means to surrender 100 percent of our lives to God. It also means we will have a heart willing to serve God and be used by Him to share the gospel with the world. Growing weary or weak may come from physical, mental, or spiritual overload. God knows each of us and our limitations. He won't call us to do more than what He knows we are capable of doing, and He will equip us with renewed energy for what He does call us to do. It's normal to grow weary and tired; that's why God Himself took one day off a week to rest. He rested and knew we, too, would need rest.

In our life with Christ, there must be a time for giving and a time for receiving. Giving is serving in those areas where God called us, and receiving is submitting ourselves to Jesus and feeding on His love, His Word, and His rest. This produces hope, and hope produces strength. We serve a mighty God, One who, unlike the world, does not pressure us to perform beyond our abilities. When we wait upon the Lord, we have the assurance that our strength will be renewed by the power of God's love.

Dear Lord: Help me to stay focused and not give up, even when the conditions appear hopeless. You alone are my hope and source of power. As I wait on You, may I soar high as the eagles, trusting You to renew my strength. In Jesus' name, Amen.

SOUTHWEST CHICKEN CASSEROLE

2 cups uncooked instant rice
2 cups chicken broth (bouillon and water okay)
1 cup diced, cooked chicken
1 small onion, chopped
1 (10-ounce) can mild Rotel tomatoes and green chiles
1 teaspoon chili powder
1 can cream of chicken soup
1 cup sour cream
8–12 ounces grated cheddar cheese

Mix all ingredients together except cheese. Pour into greased baking dish. Bake at 350 degrees for 30 minutes or until bubbly. Remove from oven; spread cheese over the top. Return to oven until cheese melts.

March 27

So do not fear, for I am with you; do not be dismayed, for I am your God. I will strengthen you and help you; I will uphold you with my righteous right hand.

—Isaiah 41:10

WHAT AN ENCOURAGEMENT this is as we encounter the storm and trials of life! Our fears are instantly eased with a promise from God. Israel was in captivity, and God spoke these words through Isaiah to let the people know He was with them and knew exactly what they were enduring. At times, we may feel all alone and wonder if anyone really cares. The pressures of life are overwhelming, and whether it is a financial, physical, spiritual, family, or any type of circumstance or affliction, God wants to lift our fears and discouragement. His hand is strong, willing, and able to help us with any ordeal or threat from the evil one. God's will is that His people will not live in fear but in victorious faith and trust in Him. We are to be dependent upon God's presence in the best of times and in the worst of times. His tenderness and compassion is available when we admit we no longer can conquer the battle ourselves but are ready for God's help. In humility, we must cry out to Him for forgiveness and then receive His counsel and comfort. God's hand is strong, and His love is everlasting.

Father: I praise and thank You for Your willingness to provide strength when I am weak and comfort when I am in the midst of a storm. Your hand is mighty, and You are willing to help me at all times. You are my comfort and the peace that replaces all my fears. Help me to trust You more and reach for Your hand when I feel like I am falling. In Jesus' name, Amen.

CORN AU GRATIN

2 eggs, well beaten
1 cup cooked corn
1 small onion, chopped
1 small green pepper, chopped
2 tablespoons butter
1 cup cooked rice
½ cup grated cheddar cheese
¼ teaspoon salt
¼ teaspoon pepper
¼ teaspoon paprika
3–4 bacon strips, fried and crumbled

Mix together beaten eggs and corn. Sauté onion and green pepper in butter; add to corn mixture. Fold in rice, half the grated cheese, salt, and pepper. Pour into greased baking dish; cover with remaining cheese, paprika, and bacon pieces. Bake uncovered at 375 degrees for 20–25 minutes.

March 28

Seek ye the Lord while He may be found, call ye upon him while he is near.

—Isaiah 55:6, KJV

EVERYONE IS BORN with a sinful nature and never has to be taught how to be disobedient to authority; it just comes natural to us. Because of that, God provided for us a Savior. He also gave us a free will to either accept His Son as our personal Savior or reject Him and face the consequences of eternal hell.

God's Holy Spirit speaks to us and convicts us of sin. If we ignore the still, small voice that speaks deep within our soul, our hearts will gradually grow hard and no longer be sensitive and yield to the Spirit's call. When this happens, living a righteous life no longer has priority. Instead, we seek more worldly pleasures and compromise the morals and values we once knew.

God warns us in His Word to seek Him while He may found and call on Him while He is near before it is too late. There is a point of no return—a place we never want to be. God is not the one who leaves us, but it is a choice of our own to accept or reject Him. May we all choose to find Christ while there is still yet time.

Dear Lord: I love You and seek You with all my heart. Your Word is true and explains so well how I should live my life. Thank You for sending Your Holy Spirit to speak, guide, direct, listen, convict, and comfort my heart. Without You, life would have no meaning; with You, I have purpose and a reason to live. Help me be a witness to my neighbors so they might seek You and know You while You still may be found. In Jesus' name, Amen.

TORTELLINI SOUP

1 pound lean ground meat
4 cups beef broth (water and bouillon okay)
1 (14.5-ounce) can Italian diced tomatoes
½ teaspoon dried basil
½ teaspoon dried oregano
1 (9-ounce) package refrigerated cheese or meat tortellini
Parmesan or mozzarella cheese, grated

Brown ground meat in pan; drain. Add broth, tomatoes, basil, and oregano. Bring to boil; add tortellini. Boil 6–8 minutes, until tortellini tender. Serve in bowls; top with grated cheese.

March 29

Behold, the LORD's hand is not shortened, that it cannot save; neither his ear heavy, that it cannot hear: But your iniquities have separated between you and your God, and your sins have hid his face from you, that he will not hear.

—ISAIAH 59:1–2, KJV

JUST AS THE psalmist warned us in Psalm 66:18, so does God tell us through the prophet Isaiah that He does not hear our prayers if we have sin in our heart. Sin is any offense done or not done that is contrary to the Word of God. If we live our lives apart from the teachings of the Bible, we cannot expect God to answer our prayers when we call on Him. When living in a sinful state, the only prayer God hears is the prayer of repentance. Psalm 91:14–15 (KJV) says: "Because he hath set his love upon me, therefore I will deliver him: I will set him on high, because he hath known my name. He shall call upon me, and I will answer him: I will be with him in trouble; I will deliver him, and honor him." Psalm 145:19 (KJV) says: "He will fulfill the desire of them that fear (love) him: he will also hear their cry, and will save them."

God loves us and wants to hear and answer our prayers, but He gave us a free will to either choose to serve Him or choose the way of sin and remain apart from Him. May we each decide today to repent of our sin and invite Jesus to be our Savior and Lord, knowing for sure that God will indeed hear our prayers.

Father in heaven: Forgive and pardon me from the things I knew were wrong but did anyhow and for the things I didn't do that I knew I should have done. Cleanse me within, and hear my plea for repentance. Lead me with Your Holy Spirit to do only those things that bring You glory. May You be pleased with my life and hear my every prayer. In Jesus' name, Amen.

CHICKEN ENCHILADAS

1 can cream of chicken soup
4 ounces chopped green chiles (optional)
2 cups cheddar cheese
½ cup sour cream
2 cups (2–3 breasts) cooked chicken breasts, diced
¼–½ cup butter, melted
8 small flour tortillas
2 cups Monterey Jack cheese

In large bowl, combine soup, chiles, cheddar cheese, sour cream, and chicken. Melt butter in 9x13-inch baking dish (warm oven works well). Dip both sides of tortillas in butter. Add spoonful of chicken mixture to each tortilla; roll up and place in baking dish. Sprinkle Monterey Jack cheese over top. Cover with foil; bake 30 minutes at 350 degrees. Serve with salsa.

March 30

The Spirit of the Lord God is upon me; because the Lord hath anointed me to preach good tidings unto the meek; he hath sent me to bind up the brokenhearted, to proclaim liberty to the captives, and the opening of the prison to them that are bound; To proclaim the acceptable year of the Lord, and the day of vengeance of our God; to comfort all that mourn; To appoint unto them that mourn in Zion, to give unto them beauty instead for ashes, the oil of joy for mourning, the garment of praise for the spirit of heaviness; that they might be called trees of righteousness, the planting of the Lord, that he might be glorified.

—Isaiah 61:1–3, kjv

WHEN JESUS STARTED His ministry on earth, after He had been tested for forty days in the wilderness, He went to the synagogue and read this passage from the prophet Isaiah (Luke 4:17–19). Then He said, "This day is this scripture fulfilled in your ears" (Luke 4:21, kjv).

Christ means "the Anointed." But what was He anointed to do? Indeed, He was the sacrificed Lamb—sacrificed to atone for sin—but much of Jesus' earthly ministry was devoted to preaching and healing. That's why He was anointed with the Spirit of God.

If we claim to be followers of Christ, then we too have the Spirit of the Lord upon us and are anointed to do God's work. Our purpose is the same as Christ's: to preach the gospel to the poor, afflicted, brokenhearted, imprisoned, blind, oppressed, and all who mourn and grieve and to proclaim the time of true freedom and salvation to all who are still bound by sin and the power of Satan. It is our privilege and duty to offer the oil of gladness and a garment of praise to those who still need freedom from death, freedom from sin, and freedom to joyfully and blamelessly enter into God's presence.

Sovereign Lord: You have called me to share Your good news with the poor and brokenhearted. Equip me for Your service as I tell others about Your love and strive to meet their needs. In turn, may they accept You as Lord and Savior. In Jesus' name, Amen.

BAKED CHICKEN STRIPS

4 boneless, skinless chicken strips
¼ cup butter, melted
3 cups crushed cheese-flavored butter crackers

Lightly grease a 9x13-inch baking dish. Roll chicken strips in melted butter, then in cracker crumbs; place in dish. Bake at 350 degrees for 50 minutes or until chicken is done, turning once.

March 31

Before I formed thee in the belly I knew thee; and before thou camest forth out of the womb I sanctified thee, and I ordained thee a prophet unto the nations.

—Jeremiah 1:5, KJV

J EREMIAH WAS A prophet of the southern kingdom of Judah almost six hundred years before Jesus was born. He was a great man and was called by God to encourage the rebellious people of Judah to repent and turn to Him. Jeremiah felt inadequate to do the job that God called him to do, though he loved God very much and had a burden for the lost. When Jeremiah questioned God's call, telling Him of his inadequacies and limitations, the Lord spoke the words of Jeremiah 1:5. Before Jeremiah was even born, God knew him and had a purpose and a plan for his life.

Oftentimes in our own lives we hear of the great needs there are to meet the commands of spreading the good news in our churches, communities, and throughout the world, but we feel incompetent and inadequate to help, just like Jeremiah. If we are called, God will equip us, just as He did Jeremiah. He has a plan and purpose for each of us. Remember this: God equips the called; He doesn't necessarily call the equipped.

Heavenly Father: You knew me before I was born, and You have a great plan for my life. What a joy this brings to my heart! Thank You for caring about me and for orchestrating my life so my purpose would be real and exciting as I follow after You. Equip me to do Your work, and help me show others how they too might follow after You. In Jesus' name, Amen.

POTATO SOUP

4 strips bacon, diced
1 onion, chopped
2 quarts water
1 teaspoon garlic salt
1 teaspoon pepper
8–10 potatoes, peeled and diced
6 chicken bouillon cubes
1–2 cans evaporated milk
1 (8-ounce) package cream cheese
4 ounces Velveeta cheese
8 ounces sour cream
Potato flakes (optional)

Fry bacon in large pan until crisp; add onion and cook until tender. Add water, salt, pepper, potatoes, and bouillon; bring to boil. Turn heat to low; simmer until potatoes are soft. Add milk, cheese, and sour cream; stir until melted. If too thin, add small amount potato flakes. If too thick, add milk or broth.

He
is Risen

April

April 1

Oh, my anguish, my anguish! I writhe in pain. Oh, the agony of my heart! My heart pounds within me, I cannot keep silent.

—Jeremiah 4:19

GOD CALLED JEREMIAH to minister to the sinful people of Judah. He had a very sensitive and broken heart for the lost and often wept before the Lord on their behalf. Though he was a lonely and rejected man, he was one of the boldest and bravest of all the prophets. Because of his deep compassion and burden for those who rejected God, Jeremiah was often called the "weeping prophet." He frequently expressed his grief and loyalty to God by weeping and wailing before Him. Jeremiah knew God's judgment would be upon the people if they didn't repent, and this deeply saddened him. The sorrow and agony he felt because of sin, idolatry, and rebellion is also what we should feel for those without Christ. The very thought of people being destroyed by sin and spending eternity in hell should be enough to cause our hearts to pound with agony and our lips unable to be kept silent of proclaiming God's Word.

O God: You called Your children to take the good news of Your love and grace to a lost and dying world. Without You, we have no hope. I repent of the times in my life when I held back and did not proclaim Your truth to those You placed in my path. Help me to be stronger with my testimony and witness so You are glorified in the lives of those once lost. In Jesus' name, Amen.

SHRIMP AND VEGETABLE STIR-FRY

1 garlic clove, minced
1 tablespoon vegetable oil
1 large onion, cut in chunks
1 bell pepper, cut in slices
1 cup fresh or frozen snow peas
1 cup fresh mushrooms, sliced
1 (8-ounce) can water chestnuts, sliced and drained
1 cup chicken broth
1 tablespoon corn starch
2 tablespoons soy sauce
1 pound cooked shrimp
3 cups hot cooked rice

Heat oil with garlic in large skillet or wok over high heat. Add onion, pepper, snow peas, mushrooms, and water chestnuts; stir-fry until vegetables are crisp-tender. Mix broth, cornstarch, and soy sauce together. Add mixture and shrimp to pan; cook until sauce is thick and bubbly. Serve over hot rice.

April 2

Are they ashamed of their loathsome conduct? No, they have no shame at all; they do not even know how to blush. So they will fall among the fallen; they will be brought down when they are punished, says the LORD.

—JEREMIAH 8:12

THE PEOPLE OF Judah lived in sin and disobedience to God's law. The leaders of that day made things worse because they distorted the Word of God so severely that the people believed they could live any way they wanted without condemnation from God. They eventually abandoned any desire they once had to serve God, were unrepentant, and showed no shame or remorse for their sin. Just because they thought there would be no judgment for their sinful lives didn't mean that one day the Almighty would not come and be their judge.

There are many of us today who believe the same way the people of Judah did and no longer feel a sense of conviction or shame for disobedience to God's Word. We become desensitized to the blatant sin and immorality all around us. No longer do we blush at nudity, profanity, or illicit sexual scenes in movies, magazines, or on television; shame is a thing of the past. Many churches have accepted sin and sugarcoated it so to not step on any toes.

The apostle Paul warned us in Romans 1:24–32 that if we continue to reject the Holy Spirit's conviction concerning sin, our souls will eventually become hard and unable to be converted. We must come to God through the redemption plan that He gave us in His Son Jesus before it is too late.

Dear Lord: Forgive me for any unconfessed sin in my life. I want only to be found acceptable in Your sight. Show me Your way, and help me to do my part in bringing morality back to this nation. Thank You for Your Holy Spirit who convicts me when I am tempted to sin. You are a wonderful Lord! Thank You for redeeming my soul. In Jesus' name, Amen.

PIEROGI CASSEROLE

1 pound lasagna noodles
6 cups diced potatoes
8 ounces cream cheese, softened
3–4 large onions, sliced
2 sticks butter
Salt and pepper to taste

Cook noodles according to package directions. Cook potatoes in salted water until done; drain and mash with cream cheese. Brown onions in pan with 1 stick butter. Melt ½ stick butter in bottom of 9x13-inch pan. Layer with noodles, potatoes, onions, and remaining butter. Cover with foil and bake at 325 degrees for 15 minutes. Remove foil and bake an additional 10–15 minutes.

April 3

Blessed is the man that trusteth in the LORD, and whose hope the LORD is. For he shall be as a tree planted by the waters, and that spreadeth out her roots by the river, and shall not see when heat cometh, but her leaf shall be green; and shall not be careful in the year of drought, neither shall cease from yielding fruit.

—JEREMIAH 17:7–8, KJV

D O YOU HAVE a green thumb? I certainly don't, and every plant that enters my home eventually dies. Perhaps it gets watered too much or too little. Maybe it gets too much sun or not enough. Whatever the case may be, it always dies. Obviously, I am not the plant's source of life. God said we are like trees planted along the water if we trust in Him. God is our source of life. If we are rooted in the Word by reading our Bibles, praying, obeying, and trusting, our spiritual roots will grow deep and nothing will be able to move us away from our Lord. Though trials and circumstances may come, we will continue to produce good fruit—*if we trust in the Lord.*

O Father: I love You so much. You are my source of life and the joy of my salvation. In You are my roots planted and nourished. Forgive me when I become weak and begin to waver in my relationship with You. Help me to not allow anything to rob me of my time with You because with You my soul is fed and nurtured and my life full and fruitful. In Jesus' name, Amen.

CHICKEN TORTILLA SOUP (Tex-Mex style)

3–4 boneless, skinless chicken breasts
2 cups water
2 (14.5-ounce) cans chicken broth
1 (14.5-ounce) can diced tomatoes
1 (14.5-ounce) can black beans, rinsed/drained
1 medium onion, chopped
1 can diced green chiles
1 (14.5-ounce) can whole kernel corn; drained
1 teaspoon chili powder
1 teaspoon cumin
1 teaspoon garlic salt
1 bag tortilla chips or corn chips
1 cup grated Monterey Jack cheese
¼ cup chopped fresh cilantro *or* 1–2 tablespoons dry cilantro flakes
1 lime, cut in wedges (optional)
1 avocado, peeled and diced (optional)
Dollop of sour cream (optional)

Boil chicken in water until done; remove, dice, and return to pan. Add broth, tomatoes, beans, onions, chiles, corn, and seasonings; cover and simmer 30 minutes. To serve, crush few chips in individual bowls; pour soup over top. Top with remaining ingredients as desired.

April 4

"For I know the plans I have for you," declares the LORD, "plans to prosper you and not to harm you, plans to give you hope and a future."

—JEREMIAH 29:11

JEREMIAH TOLD THE people of Judah that after their seventy years of captivity, God would deliver them and restore their lives. Though the people had turned their backs on God many times, He did not abandon them. Instead, God planned to bring peace and prosperity to those who had separated themselves from the people who wanted nothing to do with Him. The Lord wanted His people to know that no matter what they were going through, He was still in control.

God is sovereign and works out His purposes, at times even using the evil plans of wicked men. He redeems our suffering and trials and uses them for His glory. We have the promise from Jesus that He is with us, having overcome the world. Every believer can have the peace of God, and we can also have confidence in His sovereign control of all events. As we do, God will give us peace. No matter what the circumstances may be, we are aliens and strangers here, and our hope is not in this world. Rather, our hope is Jesus Christ! So we must delight in Him, seek His face, and know the peace of God.

Dear Lord: There are times when I am weary and discouraged, but You are there, loving, forgiving, and bringing me hope. Grant me faith to not waver in my trust of You and courage to press on and not give in to circumstances and feelings. Thank You for loving me and for giving me a bright future with You. In Jesus' name, Amen.

PARTY POTATO CASSEROLE

10–12 medium potatoes, peeled and quartered
1 (8-ounce) package cream cheese, softened
1 (8-ounce) carton sour cream
½ teaspoon garlic powder
½ teaspoon salt
½ teaspoon pepper
2 teaspoons chopped chives
2 teaspoons dried parsley
½ stick butter, melted
Paprika

Cook potatoes in boiling water until tender, about 15 minutes; drain and mash. Add cream cheese, sour cream, garlic powder, salt, pepper, chives, and parsley; beat with electric mixer until smooth. Pour into baking dish; brush with melted butter; sprinkle with paprika. Bake at 350 degrees for 30 minutes.

April 5

I have loved thee with an everlasting love: therefore with lovingkindness Have I drawn thee.

—Jeremiah 31:3b, KJV

GOD LOVES US! He loved us before; He loves us now; and He loves us forever. God's love for us is tender, deep, warm, intense, caring, sweet, and beyond what human expression can describe. God is never-ending love, and therefore, He is the God of gods, Lord of lords, King of kings, and the Father of all. We are His descendants from His own breath that He breathed into His first son, Adam. God the Father has come to bless us with His eternal love. It is the same love with which He surrounds the other two persons of the Godhead: Jesus Christ and the Holy Spirit. God's love is unconditional, absolute, eternal, and He will never forget or forsake those who trust in Him for their salvation. The world and its beings stand as a testimony of the Almighty's unfailing love. Every one of His creatures—angels, men, women, children and infants—breathe and live through the heartbeat of God's love. His love gives all of us life, peace, hope, faith, and love. Psalm 36:7 (KJV) says, "How excellent is thy lovingkindness, O God! Therefore the children of men put their trust under the shadow of thy wings." God demonstrated His love toward us two thousand years ago with the gift of His Son. Romans 5:8 (KJV) says, "But God commendeth his love for us, in that, while we were yet sinners, Christ died for us." In John 3:16, we are told that God loved the world so much He sent His only Son to die for us so we might experience eternal life. Today and every day, we rejoice that God sent His divine gift to us and reminds us, once again, that He loves us with an everlasting love.

Dear Lord: I praise and thank You for loving me with an unconditional and everlasting love. Though no one deserves the gift of Your Son, You saw fit to bless us anyhow. As I pattern my life after Yours, may I faithfully show love and kindness to others. In Jesus' name, Amen.

CAULIFLOWER LETTUCE SALAD

¾ cup Miracle Whip
½ cup ranch dressing
¼ cup grated Parmesan cheese
¼ cup sugar
2 tablespoons red onion
Bacon bits (desired amount)
1 head cauliflower (cut up)
1 bunch of loose-leaf lettuce

Mix together all ingredients except lettuce. When ready to serve, add lettuce. (Don't combine too soon as lettuce will wilt and become soggy.)

April 6

Babylon must fall because of Israel's slain, just as the slain in all the earth have fallen because of Babylon. You who have escaped the sword, leave and do not linger! Remember the LORD in a distant land, and think on Jerusalem.

—JEREMIAH 51:49–50

BABYLON WAS ONE of the most splendid cities of the ancient world when it was under the rule of King Nebuchadnezzar. Israel's chosen people were held in captivity there until God freed them. While there, they lived ungodly, immoral lives and committed every kind of sin known to man. Babylon became known as a place of wickedness and moral decay; it still represents a place of spiritual lostness today.

The opposite of Babylon is Jerusalem, the city where God freed and restored the people who were willing to repent and turn back to Him.

Here on earth, we have two spiritual places to be—either Babylon or Jerusalem. Being in Babylon is the place where we are before accepting Jesus as our Savior. Jerusalem is the place we are when we have chosen to repent and turn from our sin. Jesus is the only One who is able to lead us out of Babylon and into Jerusalem. He was appointed by God, and without following Him out of our spiritual bondage and captivity, we will be eternally lost and left behind in a spiritual Babylon.

The Babylonian captivity is symbolic. It simply gives a name to sin's captivity and illustrates our human attachment to wickedness. Christianity is the only road out of Babylon; it is the only way out of sin. But where paganism (secularism) rules, Babylon remains and salvation is rejected. Jesus will return one day after the entire world has been warned to change its ways and turn to embrace Him. The Lord will gather all mankind into judgment for the way in which we lived our lives. The choice is ours—Babylon or Jerusalem.

Dear Lord: Thank You for rescuing me and leading me out of Babylon and into Jerusalem. I was spiritually dead, but You restored me and now I live. Strengthen my walk with You and help me to lead others to know You also. In Jesus' name, Amen.

BUSY WOMAN'S DREAM

1 ½ pounds ground chuck
1 can cream of chicken soup
1 (16-ounce) bag frozen Tater Tots

Crumble raw meat in bottom of baking dish; spread soup evenly over top. Place Tater Tots on top of soup. Bake uncovered at 350 degrees for 45 minutes, until bubbly and Tater Tots are browned.

April 7

This I recall to my mind, therefore have I hope. It is of the Lord's mercies that we are not consumed, because his compassions fail not. They are new every morning: great is they faithfulness.

—Lamentations 3:21–23, KJV

THE PROPHET JEREMIAH wrote the five chapters of Lamentations to express his intense sorrow and emotional pain over the tragic devastation and downfall of Jerusalem and Judah. The tragedy was a result of God's judgment for their centuries of rebellion against Him. Jeremiah acknowledged that God was righteous and just in his wrath toward these unrepentant people, but he also recognized there was hope in the midst of their despair. Even though the people deserved their punishment, Jeremiah had hope and relied on God's mercy and compassion to renew his strength each and every day. He wanted the people to know that if they trusted and waited on the Lord, He would restore them and give them purpose. We too become weary with the circumstances, afflictions, and disappointments of life, but God is our portion and everything we need. If we look to Him, trust in Him, and wait on Him, His mercy and love will renew our strength and hope each and every morning.

Dear Lord: Your love and compassion renew my hope and strength each and every morning; great is Your faithfulness to Your children. Thank You for loving me, even when I am unlovely. Forgive me for allowing the enemy to rob me of precious time with You and for not trusting and waiting on You to aid me in my circumstances and afflictions. In Jesus' name, Amen.

SPINACH SALAD

1 ½ pounds spinach
1 clove garlic, slivered
¾ cup salad oil
½ cup red wine vinegar
1 tablespoon sugar
½ teaspoon salt
Dash pepper
3 hard-cooked eggs, chopped
4 slices bacon, crispy fried

Wash spinach; remove stems and tear leaves into bite-size pieces. Dry; chill 2 hours. Let garlic stand in oil 1 hour. Just before serving, mix oil, vinegar, sugar, salt, and pepper in large salad bowl. Add spinach and toss with dressing until leaves well coated. Sprinkle with chopped eggs and crumbled bacon; toss.

April 8

I will give them one heart, and I will put a new spirit within you; and I will take the stony heart out of their flesh, and will give them an heart of flesh: That they may walk in my statutes, and keep mine ordinances, and do them: and they shall be my people, and I will be their God. But as for them whose heart walketh after the heart of their detestable things and their abominations, I will recompense their way up on their own heads, saith the Lord God.

—Ezekiel 11:19–21, KJV

These were the prophetic words of God, spoken through the prophet Ezekiel concerning the people of Judah who had been taken into Babylonian captivity. They had rebelled against God and were sent away out of their homeland as a judgment from God for their sin and idolatry. A remnant of these people was being returned to their land, and because of their change of heart they would remove all the vile images and detestable idols that were there and worship the one true God. Ezekiel prophesied that God would pour out His Holy Spirit on these people and empower them to live according to His law.

Do we have the same Spirit of God to give us the wisdom and strength we need to live as God's Word tells us? When we accept His plan for our lives by inviting Jesus to be our Savior, we must abandon our old lifestyle and beliefs and follow after the decrees of God. It is then that our hearts of stone become hearts of flesh and we are forgiven, restored, and renewed by the love and grace of the sovereign Lord.

Father: Even though You knew Your children would rebel and sin against You, You still created and loved us. Thank You! Reveal to me the detestable ways in my life that disgrace Your name and help me to change. In doing so, may others be anxious to know the God I serve. Thank You for taking my heart of stone and turning it into a heart of flesh. In Jesus' name, Amen.

BRUNCH CASSEROLE

8 slices of bread, diced
1 pound sausage, cooked and drained
2 cups shredded cheddar cheese
1 dozen eggs
1 teaspoon salt
1 cup milk
1 teaspoon mustard
1 can cream of mushroom soup

Layer bread, sausage, and cheese in greased 9x13-inch baking dish. Mix eggs salt, milk, mustard, and soup; pour over top. Refrigerate 6–8 hours or overnight. Bake at 350 degrees for 45 minutes.

April 9

If it be so, our God whom we serve is able to deliver us from the burning fiery furnace, and he will deliver us out of thine hand, O king. But if not, be it known unto thee, O king, that we will not serve thy gods, nor worship the golden image which thou hast set up.

—DANIEL 3:17–18, KJV

THESE WERE THE words of Shadrach, Meshach, and Abednego, three Jewish men who loved God with all their hearts. They worked for prideful King Nebuchadnezzar in Babylon, where they had important jobs. The king made a ninety-foot golden image and demanded, at the sound of music, for everyone to stop what they were doing and bow and worship it. Whoever didn't obey would be immediately thrown into a blazing furnace.

Some of the king's workers, jealous of Shadrach, Meshach, and Abednego, saw they didn't bow down and worship the golden image and ran to tell Nebuchadnezzar of their disobedience. The king sent for the men and gave them another chance, but Shadrach, Meshach, and Abednego stood strong in their faith and refused. Immediately, they were thrown into the fiery furnace—but the fire did not destroy them. Instead, a fourth person was seen with them. The king ordered them to come out, where they were found unharmed by the fire. Nebuchadnezzar acknowledged that the fourth person was an angel God put there to protect them. The king was not only astonished that God spared the men's lives, but more so that the men were willing to die to honor their God.

Shadrach, Meshach, and Abednego did not compromise their faith, but they had such a high allegiance to God that they didn't hesitate to place their lives in His hands. Each of us is faced with daily decisions to either compromise our Christian faith or hold strong to our convictions, too. We may face peer pressure, persecution, or ridicule if we choose to worship God. But He will be there with us in our fiery furnace if we choose to follow God, believing that He is able to save us from it, but even if not, we will still serve Him and none other.

Lord: You are wonderful and You are amazing! When pressures come and the heat starts to rise, may I be as these three men and choose to serve You, no matter of the outcome. Teach me how to walk and talk the life that honors only You. In Jesus' name, Amen.

BARBECUE PORK ROAST (crockpot)

3 pounds boneless pork roast
1 cup barbecue sauce
1 cup water

Combine all ingredients in a crockpot. Cook on high 6–8 hours, until pork is thoroughly cooked.

April 10

For he is the living God, and steadfast for ever, and his kingdom that which shall not be destroyed, and his dominion shall be even unto the end. He delivereth and rescueth, and he worketh signs and wonders in the heaven and in earth, who hath delivered Daniel from the power of the lions.

—Daniel 6:26–27, KJV

D ANIEL WAS A bright young man living in Jerusalem when he was taken captive and deported to Babylon to work in the royal courts under King Nebuchadnezzar. The other elites he worked with became jealous of Daniel because the king showed him favor due to his integrity, hard work, and prophetic giftings. They wanted Daniel killed but knew he had no fault except that of honoring his Lord. The men convinced the king to create a law where no one could pray to any god or man but could only worship him (the king). If anyone broke the law, they would be thrown into the lion's den.

Daniel refused to obey the decree and continued to pray to the one true God three times a day, as was his custom. The jealous men reported this to the king, and Daniel was thrown into the den of hungry lions. When the king went to the den the next morning, he found Daniel unharmed and giving praise to God for sending an angel to keep the lions' mouths shut. The king acknowledged that Daniel's God had saved him. In turn, the king had the men who were jealous of Daniel thrown into the lion's den, where they were devoured.

Daniel was not afraid to pray, even knowing he might lose his life. In America, we are free to pray and worship as we desire but don't always take advantage of it. Daniel is an example for us to stand up for our religious freedom and be faithful to God, no matter the cost.

Dear God: Thank You for Your faithfulness and love. You care for us and perform signs and wonders like none other. Help me to live my life totally focused on You and do as Daniel did and not be ashamed to honor You, no matter the cost. In Jesus' name, Amen.

MAC AND CHEESE (3-ingredient)

2 cups uncooked macaroni
4 tablespoons butter
8 ounces Velveeta cheese, cubed

Cook macaroni according to directions; drain and leave in pan. Add butter and cheese; stir constantly over low heat stirring until melted. Add a little milk if too thick.

April 11

O Lord, the great and awesome God, who keeps His covenant of love with all who love Him and obey His commands.

—Daniel 9:4

THIS IS HOW Daniel began His plea to God on behalf of the desolation of his homeland, Jerusalem. He was troubled because the prophet Jeremiah prophesied that restoration would begin soon, but there was no indication it was happening. Being the man of God Daniel was, he turned to God and pleaded with Him in prayer and fasting for the fulfillment of the prophetic word given in the Scriptures. In his prayer of intercession, Daniel recognized God's awesomeness, greatness, faithful love, and covenant mercy for all who love Him and obey His commands. God's unconditional love for us should be celebrated every day.

Probably the most familiar verse in the Bible is John 3:16 (KJV): "For God so loved the world, that he gave his only begotten Son, that whosoever believeth in him should not perish, but have everlasting life." This reveals God's heart and purpose. He gave His Son as an offering for our sin, and the Son willingly and lovingly accepted the call. God's love is supernatural, kind, unconditional, eternal, genuine, patient, free, merciful, selfless, fulfilling, long-suffering, spontaneous, deliberate, sacrificial, endless, and the list goes on. God is love all the time, and He keeps His covenant of love with all who love Him and keep His commands.

Father: Thank You for sending Your Son to die on the cross for me as a payment for my sin and disobedience. In turn, I choose to love You by being obedient to Your Word. Forgive me for my sin and show me how to not only love You but also love others. Help me to see the world through Your eyes and love and serve others unconditionally, as You do. In Jesus' name, Amen.

CHEESY RICE CASSEROLE

1 stick butter
4 green onions, chopped
2 cans cream of mushroom soup
1 (4-ounce) can mushrooms, undrained
4 cups rice, cooked
1 cup slivered almonds
8–10 ounces cheddar cheese, grated

Melt butter in saucepan; add onions; sauté until soft. Add soup, mushrooms, rice, and almonds; mix well. Pour half of mixture into greased baking dish; cover with half of cheese. Add rest of rice mix; top with remaining cheese. Bake at 350 degrees for 20 minutes or until cheese is melted.

April 12

I led them with cords of human kindness, with ties of love.

—HOSEA 11:4

THE PRODIGAL SON in Luke 15 rejected his father's values. He made foolish decisions and got into trouble. The father was deeply disappointed but never gave up on him. No matter what he had done, the father said, he was still his son and he would never stop loving him. The joyful day finally came when father and son were reunited.

The people in Hosea's day followed a similar pattern. Although God had rescued them from Egypt and nourished them, they turned their backs on Him. They insulted God's name by worshiping the gods of the Canaanites, but still God loved them and longed for their return (Hosea 11:8).

Do you ever wonder if you may have strayed too far from God to be restored? He who loves and cares for you longs for your return. His arms are open in forgiveness and acceptance. Come to the Father today and give Him your life totally, 100 percent, 24/7, always, and forever.

Father: Pardon my sins and restore my relationship with You. Cleanse my heart and life from all the impurities I have put into it and make me white as snow. Help me, Lord Jesus, to live for You every day and not return to my old ways. In Jesus' name, Amen.

SPAGHETTI LASAGNA

1 pound ground meat or Italian sausage (or combination of both)
3 cups spaghetti sauce (homemade or store bought)
1 pound spaghetti noodles, cooked according to package minus 2 minutes; drained
1 (16-ounce) container ricotta cheese
8 ounces grated mozzarella cheese
¼ cup Parmesan cheese
1 egg
¼ teaspoon pepper
¼ teaspoon salt
1 tablespoon chopped parsley

Brown meat in skillet; add spaghetti sauce and cook on low for 30 minutes. Pour noodles into large greased baking dish. Add spaghetti meat sauce and mix well. Mix 3 cheeses together with egg, salt, pepper, and parsley. Mix with noodles, saving some to spread over top. Cover with lid or foil and bake for 30 minutes at 350 degrees, or until cheese is melted. Cut into serving sizes; serve.

April 13

Who is wise? He will realize these things. Who is discerning? He will understand them. The ways of the LORD are right; the righteous walk in them, but the rebellious stumble in them.

—HOSEA 14:9

THE NATION OF Israel had finally repented for their sin and rebellion toward God. Restoration could now take place. The people had suffered a spiritual death because they worshiped idols and engaged in ever-increasing sin. But now they were ready to repent and turn back to God. Before they could be restored, though, they had to recognize they were lost, broken, ruined, and needed God's divine presence and intervention in their lives. God yearned to care for them, even in their time of sin, but until they sought Him with repentant hearts, His hands were tied.

God has a wonderful plan for all of us, but unless we come to Him the same way the Israelites came, with broken and contrite hearts, we will remain lost. True wisdom, discernment, and understanding come from knowing God and walking in His truth and righteousness. It's only when we draw strength and direction from the Lord that we can be fruitful and have a productive and meaningful life.

Dear Lord: You are wise and wonderful and know what's best for Your children. At times we run to and fro looking for love, peace, joy, and understanding, but without totally surrendering our lives to You, we stumble and remain unsettled. Help me to stay focused on You so I might be wise in the decisions I make and live a fruitful, productive, and meaningful life. In Jesus' name, Amen.

CHEESY CAULIFLOWER

1 head cauliflower
1 small onion, chopped
3 tablespoons water
½ cup Miracle Whip
1 tablespoon mustard
1 cup grated cheddar cheese

Cut cauliflower into large pieces; discard core. Place in microwaveable baking dish along with onion. Add water; cover with lid or plastic wrap. Microwave on high for 10 minutes, stirring every two minutes; drain. Mix Miracle Whip and mustard. Spread over cauliflower; sprinkle with half the cheese; cover. Microwave 2–4 minutes, or until all cauliflower pieces are tender. Spread rest of cheese over top and microwave 1–2 minutes, until cheese is melted.

April 14

Blow ye the trumpet in Zion, and sound an alarm in my holy mountain: let all the inhabitants of the land tremble: for the day of the LORD cometh, for it is nigh at hand.

—JOEL 2:1, KJV

THESE WERE THE inspired words of the prophet Joel to the people of Judah and Jerusalem, warning them that the day of the Lord was near. Because of the sin of the people, God had allowed a plague of locusts to overcome the land. They ate and destroyed all the vegetation, and the people faced a severe famine. Joel wanted the people to repent and return to the Lord with fasting, weeping, mourning, and intercession. He knew there was no other hope, outside of God, and Joel was intense in his proclamation to the people. In his anguish, Joel cried out for the trumpet to be sounded, warning the people that the conditions were serious and severe. This was usually done when an advancing army was coming, but the impending plague was just as crucial. Joel knew the people would tremble with fear because they were not prepared for the locust invasion, nor were they prepared for the coming of the Lord.

We too must be prepared for the day of the Lord and the final judgment. If Jesus is going to be the Judge and His words are going to be the standard or rule by which we are judged, it becomes very important that we learn what His words are. In the great Sermon on the Mount in Matthew 7:21, Jesus said, "Not everyone who says to Me, Lord, Lord, will enter the kingdom of heaven, but only he who does the will of my Father which is in heaven." This happens only as we study God's Word and do what it says. When the day approaches and we hear the trumpet sound presenting our Lord and Savior, we will tremble only with anticipation and joy as we give account of the way we lived our lives here on earth.

Dear Lord: I praise You for Your marvelous plan of hope. May I live to not be ashamed to meet You on Judgment Day. Show me ways to love and serve others with hope that they come to know You as Savior and also wait with anticipation for the trumpet to sound. In Jesus' name, Amen.

BEEF TIPS (crockpot)

1 pound stew meat or cut up roast pieces
6–8 tablespoons butter, melted
1 envelope dry onion soup mix
Cooked noodles, mashed potatoes, or rice

Put meat in crockpot; pour over melted butter and then add soup mix. Cook on low 8 hours, stirring once. Serve over noodles, mashed potatoes, or rice.

April 15

I will restore to you the years that the locusts hath eaten.

—Joel 2:25, KJV

THE NATION OF Israel had separated itself from God even though they were His covenant people. Because of their sin and rebellion, God sent a plague of locusts to destroy their land. Their only hope was repentance and a total change of heart. The prophet Joel told the people that if they turned from sin and sought God, He would restore their land and repay them for the time they had suffered.

Sometimes it takes drastic measures for God to get our attention. Just as He loved the people of Israel, He loves us. It is not His intention to destroy, punish, or inflict horrible consequences on us, but God is sovereign and has the ability and right to do whatever it takes to stir our hearts with conviction and repentance. God's character is one of love, compassion, grace, and mercy that He pours out upon us. It is our choice whether or not we want to receive His free gifts. God was merciful to the Israelites who had turned from Him, and He is merciful to us also in our sin. But God wants us to know that if we come to Him in true repentance, His love and grace is great enough to receive us. With His heart of compassion, He restores our lives and repays us for the years the enemy has stolen.

Father: I praise You for the heart of mercy You had for me, even when I was deep in sin. You loved me unconditionally and were compassionate toward my soul. When I came to You and turned from a life of sin, You poured out Your love and grace upon me. Now I rest in Your loving arms, trusting You to guide my every step and meet my every need. In Jesus' name, Amen.

TUNA NOODLE CASSEROLE

1 (8-ounce) bag egg noodles
2 small cans tuna, drained
1 can cream of mushroom soup
1 can evaporated milk
½ cup sour cream
1 small can mushroom pieces (optional)
1 cup frozen peas (optional)
¼ teaspoon salt
½ teaspoon pepper
8 ounces grated cheese (cheddar or Colby)

Cook noodles according to directions on bag; drain. Mix together all ingredients and pour into greased 2-quart baking dish. Bake 20 minutes at 350 degrees. Remove from oven and sprinkle grated cheese over it. Return to oven and bake 10–15 more minutes or until cheese is melted.

April 16

Seek good, and not evil, that ye may live: and so the Lord, the God of hosts, shall be with you, as ye have spoken.

—Amos 5:14, KJV

THE PROPHET Amos, whose name in Hebrew means "burden-bearer," was a shepherd and fig farmer but was called by God to prophesy to the sinful people of Northern Israel. God's chosen people had broken their Jewish covenant with Him and were living sinful, selfish lives. The wealthy floundered on their own riches and glory while the poor and weak were ignored. They disregarded the fact that it was God who had blessed them. Their pride and lack of compassion for the needy caused them to fall deeper into sin and pagan worship. They were involved in corrupt religious ceremonies and festivals that God abhorred. The people felt that because they occasionally sought God and followed Him, they could live how they wanted the rest of the time. So God called Amos, a layperson, to try to convince them to turn back to Him. Amos warned the people they not only have to say that the Lord God Almighty is with them, but they must prove it by abandoning their evil lifestyle for one that is good and pleasing to Him.

Many of us today are just like the people of Northern Israel. We want to live any way we like, dabbling in this sin and that one, but show up for church once in a while out of duty. Just as Amos warned the Israelites, we must make a decision to either seek good and follow God all the way, all the time, or choose evil and suffer the consequences of an eternal hell. God is instantly ready to give us pardon if we are serious about committing our lives to Him.

Almighty God: Thank You for sending pastors, teachers, and many wonderful people into our lives to warn us about the consequences of sin. You have loved us with an everlasting and unconditional love, yet at times we are unlovely and choose to do evil and not good. I repent of my sin and ask You to help me to always seek that which is right. In Jesus' name, Amen.

HAM BARBECUE (easy as 1-2-3)

1 tablespoon butter
2 tablespoons brown sugar
3 tablespoons ketchup
½ pound chipped (shaved thin) ham
4 hamburger buns
Pickles, as desired

Combine first 3 ingredients in small non-stick pan over medium heat until butter is melted and mixture is smooth (takes only 2–3 minutes). Add ham and heat through; serve on buns.

April 17

The day of the LORD is near for all nations. As you have done, it will be done to you; your deeds will return upon your own head.

—OBADIAH 1:15

O BADIAH, WHOSE NAME means "servant of the Lord," was chosen by God to proclaim His judgment on the land of Edom. When Israel was attacked, the Edomites refused to help them and even acted as though they were an enemy. When twin brothers Esau and Jacob, parted their ways, Esau went to Edom and Jacob to Israel, causing a common bloodline between the two nations.

Because of Edom's lack of support to its brother-nation when in need, the land would be completely destroyed, leaving no survivors. Obadiah's prophetic message is different from the other prophets in that he did not offer an opportunity for them to repent and avoid the penalty. They were beyond redemption because of their sin, hatred, jealousy, and mockery of the Israelites; and now God's wrath would be upon them. They had been given ample opportunity to change, and their destiny was determined by their own volition.

The day of the Lord is near, when we all will face the judgment of God. We too have been given ample opportunity to accept Christ, and one day it will be too late. Just like the Edomites, we who are without Christ will face eternal judgment and destruction while we who have chosen to follow Christ will be rewarded for being a good and faithful servant.

Soon-returning Lord: You are my Lord and the Savior of my soul; for this I praise You. Forgive me for any pride, jealousy, or hostility I may have against my brother, and help me to change while there is time. When I see those in need, show me ways to help them so I might prove my love to them in Your name. In Jesus' name, Amen.

LIMA BEAN CASSEROLE

2 (10-ounce package) lima beans
8 slices diced bacon
½ cup chopped onion
½ cup chopped celery
1 ½ cups shredded Monterey Jack *or* mild cheddar cheese
¼ teaspoon pepper
1 teaspoon Worcestershire sauce

Cook beans according to package directions; drain, reserving ½ cup liquid. Fry bacon until crisp; drain all but 3 tablespoons grease. Cook onion and celery in grease until tender. Mix everything except bacon; put in 1 ½-quart baking dish; top with bacon. Bake at 350 degrees for 25 minutes.

April 18

From inside the fish Jonah prayed to the LORD his God. He said: "In my distress I called to the LORD, and He answered me. From the depths of the grave I called for help, and you listened to my cry. You hurled me into the deep, into the very heart of the seas, and the currents swirled about me; all your waves and breakers swept over me." I said, "I have been banished from your sight; yet I will look again toward your holy temple. The engulfing waters threatened me, the deep surrounded me; seaweed was wrapped around my head. To the roots of the mountains I sank down; the earth beneath barred me in forever. But you brought my life up from the pit, O LORD my God. When my life was ebbing away, I remembered you, LORD, and my prayer rose to you, to your holy temple. Those who cling to worthless idols forfeit the grace that could be theirs. But I, with a song of thanksgiving, will sacrifice to you. What I have vowed I will make good. Salvation comes from the LORD." And the Lord commanded the fish, and it vomited Jonah onto dry land.

—JONAH 2:1–10

JONAH PRAYED THIS heartfelt prayer of repentance, deliverance, and thanksgiving when he ran from the God he loved but nonetheless disobeyed and ended up in the belly of a huge fish for three days. Jonah was astonished to be alive but knew it was a miracle of God. He felt God had removed him from His sight, mainly because he disobeyed God's call to go to Ninevah. Jonah's only hope was that God would hear his cry and have mercy on him. God did hear Jonah's prayer that day of confession and promise and gave him another chance. We too, like Jonah, have times of disobedience and once again need God's mercy and grace. If we repent as Jonah did and look again to God's holy ways, He will hear our prayers, lift us up from the pit we are in, rescue us from the raging sea, give us a second chance, and put us back on dry land.

Father: You are the One who is able to lift us from our pit and put us on solid ground. When You call, our choice is to listen and follow or run the other way. Forgive me for the times I choose to ignore Your voice. Help me to listen and follow Your instructions so I might avoid the consequences that come with disobedience. In Jesus' name, Amen.

SWEET AND SOUR MEATBALLS (crockpot)

2 pounds precooked frozen meatballs
2 cups cocktail sauce
1 cup grape jelly

Put all ingredients in crockpot. Cook on high 4 hours. Serve alone or with rice.

April 19

Then the word of the LORD came to Jonah a second time: "Go to the great city of Nineveh and proclaim to it the message I give you."

—JONAH 3:1–2

WHEN JONAH DISOBEYED God's first call to go to Nineveh and prophesy to the people there, he was given a second chance. Jonah's prayer of repentance from the stomach of the big fish proved to God that he was serious and willing to change. Jonah accepted the call to go, and while in Nineveh preaching, a remarkable revival broke out. The entire city repented when they heard that God's wrath was upon them because of their sin and wicked lifestyles. When God saw that the Ninevites truly did turn from their evil ways, He had compassion and didn't bring the judgment on them that He had threatened. God is a God of love, mercy, compassion, and grace, but He also is fair and just when it comes to obedience of His Word. His plan is that no one would perish but that all would come to know His Son as Savior and have eternal life. God was patient and forgiving of Jonah, even giving him a second chance to do His will. He will do the same for us if we call on His name, repent, and turn from our wicked ways while there is yet time.

Dear Lord: Thank You for all the times You forgave me and granted me another chance to serve You. In my sin, You still loved me, and when my heart was ready to turn back to You, You were there, forgiving and bringing me back home. I praise You for Your patience as I travel the road of life. Help me to not stumble and fall but to walk upright, steady and focused on You all the days of my life. In this, may You be glorified. In Jesus' name, Amen.

CREAMY SOUTHWESTERN SOUP (low-carb)

1 pound ground beef
½ cup chopped onion
2 garlic cloves, minced
1 tablespoon cumin
1 teaspoon chili powder
½ cup heavy cream
2 (10-ounce) cans Rotel tomatoes
2 cans beef broth
8 ounces cream cheese, softened
Salt to taste

Brown ground beef; drain. Add onion and garlic; sauté 3–4 minutes. Add remaining ingredients, except cream cheese. Bring to boil; reduce heat and cook 15 minutes; add cream cheese. Stir until cream cheese blended. Serves 6.

April 20

But Jonah was greatly displeased and became angry. He prayed to the LORD, "O LORD, is this not what I said when I was still at home? That is why I was so quick to flee to Tarshish. I knew that You are a gracious and compassionate God, slow to anger and abounding in love, a God who relents from sending calamity."

—JONAH 4:1–2

BECAUSE OF GOD's compassion on the people of Nineveh, He spared their lives when they repented of their sin. Even though it was Jonah's message that brought the people to repentance, he was angry that God relinquished His plan of destruction for them. He didn't think God should be so forgiving of the Ninevites because they had been so wicked and disobedient prior to this time. Jonah was so angry, he wanted to die. He went outside of town and made himself a shelter, where he waited to see what would happen next to Nineveh. God thought it necessary to teach Jonah a lesson, so he provided a vine and caused it to grow up over Jonah's head to give him shade and support. This made Jonah happy, so God provided a worm that ate the vine and caused it to die. God then brought about a scorching hot wind that beat on Jonah's head. With the pain and weakness this brought, Jonah really wanted to die. But God scolded Jonah and told him he had no right to be angry, because all he cared about was himself and his own comfort. God reminded him how the vine sprang up overnight and died the next day, without any care on his part. Weren't the Ninevites more important than the physical and mental comfort of Jonah? God's unconditional compassion and love for the lost is always His top priority. This was proven when He gave His only Son to die so that we might live.

Forgiving God: You are great and compassionate, always ready to forgive and restore. Just as You forgave the people of Nineveh, so do You forgive me when I ask. I repent of the times when I thought only of my own comfort and desires. Help me to put others first, no matter the cost, to see You glorified. In Jesus' name, Amen.

PORK CHOP CASSEROLE

1 box of Stove Top pork stuffing mix
4–6 pork chops
1 can of cream of mushroom soup
½ soup can of milk

Prepare stuffing mix according to directions. Place in greased baking dish. Lightly brown pork chops and place on top of stuffing. Mix soup with milk and pour over chops. Cover; bake at 350 for 45–60 minutes, until pork is thoroughly cooked.

April 21

He has showed you, O man, what is good. And what does the LORD require of you? To act justly and to love mercy and to walk humbly with your God.

—MICAH 6:8

GOD USED MICAH to speak to the people of Judah about sin, judgment, and righteousness. The people were convicted of their transgressions but were convinced their iniquities were beyond what God would forgive. What would they have to do to gain God's favor again? If they bowed before Him, brought Him burnt offerings or calves, rams, rivers of oil, their own children, or even their own bodies, would this save them from God's wrath? All these proposals showed interest and zeal but lacked wisdom and knowledge of God's Word.

Are we not sometimes like these ones who want to buy or earn God's pardon and acceptance rather than repent and turn from sin? God makes it quite clear that there is nothing and no one that can be offered to Him that will buy His love and forgiveness. Instead, He asks us to act justly (live morally according to His Word), to love mercy (repent and rely on Christ's atonement), and walk humbly with our God (daily fellowship with the Father and obedience to His will). Our thoughts and actions must be in accordance with God's Word. This is what the Lord requires of us.

Merciful Father: You are holy and good, and I want to pattern my thoughts and actions after You. Show me the areas in my life I need to change, and help me to act justly, love mercy, and walk humbly with You, always and forever. May You be glorified as I strive to do those things You require me to do. In Jesus' name, Amen.

PIZZA BITES

1 cup shredded pizza-blend cheese
½ cup grated Parmesan cheese
1 (10-ounce) tube refrigerated flaky biscuits
Nonstick vegetable spray
40 slices pre-sliced pepperoni
7 tablespoons pizza sauce

Combine cheeses; set aside. Cut each biscuit into quarters; roll each quarter into a ball. Using lightly floured rolling pin, roll each ball into a 2 ½–3-inch circle on lightly floured surface. Fit circles into greased miniature muffin cups. Place one pepperoni slice snugly in bottom of each biscuit-lined cup. Spoon ½ teaspoon pizza sauce on top of each pepperoni; sprinkle with 1 ½ teaspoons of cheese mixture. Bake at 400 degrees for 10–12 minutes or until golden. Serve warm. Makes 40.

April 22

The LORD is good, a refuge in times of trouble. He cares for those who trust in Him.

—NAHUM 1:7

GOD USED THE prophet Nahum to proclaim the impending destruction of Nineveh, the capitol city of Assyria. The Ninevites had repented of their sin and corruption a century earlier when Jonah was sent there to preach. But they soon fell back into their wicked ways and were known for their cruelty and ruthless slaughter of the people they conquered. Their day of judgment was fast approaching, though.

At the same time, Nahum delivered a message of comfort and hope to those who remained faithful to God. He assured them that no matter what injustice seemed to be going on all around them, God would one day establish His kingdom of peace.

In our world today, we see injustice and unfairness taking place. But just as God used Nahum to bring hope to those who trusted in Him, that same message is for us. In our times of trouble, weariness, persecution, loneliness, and whatever the circumstances may be, our Lord is good and will care for us in our times of need if we put our trust in Him.

Caring Lord: You are my hiding place and shelter in the time of need. When I am weary and lonely, You are there. When unfairness or injustice is done to others or myself, You are there, rightfully judging. Forgive me if I have been unkind or cruel to anyone and help me to forgive those who have been unkind to me. In Jesus' name, Amen.

POTATO SOUP

4 strips bacon, diced
1 onion, chopped
2 quarts water
1 teaspoon garlic salt
1 teaspoon pepper
8–10 potatoes, peeled and diced
6 chicken bouillon cubes
1–2 cans evaporated milk
1 (8-ounce) package cream cheese
4 ounces Velveeta cheese
8 ounces sour cream
Potato flakes (optional)

Fry bacon in large pan until crisp; add onion and cook until tender. Add water, salt, pepper, potatoes, and bouillon; bring to boil. Turn to low; simmer until potatoes soft. Add milk, cheese, and sour cream; stir until melted. If too thin, add small amount potato flakes. If too thick, add milk or broth.

April 23

Although the fig tree does not blossom, neither shall fruit be in the vines; the labor of the olive shall fail, and the fields shall yield meat; the flock shall be cut off from the fold, and there shall be no herd in the stalls: Yet I will rejoice in the LORD, I will joy in the God of my salvation.

—HABAKKUK 3:17–18, KJV

UNLIKE SOME OF the other prophets whom God used to warn the people about His impending wrath due to their sin and disobedience, the prophet Habakkuk was used to encourage those in Judah who remained faithful and obedient to God. But Habakkuk was appalled as to why it appeared as though God were merely turning His head from the sin and ungodliness that was taking place. At times, he even got impatient and complained to God about His tolerance of such perverse wickedness. The answers God gave Habakkuk confused him even more, but regardless, he trusted God to do the right thing.

God made it clear that those whose hearts are turned to Him must live in this world by faith and a steadfast trust in Him. Even in their despair, they should hold strong to their faith, knowing God's ways are always right. No matter what happens in life, to others or to us, God is aware and has not hidden His face. Habakkuk trusted God in spite of the evil and injustice that he witnessed and testified that he would serve God and be joyful, no matter what the circumstances were.

We too have our fig trees that don't bud or fields that produce no food and all the other losses and hurts that life may bring. No matter what, we must make the decision to rejoice in the Lord and serve Him with joy, just as Habakkuk did.

Lord and Savior: At times I am weary and wonder how all the injustice can continue not only in my life, but in this world. Sometimes it seems as though those living outside of Your will are not paying the consequences for their actions. You are a righteous Judge and have everything under control. Help me to focus only on the wonderful God You are. Grant me strength to go on and win this race called life. Today I choose joy because I choose You. In Jesus' name, Amen.

BAKED ONION-MUSHROOM STEAK

1 ½ pounds (½-inch thick) round steak
1 can cream of mushroom soup
½ cup water
1 (1-ounce) packet onion soup mix

Place steak in greased baking dish. Mix mushroom soup and water; pour over steak. Sprinkle onion soup mix on top. Cover and bake at 325 degrees for 2 hours.

April 24

The LORD thy God in the midst of thee is mighty; he will save, he will rejoice over thee with joy; he will rest in his love, he will joy over thee with singing.

—ZEPHANIAH 3:17, KJV

THE PROPHET ZEPHANIAH was used by the Lord to warn Judah and Jerusalem of the impending judgment of God called "the great day of the Lord." Though he saw a worldwide judgment coming one day, he especially focused on the judgment of Judah because of its sin and disobedience to God. Zephaniah's prophetic appeal was to see Judah humbly repent and seek the righteousness of God before it was too late. He also had a great message for those who loved God and followed His ways. With the prophetic words of His Lord, Zephaniah proclaimed the message of God's saving power and the delight God has in knowing that His children love Him. When the great day of the Lord comes, it will be then that the supernatural joy that only God can give will reach its pinnacle as He manifests His glory and majesty over the whole earth.

Mighty God: Thank You for loving me and for saving my soul. It is my desire that You rejoice over me with singing and are pleased with my life. Pardon me for any sins of which I have not yet repented. Help me to keep my eyes on You and off the world and the things in it. With joy I look forward to the day of the Lord when You will return in Your glory and majesty. In Jesus' name, Amen.

SESAME GINGER SALMON

1 tablespoon soy sauce
¼ cup orange juice
1 tablespoon horseradish mustard
2 dashes cayenne pepper
½ teaspoon ground ginger
1 teaspoon minced garlic
1 tablespoon honey
4 boneless salmon fillets
1 teaspoon toasted sesame seeds

In small bowl, whisk together everything except salmon and sesame seeds. Place salmon in large ziplock bag. Add marinade; seal and gently distribute to coat fillets. Refrigerate one hour, turning occasionally. Cook in pan without marinade on medium heat until flakey (about 6 minutes each side); baste occasionally with juices. Add marinade to pan and bring to boil; cook 2–3 minutes. Serve with marinade drizzled over top and sprinkle with toasted sesame seeds.

April 25

Be strong, all ye people of the land, saith the LORD, and work: for I am with you, saith the LORD of hosts.

—HAGGAI 2:4, KJV

THE JEWS HAD returned to Jerusalem after being in exile for a long time in Babylon, and the prophet Haggai urged them to finish building the temple they started sixteen years prior. They were reluctant because they thought building their own homes took precedence. It's not that they didn't want to restore the temple, but they merely got complacent and selfish. Haggai rebuked them for being preoccupied with their own homes while God's house remained a ruin. He reminded them that the reason they didn't have God's blessings was because of their self-seeking ways. The leaders and the people took Haggai's message seriously and completed the temple, and God blessed them. But some of the people viewed the temple as nothing in comparison with the previous temple that Solomon built. God encouraged them and told them to be strong because He, the Lord Almighty, was with them. The greatness of the building was not to be viewed by its magnificent building structure but by His manifested presence and power inside, among the people. God declared His glory would be even greater in the new temple than in the former one.

We too may think like the Jews and neglect the house of the Lord because of work that needs done around our own homes. God looks at this as selfishness and complacency toward Him. If we seek His will and work for Him, He will honor our endeavors and bless our lives by seeing that our needs are met.

Lord Almighty: You are the Holy One and the Conductor of my life. Show me what You want me to do and help me to stay on track to complete my work. You are with me all the time; when I am weak, You strengthen me and help me to persevere until the end. Help me to organize and prioritize my work so I might serve my church in a greater way. In Jesus' name, Amen.

CRISPY NUTTY CHICKEN

⅓ cup dry-roasted peanuts, minced
1 cup corn flake crumbs
½ cup ranch buttermilk salad dressing
6 boneless, skinless chicken breast halves

Combine peanuts and crumbs on wax paper; pour dressing into small dish. Dip chicken pieces in dressing and then roll in crumb mixture to coat. Arrange chicken in shallow 9x13-inch baking dish. Bake uncovered for 50 minutes or until light brown.

April 26

Therefore tell the people: This is what the LORD Almighty says: "Return to me," declares the LORD Almighty, "and I will return to you," says the LORD Almighty. Do not be like your forefathers, to whom the earlier prophets proclaimed; This is what the LORD Almighty says: "Turn from your evil ways and your evil practices." But they would not listen or pay attention to me, declares the LORD.

—ZECHARIAH 1:3–4

To help the prophet Haggai encourage the remnant of Jews to rebuild the temple in Jerusalem that had been destroyed, God raised up a younger man named Zechariah. Through this prophet, God proclaimed His anger concerning the complacency and apathy the people had toward His commands. God wanted them to be different than their ancestors, repent of their sin, and turn back to Him.

Throughout the Word of God, from the beginning to the end, God uses circumstances, good and bad, people, prophets, dreams, visions, and even the death of His only Son to proclaim His Word and will for our lives. He loves us that much! God is saddened when He sees His children walk in disobedience. If we don't repent and come to God by accepting Christ as Savior, we too will miss God's plan for our lives and forever be denied the ultimate blessings He intended for us to have. The Lord Almighty assures us that no matter how far into sin we have gone, if we return to Him, He will return to us.

Almighty Lord: I praise You for Your Word and the many wonderful prophets You used to encourage the people to serve You. Thank You for all those You put in my life many years ago that encouraged me to turn from my sin and follow You. As I study and learn more about You, may I too be filled with wisdom and power to lead others to Christ. Show me the sin in my life I need to turn from and give me strength to lay it all aside. In Jesus' name, Amen.

BEEF AND NOODLES

1 ½ pounds stew beef or lean ground beef
1 can beef broth
1 package dry onion soup mix
1 can cream of mushroom soup
1 can mushrooms (optional)

Put all ingredients in crockpot; cook on low 8 hours. (May cook on stovetop over low heat for 3–4 hours instead.) Serve over buttered cooked noodles or rice. If beef stew is too thick, add some water, bouillon, or more beef broth.

April 27

And it shall come to pass, that in all the land, saith the LORD, two parts therein shall be cut off and die; but the third shall be left therein. And I will bring the third part through the fire, and will refine them as silver is refined, and will try them as gold is tried: they shall call on my name, and I will hear them: I will say, It is my people: and they shall say, The LORD is my God.

—ZECHARIAH 13:8–9, KJV

THESE VERSES PROBABLY refer to the tribulation—the seven-year period of time when God will finalize His judgment on the unbelieving world. The Jews who didn't believe in Christ represent the two-thirds who will be killed. The remnant one-third represents those who are believers, and they will be saved. They are the ones who will realize that Jesus truly is the Messiah and will grieve and mourn because of the part they had in His crucifixion.

Though we all have pierced the side of Jesus with our deliberate sin and disobedience to His Word, God will forgive us if we ask. If we repent and choose to follow Him, usually a life of trials and tribulations results. But if we are His people, we shall be refined as gold, and the end of all our trials and sufferings will be praise, honor, and glory at the appearing of our Lord Jesus Christ.

Lord God: I believe in You and honor You as my Lord and Savior. You are with me in the good times and in the bad. You say in Your Word that You will hear me when I call on Your name. Thank You! When I go through trials and difficult times, I know You are refining me and testing my true faith. I look forward to the day when You return and I stand with You, forever and always, never to experience pain or suffering again. In Jesus' name, Amen.

POTATOES AU GRATIN

8 ounces Velveeta cheese, cubed
1 (16-ounce) carton half-and-half (or milk)
1 cup shredded cheddar cheese
1 stick butter
1 (32-ounce) package frozen hash brown potatoes, thawed

Melt Velveeta, half-and-half, cheddar cheese, and butter in pan over low heat. Put hash browns in greased 9x13-inch baking dish; pour melted cheese mixture over top. Bake uncovered 1 hour at 350 degrees.

April 28

For from the rising of the sun even unto the going down of the same my name shall be great among the Gentiles.

—MALACHI 1:11, KJV

THE PROPHET MALACHI prophesied that there would be a time that would come when people from all over the world would worship God in sincerity and in truth. But he was disturbed that the people who had once been zealous in their worship of God had become cynical and indifferent and were now living a life of sin. Where they once sacrificed their best to the Lord, they were now giving Him their worst. God was displeased with their contempt toward His law and used Malachi to confront them regarding their hypocrisy and disobedience.

As believers in Christ, we must give God our very best. Our daily devotions should be done when we are alert and not when we are tired and unable to stay awake. The decisions we make, the places we go, the movies or TV programs we watch, the music we listen to, the words we speak, and everything we do should honor God. Our lives should be given to Him as living sacrifices. One day, God's name will be great among the nations; may it be so even now in our lives.

Dear Lord: Your name is great and greatly to be praised—not only in the future, but in my life today. You are my God, my Redeemer, and the Savior of my soul. Thank You for making that possible for me. Forgive me when I become complacent and careless. Help me always to have the zeal I need so that You would be greatly exalted in my life. In Jesus' name, Amen.

PORK CHOPS IN SOUR CREAM SAUCE

6 loin chops
½ cup water
2 tablespoons brown sugar
2 tablespoons chopped onion
2 tablespoons ketchup
2 cloves garlic, minced
1 beef bouillon cube
2 tablespoons flour
¼ cup water
½ cup sour cream

Brown chops in greased pan. Add water, brown sugar, onion, ketchup, garlic, and bouillon. Cover and simmer 30–40 minutes. Remove chops to platter; keep warm. In bowl, combine flour with ¼ cup water. Slowly add to pan, stirring constantly; cook until thickened. Stir in sour cream; serve over chops.

April 29

Will a man rob God? Yet ye have robbed me. But ye say, Wherein have we robbed thee? In tithes and offerings. Ye are cursed with a curse: for ye have robbed me, even this whole nation. Bring ye all the tithes into the storehouse, that there may be meat in mine house, and prove me now herewith, saith the LORD of hosts, if I will not open you the windows of heaven, and pour you out a blessing, that there shall not be room enough to receive it.

—MALACHI 3:8–10, KJV

MALACHI WAS A man of strict integrity and devotion to God. He believed God should be honored above all and our covenant with Him be made with a sincere, obedient heart. Malachi was aware of the Jews' failure to give to God what was due Him (one-tenth of their income), and God used him to inform them of their disobedience. The people were robbing God by not bringing to Him 10 percent of their earnings. Tithing was set up in the law of Moses (Leviticus 27:30) many years prior, and the people gave willingly back to God what was already His. Now there were many who became selfish, and God was not pleased. The Lord, through Malachi, told the people that if they repented, turned back to Him, and began to give their tenth to the support of His work, He would bless them abundantly. If they did not give, they would be under a curse, and their covenant with God would be broken.

Many of us feel today that we cannot afford to tithe, but the truth is, we cannot afford to not tithe. God asks us to test and trust Him to provide for us if we are obedient and give back to Him what is already His. As New Testament Christians, God expects and requires us to prove our love for Him by giving our tithes and offerings to further His kingdom.

Dear God: You are my provider, and everything I have is Yours. I'm sorry for the times I withheld what You asked me to give. As I prove my love to You by giving my tithes and offerings to Your work, I trust You to meet my needs. Show me how I might make changes in my life so You would be glorified by my obedience to Your will. In Jesus' name, Amen.

CHILI CON QUESO

1 (10-ounce) can tomatoes and green chiles
1 pound Velveeta, cubed
1 can chili with or without beans
Chips

Put first 3 ingredients in crockpot or pan; heat on low until cheese melts. Serve with chips.

April 30

Now the birth of Jesus Christ was on this wise: When his mother Mary was espoused to Joseph, before they came together, she was found with child of the Holy Ghost.

—MATTHEW 1:18, KJV

And she shall bring forth a son, and thou shalt call his name JESUS: for he shall save his people from their sins. Now all this was done, that it might be fulfilled which was spoken of the Lord by the prophet, saying, Behold, a virgin shall be with child, and shall bring forth a son, and they shall call his name Emmanuel, which being interpreted is, God with us.

—MATTHEW 1:21–23, KJV

MATTHEW PRESENTS JESUS' birth as the fulfillment of Isaiah's prophecy for Israel. About seven hundred years previous, the prophet Isaiah spoke the same words in Isaiah 7:14. He told the Jewish people a Messiah would come and give them hope for their future. The emphasis in these verses is put on the fact that Jesus was born of a virgin. This was necessary because in order for Christ to be our Savior, He had to be, in one Person, fully human yet sinless and fully divine. The virgin birth qualifies Jesus for all three requirements. To be fully human, He had to be born of a woman; to be sinless, He had to be conceived by the Holy Spirit; and the only way He could be divine was to have God as His Almighty Father. Therefore, Jesus' conception and birth was not a natural one, but supernatural. Jesus is one divine Person with two natures—a divine and sinless human. He has feelings and pain just like the rest of us, but He also has the power to deliver us from the sin and bondage of the enemy. Jesus is the wonderful Intercessor for all who come to God. Hallelujah!

Dear Jesus: You are holy and anointed, born of a virgin, human, yet sinless and divine. You are the Savior of my soul, and You intercede before the Father when I come to Him. Thank You, God, for the birth of Your Son and for His redeeming love for all. Open the eyes of those who doubt the supernatural birth of Christ and convict them of their sin and pride. In Jesus' name, Amen.

HONEY-BAKED CHICKEN

⅓ cup honey
⅓ cup melted butter
1 tablespoon mustard
2–4 boneless, skinless chicken breasts

Combine honey, melted butter, and mustard in bowl. Pour over chicken in greased baking dish. Cook 1 hour at 350 degrees. Baste every 15 minutes.

May

Forget~Me~Not

May 1

But he [Jesus] answered and said, It is written, Man shall not live by bread alone, but by every word that proceedeth out of the mouth of God.

—MATTHEW 4:4, KJV

JESUS SPOKE THESE words after He had completed a forty-day fast to prepare Himself spiritually to do the work of His heavenly Father. Satan, thinking he could entice Jesus to sin with hunger, came and tempted Him to turn stones into bread.

Jesus said unto him [devil], It is written again, Thou shalt not tempt the Lord thy God.

—MATTHEW 4:7, KJV

When Satan saw that Jesus would not give in to sin, he took him to the holy city and had him stand on the highest point of the temple. Satan told Jesus to throw Himself off and let His angels save Him from the fall. Jesus again quoted the Word to not tempt God.

Then saith Jesus unto him, Get thee hence, Satan: for it is written, Thou shalt worship the Lord thy God, and him only shalt thou serve. Then the devil leaveth him, and, angels came and ministered unto him.

—MATTHEW 4:10–11, KJV

Again, Satan tempted Jesus and took Him to a high mountain where he showed Him all the kingdoms of the world and their splendor. Satan gave Jesus the opportunity to have it all if He would bow down and serve him (Satan). Jesus emphatically again quoted the Word to Satan, and this time he (Satan) left.

Satan is our greatest enemy and will do everything in his power to tempt us and see us turn from following Christ. It is imperative that we know God's Word so we are able to resist and overcome the temptation. If Jesus fought the enemy this way, we certainly should follow suit and do the same. As believers, we must continually be in prayer, be on the alert for Satan's attack, and remain strong and victorious by meditating on God's Word.

Father: Thank You for Your Holy Scriptures that equip us to resist the temptations of this world and follow You. Help me to learn and memorize the wonderful promises that give me power to walk in obedience. Forgive me for the times I yielded to temptation and didn't do what was right. May I live victoriously as I meditate on You and learn Your Word. In Jesus' name, Amen.

Today's recipe found on page 384 ITALIAN CHICKEN

May 2

Who of you by worrying can add a single hour to his life?

—Matthew 6:27

A s adults, we feel it's our job to worry. After all, if we don't worry about our families, who will? Someone has to worry about their health, finances, jobs, schools, and future, and it may as well be us. Right? Wrong! Actually, God tells us in His Word that worry is a profitless activity. Worry may feel natural, but in reality it's sin. If we constantly worry about our loved ones, that means we are not trusting God to take care of them. It's like saying to God, "I know You created the universe, but I'm not sure You know how to run it. You'll need my help, so I'll do that by worrying." This sounds ridiculous because we would really never say that to God on purpose. Yet we say this in our actions and in our hearts when we give in to worry. Instead, we must pray for our loved ones and trust God to cover them with His outstretched arms of love. Let's do what the song says: "Don't Worry! Be Happy!" It's not always easy, but it's the right thing to do.

Dear holy Father: Thank You for carrying all my burdens so I don't have to. Because of Your magnificent power and love, You do this for Your children. You know best what we need, and I ask You to bless us accordingly. Forgive me for worrying and not trusting You more. Strengthen my weak areas so I don't entertain worrisome thoughts. I love You, Lord Jesus, and praise You for hearing and answering my prayers. In Jesus' name, Amen.

BAKED KRISPIE CHICKEN

4 cups Rice Krispies
1 teaspoon paprika
1 egg
¼ cup milk
¾ cup flour
1 teaspoon poultry seasoning
1 ½ teaspoon salt
¼ teaspoon pepper
3 pounds chicken pieces, clean and dry
3 tablespoons butter, melted

Crush Rice Krispies and place in shallow dish; stir in paprika. In another dish, beat eggs and milk slightly. Add flour, poultry seasoning, salt, and pepper. Mix until smooth. Dip chicken in wet batter and then into Rice Krispie mix. Place chicken, skin side up, in greased baking dish. (Do not cover.) Drizzle with melted butter. Bake at 350 degrees about 1 hour or until chicken is thoroughly cooked.

May 3

Come unto me, all ye that labor and are heavy laden, and I will give you rest.

—MATTHEW 11:28, KJV

WHAT A MAGNIFICENT promise! Our burdens often involve worry when we should trust God with the future. But how is that done? How do we really find the rest that God promises? The call of Jesus for us to lay down our burdens is a call of hope. Bible commentaries say this verse was written to instruct us to respect the Sabbath and put aside our work details on that day. Oftentimes we want God to perform the miraculous and keep our bodies going 24/7, and He certainly is able, but He also wrote the Ten Commandments for a purpose. He expects us to obey His Word, and by doing so live life abundantly. God is our burden-bearer and wants us to come to Him with our cares. He also is the Creator of the world, and after doing so for six days, He took a day to rest. If it's good enough for God, it's good enough for us. Let's be more cautious about how we spend our Sabbath, and as we come together in the house of worship and bring our burdens to the Lord, we will find the rest that we need.

O God: You are everything I need. When I am weary and heavy with the weight of the world on my shoulders, You are there. Your Word brings comfort to my soul, and when I obey You, I find rest. Thank You for showing me by example to take a day to rest and worship You. When I do, You are faithful to provide me with the rest I need. Thank You for walking with me through the storms of life and for carrying me when I am weak. In Jesus' name, Amen.

CHICKEN RANCH JACK

3 boneless, skinless chicken breasts, cut into strips
2–3 tablespoons butter
¼ cup ranch salad dressing (or chipotle-flavored ranch)
6 slices bacon, crisply cooked and crumbled
⅓ cup shredded Monterey Jack cheese

In a skillet over medium heat, sauté chicken strips in butter until thoroughly cooked. Pour into lightly greased 2-quart baking dish. Pour dressing over chicken; mix well. Sprinkle with bacon and cheese; bake in 375-degree oven until cheese is melted and golden, about 10 minutes.

May 4

And Jesus came and spake unto them, saying, All power is given unto me in heaven and in earth. Go ye therefore, and teach all nations, baptizing them in the name of the Father, and of the Son, and of the Holy Ghost: Teaching them to observe all things whatsoever I have commanded you: and, lo, I am with you always, even unto the end of the world. Amen.

—MATTHEW 28:18–20, KJV

JESUS SPOKE THESE words to His eleven disciples after His crucifixion and resurrection. This is known as the Great Commission and was not only the responsibility of the disciples but of each and every one of us who call ourselves followers of Christ. We are commanded to go and tell everyone everywhere about the good news of Jesus. He wants us to make disciples of every believer who will, in turn, not only obey the commands of Christ but will teach and train others to do the same. We are to become missionaries and evangelists in our homes, communities, schools, places of employment, and other nations. Though we all can't travel to faraway places, we can prayerfully and financially support others who have this call on their lives. As we evangelize our world, Jesus assures us that He will be with us all the time. He is alive in our hearts and cares deeply about each one of us. The power of the Holy Spirit will be evident in our lives if we live for Christ, obey His commands, and seek Him with all our heart, mind, and soul.

Teaching Father: Help me to pattern my life after You so I can teach and train others to become Your disciples. Grant me boldness to tell the lost about their need for a Savior, and show me ways I might financially support missionaries to go where I am unable to go. Thank You for the promise that You are with us as we take Your message to the world. In Jesus' name, Amen.

CRAB QUICHE

2 eggs, beaten
½ cup mayonnaise
2 tablespoons flour
½ cup milk
1 cup crab meat (canned okay)
1 cup diced Swiss cheese
½ cup chopped green onions
1 (9-inch) unbaked pie crust

In bowl, beat together eggs, mayonnaise, flour, and milk until thoroughly blended. Stir in crab, cheese, and onion. Spread into pie shell. Bake at 350 degrees for 40–45 minutes, or until knife inserted in center comes out clean.

May 5

As it is written in the prophets, Behold, I send my messenger before thy face, which shall prepare thy way before thee. The voice of one crying in the wilderness, Prepare ye the way of the Lord, make his paths straight.

—MARK 1:2–3, KJV

THE PROPHET ISAIAH spoke these same words in Isaiah 40:3 as he prophesied that one would come and clear the way for the coming Messiah. This one is known as John the Baptist, described in the Gospels. He was the greatest of all prophets and was called by God to be His messenger. John would be the one to encourage the people to purify themselves and repent of their sins. John, preparing the way before Jesus came, is like a farmer plowing the soil before he plants the seeds. Appointed by God, John knew the importance of getting hearts ready to repent and accept the atonement of Jesus for their sins.

God wants all of us also to prepare the way or plow the soil so others may receive Christ. Living righteous lives before fellow employees, classmates, neighbors, family members, and so forth, is one way of preparing the way. If we show concern, kindness, love, and the fruit of the Spirit to others, whether we feel they deserve it or not, we are also preparing the way. It is then that they will be open to God's Word and be ready to receive Him into their hearts and lives.

Dear Lord: You are the only way to find forgiveness and eternal life. Thank You for calling me to be a messenger of Christ. Help me to use my resources to minister to others. As the way is prepared, I pray many come to know You as Savior. In Jesus' name, Amen.

CHICKEN CORDON BLEU

4 tablespoons butter
4 boneless, skinless breasts of chicken
4 very thin slices smoked ham
6 slices Swiss cheese
1 cup flour
2 eggs, lightly beaten
2 cups bread crumbs

Melt butter in glass baking dish. Lightly flatten chicken breasts between plastic wrap with mallet or dull heavy object. Lay 1 slice of ham and cheese on flattened breast; roll and seal with toothpicks. Repeat process. Coat each piece with flour, then eggs, and then bread crumbs. Place chicken pieces in dish. Turn to coat with butter. Bake at 375 degrees for 40–45 minutes, or until golden brown.

May 6

And Jesus said unto them, Come ye after me, and I will make you to become fishers of men.

—MARK 1:17, KJV

JESUS WAS WALKING along the Sea of Galilee, teaching the good news of God, when He saw two fishermen, Simon and his brother Andrew, casting their nets into the water. Jesus called them to come and follow Him, where He would teach them to become fishers of men. The men immediately dropped their nets and went to be with Jesus. A short time later, they came upon two more men, James and John, who were fishing in a boat with their father and some other men. Jesus called to them, and they also dropped what they were doing and came to Jesus. These four fishermen were the first to become Jesus' disciples.

How fitting it is that Jesus used the concept of fishing to identify with the need for them to become fishers of men. The four men all had a decision to make—they could either ignore the call of Jesus to come and follow Him and remain fishers of fish, or they could accept the invitation of the Master Fisherman and learn to become fishers of men. We have all been invited to follow Jesus and, like the four fishermen, have to make the choice. God wants everyone to follow His Son and live according to His teachings. Though it's not always easy to abandon the old life and follow Christ, it's always right.

Heavenly Father: I praise You for calling my name and inviting me to follow You. Thank You for giving us the Living Word, where we get our instructions on how to live. I want to be a follower of You and a fisher of men. Help me to see the world through Your eyes that I might show them how to also follow You. Thank You for the example You are as the Master Fisherman. In Jesus' name, Amen.

BAKED PARMESAN CRUSTED FISH FILLETS

4–6 fish fillets
⅓ cup grated Parmesan cheese
¼ cup bread or cracker crumbs
½ teaspoon garlic or seasoned salt
¼ teaspoon pepper
3 tablespoons butter
3 tablespoons lemon juice
Parsley or dill (optional)

Place clean and dry fillets in buttered baking dish. Mix together Parmesan cheese, crumbs, garlic salt, and pepper; sprinkle over fish. Mix butter and lemon juice together and drizzle over crumbs. Bake 20–30 minutes at 350 degrees, until fish is flaky. Sprinkle with parsley or dill, as desired.

May 7

Some people are like seed along the path, where the word is sown. As soon as they hear it, Satan comes and takes away the word that was sown in them.

—MARK 4:15

JESUS WAS SPEAKING to His disciples about the four different types of people in the world and how each receives the gospel. One type is like seed that has been thrown by a farmer along a path—the birds come along and eat it. The Word of God is also stolen away by Satan if not taken seriously and allowed to regenerate one's soul. Another type is like seed that lands on rocky places where there is little soil. The seed grows quickly but dies because it cannot take root in such shallow soil. Some of us hear and believe the Word but do not grow because the Word never takes root. Personal devotions, time spent in fellowship with believers, and true separation from the world never take place or begins to wane away, and eventually the relationship we once had with Christ is gone. A third type of person receives the gospel like seed that falls among thorns—the seedlings are choked before they produce grain. This happens to those who hear the Word, believe, and accept it, but because of worries, circumstances, or worldly desires, they never grow to become fruitful. Then there are the seeds that are sown in good soil—they grow and produce good crops. We too will grow to become fruitful Christians if we obey God's Word and make Him not only our Savior, but also the Lord of our lives.

Father: Thank You for the stories and illustrations in Your Word that help us understand the principles of mere Christianity. I want to be like good soil so Your Word grows inside of me. Help me to be faithful and ready to receive everything that is of You. In turn, may I teach others how to be good soil so they, too, will reap a harvest of blessings. In Jesus' name, Amen.

FRIED CHICKEN

Cut up chicken pieces (as many as needed)
Large pan of water with 2–4 tablespoons salt added
1–2 cups flour (depends on amount of chicken)
1 teaspoon salt per cup of flour
1 teaspoon pepper per cup of flour
1 teaspoon seasoned salt per cup of flour
½–1 stick butter and equal amount of oil

Soak chicken pieces in salt water at least 4 hours. Drain and pat dry. Mix flour with seasonings; dip chicken into flour mixture then put into large skillet with hot oil and butter mixture. Brown slowly on all sides until no longer pink inside. Drain on paper towels before serving.

May 8

And he [Jesus] arose, and rebuked the wind, and said unto the sea, Peace, be still. And the wind ceased, and there was a great calm.

—MARK 4:39, KJV

ONE EVENING AS Jesus was out with His disciples teaching God's Word, He decided to leave the crowd of people and go to the other side of the lake. The disciples escorted Him into the boat and prepared to cross the water.

While in the boat, a furious storm came, and though Jesus was asleep and unaware, the disciples were very frightened. More so, they were annoyed that Jesus was sleeping through the storm and felt He didn't care if they drowned. When the disciples awakened Jesus, He stood and rebuked the storm, and it immediately stopped. Jesus asked the disciples if they were afraid because of their lack of faith.

We oftentimes experience storms in our lives, though not necessarily weather related. They come in the way of circumstances and calamities, and like the disciples in the boat, we too might feel we aren't going to survive the storm. It is during these times that we need to call upon our Savior to quiet the wind and the waves that seem to be trying to pull us under. Jesus is the Storm Watcher and knows exactly what we are going through, but He wants us to come to Him and ask for His help.

Dear Lord: You are the calm in every storm and the One who is able to bring peace and stillness into our lives. I praise You for watching over me day and night and hearing me when I call. Help me to not become weary when I am faced with situations and circumstances that are so trying. May I become strong in my faith and trust You to calm my every storm. In Jesus' name, Amen.

PARSLEY POTATOES

10–12 small new or red potatoes *or* 3–4 large red or white potatoes
3 tablespoons butter at room temperature
½ teaspoon garlic salt (or plain salt, if you prefer)
⅛ teaspoon pepper
1 tablespoon fresh parsley *or* 1 teaspoon dried parsley

Wash potatoes; remove dark spots. Leave small red potatoes whole with skin; pare large white potatoes and cut into fourths or eighths. Boil in salt water 20–30 minutes or until done. Drain; put in bowl. Add butter, salt, pepper, and parsley; gently toss.

May 9

When she had heard of Jesus, came in the press behind, and touched his garment. For she said, If I may touch but his clothes, I shall be whole.

—MARK 5:27–28, KJV

JESUS WAS ON His way to the home of a little girl who was very sick, and a large crowd of people closely followed Him. In that crowd was also a very sick lady who had been bleeding for twelve years. She had spent all her money on doctors and continued to get worse. She believed that if only she could get close enough to Jesus to touch His clothing, she would be healed. Pressing in, possibly even being knocked to the ground because of her illness and lack of strength, she made her way to Jesus. Immediately upon touching His cloak, the bleeding stopped. Jesus announced to the crowd and to the woman that it was her faith that made her well.

Many people touched Jesus that day; however, because they didn't expect anything to happen, nothing did. Jesus' power is the same for everyone; we are the ones who determine whether or not to seek Him and allow His power to work in our lives. It is the same as plugging a small appliance into an electric outlet. We believe that when the two units touch, power will flow into the appliance and make it work. Jesus is our power source. He is the One who has the ability to change our lives if we allow Him. We plug ourselves into God when we seek Him first no matter how we feel, how busy we are, or how others feel toward us. The woman with the issue of blood was made whole because she was determined to touch Jesus, no matter what. Shouldn't we do the same?

Loving Father: You are my Healer and Provider. Everything I need is in You. I give You glory for the awesome provisions You have made for me in Your Son, Jesus. Help me to press on in my times of weakness so I might touch Jesus and be made whole. In Jesus' name, Amen.

CHICKEN AND MUSHROOM RICE AU GRATIN

1 can cream of mushroom soup
1 cup milk
1 ½ cups cooked long-grain white rice
2 cups cubed cooked chicken breast
¼ cup breadcrumbs
¼ cup shredded cheddar cheese
2 tablespoons butter, cold

In saucepan, heat soup and milk; stir until smooth; keep warm. Put rice and chicken in greased 8-inch baking dish. Pour soup mixture over rice. Sprinkle with breadcrumbs and cheese. Top with small bits of butter. Bake 20 minutes, until heated through and cheese is bubbly.

May 10

He [Jesus] went on: "What comes out of a man is what makes him 'unclean.' For from within, out of men's hearts, come evil thoughts, sexual immorality, theft, murder, adultery, greed, malice, deceit, lewdness, envy, slander, arrogance and folly. All these evils come from inside and make a man 'unclean.'"

—MARK 7:20–23

JESUS WAS SPEAKING to a crowd of people about the traditions of men and how they should not place guilt on those who do not follow them, especially if they conflict with God's Word. He wanted them to know that God's commands must be observed, but not necessarily man-made rules. Jesus explained how we become separated from Christ when our hearts are unclean. Our heart is responsible for our thoughts, feelings, words, and actions. When we sin and disobey God's Word, our hearts become impure and corrupt, separating us from sweet fellowship with our Lord. Jesus named the various evils that come from within that make us unclean. To remain in this state of impurity or uncleanness demonstrates spiritual lostness. A conscious decision to repent and restore a relationship with Christ is the only hope of spiritual regeneration. When we come to Christ this way, He is faithful and just to forgive us and give us the spiritual cleansing we need. It is then that our hearts are once again pure and right with God and our fellowship with the Savior restored.

Righteous Deliverer: I praise You for convicting my heart of sin and uncleanness. Forgive me for my iniquities and renew a right spirit within my heart. Show me the ways of righteousness and pure living so that my fellowship with You is sincere. In Jesus' name, Amen.

CREAMY SPINACH PARMESAN (low-carb)

2 tablespoons butter
1 small clove garlic, minced
1 large bunch of spinach, washed well, drained, and chopped
½ cup heavy cream
3 tablespoons Parmesan cheese (fresh grated is best)

Melt butter in skillet on medium-high heat. Add garlic; sauté 1 minute. Add spinach; reduce heat to medium. Cook uncovered until spinach wilts and most of moisture gone (about 2–3 tablespoons juice remaining). Add cream; cook 1–2 minutes. Add Parmesan cheese and mix.

May 11

And when he had called the people unto him with his disciples also, he said unto them, Whosoever will come after me, let him deny himself, and take up his cross, and follow me.

—MARK 8:34, KJV

THE CROSS OF Christ is a symbol of suffering, ridicule, self-denial, rejection, shame, and death. It represents the selfless act of love Jesus demonstrated for us all. In Bible times, a condemned person was forced to carry his own cross to where he would be nailed while crowds watched. For Jesus to tell His followers to take up their cross and follow Him would be the same as telling them to be prepared for public execution if they wanted to come after Him.

Though we aren't expected to literally pick up a heavy cross and carry it to a place where we will be crucified, Jesus does want us to crucify our sinful fleshly desires and live according to His will. Carrying our cross means standing up for what we believe, even in the midst of ridicule and persecution. It is denying our own desires and doing what God's Word says to do. It is refusing to accept the world's standards by holding on to the morals of what a godly Christian should be.

After Jesus spoke to His disciples and the people in the crowd, He went on to say that if anyone is ashamed of Him and His teachings in the sinful and adulterous generation in which we live, and doesn't follow His teachings, He too will be ashamed of them when He returns one day for His church. What a tragedy this would be. We must this moment purpose in our hearts to live for God.

Father: Thank You for the Cross! Thank You for sending Jesus to die in my place. I repent of my sin and shame. Cause me to purpose in my heart to live daily as Your child. May I never be ashamed to carry my cross for You, no matter the cost. In Jesus' name, Amen.

HAMBURGER MAC AND CHEESE

1 pound ground beef
1 small onion, chopped
1 box/package macaroni and cheese
2 tablespoons butter
4 ounces Velveeta cheese
½ cup milk
1 packet of cheese mix from box
1 can cream of mushroom soup

Brown ground meat; drain. Add onion; cook until tender. Boil macaroni until almost done (al dente). Drain and add to ground meat in skillet. Add butter, cheese, milk, packet of cheese, and soup. Simmer on low for 15 to 20 minutes.

May 12

Verily I say unto you, Whosoever shall not receive the kingdom of God as a little child, he shall not enter therein.

—MARK 10:15, KJV

RECEIVING THE KINGDOM of God like a child means coming to Him with a humble, simple, and trusting heart. Just as children jump into their earthly father's arms, trusting him to catch them, we too should have that same childlike faith to trust our heavenly Father when we need Him. Receiving the kingdom of God comes as we accept Jesus as our personal Savior. It means turning away from everything that is sinful or ungodly and turning to God and obeying the works of righteousness. Children must be taught the Word of God and trained to do what it says so that when they are old enough to make the choice, they will not only ask Christ to be their Savior, but they will choose to follow in His ways. Jesus loves the little children, and His arms are always open wide, ready to receive them unto Him. This is how each of us must also come to God.

Heavenly Father: I come to You today as a little child, trusting You with my life. I'm sorry for the times I made ungodly decisions and disobeyed what I knew was right. Show me the areas of my life I need to change and grant me the strength to do so. May I always have a childlike faith with a humble heart so You are honored in everything I do. In Jesus' name, Amen.

CLASSIC CRAB CASSEROLE

1 (8-ounce) package small shell macaroni
½ cup diced green onion
1 container fresh mushrooms, sliced
½ cup butter
½ cup all-purpose flour
1 teaspoon salt
1 teaspoon dry mustard
¼ teaspoon pepper
1 quart milk
3 cans crabmeat
2 teaspoons Worcestershire sauce
¼ teaspoon Tabasco sauce
2 cups grated cheddar cheese

Cook macaroni according to package; drain. Sauté onions and mushrooms in butter until tender. Stir in flour, salt, mustard, and pepper until blended; gradually stir in milk. Bring to boil, stirring constantly. Reduce heat; simmer 3 minutes; remove from heat. Add macaroni, crab, Worcestershire sauce, and Tabasco; blend well. Top with cheese; bake uncovered 30 minutes or until bubbling hot and cheese is melted.

May 13

My house shall be called of all nations the house of prayer but ye have made it a den of thieves.

—MARK 11:17, KJV

JESUS AND HIS disciples arrived in Jerusalem to attend the annual Passover feast. When they got to the temple, they found that merchants had turned it into a marketplace and were selling animals to be used for sacrifice. This angered Jesus because the house of God was being disrespected and wrongly used. He drove out the money-changers and their animals with whips, turned over the tables, and poured the money out onto the temple floor. In those days, they used animals as sacrifices to God, so it wasn't wrong to buy and sell animals. The wrong was the disrespectful use of the temple. The temple is a place of spiritual devotion, prayer, and worship. Being made into a place of entertainment, showmanship, or monetary gain profanes it. Our churches today must also be careful to not allow them to become anything but God-honoring places, where He is central and foremost. Just as Jesus stood up for what He believed, so should we be intolerant of the things done to defame our Lord and His house.

Precious Lord: I praise You for all You've done to prove Your holiness and righteousness. Thank You for the church that You sanctioned to be a place of prayer and spiritual devotion. Help me to do my part in seeing that it is never taken for granted and misused. May I always be found faithful to Your house and give You the honor and praise You so deserve. In Jesus' name, Amen.

BREAKFAST SOUFFLÉ (serves 8 people)

3 slices white bread, cubed
1 ½ cups grated/shredded cheddar cheese
9 eggs, slightly beaten
3 cups milk
1 ½ teaspoons dry mustard
½ teaspoon salt
2 (8-ounce) packages sausage links, browned (Brown 'n Serve or other brand)

Put bread and cheese in greased 9x13-inch baking dish. Mix other ingredients, except sausage, and pour over bread. Place sausage on top. Bake at 350 degrees for 45 minutes, or until browned.

May 14

Therefore keep watch because you do not know when the owner of the house will come back—whether in the evening, or at midnight, or when the rooster crows, or at dawn. If he comes suddenly, do not let him find you sleeping. What I say to you, I say to everyone: "Watch!"

—MARK 13:35–36

WE HAVE NO idea when Jesus will return in the clouds with His power and glory to take His children home to be with Him forever. We are told that no one knows the day or the hour—not the heavenly angels, and not even Jesus Himself. Only the Father knows when that time will be. Therefore, Jesus warns us to be alert and ready every moment of the day. He tells us to watch as though we have been left in charge of a house not knowing the exact time of the owner's return. The responsibility of having all the household chores is ours, and we are expected to have everything done in a way that will be pleasing and acceptable to the owner.

We all have had the opportunity to be left home alone while our parents stepped out for a time. The moment we heard them return we began to do some quick or last minute housekeeping. Sometimes it was too late and they returned to find us sleeping or negligent of our duties. That's how it will be when Jesus returns to rapture (take up) His church (His followers). Jesus is coming at any time, and only the faithful to His Word will inherit eternal life with Him. May we all watch and wait for His imminent return, no matter the day or hour.

Heavenly Father: With anticipation and expectation, I watch for You. Help me to have my housework done so that when You come I am not ashamed of the condition of my life. Forgive me for ignoring Your warning to watch and be ready to meet You when the clouds portray Your coming. Give me strength to rid those things from my life that are displeasing and disrespectful to You. In Jesus' name, Amen.

CITRUS BAKED SALMON

⅓ cup orange juice
1 tablespoon teriyaki or soy sauce
⅓ cup honey
Pinch of salt and pepper
1–2 teaspoons horseradish (optional)
2–2 ½ pounds salmon fillets

Mix first 5 ingredients in small bowl. Place salmon, skin side down, in greased baking dish. Pour sauce over top; bake 10–12 minutes at 400 degrees, or until fish flakes easily with fork.

May 15

And at the ninth hour Jesus cried with a loud voice, saying, Eloi, Eloi, lama sabachthani? which is, being interpreted, My God, My God, why have You forsaken me?

—MARK 15:34, KJV

FOR ALL TIME past, Jesus and the Father were One. They had perfect fellowship, perfect communication, and acted and thought in unison. Jesus even knew He was going to be crucified in perfect obedience to God the Father. He knew the pain He would suffer and, above all, the agony that would come once God's Spirit left Him. In spite of this, Jesus remained loyal to His call.

Why then did He feel God had forsaken Him? God's Word says Jesus was pure, holy, and never committed sin, but He bore our sins and died a horrific death as if a sinner. At the moment of His death, the sins of the entire world came on Jesus, and God could no longer look upon His Son. Jesus' cry on the cross was not an expression of lack of confidence in God the Father but an expression of real suffering because God had really and truly forsaken Him. Even so, Christ paid the price once and for all so we might have eternal life. Isaiah 53:6 (KJV) says, "All we like sheep have gone astray; we have turned every one to his own way; and the LORD hath laid on Him the iniquity of us all." Our sins could be in one of two places: either on our own head or nailed to the cross. If we carry our sins to the grave, they will carry us to hell. If we believe in Christ, when we die He will carry us in His arms to heaven.

Dear God: Thank You for sending Your Son to pay a debt He didn't owe, all because of love. Forgive me for my sin, and show me ways to share the message of the Cross with the lost, that they too might believe in You and be saved. In Jesus' name, Amen.

CHICKEN BREAST SUPREME

4 bacon strips
4 boneless, skinless chicken breast halves
1 can cream of mushroom soup
½ cup sour cream
4 ounces sliced fresh mushrooms *or* 1 (4-ounce) can sliced mushrooms

Cook bacon until done but not crisp; drain on paper towel. Wrap strip of bacon around each piece of chicken. Place in greased baking dish. Mix together soup, sour cream, and mushrooms; pour over chicken. Cover and bake at 350 for 30 minutes or until chicken juices run clear.

May 16

"Why were you searching for me?" he [Jesus] asked. "Didn't you know that I had to be in my Father's house?"

—LUKE 2:49

WHEN JESUS WAS twelve years old, He was found missing while returning from a trip. Three times a year, devout Jewish families traveled to Jerusalem for religious festivals. They loaded their camels, and families caravanned together. On one journey back home, Mary and Joseph realized that Jesus was not with them. The custom was that both girls and boys traveled with their mothers, but when they turned thirteen, boys would stay with their fathers and girls with their mothers. Jesus, being twelve, probably could have chosen to travel with either one, so this could be why He wasn't missed right away. Each parent thought Jesus was with the other. Mary and Joseph had already traveled one whole day and had to turn back and go to Jerusalem to look for Him. There they found Him in the temple listening to the teachers and asking questions. Mary quickly scolded Jesus for causing them to worry. In turn, Jesus showed His surprise that His parents hadn't realized where He was. They had taken Him to church all His life, and when they left for their journey back home, Jesus stayed behind at the temple. It was the place He wanted to be, learning about His heavenly Father. For Jesus, it seemed right to be there. Joseph was a very busy man, but he made sure his family was in church. He was a carpenter and had a large family to support, but he was faithful to God. When Jesus was found, He could not believe His parents were searching for Him. Was not being in the temple so common to Jesus that He thought it was okay to be there?

Where would our children want to be if given the opportunity? Is our Father's house honored, respected, and a place of priority, where we talk about loving to go and learn about God? Or do we teach our children that it's a place to go only when convenient and nothing else is on our schedules? Jesus had to be in His Father's house. Shouldn't we?

Father: Just as Jesus wanted to be in the house of God, I too yearn to be there in Your presence, learning about You and having fellowship with like-minded believers. Help me to prioritize my time so I don't neglect the privilege of gathering with others to worship You. In Jesus' name, Amen.

PORK BARBECUE (crockpot)

1 (2–3 pounds) pork loin roast
1 (12-ounce) jar pepperoncinis and juice
Barbecue sauce

Put meat and pepperoncinis in crockpot for 8 hours on low. Shred meat; serve on buns with barbecue sauce.

May 17

But I say unto you which hear, Love your enemies, do good to them which hate you. Bless them that curse you, and pray for them which despitefully use you.

—LUKE 6:27–28, KJV

JESUS SPOKE THESE words to His disciples and a crowd of followers concerning how they should treat those who mistreat them. As Christians, we are obligated to follow a different standard than that of the world. This doesn't mean we should agree with the way they treat us, but it does mean that we are to be concerned for their welfare and souls. Knowing those without Christ will perish and forever endure an eternal hell should be enough to motivate us toward reaching the lost. Loving, doing good deeds, blessing with thoughts and words, and praying for all those who mistreat us is what God expects each of us to do. If we will do good when we find opportunities and pray and intercede for others earnestly before the Lord, we will find that God will begin to put love in our hearts toward our enemies. Just as Jesus loved those who nailed Him to the cross, we are to do the same to those who mistreat us.

Heavenly Father: When life is challenging and circumstances are overwhelming, it's You I need to embrace. I desire Your wisdom, guidance, and healing as I face certain situations and difficulties. You are my Shepherd and my Comforter, and I praise You for caring for me. Help me to love and forgive those who have mistreated me. In Jesus' name, Amen.

TEXAS CAVIAR

1 can black-eyed peas or black beans, drained and rinsed
1 can Mexican corn
1 sweet or red onion, finely chopped
1 green pepper, chopped
½ of each red, yellow, and orange pepper
4–6 jalapenos, finely chopped
3–4 tomatoes, diced
1 (8-ounce) bottle Italian dressing
½ of 1 lemon, squeezed, or 2 tablespoons lemon juice
1 fresh bunch cilantro, washed and diced

Mix everything together; refrigerate until ready to use. Great dip for chips or as a salad.

May 18

Do not judge, and you will not be judged. Do not condemn, and you will not be condemned. Forgive, and you will be forgiven. Give, and it will be given to you. A good measure pressed down, shaken together and running over, will be poured into your lap. For with the measure you use, it will be measured to you.

—LUKE 6:37–38

JESUS LOVES US! Everything He did, taught, and stood for was because of His vast amount of love for His children. He desires that we each walk in obedience to His teachings and love one another as He loves us. When Jesus instructs us to not judge, He doesn't mean that we should turn our heads to sin and act as though we aren't moved to sadness because of sin's perverse effects. Jesus wants us to judge but do so righteously. That means to use the truth of the Word to discern sin and not only the appearance.

In 1 Corinthians 6:2–3, Jesus authorizes us to judge. If we didn't, we could not discern good from bad, proper from improper, or righteousness from evil. We must judge behavior and not the individual; the deed, not the doer; the choice, and not the chooser. The individual, doer, or chooser is accountable for his or her deed or choice. We are to judge only the deed or choice. Jesus could see a king in a shepherd boy and an apostle in a murderer. So, while we must judge one's behavior, we must also try to see and nurture the goodness in that one. This is how Jesus sees each of us.

Heavenly Father: Help me not to judge others in a way that is not pleasing to You. Instead, show me ways I might help others to draw closer and live according to Your Word. Forgive me when I condemn others, even if they are wrong. Help me see them through Your eyes and love them accordingly. In Jesus' name, Amen.

KROPSU (Finnish baked pancake)

3 tablespoons butter
3 eggs
1 ½ tablespoons sugar
½ teaspoon salt
1 cup milk
½ cup flour

Melt butter in heavy 9- or 10-inch cast-iron or glass pan (lightweight pan will burn bottom of pancake). Beat eggs in bowl; add sugar, salt, and milk. Slowly add flour; mix well. Pour into hot butter in pan. Bake 20 minutes at 400 degrees. Cut into wedges; serve with syrup, powdered sugar, or fruit topping.

May 19

And why call ye me, Lord, Lord, and do not the things which I say?

—LUKE 6:46, KJV

JESUS LOVED TO walk with His disciples and teach the crowds who followed them about the way they should live. He used parables, stories, and any means He could to convey God's Word so they would understand it. In this verse, Jesus questioned the disciples' relationship with Him. How could it be that they would call Him Lord and yet disobey His commands? How is it that we too call Him Lord and yet disregard what He asks of us?

Jesus went on to say in the following verses that one who hears His Word and puts it into practice is like a man who built his house with a deep and firm foundation on rock. When a flood or storm comes, the house will stand firm and not fall. But the one who hears God's Word and does not obey it is like a man who builds his house on the ground without a foundation. When the storm comes, the house will not stand and is destroyed.

Calling Jesus Lord means we have repented of our sins and have asked Him to come and dwell within our hearts. It means we hunger and thirst to know Him more. It means that Jesus is our Rock, and upon Him we build our lives. May we all live in a way that Jesus never has to ask us why we call Him Lord and yet do not obey Him. Our words and actions should be enough evidence to prove to Him that He truly is Lord!

My Lord: You are the Rock of my salvation; upon your Word I build my house. When the trials, circumstances, and perils of life come, I am then grounded in You and do not fall. I repent of the times I called You Lord yet did not obey Your Word. Help me to come before You with the decisions I need to make so they line up with Your Word. In Jesus' name, Amen.

SHRIMP CASSEROLE

4 ounces (3 cups) medium noodles
1 (10-ounce) can cream of shrimp soup
¾ cup milk
½ cup mayonnaise or salad dressing
2 chopped green onions
¼ cup diced celery
¼ teaspoon salt
⅓ cup grated cheddar cheese
1–2 cups shrimp
10 Ritz crackers, crushed

Cook noodles according to package; drain. Mix rest of ingredients together, except cracker crumbs, and pour into greased baking dish. Bake at 350 degrees for 30 minutes. Sprinkle cracker crumbs overtop and bake 10–15 minutes longer.

May 20

And whosoever will not receive you, when ye go out of that city, shake off the very dust from your feet for a testimony against them.

—LUKE 9:5, KJV

THIS SCRIPTURE REFERS to the sending forth of Jesus' disciples to minister to those who are lost and living sinful lives. Jesus taught that if they are not welcome and the people will not listen to their message, they should merely go to another place where the people are receptive. When we surrender our lives to Jesus Christ and experience forgiveness, redemption, and restoration, we want others to turn their lives over to Him and also experience abundant life. Though we must do everything possible to present Christ, there are times when it is obvious that we are speaking to deaf ears. Some people are determined to not follow the Lord and obey His holy Word, regardless of what we say or do. We must do all we can to plant the seed of salvation and trust others to come along and water it. When others do not accept the message, Jesus instructs us to gently remove ourselves from their lives and move on to be a witness to others who are hungry for Him. We can still persist in prayer for those who have rejected Christ and consistently set a Christlike example before them, hoping that one day they will be saved.

Dear Lord: Forgive me for the times I reacted badly toward those who seemed to reject the message of salvation. Remind me that I am to love people and witness Christ to them; it is Your Holy Spirit who speaks to their hearts. I pray for lost family and friends who do not know You as Savior and Lord. May they come to a place of conviction and conscious recognition of their need for You in their lives. In Jesus' name, Amen.

BLT LINGUINE

8 ounces uncooked linguine
8 bacon strips, cut into 1 ½ inch pieces
2 plum tomatoes, cut into 1 inch pieces
2 garlic cloves, minced
1 tablespoon lemon juice
½ teaspoon salt
½ teaspoon pepper
4 tablespoons Parmesan cheese
2 tablespoons fresh parsley, minced

Cook linguine according to package. In large pan, cook bacon until crisp; remove to paper towels and crumble. Discard all but 1 tablespoon grease. Add tomato and garlic to pan; sauté 1–2 minutes. Stir in lemon juice, salt, and pepper. Drain linguine; add to skillet. Sprinkle with cheese, parsley, and bacon; toss.

May 21

For whosoever shall be ashamed of me and my words, of him shall the Son of man be ashamed, when he shall come in his own glory, and in his Father's, and of the holy angels.

—LUKE 9:26, KJV

JESUS HAD JUST spoken to His disciples about denying themselves and taking up their crosses to follow Him. He then gave them another word of caution: if they (or any of us) are ashamed of Him (Jesus), when He comes in His glory to take His children home, He will be ashamed of them (and us). Thus, we would be eternally lost and go to a place designed for Satan and his followers. To be ashamed of Jesus means to be embarrassed, uncomfortable, or fearful about being a believer and follower of His, whether it be at home, work, in the neighborhood, out in the community, at school, or around friends and family. We must heed the words of Jesus when we are tempted to hide our faith because of fear or embarrassment. Our world is filled with lost souls dependent upon our witness to lead them to Christ. If we don't...then who will?

Glorious Father: Thank You for the awesome way You show us how to live and for the guidelines You give us to do Your will. Strengthen my witness in the world around me and show me ways to be bold and zealous when sharing Jesus with the lost. Help me to live my testimony before them and not just talk with empty words. Open ears and soften hearts to receive the true and only message of salvation. May I never be ashamed of serving You. In Jesus' name, Amen.

CHICKEN CRESCENT BAKE

¼ cup diced onions
1 (4-ounce) can sliced mushrooms
4 tablespoons butter, separated
2 chicken breasts, cooked and diced
½ cup mayonnaise or Miracle Whip
1 can cream of chicken soup
½ cup sour cream
1 can crescent rolls
4 ounces Monterey Jack cheese, grated
3–4 tablespoons sliced almonds (optional)

Sauté onions and mushrooms in 2 tablespoons butter until tender. Add chicken, mayonnaise, soup, and sour cream. Heat until bubbly. Pour into a 9x13-inch baking dish. Top with crescent rolls to form a top crust. Sprinkle grated cheese over top. Sprinkle with sliced almonds. Drizzle 2 tablespoons melted butter over top and bake at 375 minutes for 30 minutes, or until done.

May 22

Then he said to them, "Whoever welcomes this little child in my name welcomes me; and whoever welcomes me welcomes the one who sent me. For he who is least among you all—he is the greatest."

—LUKE 9:48

JESUS' DISCIPLES WERE arguing about which one of them might be the greatest. Did they not grasp the true meaning of what Jesus had recently told them about sacrificially denying themselves of their own selfish desires to follow Him? Did they not understand that the choice to do or not do this determined their eternal destiny? Perhaps the disciples were like many of us today who are still caught up in our own selfish desires, unwilling to make the sacrifices we need to follow Christ. Serving the Lord is not a contest or competition. The world defines greatness in terms of status—power, wealth, or fame—but Jesus defines greatness in terms of service—humility, love, and self-denial. Greatness, according to the Lord, comes when we accept Christ as our Savior, crucify our fleshly desires and motives, surrender fully and completely to the Cross, and are willing to do whatever God asks us to do, no matter how small or large the task may be. It is then that we have the right to call ourselves great.

Wonderful Lord: You are an awesome example of love and humility. My desire is to be like You and serve whenever and wherever I am needed. Show me what it is You would have me to do, and help me to always be humble and willing to carry out those tasks. Forgive me for the times I am prideful and desirous of status and power. May I be faithful to Your Word and always willing to be least in the world so I might be found great in Your eyes. In Jesus' name, Amen.

THREE-BEAN SALAD

2 medium onions, thinly sliced
1 small green pepper, diced
1 can green beans, drained
1 can yellow waxed beans, drained
1 can kidney beans, undrained

Dressing:

¾ cup sugar
⅔ cup oil
⅔ cup vinegar
¼ teaspoon salt
¼ teaspoon pepper

Mix all beans, green pepper, and onion together. Mix dressing ingredients together and pour over vegetables. Refrigerate several hours before serving, if time allows.

May 23

And he answering said, Thou shalt love the Lord thy God with all thy heart, and with all thy soul, and with all thy strength, and with all thy mind; and, thy neighbor as thyself.

—Luke 10:27, KJV

THIS IS THE answer Jesus gave when He was asked what one had to do to inherit eternal life. It is also a question each one of us should ask. What does it mean to love the Lord with all our heart, soul, and strength and our neighbor as ourselves? It means that God is more important than anyone or anything else in the world. It means that worshiping the Lord has priority above everything else in our lives. But it doesn't end there. Not only are we to love God, we must love our neighbor as ourselves.

The same person who asked Jesus how to have eternal life also asked Him to define what He meant by neighbor. Jesus answered by telling him the parable of the Good Samaritan. Jesus wants us to know that a neighbor is anyone who is in need. It does not necessarily mean those who are in our direct vicinity, though they could be. The more time we spend reading our Bible, praying, thinking about God, being with other Christians, and helping those in need, the more natural it becomes to love God the way we should. We must remember to praise Him for all that He does for us and how He sent His only Son to die a cruel death on the cross so we might have eternal life.

Dear Lord: Thank You for the provision You made on the cross so I might experience eternal life. As I choose to serve, honor, and love You with all my heart, mind, soul, and strength, I am guaranteed a home in heaven. I praise You for allowing me the privilege of serving You. Help me to love my neighbor in ways that would glorify You. In Jesus' name, Amen.

CAULIFLOWER CASSEROLE

1 (l-pound) bag frozen cauliflower
½ pound Velveeta cheese (cubed)
25 Ritz crackers (crushed)
1 stick melted butter

Cook cauliflower in microwave as directed on package; drain off all water. Spread half of cauliflower in an 8x8-inch casserole dish. Top with half the cheese. Make another layer of each. Put crushed Ritz crackers on top. Drizzle melted butter on top of crackers. Bake uncovered at 350 degrees for 20 minutes.

May 24

And he said unto his disciples, Therefore I say unto you, Take no thought for your life, what ye shall eat; neither for the body, what ye shall put on. The life is more than meat, and the body is more than raiment. Consider the ravens: for they neither sow nor reap; which neither have storehouse nor barn; and God feedeth them: how much more are ye better than the fowls? And which of you with taking thought can add to his stature one cubit? If ye then be not able to do that thing which is least, why take ye thought for the rest?

—LUKE 12:22–26, KJV

THIS IS ONE of those self-explanatory passages where Jesus simply tells it like it is. The main thing He wants us to know is that God loves us and will take care of us. He also wants us to know that we should not worry. If God knows our needs even before we do, He will meet our needs.

Though Jesus' words have a rather sharp tone to them, they are ironically comforting to our hearts. God knows what is best for us and will provide the things we need and not necessarily the things we want. We have the choice to either trust God and not be consumed by worry and fear or not trust Him and be anxious and fearful. Throughout Scripture, we are reminded over and over that if we trust in the Lord with all of our hearts, lean not on our own understanding, and acknowledge Him with our hearts, minds, souls, and spirits, He will meet our needs according to His riches in Christ Jesus.

Dear God: I am sorry for the times I doubted and became fearful about life. Thank You for showing me in Your Word how I should trust You always. When times are hard, help me to focus on Your grace and take comfort in knowing You are in control. Show me ways I might serve You better by doing without worldly pleasures I really don't need. In Jesus' name, Amen.

BAKED BEANS

4 slices bacon
1 small onion, chopped
2 (15 ¾-ounce) cans pork and beans
¼ cup brown sugar
2 teaspoons mustard
¼ cup ketchup or barbecue sauce

Cook bacon in pan until crisp; remove and crumble. Discard half the grease; add onion to skillet and cook until tender. Stir in beans, brown sugar and mustard; pour into greased baking dish. Bake at 350 degrees for 60–90 minutes.

May 25

Be dressed ready for service and keep your lamps burning, like men waiting for their master to return from a wedding banquet, so that when he comes and knocks they can immediately open the door for him.

—LUKE 12:35

JESUS IS COMING soon, and we are to be eagerly ready and waiting for Him. Everything that needs to take place before He returns for His church has been done; nothing more needs to happen. With that in mind, we who are true believers and followers of Christ should be spiritually ready to greet Jesus when He comes knocking at the door of eternity. If Jesus is our greatest treasure and we are daily seeking His righteousness and will for our lives, then we are dressed and ready for service. The hope of our Savior coming to take us out of this world to be with Him forever is the blessed hope of all the redeemed and the source of comfort we all need to press on in an unrighteous world.

Dear Lord: I praise and thank You for the promise of Your imminent return. Knowing that You will soon come and rapture the church brings joy to my heart, and I find strength to face each day. Reveal to me ways I might change areas of my life to prove my love and readiness to serve You. You are my treasure, my hope, and the joy of my salvation, and I long for You to come and take me to my eternal home. In Jesus' name I pray, Amen.

CHICKEN ENCHILADA PIE

3 boneless, skinless chicken breasts
4 cups corn chips
1 can cream of chicken soup
1 can cream of celery soup
1 cup sour cream
1 cup salsa (smooth or chunky)
4 teaspoons minced onion
1 cup chicken broth (or water and bouillon)
1 small can mild green chiles
2 teaspoons chili powder
¼ teaspoon garlic powder
1 (8-ounce) package grated cheddar cheese

Cook chicken in pan with small amount water until done; remove and dice. Cover bottom of greased 9x13-inch baking dish with half of the corn chips. Spread half of the chicken over chips. Mix together rest of ingredients, except cheese, and cover meat with half of mixture. Then sprinkle half the cheese over top; repeat process of corn chips, sauce, ending with cheese. Bake at 350 degrees for 25–30 minutes or until hot and bubbly.

May 26

Then Jesus asked, "What is the kingdom of God like? What shall I compare it to? It is like a mustard seed, which a man took and put in his garden. It grew and became a tree, and the birds of the air perched in its branches."

—LUKE 13:18–19

THIS PARABLE IS one we can all understand, even small children. If we take a tiny seed from a packet and plant it in soil, it will grow into a beautiful tree, bush, or whatever it is meant to be. The main thing to understand is that it requires opening the packet, taking the seed out, and planting it in the garden. If the seed were to remain in the packet, it would never have the opportunity to grow and have purpose. Such is the same for the gospel of Christ. We must take the seed of the gospel out and plant it into the hearts of those who are without Christ. Just as the little mustard seed planted in the garden grows to produce branches large enough to hold the birds of the air, so will our gospel seeds do the same. When we share God's love with a lost person and he receives it, he will begin to grow and fulfill God's purpose. He, in turn, must share the gospel with others. Every word we speak, every act of kindness and love we do, and every cent we give to church and missions are seeds planted to see the kingdom of God grow.

Dear God: Thank You for this story that helps us all to understand the need to sow Your holy Word to a lost and dying world. Forgive me for not sowing seed when I had every opportunity to do it, especially when Your Holy Spirit was nudging me. Please give me boldness to share Your love with my neighbors, friends, family, and the people I meet day to day. In Jesus' name, Amen.

REUBEN CASSEROLE

½–1 pound cooked corned beef, sliced or diced
¼ cup Thousand Island salad dressing
1 can or 1 (16-ounce) bag sauerkraut, drained well
8 ounces Swiss cheese, shredded or torn into small pieces
6 slices rye bread, crumbled
1 stick butter, melted

Place corned beef in lightly greased 9x13-inch baking dish. Dot with dressing; spread sauerkraut on top and top with cheese. Melt butter and toss with bread crumbs; sprinkle over top. Bake at 350 degrees for 30 minutes.

May 27

Then Jesus said to his host, "When you give a luncheon or dinner, do not invite your friends, your brothers or relatives, or your rich neighbors; if you do, they may invite you back and so you will be repaid. But when you give a banquet, invite the poor, the crippled, the lame, the blind, and you will be blessed. Although they cannot repay you, you will be repaid at the resurrection of the righteous."

—LUKE 14:12–14

JESUS WAS DINING at a prominent Pharisee's house with a group of other guests when He spoke these words to them. He wanted them to know there was a better way of giving a banquet, and though they would not be repaid while on earth, they would reap heavenly rewards. Jesus encouraged them to invite the poor and sick to their homes to dine. Even though they could not reciprocate, the blessing of this humble act would be great. Jesus wants us to do the same and open our hearts and lives to helping those who are in no condition to return the favor. This act of love and servanthood is definitely contrary to the practice that we are most familiar with in our world today, where we are guests of someone and then they become our guests. How much greater it is to bless those who are unable to return the favor. It is then that God is glorified and our heavenly rewards await us.

Thank You, Lord Jesus, for teaching us how to be humble, gracious, and a servant to those in need. Because of Your love and compassion, I am encouraged to open my heart to the sick and poor. Knowing my reward will be given in heaven is all I want. In Jesus' name, Amen.

BLT SALAD

½ pound bacon
½ cup mayonnaise
2 tablespoons red wine vinegar
4 slices French or Italian bread, cubed
½ teaspoon salt
½ teaspoon pepper
1 tablespoon oil
1 pound romaine lettuce, torn into bite-sized pieces
1 pint cherry tomatoes, quartered

Fry bacon until crisp; drain grease, reserving 2 tablespoons. Mix bacon drippings with mayonnaise and vinegar; whisk and set aside. Crumble bacon. Toss bread cubes with salt and pepper in large skillet; drizzle oil over them while cooking on medium heat until golden brown. Combine all ingredients and toss with dressing.

May 28

Jesus said to His disciples: "Things that cause people to sin are bound to come, but woe to that person through whom they come. It would be better for him to be thrown into the sea with a millstone tied around his neck than for him to cause one of these little ones to sin."

—LUKE 17:1–2

SIN IS ALL around us and comes in many forms of temptation and enticement. Jesus told His disciples there would be things that would cause people to sin, but the real problem would be if they in turn caused another one to sin. Jesus was so emphatic about this that He gave a mental picture of someone being pulled under water to their death because of an anchor around their neck. God's wrath will be upon anyone who is responsible for the spiritual destruction of a soul. Pastors, teachers, and especially parents should consider this teaching of Christ. We all must consider the things we do and say that might cause another to sin. It may be how we dress, our involvement with worldly entertainment, immoral films and relationships, humanistic teaching, literature, drugs, alcohol, and anything else contrary to what God's Word teaches. We should strive to remove from our lives all the things that might cause others to be tempted to sin. Knowing the consequences of this because of our example, attitude, or neglect should be enough reason to strive to live according to the holy principles of God's Word.

Dear Lord: You know my heart and how I long to live according to Your will and way. Show me the areas that need attention so I might not be a stumbling block in the path of others. Forgive me for my sin, and help me to avoid falling into temptation when it comes. In Jesus' name, Amen.

BREAD AND BREAKFAST CASSEROLE

1 pound ground pork sausage
1 teaspoon mustard, regular or powder
½ teaspoon salt
4 eggs, beaten
2 cups milk
6 slices white bread, cut into cubes
8 ounces mild cheddar cheese, grated

Cook sausage in skillet until done; drain. In bowl, mix mustard, salt, eggs, and milk; add sausage, bread cubes, and cheese. Mix well; pour into greased 9x13-inch baking dish. Cover; chill in refrigerator 8 hours or overnight. In morning, bake covered in 350 degree oven for 45–60 minutes. Uncover; reduce temperature to 325 degrees. Bake additional 30 minutes, until set.

May 29

As he approached Jerusalem and saw the city, he wept over it and said, "If you, even you, had only known on this day what would bring you peace—but now it is hidden from your eyes."

—LUKE 19:41–42

JESUS WAS APPROACHING Jerusalem, riding on a donkey, just one week before being crucified on a cross for the sins of all. As He looked over the city, great sorrow and compassion filled His heart because He realized the people and their leaders would reject Him as God's promised Messiah. His heart was broken over the lostness of the human race and their refusal to repent and accept His plan of salvation. Jesus came to bring the people of Jerusalem the opportunity to have peace like they have never known before. This peace would be the result of having Christ live within their hearts, but they were blinded and did not receive Him.

The story is the same today; we all seek peace, but we seek it in the form of happiness, security, rest, comfort, and satisfaction. This type of peace is merely temporary. True peace is a Person, and that Person is Jesus. It has nothing to do with people, places, events, or things. No matter what the circumstances are in life, God's peace can be with us. Jesus still weeps as He looks over our cities and sees the condition of our souls in quest for peace. As long as we seek the peace that the world defines, we will never experience the true peace of God, for it can only be found in a personal relationship with Him.

Heavenly Father: Thank You for sending Your only Son to be my peace. May I not look to the world for contentment and happiness but only to Jesus Christ. It is in Him that I find true eternal peace and that is what my heart desires. In Jesus' name I pray, Amen.

ORIENTAL SALAD

1 package cole slaw mix or 1 small head of Napa cabbage, chopped
1 bunch green onions, chopped
1 package Oriental Ramen noodles, crushed in bag
1 (4-ounce) package slivered almonds

Dressing:

⅓ cup sugar
⅓ cup vinegar
½ cup oil
1 seasoning packet from the Ramen noodles

Mix together cabbage and green onions; refrigerate. Heat oil in skillet and toast almonds and dry noodles until lightly browned; set aside. Mix dressing ingredients together in small pan and boil 1 minute. Mix everything together and serve.

May 30

The Son of Man must be delivered into the hands of sinful men, and be crucified, and the third day rise again.

—LUKE 24:7, KJV

ON THE THIRD day, which was the first day of the week, Mary Magdalene, Mary, mother of James, and another lady, Salome, went to the tomb where Jesus was laid. They wanted to anoint His body with spices and wondered how they would move the large stone that blocked the doorway of the tomb. But when they got there, they saw the stone had already been moved. Upon entering the tomb, they saw an angel sitting there, but Jesus' body was gone. The women became alarmed and trembled. Once the angel explained that Jesus had risen, just like He said He would, joy began to fill their hearts. The angel then instructed them to go and tell what they had seen, so they did. But the story doesn't end there. Would everyone believe their story that Jesus, who just two days prior was crucified and buried in a tomb, was now resurrected and alive? Or would they make fun and deny this miraculous act of God? It is a decision that we all have to make. Is the tomb empty because Jesus now resides in our hearts, or is He still there waiting for us to remove the stone that blocks the entrance to our hearts and allow Him to come in?

Our Father in heaven: You are holy, and Your name is above all names. I praise You this day for allowing Your only Son to give His life so I might be forgiven and have eternal life. I believe You conquered death because of Your great love and compassion. Search my heart, Lord, and remove any barriers I might have that would keep You out of my life. In Jesus' name, Amen.

MEXICAN CORNBREAD CASSEROLE

2 boxes Jiffy cornbread mix
1 can cream corn
2 pounds ground beef
1 onion, chopped
1 package taco seasoning mix
1 (13–16-ounce) jar salsa
12 ounces cheddar cheese, grated

Make Jiffy mixes according to directions; add creamed corn. Brown ground beef; drain. Add chopped onion and cook 5 minutes. Add taco seasoning and salsa. Mix and cook another 5 minutes. Pour half the Jiffy mix into greased 9x13-inch baking dish. Spread ground meat mix over top; sprinkle cheese on top of meat. Top with rest of Jiffy mix. May also sprinkle additional grated cheese on top, if desired. Bake at 375 degrees for 30–40 minutes, until browned.

May 31

He [Jesus] told them [His disciples], "This is what is written: The Christ will suffer and rise from the dead on the third day, and repentance and forgiveness of sins will be preached in His Name to all nations, beginning at Jerusalem."

—LUKE 24:46–47

WHILE THE DISCIPLES were together, discussing the possibility of Jesus' resurrection, He suddenly appeared in their midst. At first they were afraid because they thought Jesus was a ghost, but when they saw the nail prints in His hands and feet they were overwhelmed with excitement and joy. Jesus assured them that He truly was the Christ who came to suffer death on a cross and then rise on the third day. The real meaning of His resurrection was prophetically spoken when Jesus stated that repentance and forgiveness of sins would be preached in His name throughout the world. Repentance is the feeling of remorse for sinning or breaking God's law and then turning away from that action and pursuing a holy walk with God. Forgiveness is the absolution or pardon of our sins by God after we have consciously asked Him in Jesus' name to do so. Both repentance and forgiveness are required to complete Christ's purpose for His death and resurrection. Repentance is a prerequisite for salvation; without it, there is no forgiveness of sin. It is an ongoing experience in a Christian's life to remain in constant fellowship with the Father.

Father: For everything I've done that dishonored Your holy Word, I repent. I choose to turn away from those things that separate me from having a holy fellowship with You. Help me to follow You all the days of my life. In Jesus' name, Amen.

HOT CHICKEN SALAD

2 cups diced cooked chicken
1 cup chopped celery
1–2 tablespoons grated onion
2 tablespoons lemon juice
¼ teaspoon salt
¼ teaspoon pepper
1 cup mayonnaise
Dash of Tabasco sauce
⅓–½ cup slivered almonds
¼ cup grapes, quartered
1 ⅓ cups crushed potato chips
1 cup grated cheddar cheese

Mix all ingredients, except for cheese and potato chips. Pour into greased baking dish. Combine potato chips and cheese; spread over the top. Bake at 350 degrees for 20 minutes or until bubbly.

Summer Fest

June

June 1

In the beginning was the Word, and the Word was with God, and the Word was God. The same [Jesus] was in the beginning with God.

—JOHN 1:1–2, KJV

JOHN OPENS HIS Gospel by letting us know that God, the Word, and Jesus are all the same. They were! They are! They always will be! The love, honesty, joy, peace, meekness, and patience that we see in the life of Jesus are the very same wonderful qualities and characteristics that God has. Jesus is God in the flesh; He is God's ultimate message to us. He did not speak His own words; He spoke the words of His Father. He did not do His own will; He did the will of His Father. In everything He said and in everything He did, He faithfully showed forth the heart of His Father God. And just like Jesus reflected his Father, we are to reflect Jesus. As we walk by the Spirit of God and in His light, rather than by our own corrupt desires, God's Word is made flesh in us, just as God's Word was made flesh in Christ.

Dear God: You were! You are! You always will be! As I seek to know You more, I am amazed at the wonderful blessing of Your grace and mercy. When my days are over on earth, You will be there to usher me into heaven, where I will forever be with You. For this, I am so thankful. In Jesus' name, Amen.

CRAB CAKES

1 pound crabmeat (canned or fresh)
⅓ cup crushed crackers (Ritz best)
3 green onions, finely chopped
¼ cup finely chopped bell pepper
¼ cup finely chopped celery
¼ cup mayonnaise
2 eggs
1 teaspoon Worcestershire sauce
1 teaspoon mustard
3 tablespoons lemon juice
¼ teaspoon garlic powder
1 teaspoon salt
2 tablespoons melted butter
¼ cup grated Parmesan cheese
Dash cayenne pepper
Flour, for dusting
½ cup peanut or canola oil
Favorite dipping sauce

In large bowl, mix together all ingredients, except flour and oil. Shape into patties; dredge in flour. Heat oil in large skillet over medium heat. When hot, carefully place crab cakes in pan; fry until browned, about 4–5 minutes. Flip and brown other side. Serve with dipping sauce or lemon.

June 2

In him was life; and the life was the light of men. And the light shineth in darkness; and the darkness comprehended it not.

—John 1:4–5, KJV

Jesus, the Holy Spirit, and God the Father have always been in fellowship with one another from the beginning of time. They are the three Persons of the blessed holy Trinity, each one having a distinct purpose yet sharing a common divine nature. The beloved disciple John wanted it known that Jesus is the Christ, the Son of God, and that by believing in Him, there is life in His name. Jesus came to be a light to all men—a light that shines in the darkness of an evil, sinful world controlled by Satan. Most of the world has not accepted this light; therefore, they stumble around in darkness and defeat. It is the responsibility of every one of us who are believers to shine our lights and illuminate the darkness with the love of Christ. By doing so, a gospel of hope and grace might be imparted to the hearts of the lost in order that they may freely choose to accept or reject the message of salvation. Apart from this, there is no other way to find the truth and be saved.

Dear God: Thank You for Your unconditional love and grace. You are my life and the light that brings me hope and peace even in the darkest night. Give me strength to overcome obstacles that arise, and I will give all the glory to You. In Jesus' name I pray, Amen.

TWICE-BAKED POTATOES

4 large baking potatoes
4 ounces cream cheese
4 tablespoons butter
¼ cup grated Parmesan cheese
2 tablespoons sour cream
1 egg
½ teaspoon garlic salt
½ teaspoon pepper
Dash paprika
Bacon bits
Grated cheese
Chives or green onions (optional)

Bake clean potatoes in 350-degree oven for 60–90 minutes, until done. Cut in half lengthwise and scoop out potato into mixing bowl. Add cream cheese, butter, Parmesan cheese, and sour cream; mix well with electric mixer. Add egg, garlic salt, and pepper; beat one minute or until smooth. Fill empty potato skins with mixture; sprinkle with paprika. Arrange on shallow dish or pan. Bake at 375 degrees for 5–10 minutes or until fluffy and browned. Garnish as desired.

June 3

Jesus answered and said unto him [Nicodemus], Verily, verily, I say unto thee, Except a man be born again, he cannot see the kingdom of God.

—JOHN 3:3, KJV

RECEIVING AND BELIEVING in Jesus Christ assures us of our salvation and life eternal in heaven. In this verse, Jesus was speaking to Nicodemus, a Jewish ruler, who was eager to know how to be born again. Nicodemus asked Jesus if it meant entering a second time into his mother's womb. Jesus explained that regeneration, or the second birth, is a spiritual birth that comes to those who repent of their sin and put their faith in Him as Savior and Lord. Being born again involves a transition or turning away from the old life of sin to a new life of obedience to God's Word. This happens only through the grace of God given to all who sincerely desire to know Him and walk in His ways. Once a decision has been made to come to Christ and be born again, it is necessary to repent and ask God for His forgiveness for living a life of sin and disobedience to Him. It is then that the Holy Spirit comes in and guides and directs our lives. This relationship is conditional on our faith in Christ and demonstrated by a life of obedience and love for God's Word.

Dear Lord: I know I have sinned and disobeyed Your Word; please forgive me. By faith I receive You into my heart and believe that my life is redeemed because of the price You paid on the cross for my sins. Fill me with Your Holy Spirit and give me the strength and power I need to walk in the ways of holiness and righteousness all the days of my life. In Jesus' name, Amen.

MAC AND CHEESE LASAGNA

1 (7.25-ounce) package Kraft macaroni dinner
1 ½ cups spaghetti sauce
½ pound lean ground beef, browned and drained
1 cup mozzarella cheese
2 tablespoons grated Parmesan cheese

Prepare macaroni dinner according to package. Spoon half on bottom of greased 8-inch square baking dish. Top with half the spaghetti sauce. Top that with half the ground meat and top that with half the mozzarella cheese. Repeat layers. Top with Parmesan cheese. Bake at 350 degrees for 20 minutes, or until thoroughly heated.

June 4

For God so loved the world that he gave his only begotten Son, that whosoever believeth in him should not perish but have everlasting life.

—John 3:16, KJV

THIS IS PROBABLY the most popular verse in the Bible; more people know this one than any other. It is our hope that one day this life will be over and we will live eternally with our Lord. But it is a choice, and only those who have accepted Christ will enter into the Promised Land. God already paid the price of sacrificing His Son, and now it is up to us to receive it. How many *whosoevers* do you know? They are in our world, and it is up to us to share the message of hope in Jesus with them.

Dear God: Thank you for sacrificing Your Son on the cross for me. Because of Your love for the world, You so graciously did this. You first chose us, and now it is our decision to choose or reject You. I choose to follow You by being obedient to Your Word and making it alive in my heart and life. At the end of my life here on earth, I want to go and live eternally with You. Help me to share my faith with others so they too might choose You. In Jesus' name, Amen.

CABBAGE ROLLS

1 large or 2 small heads cabbage
1 pound ground beef
1 pound ground pork
1 large onion, chopped
1 teaspoon garlic salt
1 teaspoon black pepper
1 cup uncooked rice
1 tablespoon Worcestershire sauce
1 bag sauerkraut, drained (optional)
1 large onion, thinly sliced (optional)
1 tablespoon lemon juice
1 tablespoon brown sugar
1 (48-ounce) can tomato juice
2 (10.75-ounce) cans tomato soup
Mashed potatoes (optional)
Sour cream (optional)

Remove core of cabbage with knife. Put cabbage in large pot of boiling water; remove leaves as they get slightly tender. Mix well beef, pork, onion, garlic salt, pepper, rice, and Worcestershire sauce. Place 2–3 tablespoons at base of each cabbage leaf. Roll, folding in sides until mixture completely encased. Place in large greased deep baking dish; stack as necessary. Place sauerkraut and sliced onion evenly over rolls. Mix lemon juice, sugar, tomato juice, and soup together; pour over top. Cover with lid or foil. Bake at 325 degrees for 2–3 hours until thoroughly cooked. Serve with mashed potatoes and dollop of sour cream.

June 5

Everyone who does evil hates the light, and will not come into the light for fear that his deeds will be exposed. But whoever lives by the truth comes into the light, so that it may be seen plainly that what he has done has been done through God.

—JOHN 3:20–21

ALMOST ALL EVIL deeds and intents begin with a thought that can be hidden by deceit. The kingdom of evil is built on lies, secrets, and darkness and requires the absence of light to survive. Everyone who lives without Jesus Christ in their heart and life, lives in darkness…for Jesus is the Light that comes within and drives out the darkness of sin. This happens when we confess our sins to God and ask for His forgiveness. Before we come to Christ, our sins are not only known by God but are eventually exposed to the world as well. There is a payday for sin on this earth and also after death if we have not confessed them to the Lord. We must count the cost. If we resist the temptation of sin, God will help us and He is glorified. If we yield to the temptation, God's light will illuminate the sin, and sooner or later the consequences will come. When we come to Christ and then testify to others how God has turned our darkness into light giving us a hope and a future, we are doing the will of God.

Heavenly Father: I'm sorry for the things I have done that were contrary to what Your Word asks of me. I want to be clean and pure so I will be ready to meet You in the air when You return. I need You to help me be strong when temptation comes. Thank You for hearing and answering my prayers according to Your will. In Jesus' name, Amen.

GROUND BEEF STROGANOFF

1–2 pounds lean ground beef
½ stick butter
1 onion, chopped
2 cloves garlic, minced
1 can cream mushroom soup
1 can beef broth
¼ cup ketchup
½ teaspoon salt
½ teaspoon pepper
2 teaspoons Worcestershire sauce
8 ounces fresh sliced mushrooms *or* 1 (8-ounce) can mushrooms, drained
1 cup sour cream
1 (8-ounce) package egg noodles, cooked and drained

Brown ground meat in large pan; drain. Add butter, onion, and garlic; cook 5 minutes. Add rest of ingredients, except sour cream and noodles. Cook on low 20–30 minutes. Add sour cream and mix well. Mix with noodles or serve over noodles on plate.

June 6

Jesus answered and said unto her, Whosoever drinketh of this water shall thirst again: But whosoever drinketh of the water that I shall give him shall never thirst; but the water that I shall give him shall be in him a well of water springing up into everlasting life.

—JOHN 4:13–14, KJV

JESUS WAS ON his way from Judea to Galilee when He stopped in Samaria to rest by a well. While there, a Samaritan woman came to draw water. Jesus, being thirsty from His long trip, asked her for a drink. With Jesus' consuming passion for the lost, He used the conversation with the woman to witness to her spiritual needs. We are to follow Jesus' example and do the same in our lives. All around us are hungry, thirsty people needing and wanting to hear the good news of Jesus. Within each of us is an empty void that can only be filled by receiving and believing in Christ. A physical thirst is met by drinking real water, and a spiritual thirst is satisfied by partaking of real spiritual food and water: Jesus Christ.

Father: Thank You for being a spring of water to my soul. You alone are able to quench my spiritual thirst. As I walk with You, talk with You, and serve You, my life becomes more satisfied. Help me to be a witness like You were with the Samaritan woman and be ready and eager to minister Your love and grace to everyone I meet. In Jesus' name, Amen.

CASHEW CHICKEN

4 boneless, skinless chicken breasts, diced
½ teaspoon salt
1 tablespoon sugar
¼ cup teriyaki sauce
2 eggs, beaten
⅓ cup cornstarch
Cooking oil
1 teaspoon garlic salt
1 teaspoon ginger
2 cups boiling water
2 tablespoons Accent
1 cup cashew nuts
¼ cup chopped green onions

Mix chicken with salt, sugar, and teriyaki sauce; marinate in refrigerator 1–4 hours. In small bowl, mix beaten eggs with cornstarch. Remove excess marinade from chicken, and dip pieces in cornstarch mixture. Put small amount oil in large pan; fry chicken pieces over medium-high heat until thoroughly cooked. Remove to paper towels. To same pan, add garlic salt, ginger, boiling water, and Accent. Cover and simmer 15 minutes; add cashews and chicken; thoroughly heat. Serve over hot rice. Sprinkle with chopped green onions.

June 7

Then said Jesus unto him [nobleman], Except ye see signs and wonders, ye will not believe.

—JOHN 4:48, KJV

THESE WERE THE words of Jesus when He was approached by a government official while visiting Cana in Galilee. This is the place where Jesus performed His first miracle by turning water into wine at a wedding. The official heard Jesus was there and begged Him to come to Capernaum where his ill son lay nearly dead.

Signs and wonders are an authentic work of God, but Jesus wants our faith to be focused on Him rather than the miracle. We must seek Him because He is God's Son and our Lord and Savior. Jesus was pleased to heal the official's child, and in turn the man's faith was strengthened and his family became believers. But it seems apparent that Jesus wants us to esteem Him for who He is and not for what He can do. Jesus' character is loving, merciful, and righteous, and we are to worship Him because of who He is in the Father and not just for what He can do for us in a supernatural way.

Lord Jesus: You are the One who is able to do miraculous signs and wonders. Thank You for saving my soul, the most miraculous wonder of all. I believe in You and honor You as my Savior and Lord. Help me to stay focused on You for who You are and give You the praise You deserve. In Jesus' name, Amen.

CREAM OF CHICKEN AND POTATO SOUP

1 small onion, chopped
1 tablespoon butter
3 cups water and 3 chicken bouillon cubes
3 carrots, diced
2 potatoes, peeled and diced
2 cups cooked chicken (leftovers fine)
1 teaspoon parsley flakes
1 teaspoon salt
½ teaspoon pepper
¼ cup flour
1 cup milk
1 (8-ounce) package cream cheese

Sauté onion in butter 2 minutes; add water, bouillon, carrots, potatoes, chicken, parsley, salt, and pepper. Cover; boil 15 minutes. Mix milk and flour together until smooth. Add slowly to soup, stirring until blended. Bring to simmer; cook 2 minutes, stirring constantly. Add cream cheese and heat until cheese is melted.

June 8

Verily, verily, I say unto you, He that heareth my word, and believeth on him that sent me, hath everlasting life, and shall not come into condemnation; but is passed from death unto life.

—JOHN 5:24, KJV

As the Son of God, Jesus maintains unity, communion, and authority with the Father. God has given Him the power to give life, the right to judge, the right to divine honor, and the power to give eternal life. Jesus tells us that whoever hears and believes His Word will not face eternal judgment and death but will be granted pardon and life eternal. To hear and believe are not to be one-time actions but an ongoing process. Our assurance of eternal life is conditional, according to our present faith, and not by an experience we had long ago. God's grace is free and available for any who follow the guidelines He has given us in His Word. It is imperative that we daily walk in His truth and live in obedience to the Father's will. This is what it means to cross over from death to life.

Father: Thank You for sending Your Son to give me eternal life and the power to live according to Your will. Forgive me if there is any unconfessed sin in my heart and help me to live in accordance to Your will and way. Show me those things that weaken my relationship with You and help me to abandon them. May I be found faithful to Your Word and receive eternal life when You return to judge our lives. In Jesus' name, Amen.

CARIBBEAN CHICKEN WINGS

3 pounds chicken wings, separated at joints
½ cup melted butter
1 ¼ cups fine dry bread crumbs
1 (14-ounce) can pineapple chunks
⅓ cup honey
1 clove garlic, crushed
1 tablespoon lemon juice
1 tablespoon Worcestershire sauce
¾ cup ketchup
½ teaspoon ground ginger

Roll wings in butter, then crumbs; put in greased baking dish. Bake 30 minutes at 400 degrees. Drain pineapple; reserve juice. Add water to make ¾ cup. Combine juice with other ingredients except pineapple; pour over wings. Bake 30 minutes more until chicken tender. Add pineapple during last 5 minutes.

June 9

And Jesus said unto them, I am the bread of life: he that cometh to me shall never hunger; and he that believeth on me shall never thirst.

—JOHN 6:35, KJV

I N THE GOSPEL of John, Jesus refers to Himself as *I Am* seven different ways, and in this particular verse He invites us to experience Him as the *Bread of Life*. Jesus had just performed the miracle of feeding five thousand people with only two fish and five loaves of bread when the people began trying to coerce Him into feeding them again. The crowd had eaten until they were satisfied, but their minds were focused on physical food and not spiritual food. Jesus had compassion on them, but He knew they needed something more than edible food. He reminded them again that He, the Christ, is the Living Bread from heaven and the sustenance that nourishes our souls. The bread is His flesh that He sacrificially gave for each one of us so that we might have life eternal. Just as physical food has to be eaten to bring satiety and nourishment to the body, so does spiritual food have to be eaten. This is done by reading the Bible, praying, and following the plan God has for our lives.

Lord Jesus: You are the great I Am and the Bread of Life that satisfies our hungry and thirsty souls. When we come seeking to know You as Savior and Lord, our needs are met and You are glorified. Help me always to be satisfied with the daily food that I receive from You. In Jesus' name, Amen.

BAKED FRENCH TOAST

1 (1-pound) loaf French bread, cut into 1-inch slices
8 eggs
2 cups milk
1 ½ cups half-and-half cream (milk okay)
2 teaspoons vanilla extract
¼ teaspoon cinnamon
¾ cup butter
1 ⅓ cups brown sugar
¼ cup light corn syrup

Butter a 9x13-inch baking dish; arrange slices of bread on bottom. In large bowl, beat together eggs, milk, cream, vanilla, and cinnamon. Pour over bread slices; cover and refrigerate overnight or 6–8 hours. Next morning, in small saucepan, combine butter, brown sugar and corn syrup; heat until bubbling. Pour over bread and egg mixture. Bake at 375 degrees, uncovered, 40 minutes.

June 10

For my Father's will is that everyone who looks to the Son and believes in him shall have eternal life, and I will raise him up at the last day.

—JOHN 6:40

JESUS DIED FOR one and all! It is His perfect will, along with the Father's, that none should perish. When He went to the cross, He had each and every one of us on His mind. This verse so clearly reiterates what we are told in John 3:16 that God loved the world so much He sent His only Son to die so that whoever believes in Him shall live forever. It is the Father's desire that we all accept His plan of salvation and never forsake it. However, it is our choice whether or not we look to Jesus and believe in Him or reject Him and perish. Our hearts are joyful in knowing that by receiving and believing in Christ we receive spiritual life and share in the redemptive benefits of His death on the cross. We are saved by God's grace and the regenerating power of the Holy Spirit when we first hear and receive Christ as our Savior. We continue to be saved and receive grace by reading, obeying, and absorbing the truth of His Word into our hearts and lives.

Saving Father: Thank You for thinking about me when You sent Your only Son to the cross to die for my sins. Thank You for Your Holy Spirit who guides and directs me to follow after You. Help me to keep my faith in You strong, never to take advantage of Your wonderful mercy and grace. It is my desire to serve You all the days of my life. In Jesus' name, Amen.

BUFFALO CHICKEN DIP

1 (8-ounce) package Philadelphia cream cheese, softened
¼ cup blue cheese dressing + ¼ cup ranch dressing *or* ½ cup of one type dressing
⅓ cup buffalo wing sauce (Frank's preferred)
1 ½ cups finely chopped cooked chicken (canned chicken okay)
4 ounces cheddar cheese, grated

In a bowl, mix well the cream cheese, dressing, and wing sauce. Microwave 1–2 minutes or until cream cheese is melted and mixture thoroughly heated. Add chicken; mix well and either microwave for 3–4 more minutes or pour mixture into a pie dish and bake at 350 degrees for 15 minutes. Sprinkle with cheddar cheese and either microwave until cheese is melted or return pie dish to oven until cheese is melted. Serve hot with crackers, tortilla chips, scoops, or veggie sticks.

June 11

Then said Jesus to those Jews which believed on him, If ye continue in my word, then are ye my disciples indeed; And ye shall know the truth, and the truth will make you free.

—JOHN 8:31–32, KJV

JESUS WAS IN Jerusalem speaking to a group of followers comprised of believers and some who doubted that He was the Son of God. Just as He spoke to the people then, Jesus also wants us to know that there is only one truth that will set us free from sin, destruction, and Satan's bondage: the truth of God's teaching found in the gospel. God provided a way of redemption for all mankind in His beloved Son. We have the opportunity to believe the truth that is in God's Word and apply it to our lives or reject it and pay the consequences of sin. Sin is like quicksand—it may be fun at first to play in it, but then it sucks us steadily downward and soon we are enslaved to its death grip. Yes! We were once bound in sin, but Jesus came and set us free. He lived, died, rose again, and has defeated sin, death, and Satan. He has won freedom for the world, and He offers that freedom to all who desire to have it through the gospel of Jesus.

Dear Lord: For the times I didn't walk in Your ways and was deceived by the enemy, being pulled into the quicksand of sin, I repent. As I continue to read and study Your Word, may I become stronger and more steadfast in my relationship with You. For my family and friends, I pray they too receive Your mercy and grace for their transgressions and be set free by the truth of Your Word. In Jesus' name, Amen.

STUFFED GREEN PEPPER SOUP

2 pounds ground beef
1 small onion, diced
2 green peppers, chopped
1 ½ cups water
1 (28-ounce) can tomato sauce
1 (28-ounce) can diced tomatoes
1 cup long-grain uncooked rice
2 beef bouillon cubes
2 tablespoons brown sugar
2 teaspoons salt
1 teaspoon pepper
1–2 teaspoons Worcestershire sauce

Brown ground beef; add onion and green pepper; sauté for 2–3 minutes. Add rest of the ingredients and simmer for 30–45 minutes, until rice is done.

June 12

Then said Jesus unto them again, Verily, verily, I say unto you, I am the door of the sheep. All that ever came before me are thieves and robbers: but the sheep did not hear them. I am the door: by me if any man enter in, he shall be saved, and shall go in and out, and find pasture. The thief cometh not, but for to steal, and to kill, and to destroy: I am come that they might have life, and that they might have it more abundantly.

—John 10:7, 9–10, KJV

JESUS CAME TO the world to give us life. He didn't come to condemn us or make our lives miserable. He loves us and wants our lives to be filled with His mercy and goodness. Though He is preparing a beautiful heavenly home where we will live eternally, God wants us to be victorious and prosperous here on earth. Satan, the thief, wants to destroy our lives and rob every good thing from us. He doesn't get blamed enough for the evil of the world and sometimes God is the one we blame instead. But Jesus assures us throughout His Word that He is the giver of life and wants good things for His people. Have you entered the gate and accepted the salvation that God gave us by knowing His Son? Are you enjoying the green pasture that represents the good food we need for our soul? The gate is open; why not enter in?

Thank You, Father, for the open gate that leads to the pasture of bountiful living. You are the giver of life and want only good things for Your children. The enemy has no power to rob and steal from our lives when we put our trust in You. Thank You for saving my soul and for loving me enough to send Your Son so I might have abundant life. In Jesus' name, Amen.

STRAWBERRY LETTUCE SALAD

½ cup slivered almonds
2 tablespoons butter
¼ cup sugar
1 bunch romaine lettuce, torn into pieces
1 pint strawberries, washed and halved
½ medium red onion, thinly sliced

Dressing:

¾ cup mayonnaise
¼ cup milk
2 tablespoons poppy seeds
2 tablespoons vinegar
⅓ cup sugar

In pan on medium heat, sauté almonds in butter and sugar until golden; cool. Combine with lettuce, strawberries, and onion. Mix dressing ingredients in blender. Pour over salad; serve.

June 13

I am the good shepherd: the good shepherd giveth his life for the sheep.

—John 10:11, KJV

A SHEPHERD IS ONE employed in tending, feeding, and guarding sheep. Jesus, the Good Shepherd, indicates the kind of shepherd He is: tender, watchful, loving, devoted, caring, and willing to die for us, His sheep. Sheep are completely reliant on their shepherd to take them where there is food and to protect them from wolves and other predators that would devour them if left unprotected. We too are reliant on our Shepherd to protect us from the evil and perverse world, but we first must be willing to follow after Him and obey His voice. Just as sheep know the voice of their shepherd because of the time spent with him while in his care, we too will know the voice of our Good Shepherd when we bask in His presence while in His care.

Father: You are the Good Shepherd, and Your desire is to protect me from all evil. You have provided a safe place for Your sheep, but only when we follow after Your voice. Thank You for laying down Your life so I might live victoriously under Your care. In Jesus' name, Amen.

CHICKEN PAPRIKA WITH DUMPLINGS

1 stick butter
1 large onion, quartered
1 tablespoon paprika
1 teaspoon salt
¼ teaspoon pepper
4–5 pounds cut up chicken pieces
1 ½ cups water
1 tablespoon flour
2 cups sour cream

In large pan, sauté onions in butter until tender. Mix in paprika, salt, and pepper. Add chicken and lightly brown. Add water; cover and simmer over low heat until chicken tender, about 45 minutes. Mix flour with sour cream; mix with chicken. Keep warm until dumplings done.

Dumplings:

3 eggs, beaten
1 teaspoon salt
2 ½ cups flour
½ cup water

Combine all ingredients. Beat with spoon until smooth. Drop by a teaspoonful into pan of boiling salted water (about 2 quarts water with 1 tablespoon salt added); cook until done, about 10 minutes. Drain dumplings and add to chicken mixture. Serve.

June 14

Jesus said unto her, I am the resurrection, and the life: he that believeth in me, though he were dead, yet shall he live: And whosoever liveth and believeth in me shall never die. Believest thou this?

—JOHN 11:25–26, KJV

MARY AND MARTHA had just lost their brother, Lazarus, and were so upset. They had sent for Jesus to come, hoping He would heal Lazarus' body before he died; but Jesus came two days later and death had already claimed their loved one's life. Jesus loved Lazarus and also was very sad. He even wept when he saw the extreme sadness of the family. Jesus comforted them by letting them know that though Lazarus was dead, because He was a believer, he would never die.

Jesus wants us also to know that if we are grieving the loss of a loved one's death, it is not a sign of weakness. If anything, it's a sign of how much we loved that individual. As much as Jesus wants to comfort us after a loss, He also wants to fill us with hope in the promise of the resurrection. Every life is in His hands; not a single sparrow falls to the ground without Him knowing. How much more would His compassion be for His children who are grieving a loss or heartache? Jesus knows and understands loss, sadness, and grief, and we must let Him embrace us with His arms of love.

Loving Father: Thank You for restoring the dead person I once was and for raising me up to live a new life in, with, and for You. Hope and joy fill my heart because of Your great love. I know I will see my loved ones again, and that is such a sustaining promise. Help my friends and family who are sad with losses and heartaches to find peace and hope. In Jesus' name, Amen.

HIDDEN VALLEY CHICKEN

2 pounds boneless, skinless chicken breasts
1 stick butter, melted
¾ cup grated Parmesan cheese
¾ cup cornflake crumbs
1 package (dry) Hidden Valley Ranch dressing

Wash and dry chicken breasts. Dip in butter. Mix dry ingredients all together; dip chicken in them, coating well. Pour extra butter in bottom of casserole dish. Arrange chicken pieces in dish; bake at 350 degrees for 45 minutes, or until juices run clear. Baste every 15 minutes.

June 15

Jesus wept.

—JOHN 11:35, KJV

MARY AND MARTHA were sisters of Lazarus, and they all were very close friends of Jesus. When the sisters went and told Jesus that their brother was very ill and dying, He showed concern but did not immediately go to him. In fact, Jesus stayed in the town where He was for two more days. Finally, when He went to see Lazarus, the sisters met Jesus with the sad news that it was too late and their beloved brother had died. They were upset that Jesus took so long to get there and fell to His feet weeping.

When Jesus saw their intense sadness, He was deeply moved in His spirit and also wept. This mere act of humility revealed the deep emotion Christ feels for all of us. Just knowing that He has compassion on us and feels the same sadness we feel when we lose someone very special to us should bring us comfort. Jesus showed sympathetic love, not only because His friend died, but because of the sadness of the sisters. Even though Jesus knew He was going to raise Lazarus from the dead, His mercy and compassion allowed Him to be sorrowful. God loves us that much, that though He is deity, He is not without feelings for His children. He is aware of everything we go through and cares deeply about our sorrow and pain.

Dear Lord: Thank You for Your understanding and sympathetic love, especially when we have lost loved ones. Just knowing You care brings comfort to our souls. Help me to grow in my faith and trust You in every situation that arises. May I have compassion for my brothers and sisters who are suffering and show them Your comfort and mercy. In Jesus' name, Amen.

CHICKEN WITH MUSHROOMS

3 cups sliced mushrooms
4 skinless, boneless chicken breast halves
2 eggs, beaten
¾ cup chicken broth
1 cup bread crumbs
2 tablespoons butter
6 ounces mozzarella cheese, sliced

Place half of mushrooms in a greased 9x13-inch baking dish. Dip chicken into beaten eggs, then roll in bread crumbs. In skillet, melt butter over medium heat. Brown both sides of chicken in skillet. Place chicken on top of mushrooms, arrange remaining mushrooms on chicken, and top with mozzarella cheese. Add chicken broth to pan. Bake in 350-degree oven for 30–35 minutes, or until chicken is no longer pink.

June 16

Then Mary took about a pint of pure nard, an expensive perfume; she poured it on Jesus'
feet and wiped his feet with her hair. And the house was filled with the fragrance of the
perfume.

—JOHN 12:3

SIX DAYS BEFORE the Passover, a dinner was given in Jesus' honor at the home of His friend,
Lazarus. We know this as "the Last Supper" because it was the last time Jesus and His disciples
would take bread together and have fellowship before He was crucified. Lazarus' two sisters, Mary
and Martha, were there; Martha was serving the meal, and her sister Mary was to be helping. But as
usual, Martha was doing all the work while Mary seemed mesmerized by the presence of Jesus. When
everyone was around the table eating and Martha was serving, Mary took a pint bottle of very expensive perfume and broke it on Jesus' feet. She then took her hair and wiped His feet. Everyone watched
in awe, but Judas Iscariot objected and became very angry. He pretended to be concerned that the perfume was wasted when it could have been sold with the proceeds going to the poor.

Though Mary probably knew she might receive ridicule and objection to her extravagant act of love for
Jesus, it was worth it to her. Jesus knew Mary would be using the perfume at His burial, but Mary was so
full of love for Jesus, she couldn't wait. Mary's love was truly outrageous and profound. In what ways do
we show Jesus our love, and what sacrifices do we make for Him? Would we, like Mary, be found guilty of
pouring out extravagant measures of love on the feet of Jesus?

*Lord Jesus: You are the great and mighty One whom I love, respect, and honor. Forgive me
when my actions don't identify what true love for You really should be. Help me to release
all that I have so my life will portray extravagant worship to You. In Jesus' name, Amen.*

ITALIAN BEEF (crockpot)

3–4 pound rump or sirloin roast
3–4 cups water
1 package Good Seasons Zesty Italian dressing mix
1 small jar pepperoncinis, undrained
1 chopped onion
4 cloves garlic, chopped
1 package brown gravy mix

Put all ingredients in a crockpot, except gravy mix. Cook on high 5–6 hours. Add gravy mix
and cook another 1–2 hours. Serve on firm buns.

June 17

I have come into the world as a light, so that no one who believes in me should live in darkness.

—JOHN 12:46

ONE OF THE great stories in the book of John is the one of Nicodemus. He would come to Jesus at night and listen to Him teach. One night, Jesus told him that those who love the truth come to the light. Later, Nicodemus spoke up for Jesus, even though he was ridiculed for it. Then at the worst possible time politically and religiously, he showed himself as Jesus' disciple when he took the broken and dead body of Jesus and helped Joseph of Arimathea place Him in a tomb. Nicodemus didn't stay in the darkness, and neither should we. Jesus is the Light of the world, and all those who believe in Him will see Him as a Light in their life. To know Jesus in this way simply requires asking God to forgive all the evil we have done in the darkness of the world. If we ask, He will cleanse us and become Lord of everything we do, say, listen to, think about, and so on. Jesus loves each of us and has overcome the darkness with His marvelous light.

Heavenly Father: Thank You for the light You are in a dark, dark world. The darkness that came when You gave Your life on Calvary could not put Your light out, and it shone even more brightly after Your resurrection. Forgive me when I don't seek the light of Your way and stumble in my own steps of self-will. You are the light of my life, and I love You with all my heart. In Jesus' name, Amen.

ZESTY ROASTED VEGETABLES

½ pound whole mushrooms
1 ½ cups baby carrots
1 medium onion, peeled, cut into ½-inch-thick wedges
1 large yellow, red, or green bell pepper, cut into 8 strips
1/3 cup Zesty Italian salad dressing
1/3 cup grated Parmesan cheese, divided

Toss vegetables with dressing and ¼ cup cheese. Spread into greased 9x13-inch baking dish. Bake 30 minutes at 375 degrees until vegetables are tender; stir after 15 minutes. Sprinkle with remaining cheese.

June 18

Simon Peter asked him, "Lord, where are you going?" Jesus replied, "Where I am going, you cannot follow now, but you will follow later." Peter asked, "Lord, why can't I follow you now? I will lay down my life for you." Then Jesus answered, "Will you really lay down your life for me? I tell you the truth, before the rooster crows, you will disown me three times!"

—JOHN 13:36–38

AT THE LAST Supper Jesus shared with His disciples before His crucifixion, He announced that one of them would betray Him. They were all astonished because it turned out to be Judas Iscariot who was indeed the betrayer. Jesus taught them about humility and love and how they must show the world they are followers of Christ by loving one another. Jesus told them He would be leaving soon and they could not come with Him. The disciples were puzzled. Peter told Jesus he wanted to go with Him and would even lay down his life for Him. Jesus knew Peter really didn't mean it and would deny Him three times before the rooster crowed in the morning. In our lives today, God knows if we are for or against Him. Just as Jesus knew Judas would betray Him and Peter would deny Him, He knows each of our hearts and if we are real or not. As we think about Jesus, His crucifixion, and His resurrection, let's be sure we are real and truly following Christ.

Precious Lord: Thank You for laying down Your life for all the world so we might receive Your mercy and grace and follow after You. Guide me with Your Holy Spirit to be real in my relationship with You. Help me to be a witness to others so they too might experience the free gift of salvation and follow after You. In Jesus' name, Amen.

SPLIT PEA SOUP

2 cups dried split peas (about 1 pound)
2 quarts water and 6–8 chicken bouillon cubes
1 ham bone (preferably with meat attached)
1 onion, chopped
1 cup celery, chopped
¼ teaspoon pepper
4–6 carrots, diced or grated

Heat peas and water to boiling; boil gently for 2 minutes; remove from heat; cover and let stand 1 hour. Add remaining ingredients; heat to boiling. Reduce heat and simmer 2 ½–3 hours or until peas are very soft. Remove bone; trim meat from bone and add to soup. If desired, thin soup with water or milk. Season to taste. May also cook in crockpot for 8 hours on low.

June 19

And I will ask the Father, and He will give you another Counselor to be with you forever—the Spirit of truth. The world cannot accept him, because it neither sees him nor knows him. But you know him, for he lives with you and will be in you.

—JOHN 14:16–17

JESUS CALLS THE Holy Spirit a Counselor or a Helper. The Greek word *Paraclete* means "one called alongside to help." The *Paraclete* is also called the Spirit of Truth, the Comforter and the Supporter because it is the Holy Spirit, or *Paraclete*, who comes alongside the Christian to provide guidance, consolation, and support throughout life's journey. In giving us the Holy Spirit, Jesus shows that leadership is not so much the ability to walk ahead of someone as it is the willingness to walk beside someone. Followers need support as well as direction—a hand that helps as well as a finger that points. Isn't it just like God to not only send us a heavenly Father in Himself, but also a Savior and a Helper? He knew we would need someone to fill that role and walk with us through the storms of life.

Heavenly Father: I praise and thank You for the awesome God You are. You sent Your Holy Spirit to walk beside me each and every day. Thank You! Forgive me when I take advantage of Your love and fail to praise You for all You have done. Help me to trust You more and rely on my Helper to guide me in everything I do and everywhere I go. In Jesus' name, Amen.

MEXICAN CHICKEN CASSEROLE

4 boneless chicken breast halves, cooked, cubed
1 (10-ounce) can tomatoes with green chiles
1 can cream of mushroom soup
1 can cream of chicken soup
1 (4-ounce) can taco sauce
½ cup chicken broth or water with 1 bouillon cube dissolved
1 (10-ounce) package taco chips or Doritos
½–¾ cup grated American cheese or Mexican blend

In saucepan, combine all ingredients, except chips and cheese; heat thoroughly. Line bottom of greased baking dish with taco chips. Pour soup mixture overtop. Top with grated cheese. Bake at 350 degrees until bubbly and hot.

June 20

I am the true vine, and my Father is the gardener. He cuts off every branch in me that bears no fruit, while every branch that does bear fruit he prunes so that it will be even more fruitful.

—JOHN 15:1–2

WHEN PRUNING A tree, two things must take place. First, all the dead wood must be removed; second, the live wood must be cut back drastically. Dead wood is ugly, unproductive, and harbors insects and disease that may cause the vine to rot. Live wood must be trimmed back in order to prevent such heavy growth that the life of the vine goes into the wood rather than into the fruit. The vineyards in the early spring look like a collection of barren, bleeding stumps, but in the fall they are filled with luxuriant purple grapes. Just as the farmer uses the pruning knife on his vines, God cuts dead wood out from among His children. Oftentimes we may feel that God has cut back too much of our living wood and has forgotten or mistreated us. We feel He has pruned us way beyond what He should have. But God knows what He is doing and sees the whole picture of our lives; we see only the present. Nevertheless, from those who have suffered the most, there often comes the greatest fruitfulness.

Wonderful Father: Thank You for pruning me and for removing from my life those things that hinder my growth and commitment. You are the great Gardener and know exactly what I need. Thank You for blessing me with good fruit so I might serve You better. Forgive me when I grumble about the pruning process. Help me to use my fruitfulness to touch other's lives so they too might come to know You personally. In Jesus' name, Amen.

POTATO SALAD

5–6 large red-skinned potatoes
4 hard-boiled eggs
½ cup celery, finely diced
1 small sweet onion, diced
1 cup Miracle Whip
1 tablespoon mustard
2 tablespoons vinegar
2 tablespoons sugar
½ teaspoon salt
¼ teaspoon pepper

Boil potatoes in water until tender, about 20 minutes. Remove skin, let cool, and dice. Boil eggs 5–6 minutes; remove shell, cool, and dice. In bowl, mix Miracle Whip, mustard, vinegar, sugar, salt, and pepper until smooth. Mix all ingredients together; refrigerate until cold.

June 21

These things I have spoken unto you, that in my ye might have peace. In the world ye shall have tribulation: but be of good cheer; I have overcome the world.

—JOHN 16:33, KJV

LIFE CAN SOMETIMES be tough. The world we live in is a place of struggle and heartache. Jesus said that in this world we *will* have trouble. Take note that He didn't say *if* we have trouble. In the midst of our struggles, we can be assured that God is with us and will be with us every step of the way. Perhaps you are struggling today with a loss or a health problem, a wayward child, financial struggles, an unfaithful spouse, or any number of other situations. Jesus reminds us to not give up ("take heart") for He has overcome the world! No matter what happens during our lifetime on earth, we will be victors in the end as long as we know and serve the Lord. Jesus already has won the battle for us. One day all our heartaches will be over and there will be no more need for tears, except tears of joy. We who know Christ will share in His great triumph and live eternally in a place called heaven.

Dear Lord: When trouble comes again and again, I often don't know which way to turn. But then I call on Your name and, as always, You are there. You comfort me and bring me peace. No matter what I go through, I know You will never forsake me. Thank You for what You did on the cross for me so that I might have peace. In Jesus' name, Amen.

BUFFALO CHICKEN SOUP

3–5 boneless, skinless chicken breasts
2 tablespoons butter
½ cup chopped celery
½ cup chopped onion
2 (14-ounce) cans chicken broth
1 ½ cups milk
1 teaspoon hot sauce (such as Frank's)
1 ½ cups (8 ounces) mozzarella cheese
1 ¼ cups (6 ounces) crumbled blue cheese
½ cup (2 ounces) shredded Parmesan cheese
⅓ cup all purpose flour

In pan with small amount water, cook chicken until done; dice. In soup pot, melt butter over medium heat. Add celery and onion; cook and stir until tender. Stir in broth, chicken, milk, and hot sauce; simmer on medium-low for 15 minutes. In a bowl, toss together mozzarella, 1 cup blue cheese, Parmesan cheese, and flour. Add gradually to soup, stirring after each addition, just until melted. Top with remaining blue cheese and additional hot sauce, if desired.

June 22

Then Pilate therefore took Jesus, and scourged him. And the soldiers platted a crown of thorns, and put it on his head, and they put on him a purple robe, And said, Hail, King of the Jews! And they smote him with their hands.

—JOHN 19:1–3, KJV

When the chief priests therefore and officers saw him, they cried out, saying, Crucify him crucify him.

—JOHN 19:6, KJV

And he bearing his cross went forth into a place call the place of a skull, which is call in the Hebrew Golgotha: Where they crucified him, and two other with him, on either side one, and Jesus in the midst.

—JOHN 19:17–18, KJV

ONCE AGAIN, THE people Jesus loved betrayed Him, mocked Him, denied Him, beat Him, spit on Him and eventually crucified Him on a cross, naked and humiliated; yet, we call it Good Friday. It was good in that Jesus, who is the very Word of God, was born to die. Ironically, His death becomes His glory. Though He appeared helpless, Christ was very much in control and knew what He was doing. As the Son of God, He had the power to completely turn things around and avoid death on a cross, but because of His great love for us, He didn't.

Did the Romans or Jews alone crucify Jesus? No! Each one of us is guilty of His brutal death, but it was the only way God could bring us into a relationship with Himself. Jesus is the mediator between God and man, and without Him paying the price He did with His death, there would be no remission of sins for us.

If each one of us is guilty of Christ's death, how do we receive pardon and not be penalized for such a horrible thing? There is only one way: we must believe the story of Christ, ask Him to forgive us of all the sin we have committed, receive Him into our hearts, and obey His holy Word.

Father: I admit that I have gone my own way and sinned in thought, word, and deed against You. I'm sorry, and I repent of all those things I did that weren't according to Your Word. I believe You died for me, took my sins upon Your own body, and paid the price I should have paid. Come into my life and fill me with Your Holy Spirit so I might forever walk in Your steps. In Jesus' name, Amen.

Today's recipe found on page 384 CORN AND SHRIMP CHOWDER

June 23

The third time he [Jesus] said to him [Peter], "Simon son of John, do you love me?"

—JOHN 21:17

PETER WAS UPSET because Jesus had already asked him twice if he loved Him and Peter said that he did. But Jesus knew in His heart that Peter's love was not real. Jesus also knows our hearts and if we are real or not. We might say we love Him, but do we really? And if we do, can we prove it? What the Lord Jesus is looking for in us is that we love Him above everything and everyone else. We may think we can impress God with our knowledge, bank accounts, or our accomplishments, but if the risen Lord were to do a heart examination on each one of us today, He would ask us one question: "Do you love Me? Do you love Me?" It isn't enough to just say the words, "I love you." The Lord enjoys hearing these words from us, just as we love to hear them from others. However, we must back up our words with our actions. Love must show action. Let's say we are going to court and have to prove our love for Christ to win the case. Would we have enough evidence to prove ourselves guilty of love? Or would the righteous Judge have to ask us a second and third time, "Do you love Me?"

Father: I love You and praise You for being the Lord of my life. Forgive me when I fall away from the truth of Your Word and go about my life as though it is all about me. Give me strength to love others and serve them, knowing this pleases You and shows my love is real. Help me to put You first above all and to love You more than life itself. In Jesus' name, Amen.

CHICKEN POT ROAST

2 tablespoons oil or melted butter
3–4 boneless, skinless, chicken breasts
3 cups flour
1 teaspoon pepper
1 teaspoon seasoned salt
½ teaspoon poultry seasoning (optional)
2 stalks celery, cut in half
6 red potatoes, left whole
1 onion, quartered
6 whole carrots *or* 12 baby carrots
1 can cream of mushroom soup
2 cups water + 2 chicken bouillon cubes

Put oil or butter in bottom of Dutch oven or large baking dish. Mix together flour and seasonings and coat chicken pieces on both sides; place in dish. Sprinkle remaining flour over chicken. Add all other ingredients and cover with lid or foil. Bake at 325 degrees for 2–2 ½ hours, or until done.

June 24

For John baptized with water, but in a few days you will be baptized with the Holy Spirit.

—ACTS 1:5

THE APOSTLE LUKE quoted these words of Jesus about a different baptism other than by water. Jesus' death on the cross did not bring His life to a final end, but after three days in the tomb He arose and showed Himself to His disciples. They spent much time together over the next forty days as Jesus told them the work they should do. He gave them the mission of carrying the gospel to the whole world but warned them that in doing so, they would not be popular. Many would hate them and try to stop them from preaching God's Word.

Jesus told the disciples they were not yet ready to go but were to stay in Jerusalem for a short time until they were baptized with the Holy Spirit. The word baptize means "to dip or immerse." Jesus meant they would be saturated or possessed fully with the Holy Spirit, much as a sponge dipped in water becomes soaked. It was essential for them to receive the Holy Spirit before they embarked on their mission to the world because they needed His power and guidance. If the disciples relied on mere human ability, they would fail, for it is impossible to accomplish any work for God without His help. God's will is that we all be baptized or filled with the Holy Spirit so we are empowered to be His witnesses.

Father: Thank You for Your Holy Spirit who comes and dwells within us when we accept Christ as our Savior. Thank You for the baptism of the Holy Spirit that gives us boldness and power to be witnesses for You. Help me to use the power and resources You have given me to do Your work. In Jesus' name, Amen.

SAUCY MEXICAN CHICKEN

1 pound boneless, skinless chicken breast halves (4 small breasts)
1 (16-ounce) jar thick and chunky salsa
1 (15-ounce) can black beans, rinsed
1 cup shredded cheddar cheese

Cook chicken in pan on medium-high heat about 4 minutes each side or until browned. Add salsa and beans. Bring to boil; cover. Simmer on medium-low 5 minutes or until chicken thoroughly cooked. Top with cheese. Remove from heat; let stand, covered, 5 minutes until cheese melts.

June 25

But ye shall receive power, after that the Holy Ghost is come upon you: and ye shall be my witnesses unto me both in Jerusalem, and in all Judea, and Samaria, and unto the uttermost part of the earth.

—ACTS 1:8, KJV

THE BAPTISM IN the Holy Spirit is the promise of the Father (Luke 24:49) given by Jesus to all believers who desire this free gift. The Holy Spirit empowers us and increases our effectiveness to be witnesses for Christ. When we are baptized in the Holy Spirit, the presence and person of Jesus becomes more intimate and real, and our desire to love, honor and please our Savior will continue to be an ever-growing desire. Our lives will also manifest the likeness of Christ, and He will be glorified in our words, deeds, and actions. It should be the goal of every Spirit-empowered believer to strive to win lost souls for Christ. This is done by witnessing in Jerusalem (our homes, schools, neighborhoods, and places of employment), Judea and Samaria (communities, cities, and states further away), and the ends of the earth (foreign countries). Our witness can be done through our prayers, words, actions, and financial support. The main thing is that we stay strong in our faith and seek the Holy Spirit's power and guidance each and every day as we proclaim the message of Christ to a lost and dying world.

Dear Lord: You have blessed me abundantly with all Your wonderful gifts, and I praise You for them. Thank You for Your Holy Spirit who gives me the strength and wisdom I need to be a witness for Your cause. As I share Your Word with those who are near and far, I ask for Your divine help and guidance. Soften the hearts of those I reach out to and prepare them to receive the message of Your great love. In Jesus' name, Amen.

NACHOS SUPREME DINNER

1 pound ground beef
1 packet of taco seasoning mix
1 can tomato soup
1 ½ cups water
1 ½ cups uncooked instant rice
Salsa (favorite kind)
Shredded cheddar cheese
Shredded lettuce
Tortilla chips
Sour cream

Brown ground beef; drain. Add taco seasoning, soup, water, and rice. Cover; cook on low 5 minutes, until rice soft. Serve with favorite toppings and chips for dipping.

June 26

Repent ye therefore, and be converted, that your sins may be blotted out, when the times of refreshing shall come from the presence of the Lord. And he shall send Jesus Christ, which before was preached unto you.

—ACTS 3:19–20, KJV

THERE ARE THOSE times in our lives when everything seems to be going well, and then there are the times when we feel a lull or low time. It may seem as though the whole world has come against us and we just don't know how we can go on. Maybe we aren't feeling well physically, sleeping well, are depressed, irritable, or tired. We just can't seem to get a handle on things and wonder if joy and peace will ever be ours to hold.

It's during these times that we need to stop, examine our hearts, and do a spiritual inventory. Is serving God our main priority in life? Are we taking time to pray and read our Bibles each day? Have we even prayed and asked Jesus to come into our hearts and forgive us of our sin? Maybe we have but really don't want Him to take precedence over the things we do, the places we go, and all the decisions we make.

Our relationship with Christ must be passionate and real. It means setting aside time each day to study God's Word and pray. It's putting God first in everything we do. If we would do the things the Lord asks of us, He will keep His Word and send Jesus Christ, who has been appointed to come and refresh our souls.

Dear God: Thank You for always hearing my pleas for help. Forgive me for not taking time to be with You as I should. Help me to organize my schedule so Your agenda takes precedence. If I do what You have asked of me, You will bring times of refreshing to my soul. Today and always I put my trust and faith in You. I want to see You glorified in my life. In Jesus' name, Amen.

SMOTHERED CHICKEN

4–6 boneless, skinless chicken breast halves
Garlic powder and seasoned salt to taste
1 tablespoon vegetable oil
8 ounces fresh sliced mushrooms
6–8 ounces shredded white cheese
½ cup chopped green onions
½ cup bacon bits (optional)

Sprinkle chicken with garlic powder and seasoned salt. In large nonstick skillet over medium heat, brown chicken in oil; turn. Top with mushrooms, cheese, green onions, and bacon. Cover and cook until chicken thoroughly done.

June 27

Neither is there salvation in any other: for there is none other name under heaven given among men, whereby we must be saved.

—ACTS 4:12, KJV

THE MEANING OF this verse permeates throughout the entire New Testament and holds the divine purpose of every believer. Each one of us is born separated from Christ and remains in a state of hopelessness and lostness until that time when we yield ourselves completely over to Christ and are saved. This is the same desolate situation the entire world is in and, unless drawn by the Holy Spirit and brought to repentance in Christ, they will spend eternity in hell. Though God's power and deity are evident all around us, the majority of mankind refuses to accept His mercy and grace and continues in a life of unrighteousness and disobedience to His Word. God, in His grace and mercy, provided a plan of salvation in His Son, Jesus. Through Him and through Him alone is God's forgiveness available. Jesus says in John 14:6 (KJV), "I am the way, and the truth, and the life: no man cometh to the Father, but by me." As Christians, it is our duty to proclaim the gospel to the whole world, trusting that God has so providentially ordered things that through us the good news will be brought to persons who God knew would respond if they heard it.

Dear heavenly Father: Thank You for Your wonderful plan of salvation in Jesus Christ. There are many religions in the world, but not one is able to save and bring hope to the lost outside of You. Your name is above all, and I rejoice at the privilege of knowing You as my Savior. Help me to be a good witness of Your love and grace so that many come to call on Your name and also experience salvation. In Jesus' name, Amen.

RICE AND SOUR CREAM CASSEROLE

3 cups cooked rice
2 cups sour cream
½ teaspoon pepper
1 cup chicken broth
2 cans green chiles, drained and chopped
1 cup Monterey Jack cheese, grated
2 cups cheddar cheese

Mix together the cooked rice, sour cream, pepper, broth, and chiles. Mix cheeses together; reserve 1 cup for topping. Stir cheeses with rice mixture. Pour into greased baking dish; top with reserved cheese. Bake at 350 degrees for 30 minutes.

June 28

Believe on the Lord Jesus Christ, and thou shalt be saved, and they house.

—ACTS 16:31, KJV

THIS WAS PAUL'S answer to a jailor who asked him how he might be saved. The apostle Paul and his assistant Silas were on a missionary journey in Philippi when they were brutally beaten and thrown into prison after Paul cast a demonic spirit out of a slave girl. Her owners used her to do fortune-telling and now she would not be able to make money for them. Paul and Silas suffered great physical pain and humiliation during that ordeal as they were severely flogged, put into chains, and thrown into a dark and deplorable prison. It was about the midnight hour, and in their distress they began praying and singing hymns to God as the other prisoners listened. All of a sudden, a great earthquake came and shook the foundation of the prison, causing all the prison doors to open and the release of all the chains that had them bound. The jailor who was commanded to carefully guard Paul and Silas nearly took his own life when he woke up, thinking all the prisoners had escaped. Paul informed him that they were all there. The terrified jailor and his family came to know Christ that day, not only because Paul and Silas prayed for that to happen, but also because of their remarkable act of love and forgiveness toward those who had wronged them. Paul and Silas demonstrated the ability we all have to *choose* to praise God in the midst of our persecution, circumstances, and disappointments. In praising God no matter what the outward conditions are, He will provide the inner peace, joy, and grace we need to live a victorious life in Christ Jesus.

Lord Jesus: Thank You for being my joy and strength even in the midst of storms. I choose to praise You, no matter how I feel and no matter how hopeless my situations seem to be. You are worthy of praise in the mornings, in the afternoons, and in the evenings of my days. In the rain and in the sunshine, I praise Your name. In Jesus' name, Amen.

BAKED GARLIC CHICKEN

4 boneless, skinless chicken breasts
4 teaspoons lemon juice
2 garlic cloves, minced
2 teaspoons vegetable oil

Mix lemon juice, garlic, and oil in bowl. Put chicken breasts in pan; pour juice over them. Bake at 375 degrees for 30 minutes until chicken done (juices run clear).

June 29

I am not ashamed of the gospel, because it is the power of God for the salvation of everyone who believes, first for the Jew, then for the Gentile.

—Romans 1:16

ARE YOU EVER embarrassed to be identified as a Christian? Do friends, coworkers, or family members know where you stand on certain moral issues? Are unholy conversations, such as gossip or indecent jokes, going places or doing things that would jeopardize your Christian testimony all because of peer pressure in a place you find yourself? Once we compromise our Christian morals and enter into the same careless behavior as our non-Christian peers, it is hard to change. It's best to take a firm stand from the very beginning and let others know what we will and will not do and why. The apostle Paul felt no shame in the message of Christ, for he saw it as the power of God that transforms lives. Everywhere he went, he shared the gospel, even though he knew it might mean imprisonment or torture. We must not delay in making things right with the Lord and repent today of all our sin. As we turn our lives over to God and begin to take a stand for righteousness, it will get easier and God will honor our efforts.

Father God: Thank You for saving my soul and for giving me the Holy Spirit to guide me in choosing right from wrong. I repent of any unconfessed sin in my life and ask for Your help in making decisions that only honor You. Your gospel is powerful, and I want it to control everything I say and do. In Jesus' name, Amen.

SOUTHWEST WHITE CHILI

1 tablespoon oil
¼ cup chopped onion
1–2 pounds boneless, skinless chicken breasts, diced
1 cup water plus 1 chicken bouillon cube
1 (4-ounce) can chopped green chiles
1 (20-ounce) can northern or cannellini white beans
1 teaspoon garlic powder
½ teaspoon oregano
½ teaspoon cilantro leaves
½ teaspoon ground red pepper
1 teaspoon ground cumin
2 green onions, chopped
Monterey Jack cheese, grated

Heat oil in large pan over med-high heat; add chicken and onions. Cook 5–10 minutes, until onions tender and chicken no longer pink; stir in broth, chiles, and spices; simmer 20 minutes. Stir in entire contents of beans; simmer 5 minutes. If more broth is desired, add 1 more cup water plus 1 chicken bouillon cube. Heat through and serve. Top with green onions and cheese.

June 30

The wrath of God is being revealed from Heaven against all the godlessness and wickedness of men who suppress the truth by their wickedness, since what may be known about God is plain to them, because God has made it plain to them.

—ROMANS 1:18–19

FROM THE BEGINNING of time, God has revealed His eternal power and divine nature in everything He did. We were created with a desire to know and serve the Lord, but some who say they know Him don't obey His Word. Instead, their thoughts are futile and foolish and their hearts have become dark and hard for the things of God. They worship the world and everything in it. The preaching of the gospel no longer moves them to repentance, and their fear of God's wrath is gone. This is not a good place to be. Unless there is a total conversion, it is probable that these ones will die and forever be in hell. What must we do, then, for those we see in this state? Pray, pray, and pray! We must pray that the Holy Spirit would quicken their hearts to repentance before it is too late. We have that hope and on it we stand with the authority given to us as heirs of Christ Jesus.

Dear God: I praise and thank You for revealing Yourself to us in such a plain and wonderful way. You created us to worship You and then lead others to do the same. I pray for my family and friends and all who say they know You but don't honor You as their Savior and Lord. Help me to pray fervently for them that their hearts don't become cold and hard before it's too late. In Jesus' name, Amen.

PIZZA PASTA SALAD

1 pound tri-color rigatoni, cooked
8 ounces pepperoni, sliced
12 ounces grated provolone or mozzarella cheese
Black or green olives to taste, sliced
3 diced tomatoes (preferably Roma)
2 diced green or red peppers
1 diced red or sweet onion
2 tablespoons Parmesan cheese

Dressing:

½ teaspoon oregano
1 tablespoon sugar
⅔ cup vegetable or olive oil
⅓ cup vinegar
Salt and pepper to taste
Garlic salt to taste

Combine all ingredients in a large bowl. Toss with dressing.

Let Freedom Reign

July

July 1

For it is not those who hear the law who are righteous in God's sight, but it is those who obey the law who will be declared righteous.

—Romans 2:13

THE APOSTLE PAUL had been preaching the gospel for about twenty-five years as a missionary and wanted to reiterate the desperate need for the people to display righteousness. He knew both Jew and Gentile alike struggled with sin and needed the justification of Jesus Christ to remove them from God's wrath. The law is the Word of God, the gospel, and the Bible, and it must be respected and obeyed, not only outwardly in the things we do and say but also inwardly in our hearts. It is not enough to *hear* the law taught, as Paul tells us; we must obey it. It's possible to attend church all our lives and listen to the teachers and pastors, but unless we allow the message to permeate our hearts and act in obedience to God's Word, we will be declared unrighteous. God's will is that everyone be saved and enter into eternity with Christ, as we are told in 2 Peter 3:9. Therefore, it is imperative that we as believers tell others about the saving power of Jesus Christ and pray for them with the assurance that God will answer our prayers for their salvation.

Dear God: Thank You for Your Word, the law that brings order and life to my soul. Thank You for the example the apostle Paul has been to the church throughout the centuries. Help me to be obedient to Your teachings so I am declared righteous in Your sight. In Jesus' name, Amen.

PARTY PASTA (similar to lasagna)

2 pounds ground beef
3 cloves garlic, minced
2 medium onions, chopped
1 (15-ounce) can tomato sauce
1 (19-ounce) can stewed tomatoes
1 (10-ounce) can sliced mushrooms
1 teaspoon oregano
1 teaspoon basil
1 teaspoon salt
½ teaspoon pepper
5 cups shell, rigatoni, or other pasta
2 cups sour cream
2 cups grated cheddar cheese
2 cups grated mozzarella cheese

Brown beef in large pan; drain. Add garlic and onions; cook 5 minutes. Add tomato sauce, tomatoes, mushrooms, oregano, basil, salt, and pepper; bring to boil. Reduce heat; simmer 20 minutes. Cook pasta according to package; drain. In large greased dish, layer ½ of pasta, ½ of meat sauce, ½ of sour cream, and ½ of cheddar cheese. Repeat layers, ending with mozzarella. Cover; bake 45 minutes at 350 degrees. Remove cover; return to oven until cheese melted.

July 2

For all have sinned, and come short of the glory of God.

—ROMANS 3:23, KJV

THE BIBLE USES the word *sin* to refer to any activity or pattern of thinking that is independent of God's standards or provisions for human life. God loves us and has our best interests in mind at all times. Because of that, He has laid out standards by which we can live happy, productive lives. These standards are known as the plan of God or the Christian way of life. To fall short of something means to completely miss it. So according to this verse, every person born will go to hell instead of heaven—but it doesn't end there. Verses 24–26 (KJV) say, "Being justified freely by his grace through the redemption that is in Christ Jesus: Whom God hath set forth to be a propitiation through faith in his blood, to declare his righteousness for the remission of sins that are past, through the forbearance of God; To declare, I say, at this time his righteousness: that he might be just, and the justifier of him which believeth in Jesus." This gives every one of us hope in that though we were born and destined to hell, if we choose God's plan of salvation by repenting of all our sin and inviting Christ to rule over our lives, we will be justified freely by His grace. Thus, we will then be destined to the glory of God and live eternally with Him. It's our choice. I've chosen Christ! Have you?

Glorious God: Thank You for Your saving grace and for providing a way of escape for all mankind. I pray for lost souls everywhere that they will be drawn by the Holy Spirit's power and choose Your glory instead of hell. Help me now to burn with passion and share the plan of salvation with the lost. In Jesus' name, Amen.

ANGEL EGGS (deviled eggs)

6 eggs
½ teaspoon onion salt
¼ teaspoon pepper
½ teaspoon mustard
3–4 tablespoons mayonnaise or Miracle Whip
2 teaspoons sugar
Paprika

Place eggs in saucepan; cover with cold water. Heat to boiling; reduce heat to simmer; cook eggs 7 minutes. Pour off water; cover with cold water. After 1 minute, pour off cold water. Remove shells; cut eggs in half lengthwise. Remove yolks; mash with fork. Add seasonings and mayonnaise; mix well. Spoon into eggs; sprinkle with paprika. Cover with plastic wrap; refrigerate.

July 3

For I am not ashamed of the gospel of Christ: for it is the power of God unto salvation to every one that believeth.

—ROMANS 1:16, KJV

THE APOSTLE PAUL was a true servant of Christ. He was a missionary who loved God with his whole heart and was passionate about preaching the gospel and encouraging people wherever he went. He was never ashamed to lift up the name of Jesus and strived to make His power known as the basis of freedom from shame. *Gospel* means "good news." It proclaims God's plan of salvation in Jesus Christ. *Salvation* means "deliverance or rescued from harm" and is received by grace through faith in Christ (Romans 3:24). Salvation is a result of God's grace on the human race and our faith to receive it. The gospel brings out shameful behavior in those who will not believe it, and it gives freedom from shame to those who do. If the gospel is the power of all who believe, that explains why many of us are weak in spirit. We probably have not spent enough time reading God's Word for it to permeate our souls and give us the strength we need to face each day. Or maybe we have been embarrassed or ashamed to stand up for our beliefs and witness Christ to others. Let us each one examine our heart and seek God's will so the power of God is evident in our lives.

Dear Lord: Thank You for the gospel that gives us the power to live victoriously. Thank You for the boldness Your Holy Spirit provides to be witnesses to others about the good news of Your Son, Jesus. Forgive me for the times I am too timid or embarrassed to stand up for what I believe. Help me to be more assertive in my endeavors to lead others to Christ. In Jesus' name, Amen.

STUFFED GREEN PEPPERS

4 green peppers
1 pound lean ground beef
1 cup cooked rice
1 small onion, finely diced
½ teaspoon salt
¼ teaspoon pepper
1–2 teaspoons Worcestershire sauce
1 (8-ounce) can tomato sauce
1 can tomato soup

Cut top off peppers; remove seeds. Combine beef, rice, onion, salt, black pepper, Worcestershire, and ½ cup tomato sauce. Pack mixture into peppers; place in greased baking dish. Mix remaining tomato sauce and soup; pour over each pepper; cover tightly. Bake at 350 degrees for 75 minutes or until peppers tender.

July 4

We also rejoice in our sufferings, because we know that suffering produces perseverance; perseverance, character; and character, hope.

—ROMANS 5:3–4

CORRIE TEN BOOM was quoted as saying, "Thank God for the fleas," because they kept the German soldiers out of the barracks in the concentration camp where she was imprisoned. This allowed her to visit and show the love of Jesus to those being persecuted. In our earthly lives, we will encounter various trials of pain and heartache. To many, this might cause bitterness and hostility toward God and others. But if we are grounded in our faith and knowledge of the Word, the Christian is able to have a completely different outlook on adversity and pain. The apostle Paul says that suffering (distress and agony) and perseverance (determination and endurance) equal character (disposition and temperament) and hope (desire and expectation). This simple equation may not make sense to the non-Christian, but it is obvious that we call on the name of the Lord more during our times of frustration, affliction, and hardship. When we persevere under pressure and stay focused on making right decisions, God rewards us with a joyful heart. That joy is our faith and trust in the Lord because we are full of hope for our future. With this we are able to look at our sufferings as merely spiritual growth spurts in becoming more of the person God intended us to be.

Father: Forgive me for getting frustrated and impatient at times when things go wrong, or at least appear that way. You may have allowed those things to happen for a reason because You see the whole picture and I see only what is before me. You know what is best for me and what will draw me closer to You. Help me to take time for You in the good times and not just in the bad. In Jesus' name, Amen.

CHINESE NOODLE SALAD

Chop and set aside:

1 large Chinese cabbage *or* 2 bags coleslaw mix
6–8 green onions

Boil 1 minute and chill:

½ cup sugar
¼ cup vinegar
¾ cup oil
2 seasoning packets from noodles

Sauté in pan over medium heat:

1 tablespoon oil
1 (2.5-ounce) bag sliced almonds
Small jar sesame seeds
2 packages Ramen noodles, broken up

Cook just until almonds begin to brown. Gently mix all ingredients in a bowl. Serve immediately to avoid noodles becoming soggy.

July 5

Consequently, just as the result of one trespass was condemnation for all men, so also the result of one act of righteousness was justification that brings life for all men.

—ROMANS 5:18

O N THE DAY Adam and Eve, the father and mother of all mankind, disobeyed God and chose to eat the forbidden fruit, they died spiritually and were then destined to die physically. From the moment they sinned, all of Adam's descendants inherited his sinful and disobedient nature. Because of this, death was passed upon all men. No one has to be trained or taught to sin; it is passed through inheritance and comes naturally. But even though one man brought sin and condemnation into the world, another has come to make us righteous before God and justify eternal life with Him. If we choose to believe and ask God to forgive us of our sin, He will do it and we will have eternal life through Jesus Christ, our Lord.

Righteous Judge and Savior: I am forgiven because You justified my sin; no longer do I have to live in disobedience and condemnation. Help me to live a life of purity and walk in the shadow of Your righteousness. In Jesus' name, Amen.

RASPBERRY SPINACH SALAD

3 tablespoons vegetable oil
2 tablespoons raspberry or balsamic vinegar
2 tablespoons raspberry jam
⅛ teaspoon pepper
8 cups torn fresh spinach
2 cups fresh raspberries, divided
4 tablespoons slivered almonds, toasted/divided
½ cup onion, thinly sliced
3 kiwis, peeled and sliced
1 cup seasoned salad croutons

In jar with tight-fitting lid, combine oil, vinegar, jam, and pepper; shake well. In large salad bowl, gently combine spinach, 1 cup of raspberries, 2 tablespoons almonds, and onion. Top with kiwi, croutons, and remaining berries and almonds. Drizzle with dressing; serve immediately.

July 6

For the wages of sin is death; but the gift of God is eternal life through Jesus Christ our Lord.
—ROMANS 6:23, KJV

WAGES ARE PAYMENT for work done, and justice demands a laborer receive them. Paul tells us there is also payment for sin. In the same way an employee has a right to his wages, the sinner also has a right to his wages. God told Adam at the beginning of time in the Garden of Eden that the wages of sin is death: "You are free to eat from any tree in the garden; but you must not eat from the tree of the knowledge of good and evil, for when you eat from it you will certainly die" (Gen. 2:16–17). Therefore, when Adam sinned, he brought two kinds of death upon himself: a physical death and a spiritual death. Physical death is the separation of the spirit from the mortal body. Spiritual death is the separation of the soul from God. When we are without Christ we are spiritually dead. When we are born again, we receive God's gift through Jesus Christ our Lord and the spiritual death is reversed (Ephesians 2:1). Jesus faced eternal death on the cross and the anguish and torment of hell, all so we wouldn't have to. He suffered separation from God during those three awful hours of darkness as He cried, "My God, My God, why have you forsaken me?" (Matt. 27:46, KJV). Because of Jesus, we who were spiritually dead are made spiritually alive and have the gift of eternal life.

Father: Thank You for the gift of eternal life in Your Son Jesus. Thank You for the provision you made by allowing Christ to die on the cross so we wouldn't have to. Forgive me for my sins and cleanse me from all my iniquities so I don't die and become eternally separated from You. In Jesus' name, Amen.

MUSHROOM-RICE CASSEROLE

1 stick butter
4 green onions, chopped
2 cans cream of mushroom soup
1 (4-ounce) can sliced mushrooms, undrained
4 cups cooked rice
1 cup of slivered almonds
12 ounces grated cheddar cheese

Melt butter in skillet and sauté green onions about 1 minute; add soup, mushrooms, rice, and almonds. Pour half of mixture into greased baking dish. Cover with half the cheese. Pour in rest of rice mixture and top with remaining cheese. Bake at 350 degrees for 20⊠30 minutes or until cheese is melted.

July 7

There is therefore now no condemnation to them which are in Christ Jesus, who walk not after the flesh, but after the Spirit.

—ROMANS 8:1, KJV

THE APOSTLE PAUL is expressing the outcome of every person who has been redeemed from the power of sin by the ransom of Christ's blood. Once a sinner (which includes every one of us) has been led by the Spirit to accept Christ's atonement by repenting and turning away from sin, we are no longer found guilty or condemned for them. Sin no longer has dominion over us, and we are free from the bondage of immorality. But we truly must be born again or all our efforts will be useless if we try to live a good moral life outside of Christ's regenerating grace. The one who has not yet accepted Christ as Savior is still a slave to sin, even though he or she may have good intentions. They are not their own master and yet they may try to follow God's commandments to the best of their ability. Only in Christ will God's grace provide a way of escape from the sinful desires of the flesh. In Him, we are set free and able to live victoriously with the Holy Spirit operating in our hearts and lives.

Heavenly Father: I praise You for setting me free from the bondages of sin and immorality. In Your Son, Jesus, is all the power I need to live a victorious life. Help me to rely on Your bountiful grace and love to live a life that pleases You. Forgive me for the times I relied on my own strength to follow Your ways. May You forever be glorified in my life. In Jesus' name, Amen.

GRILLED BASS

¾ pound bass or other fish fillets, skin removed
1 tablespoon butter, softened
4 thin red onion slices
1 lemon, sliced in thin pieces
2 tablespoons sliced almonds
¼ cup sliced green onions
⅛ teaspoon salt
⅛ teaspoon pepper
⅛ teaspoon paprika

Prepare grill for medium-direct heat. Grease center of a 20x18-inch sheet of heavy-duty aluminum foil with butter. On it, put half the red onion, lemon, almonds, green onions, and all fillets in single layer. Top with remaining ingredients; sprinkle with seasonings. Fold long sides of foil together in locked folds. Fold and crimp short ends; seal tightly. Place packet directly on cooking grate. Grill, covered, 11–15 minutes, until fish is firm, opaque, and flakey. May also bake 20 minutes in oven at 350 degrees.

July 8

Those who live according to the sinful nature have their minds set on what that nature desires; but those who live in accordance with the Spirit have their minds set on what the Spirit desires.

—ROMANS 8:5

ACCORDING TO PAUL, there are two kinds of people: those who live according to their sinful nature and those who live according to the Spirit. A sinner behaves like a sinner because he has the nature of a sinner (Psalms 51:5; 58:3). The Bible calls this the *flesh* (Romans 7:5). The flesh is the old nature we inherited from Adam, a nature that opposes God and does nothing spiritual to please Him.

It's great to know that God has given us the ability to be what He expects us to be. He sent His Holy Spirit to come and live in us so we can be empowered to do His will. When we fail to follow the Spirit and follow the natural desires of our flesh, we sin. This might include sexual immorality, adultery, anger, hatred, selfishness, obscenity, unforgiveness, gossip, and the like. To live according to the Spirit is to seek and submit to the Holy Spirit's will and focus on the things of God. From the moment we accept Christ as Savior, the Holy Spirit dwells within us, giving us the power we need to live according to the will of God. Therefore, it takes a conscious decision to choose whether to follow after our fleshly desires or that of the Spirit. As believers, we must trust God to sustain us, give us the mind of Christ, and set our minds on what the Spirit desires.

Father: I praise You for Your wonderful Holy Spirit who guides and directs my life. Thank You for the privilege of serving You with my thoughts and actions. Help me to make right choices in accordance with the Spirit and not of my fleshly natural desires. In Jesus' name, Amen.

CORNED BEEF AND CABBAGE

5 pounds well-trimmed corned beef brisket
2 cloves garlic
1 onion, quartered
8–10 carrots, left whole or cut in half
1 head green cabbage, cut into eighths
8–10 potatoes, pared and quartered

Place meat in large kettle; cover with cold water. Add garlic and onion; heat to boiling. Reduce heat; cover tightly and simmer 3 ½ hours or until tender. Add carrots and potatoes during last 30 minutes of cooking time. Place meat on warm platter; keep warm. Skim fat from liquid. Add cabbage and simmer uncovered 15–20 minutes. To carve meat, cut thin diagonal slices across the grain at a slanting angle from 2 or 3 places on the meat.

July 9

I consider that our present sufferings are not worth comparing with the glory that will be revealed in us.

—ROMANS 8:18

THE APOSTLE PAUL was very aware of the reality of suffering and reminds us that a victorious life in the Spirit is not an easy road to travel. Paul himself had been rejected by his brethren, mistreated by authorities, stoned by angry mobs, harassed by Satan, thrown into prison for preaching the gospel, and much more. He was also aware of others who faced trials of persecution, just like those throughout the ages who were mistreated and even died a martyr's death for the sake of Christ. But Paul, through the working of the Holy Spirit, puts our suffering into perspective and compares its weight to being light as a feather to that of what glory will be like.

Being people of faith does not exempt us from suffering. As members of the body of Christ, we live in hope while we wait for God's promises to be fulfilled. God has promised us a new heaven, a new earth, and a new resurrection. Everything will be made new and nothing will be broken any more. At last we will see the glory of God in all its fullness, and our deepest sorrows, our most bitter disappointments, and the sum total of all our regrets will be nothing more than a distant memory. Whatever we are facing today, our loving Father knows and cares and has a plan to redeem our lives and bring us into His glory. We must bear our burdens in hope and confidence, knowing that they soon will be over and we will stand before the Lord of all and give an account for the hope and faith that is in us.

Father: Thank You for Your plan to redeem my soul for all eternity and for the hope and confidence You have placed within me. Thank You for caring about my disappointments and suffering. Help me to rely on Your strength to see me through every situation and circumstance. In Jesus' name, Amen.

QUESADILLAS (easy)

2 flour tortillas
Vegetable oil or spray
¼ cup shredded cheese (your choice)
Toppings such as: chopped onion, green pepper, tomatoes, chicken, beef, etc.

Lay 1 tortilla on greased pizza pan or cookie sheet; cover with cheese and toppings. Cover with another tortilla. Lightly spread oil on top. Bake at 425 degrees for 10 minutes, until lightly browned.

July 10

And we know that all things work together for good to them that love God, to them who are called according to his purpose.

—ROMANS 8:28, KJV

THIS VERSE HAS brought comfort and hope to all of us, especially during those hard times. Though not everything that happens in life is good, God assures us that if we continue to love Him and look to Him for our strength, everything will work out for good. Losing a job, a loved one, or having a physical problem or family troubles may be traumatic to our lives and are oftentimes the direct result of evil. As believers, we are not immune to problems and pain, but we do have the blessed hope in Christ that the world does not have. God uses the circumstances of our lives, both good and bad, to shape outcomes that accomplish His purpose for us. Strength in this verse comes when our faith and trust in God is affirmed and our goals are focused on Him. If we do our part, God is always faithful to do His.

Dear God: Thank You for Your promises that are so honest and true. You care for Your children and love us so much. Forgive me for all my sin and help me to align my plans and goals according to Your purpose and not mine. I accept Your will for my life and want to follow Your plans so that when troubles come, I am strong in faith and trust. Thank You for taking the wrong that has come to my life and making good come from it. In Jesus' name, Amen.

ROAST TARRAGON CHICKEN

3 tablespoons olive oil
2 ½ teaspoons dried tarragon, rosemary, or thyme, crushed
2 cloves garlic, minced
½ teaspoon coarsely ground black pepper
¼ teaspoon salt
1 pound cherry tomatoes
8 small shallots, trimmed
2–3 pounds chicken pieces (breasts, thighs, legs), with or without skin

In bowl, stir together oil, tarragon, garlic, pepper, and salt. Add tomatoes and shallots; gently coat. Use slotted spoon to remove tomatoes and shallots from bowl, reserving oil mixture. Place chicken in shallow roasting pan; brush with reserved oil mixture; roast for 20 minutes at 375 minutes. Add shallots and tomatoes; roast for 15 minutes or until chicken and vegetables tender.

July 11

For I am persuaded, that neither death, nor life, nor angels, nor principalities, nor powers, nor things present, nor things to come, nor height, nor depth, nor any other creature, shall be able to separate us from the love of God, which is in Christ Jesus our Lord.

—ROMANS 8:38–39, KJV

PROBABLY THE GREATEST motivation we have to live for God is the absolute assurance of eternal life. Nothing in this life and nothing after death can separate a believer from God's love. There is no power nor anything in all of time, present or future, that can separate us from the love of God. He loves us and will never stop loving us, no matter if we have put our trust in Him or are still living a life of sin. If any of us fail in our spiritual walk, it is not because of a lack of divine grace and love, nor is it from an external force or adversity, but it is from our own decision to neglect the Spirit's call on our hearts to live for Jesus Christ. It is in Him that God chose to reveal His love for us so that we might live a victorious life here on earth while anticipating eternal life one day with Him in glory.

Heavenly Father: Thank You for Your boundless love. No matter how ugly my sins are, You still love me with an everlasting love. You have given me a free will to accept Your love or reject it. I choose to accept Your plan of salvation and make You Lord of my life. As I do this, I am promised eternal life with You. In Jesus' name, Amen.

BARBECUE MEATLOAF

1 ½ pounds lean ground beef
1 cup fresh bread crumbs
1 onion, diced
1 egg, lightly beaten
1 teaspoon salt
½ teaspoon pepper
1 (8-ounce) can tomato sauce
2 tablespoons Worcestershire sauce
2 tablespoons barbecue sauce
3 tablespoons vinegar
3 tablespoons brown sugar
2 tablespoons mustard

Mix together beef, bread crumbs, onion, egg, salt, pepper, ½ cup tomato sauce, Worcestershire, and barbecue sauce. Form into a loaf and place it in a loaf or shallow pan. Stir together remaining tomato sauce, vinegar, brown sugar, and mustard. Pour sauce over meatloaf. Bake at 350 degrees for 1 hour, basting every 15 minutes with pan juices.

July 12

That if you confess with your mouth, "Jesus is Lord," and believe in your heart that God raised Him from the dead, you will be saved. For it is with your heart that you believe and are justified, and it is with your mouth that you confess and are saved.

—ROMANS 10:9–10

THE APOSTLE PAUL summarizes the essentials of salvation in these two verses. In the first verse, he directly states that both believing and confessing are requisites for salvation. In the second, He reinforces our need to believe in our hearts that Jesus is Lord, and as we do, our confession will complete the act of salvation. Though Paul implies that a public confession justifies our salvation, God doesn't need us to confess it verbally for His benefit. He sees into our hearts and discerns our true belief and faith in Him. When we confess the Lord Jesus and His resurrection, we agree with what God said about Jesus and what Jesus said about Himself. It means we recognize that Jesus is God, that He is the Messiah, and that His work on the cross is the only way of salvation for mankind. Our confession is not only justified by our spoken words in prayer, praise, and profession of faith in Christ, but also by how we live our lives before Him. When we confess Jesus as Lord, we declare Him to be equal with God and worthy of our obedience to His Word. Our outward profession and actions are merely an inward portrayal of the true attitude of our hearts. Though salvation is a gift of God's grace, it can only be seized by the response of our hearts when we believe and confess that Jesus truly is Lord of all.

Father: I believe in my heart that Jesus is Your Son, that He died on a cross, and that He was raised from the dead. I repent of all my unrighteousness and confess with my mouth that Jesus is Lord. Help me to live a life of obedience to Your will. In Jesus' name, Amen.

TATER TOT CASSEROLE

1 (32-ounce) bag Tater Tots
1 cup sour cream
1 cup cheddar cheese
1 can cream of chicken soup
½ onion, finely chopped
½ cup (1 stick) butter, melted
1 cup corn flakes, crumbled

Thaw Tater Tots and cut into halves or thirds. Mix them with sour cream, cheddar cheese, chicken soup, and onion. Pour into greased casserole dish. Mix melted butter with corn flakes and put on top of potato mixture. Bake at 350 degrees for 45–50 minutes. This recipe can be made ahead of time, or the night before, and refrigerated. Do not add corn flake crumbs until ready to bake.

July 13

Consider therefore the kindness and sternness of God: sternness to those who fell, but kindness to you, provided that you continue in his kindness. Otherwise, you also will be cut off.

—ROMANS 11:22

THE APOSTLE PAUL was giving thought here to the destiny of Israel because of its unbelief and rejection of God's grace in Christ. Paul warned the Gentile believers about the possibility that even they could be cut off if they did not continue to trust in the kindness of God and follow in His righteous ways. God is loving and kind, but He also is stern and just. From the beginning of time, God proved to mankind that He meant what He said and said what He meant. But even in the midst of God's judgment, He shows mercy. The people who suffered destruction during Noah's Flood and those of Sodom and Gomorrah who experienced the severity of God's wrath were victims of God's judgment and also His mercy upon the world. During those times, like today, sin was so rampant in the earth that it was like a metastatic (spreading) cancer. God did radical surgery by removing the vile sinners and therefore allowed the human race as a whole to survive. If God did not spare Israel then, why would He spare those of us today who conform to the ways of the world and live in blatant sin and disobedience? The church today is guilty of becoming more and more like the world to entice outsiders to come in and have their ears tickled. God's judgment is upon them. We must have a heartfelt love for Jesus Christ, the truth of His Word, and continue to walk in both the kindness and the sternness of God. Otherwise, we face the consequences of being cut off.

Dear God: You are stern but You are kind and just. Your ways are always great, for You are a righteous and fair Judge. Forgive me when my faith weakens and I begin to conform to the ways of the world rather than to Your ways, which are holy and pure. Show me how to become more faithful to Your Word. In Jesus' name, Amen.

BARBECUE CHICKEN (on the grill)

Chicken pieces
Olive oil
Barbecue sauce

Wash chicken well; dry with paper towels. Rub chicken with small amount olive oil. Preheat gas grill to medium heat or prepare charcoal grill until fire gone. Put chicken on clean, oiled, or sprayed grill, skin-side down; cover (if lid available) 20–30 minutes, turning several times until skin golden brown and thoroughly cooked (juices run clear). Brush with barbecue sauce during last 10 minutes.

July 14

Therefore, I urge you, brothers, in view of God's mercy, to offer your bodies as living sacrifices, holy and pleasing to God—this is your spiritual act of worship.

—ROMANS 12:1

JUST ABOUT EVERYONE knows the beautiful hymn, "I Surrender All." But, do we really surrender all? Shouldn't we honestly sing something more like "I Surrender Nine Tenths" or "I Surrender One Half"? As Christians, we come to Jesus and give Him our life but then gradually take back a little bit at a time. Pretty soon, we are back to where we started and there has really been no sacrifice made at all. This happens when we make a decision to follow Christ but then fail to stay plugged into a close relationship with God. We must daily offer ourselves to Him by taking time to pray, repent, study His Word, and strive to be obedient to His will and way. God is pleased when we worship Him by living a holy lifestyle even when it means sacrificing our will for His.

God of mercy and grace: Forgive me for giving my life to You and then taking it back. I am sorry for the things I have done that weren't pleasing to You. Today, I offer myself to You once and for all. Never again do I want to walk away from Your will. Help me to live my life so I might be a living sacrifice, holy and pleasing unto You, my God. In Jesus' name, Amen.

MANICOTTI

Shells (crepes):	Filling:	Sauce:
6 eggs	2 pounds ricotta cheese	⅓ cup oil
1 ½ cups flour	8 ounces mozzarella	1 large onion, diced
½ teaspoon salt	¼ cup Parmesan cheese	2 cloves garlic, minced
1 ½ cups water	2 eggs	1 (2-pound) can diced tomatoes
	1 teaspoon salt	1 (6-ounce) can tomato paste
	¼ teaspoon pepper	2 tablespoons parsley
	1 tablespoon parsley	1 teaspoon salt
	Vegetable spray	1 tablespoon sugar
		1 teaspoon oregano
		1 teaspoon basil
		¼ teaspoon pepper
		1 ½ cups water

Beat all shell ingredients together with electric mixer until smooth. Spray an 8-inch non-stick pan; when hot on medium-high heat, pour in 3 tablespoons batter; cook until dry. Cool on racks; stack with waxed paper between them. Mix together filling ingredients. Meanwhile, sauté onion and garlic in oil over medium heat until tender; add all other ingredients and simmer 1 hour. Pour half of sauce into 13x9-inch baking dish. Spoon 3–4 tablespoons cheese filling down center of each crepe; roll and place seam side down over sauce. Pour rest of sauce overtop; top with Parmesan cheese. Cover; bake at 350 degrees for 20 minutes. Uncover; bake 20 more minutes.

July 15

Do not conform any longer to the pattern of this world, but be transformed by the renewing of your mind. Then you will be able to test and approve what God's will is—his good, pleasing, and perfect will.

—ROMANS 12:2

DON'T BE MOLDED by the world. This is not an easy task, but a reminder that *what we think* is one of the places of greatest spiritual warfare. Our minds can lead us to eternal destruction if we allow sloppy or careless thinking to control our thought process. Sloppy thinking is not *agape* thinking. Because our minds are constantly fed messages from all around us that the enemy tries to distort, God gave instructions on how we might be transformed by the renewing of our minds. The apostle Paul says in 2 Corinthians 10:5 to take *every* thought and word captive for Christ. Our present world is evil and under Satan's rule. We must despise what is evil and love what is good. The moment a word, picture, desire, or thought enters our minds, it is to be immediately analyzed. Is it of God? Is it destructive? Is it selfish? Will it encourage and build up, or will it degrade and tear down? Is God glorified in it, or is it contrary to His Word? If it is not good, we must *immediately* turn our minds to God's Word and away from the thought. This takes training, but eventually it becomes a way of life and God is pleased.

Father God: Guard my mind from the dangers of the enemy's plots and schemes to destroy me. Help me to know Your Word so well that when thoughts and temptations enter my mind, I am able to make holy and right decisions. Teach me in my heart what it means to know good from evil so that my actions are always pleasing to You. In Jesus' name, Amen.

HAWAIIAN CHICKEN

3–4 boneless, skinless chicken breasts
2 tablespoons cornstarch
¼ cup brown sugar
¼ cup vinegar
½ teaspoon salt
2 tablespoons soy sauce
1 can pineapple tidbits (do not drain)
¼ cup ketchup
½ teaspoon dry mustard (regular okay)
¼ teaspoon garlic powder
1 green pepper, cut in strips
¼ cup toasted almonds (optional)

Lay chicken pieces in large greased baking dish. Mix well all ingredients, except almonds and green pepper. Pour mixture over chicken and cover. Bake at 350 degrees for 45 minutes. Uncover; add green pepper and bake another 15–20 minutes, until chicken browned and sauce bubbly and thick. Sprinkle almonds over top; serve with rice.

July 16

Love must be sincere. Hate what is evil; cling to what is good.

—ROMANS 12:9

IF GOD IS love, is it really okay to hate? Genuine love involves hate; it means hating evil. We must detest it creeping into our lives and ruining our relationship with the Almighty. We are to abhor the evilness and wickedness in the world and what it does to our loved ones and families. The eternal destruction that evil promotes is all around us and the more we love God, the more we will hate even the appearance of evil. Loving God is hating sin or evil. Our utmost priority should be striving each day to sincerely love God by obeying His commands. In turn, as we cling to what is good, our acceptance of evil will begin to diminish and our love for God will increase.

Loving Father: You are an awesome God. Help me to walk in obedience to Your Word and protect me from the enemy's snares that pull me into his way of thinking. I want to be a witness to my friends and family and all those who cross my path; please give me wisdom and courage to pursue that goal. May You be glorified in all I say and do. In the name of Jesus, Amen

SPAGHETTI AND MEATBALLS

Sauce:

1 small piece salt pork
2 tablespoons olive oil
6–9 garlic cloves (more if desired), sliced
1 large can tomato juice
1 (12-ounce) can tomato paste
3 cups water
½ teaspoon black pepper
8 ounces sliced fresh mushrooms

Meatballs:

1 pound lean ground beef
1 egg
½ teaspoon salt
½ teaspoon pepper
3 springs fresh parsley, chopped *or* 2 teaspoons dried
1 small onion, finely chopped
½ teaspoon garlic powder
2–3 pieces bread, diced small

Dice salt pork (partially frozen works best); lightly brown in olive oil in large pan on medium heat (takes 10–15 minutes). Add garlic; sauté 2 minutes (do not brown). Add tomato juice, tomato paste, pepper, and water; simmer 1–2 hours or put in crockpot on high for 4 hours. Add mushrooms during last 30 minutes. *Do not add salt to sauce.* Mix meatball ingredients and form into balls; brown in pan on medium-high heat or in 350-degree oven for 30 minutes. They do not need thoroughly cooked. Add meatballs to sauce; simmer 1–2 hours. Before serving add 1 pound prepared spaghetti noodles to sauce.

July 17

Be devoted to one another in brotherly love. Honor one another above yourselves.

—ROMANS 12:10

BEING DEVOTED TO one another requires putting a walk to our talk. It is more than just greeting one another at church on Sundays and asking a generic, "How are you?" Devotion is entering one another's lives and getting to know them in such a way that we might serve, love, and bless them. Being devoted to one another in brotherly love requires a commitment. It starts with repentance to the Father for ignoring His wonderful command and asking for His strength and help to fulfill it. It is repenting of wanting our way instead of another's. At church, it might mean putting our desire of music aside and wanting the desires of others to be granted. Easy to do? No, but neither was dying on a cross, which was a result of our Savior honoring others above Himself. If we truly love our Lord and want to obey His commands, we must daily crucify our fleshly desires and live and pray as though it isn't about us but about others. In turn, their lives will be enriched and they too will put others above themselves in brotherly love…thus, God will be glorified.

Dear Father: Thank You for giving me a family to love. Thank You for loving me so I might love and honor others. Forgive me when I complain and grumble when my desires aren't granted but others' are. Help me to prefer my brother and sister and be joyful when their desires are supplied. Give me a heart of compassion so I might love, serve, and bless Your children. In Jesus' name, Amen.

DIRTY RICE

1 pound lean ground beef or sausage
2 garlic cloves, minced
2 celery ribs, chopped (about ½ cup)
1 medium onion, chopped
1 tablespoon chopped fresh parsley *or* 1 teaspoon dried parsley
1 green bell pepper, chopped
1 teaspoon salt
¼ teaspoon ground red pepper
¼ teaspoon ground black pepper
1 tablespoon Worcestershire sauce
1 cup uncooked rice
1 (14.5-ounce) can beef broth
¾ cup water

In large pan on medium-high heat, cook ground meat; drain. Add garlic, celery, onion, parsley, and green pepper; cook until onion tender. Add salt, peppers, Worcestershire, rice, broth, and water; stir. Bring to boil and cover; reduce heat and simmer 25–30 minutes or until rice tender.

July 18

Share with God's people who are in need. Practice hospitality.

—ROMANS 12:13

THE CHRISTIAN PRACTICE of hospitality means to welcome friends, family, and even strangers into our homes and to our tables for fellowship and the breaking of bread. This is modeled after our Lord as He took us in when we were once strangers (Deuteronomy 10:19). Jesus' identification with the stranger (Matthew 25:35) and His teaching on the necessity of welcoming the poor, the crippled, the lame, and the blind to our dinner tables (Luke 14:12–14) offers us a distinct understanding of hospitality. Although in conventional hospitality, people welcome family, friends, and influential acquaintances, Christian hospitality ought to focus on welcoming the vulnerable, poor, and needy into our homes and communities of faith. We should especially welcome the least of these (Matthew 25:45) and those unable to give anything in return. Jesus says our payment will come "at the resurrection of the righteous" (Luke 14:14). Hospitality should not be a task but a way of living. It involves responsibility and work, but the joy it brings both the giver and the receiver is immeasurable. Sharing and giving to those in need is a response of love and gratitude for God's love for us. As we give and serve, the divine blessing of hospitality is discovered: that as we welcome and serve strangers, we are ourselves the beloved guests of God's love and grace.

Dear God: Thank You for being such a wonderful example of love and grace and for living out the real meaning of hospitality. Birth in my heart a desire to welcome the needy into my home so I might practice hospitality and share Your love. In doing so, may You be glorified. In Jesus' name, Amen.

NUTRITIOUS CRUNCH SNACK MIX

2 cups Wheat Chex
2 cups Rice Chex
2 cups bite-size cheese crackers
2 cups small pretzels
1 cup Cheerios
1 cup peanuts
3 tablespoons butter
3 tablespoons Worcestershire sauce
2 teaspoons seasoned salt
1 teaspoon garlic powder
1 teaspoon onion powder

Combine all cereals plus peanuts in large roasting pan, greased or sprayed. Put butter, Worcestershire sauce, and all seasonings in a small microwavable dish and microwave for 15–25 seconds until butter melted; stir to mix. Slowly pour over cereal mixture while gently mixing. Bake at 250 degrees for 45 minutes, stirring every 15 minutes. When cool, store in containers.

July 19

Bless them which persecute you: bless, and curse not.

—Romans 12:14, KJV

Do not repay anyone evil for evil.

—Romans 12:17

Be not overcome of evil, but overcome evil with good.

—Romans 12:21, KJV

THE APOSTLE PAUL gives us a series of exhortations or warnings that concern our behavior in the midst of an evil world. In 2 Timothy 3:12 (KJV), Paul says, "Yea, and all that will live godly in Christ Jesus shall suffer persecution." How is it possible to bless and do good to those who persecute us or treat us badly? How do we even *like* these ones who are unkind and unlovely? Perhaps it's that we are not asked to have *feelings of love* for them, but to *act in love* toward them. This is not sentimental love but love in action, love in deed. This kind of love is patient and unconditional, willing to suffer or go the extra mile in order to bring about reconciliation, peace, and hopefully a convert to Christ. According to Paul, doing good eventually will overcome all evil. In order for us to love our enemies or those who have wronged us in some way, we are required to first recognize that God loves us just as we are even with all our imperfections and flaws. In that relationship with Christ, we are empowered to love our enemies as Christ loves us, and as He loved his enemies.

Dear Lord: As my heavenly Father, You already know my heart and how I feel toward those who have been unkind and unlovely. It is no surprise that I struggle with feelings of wanting to reject them instead of doing good to them. Forgive me for my insecurities and negative thoughts and help me to show Your love by doing good things to them. As I do, I believe You will give me the power and strength needed to be Your love in action. In Jesus' name, Amen.

FETTUCCINE ALFREDO WITH CHICKEN

½ pound fettuccine, uncooked
1 pound boneless, skinless chicken breasts
1 ¼ cups chicken broth
4 teaspoons flour
1 (8-ounce) package cream cheese, cubed
3 tablespoons grated Parmesan cheese, divided
¼ teaspoon garlic powder
¼ teaspoon pepper

Cook pasta according to package; drain and put in large bowl; keep warm. Cook chicken in large greased skillet on medium-high, until done; remove from pan and cut in strips. Mix broth and flour in same skillet. Stir in cream cheese, 2 tablespoons Parmesan cheese, garlic powder, and pepper; cook 2 minutes, stirring constantly until mixture boils and thickens. Stir in chicken. Pour mixture over pasta; toss. Sprinkle with remaining 1 tablespoon Parmesan cheese.

July 20

Everyone must submit himself to the governing authorities, for there is no authority except that which God has established. The authorities that exist have been established by God.

—Romans 13:1

As Christians, we are to obey the laws of the state in which we live. In this fallen world, we need restraints and laws to protect us from the evil chaos that results from sin. God has ordained the government to rule over injustice by punishing those who commit evil. Paul explains that unless the laws are contrary to God's Word, we are to protect the good in society and abide by them. There are times when governing authorities will be in direct contradiction to God's Word. Such is the case in abortion, same-sex marriage, and euthanasia. It is then that we must know what we believe and stand upon it, obeying God's law and not the state's. Obedience to speed limits and other rules of the road are there to protect us. As Christians, we cannot pick and choose to which laws we will adhere. Paul makes it clear that we need to be gracious, respectful, and thankful for the laws and those who enforce them. We are to pray for those in authority over us, that they will be led of the Holy Spirit as they make decisions on our behalf. While we can rejoice that God has given us our government, we should remember that we are citizens of a higher kingdom and subjects of a Supreme Ruler. We should submit to the government as we seek to improve it, while we yet believe that the highest calling of the Christian is to submit to the lordship of Jesus Christ.

Dear God: Blessed be Your name above all others. I praise You for taking care of us by establishing a government of laws for our protection and benefit. Forgive me when I disrespect and disobey the laws that have been put there for my own good by the governing officials. Convict me when I ignore them and do my own thing, which in turn dishonors You. In Jesus' name, Amen.

BAKED STUFFED TOMATOES

6 medium tomatoes
¼ cup grated Parmesan cheese
⅓ cup bread crumbs
½ teaspoon salt
2–3 pieces bacon, fried crisp and crumbled
Fresh parsley (optional)

Wash tomatoes; remove stem ends. With a spoon, remove pulp and chop it. Mix pulp with Parmesan cheese, bread crumbs, salt, and bacon. Fill tomatoes with mixture. Place in baking dish and bake at 350 degrees for 20–30 minutes or until done. Garnish with parsley.

July 21

This is also why you pay taxes, for the authorities are God's servants, who give their full time to governing. Give everyone what you owe him: If you owe taxes, pay taxes; if revenue, then revenue; if respect, then respect; if honor, then honor.

—ROMANS 13:6–7

PAYING TAXES IS not our favorite thing to do. No one really likes giving to Uncle Sam, but it rightfully belongs to him. If we look at it as being obedient to God, then it makes it much easier to do. Just think where we might be without the government, order, and laws. While we may not like the system and all that it entails, what if we had no system? We live in a blessed nation, and though it seems unfair that some of us seem to be paying more than what we think is the fair amount, we must thank God for meeting our needs to do so. Let's pray for our government that revival would come to the hearts of those in authority over us and that we would be a nation under God's rulings.

Father: Thank You for being the ruler of my life and the authority of all those who serve the government. Forgive me if I complain and grumble about paying taxes and obeying laws that seem unfair. You said in Your Word this is right, and I want to respect and obey Your commands. Help me to have a good attitude about paying taxes and revenue and to also give honor and respect to those in authority over me. Thank You for the privilege of being alive in this country and for being Your child. Heal our land, Lord, and bring us back to prayer and repentance so revival will come. In Jesus' name, Amen.

PEPPER STEAK (crockpot)

2 pounds beef sirloin, cut into 2-inch strips
½ teaspoon garlic powder
3 tablespoons vegetable or canola oil
1 tablespoon cornstarch
½ cup water
1 cube beef bouillon
½ cup chopped onion
2 large green bell peppers, chopped
1 (14.5-ounce) can stewed tomatoes
3 tablespoons soy sauce
1 teaspoon sugar
1 teaspoon salt

Sprinkle strips of sirloin with garlic powder. Brown meat in hot oil in large skillet over medium-high heat. Transfer to crockpot. Dissolve cornstarch in water and add to crockpot along with all remaining ingredients. Cook on high for 3–4 hours, or on low for 6–8 hours. Serve with rice.

July 22

Let no debt remain outstanding, except the continuing debt to love one another, for he who loves his fellowman has fulfilled the law.

—ROMANS 13:8

PAUL CONTINUES TO teach on the responsibility we have to love one another. He also warns us about the need we have as Christians to pay our debts. Getting out of debt requires a great deal more time and effort than it does to get into debt. It seems to take forever to pay off those financial obligations and loans. Contrary to what some may believe, the Bible does not teach that debt is evil or sinful; however, the Bible is pretty clear that we are to pay the debts we owe. We need to refrain from buying things on credit we really don't need and trust God more to meet our real needs. He already knows what we need before we ask. Making financial decisions based on the principles of God's Word rather than the world's are the way of debt management for the Christian. It will produce a simpler lifestyle and a life of joy that God intended for all of us.

Dear heavenly Father: Your Word is true and brings order to my life. Help me to want only those things I need and then trust You more to provide them for me. Forgive me when I foolishly spend money I don't have and accrue vast amounts of debt. I want to live in the freedom, power, and fullness of your Word. In Jesus' name, Amen.

COMPANY MEATLOAF

1 ½–2 pounds ground beef
1 teaspoon salt
½ teaspoon pepper
2 teaspoons Worcestershire sauce
1 small chopped onion
1 cup bread or cracker crumbs
½ (15-ounce) can tomato sauce
1 egg

Mix all ingredients; shape into loaf. Bake uncovered 45–60 minutes at 350 degrees.

Sauce:

½ (15-ounce) can tomato sauce
2 tablespoons vinegar
1 tablespoon prepared mustard
¼ cup brown sugar
¼ cup white sugar

Put sauce ingredients in small pan; bring to boil; simmer 2–3 minutes. When meatloaf has cooked 50 minutes, pour sauce over top; cook 10 more minutes. Remove from oven; let stand 10 minutes. Slice meatloaf and put on serving plate. Pour sauce over and serve.

July 23

Rather clothe yourselves with the Lord Jesus Christ, and do not think about how to gratify the desires of the sinful nature.

—ROMANS 13:14

GOD ORIGINALLY CREATED mankind to behave in a way that brings glory to Him in all the affairs of life. He expects us to do more than just worship Him in a Sunday morning church service. Our spiritual act of worship is determined by our behavior, actions, and expressions. This is done by making choices that involve dying to what we might want to do (fleshly desires) and, instead, doing as God's Word says we should do. It means we cannot even allow the first sinful thought to be entertained. By effectively defeating the first ungodly thought, we won't have to deal with the second or third one, let alone the consequences of the behavior that could result. Each of us needs to take authority over the temptations, lusts, and wrongful desires that rise up within us that try to cause us to conform to the patterns of this world. God's Word has given us the power to choose His way instead. It is possible to live a life of victory that glorifies the Lord if we daily clothe ourselves with the Lord Jesus Christ—meekness, patience, forgiveness, humility, and love.

Heavenly Father: It's with Your power and strength that I am able to clothe myself with Your Son, Jesus. I praise You for the ability You gave me to choose to obey Your Word over sinful desires. Help me in my weak areas to not submit to them, but to be strong in my faith and live in a way that brings You glory. May I be a living testimony of the power of Your Holy Word. In Jesus' name, Amen.

TACO PIE

1 ½ pounds lean ground beef
½ green bell pepper, chopped
1 (15-ounce) can Mexican stewed tomatoes
1 cup water
1 tablespoon chili powder
½ teaspoon garlic salt
1 ½ cups shredded cheddar cheese
1 (6-ounce) package corn muffin mix
1 egg
⅔ cup milk

Brown ground beef in large pan; drain. Add bell pepper; cook 5 minutes. Add tomatoes, water, chili powder, and garlic salt. Cook on medium heat about 10 minutes until most of liquid gone. Pour into greased 9x13-inch baking dish; sprinkle cheese on top. Combine corn muffin mix, egg, and milk in bowl; beat well. Pour over cheese. Bake at 350 degrees for 25 minutes until corn muffin mix light brown. Remove from oven; let stand 10 minutes before serving.

July 24

Accept him whose faith is weak, without passing judgment on disputable matters.

—ROMANS 14:1

OFTENTIMES, MORE MATURE Christians have a tendency to pass judgment on those still struggling with the excess baggage of sin that has a hold of them. The apostle Paul informs us that God has accepted both groups, the ones who have progressed in their faith and those who have not. If God has accepted them, that means He wants us to do the same. Jesus gave us a job to do—to evangelize the world and spiritually nourish the precious ones who respond favorably to the gospel message. God wants, above all else, unity in the body of Christ; and though we may have our differences, we are called to show *agape* love to one another. We are to be at peace and accept each other's level of faith as we continue our walk with Jesus! Sometimes we get impatient and pass judgment, criticize, and accuse, forgetting that we aren't the finished product yet either. God is still working in all of us and He wants to see us live in harmony and love until He comes to take us home.

Wonderful Lord: Thank You for Your Holy Spirit who comes and guides us to love one another no matter the level of each other's spirituality. Thank You for loving me, even when I was immature and not behaving according to Your will. Help me to be more patient of others who profess to know You and yet appear immature in their walk with Christ. As I live my life for You, may I be more mindful of my brother or sister whose faith is weak. In doing so, may You be glorified. In Jesus' name, Amen.

IMPOSSIBLE BREAKFAST CASSEROLE

1 pound ground pork sausage
1 small bell pepper, red or green, chopped
1 small onion (½ cup), chopped
3 cups hash brown potatoes
8 ounces cheddar cheese, shredded
1 cup Bisquick
2 cups milk
¼ teaspoon pepper
4 eggs

Cook sausage in skillet until brown; drain. Add pepper and onion; cook about 5 minutes. Add potatoes and ½ of cheese; pour into greased dish. Mix Bisquick, milk, pepper, and eggs together and pour over meat. Bake at 400 degrees for 30–40 minutes or until inserted knife comes out clean. Top with remaining cheese and return to oven for 1–2 minutes, until cheese melted.

July 25

May the God of hope fill you with all joy and peace as you trust in him, so that you may overflow with hope by the power of the Holy Spirit.

—Romans 15:13

WE LIVE IN an age where hopelessness and despair are on the increase. Satan tries to convince us that we are helpless creatures in the hands of fate with the inability to do anything about it. This is the result of rejecting God as we have placed our trust in our own systems of belief and human reason. When God is removed from the equation, there is literally no hope for the circumstances and situations that arise in our lives. Hopefulness produces joy and peace, while hopelessness is a strategy of the enemy to tear us down and destroy us. Satan wants us to live in defeat, discouragement, and despair and continue in strife with one another over jealousy, unforgiveness, selfishness, prejudice, and the list goes on and on. Paul points us again to the Source of the power that gives us hope, brings us joy and peace, and enables us to love one another. The Scripture says we overflow with hope by the power of the Holy Spirit. That's what we need—hope for the future, hope for our lives, hope for the lives of others around us, and hope that God is going to accomplish His purposes in us as we trust in Him.

Dear God: You are my hope and my strength, and I thank You for Your Word and promises. When I put my trust in You, You never fail me. Not only do You give me hope, but Your Word says it will overflow in my life. Help me to accept Your free gift of grace so I might be a person of love and compassion for a lost and hurting world. In Jesus' name, Amen.

SOUTHWEST CHICKEN SALAD

2 boneless, skinless chicken breasts, diced
2 tablespoons oil
2 tablespoons lemon or lime juice
2 tablespoons taco seasoning
1 package romaine lettuce, torn
3 tablespoons cilantro leaves, chopped
1 small can corn, drained
½ cup shredded cheddar cheese
1 cup crushed tortilla chips
½ cup ranch salad dressing
1–2 tablespoons taco seasoning
Sour cream and salsa (optional)

Put chicken, oil, lemon or lime juice, and 2 tablespoons taco seasoning in ziplock plastic bag; refrigerate at least 30 minutes. Remove chicken from bag; discard excess marinade. Sauté chicken in pan until totally cooked. Mix with lettuce, cilantro, corn, cheese, and tortilla chips. Mix ranch dressing with 1 tablespoon taco seasoning. Top each individual salad with the dressing. Add sour cream and salsa as desired. Hint: Chicken dices best when partially frozen.

July 26

I urge you brothers, by the Lord Jesus Christ and by the love of the Spirit, to join me in my struggle by praying to God for me.

—ROMANS 15:30

JUST AS THE apostle Paul needed prayer for his ministry, our leaders, missionaries, and pastors also need our intercession. Paul was persecuted for spreading the good news, and so are many of our missionaries and pastors today, regardless of where they are in the world. Satan does not sit idly back while the message is being proclaimed. Those on the front lines need prayer for protection, strength, and wisdom as they battle for the Lord. We must call out their names daily and join forces with them in their struggle of taking the love of Christ to all people.

Dear Lord: Please bless, strengthen, and protect your servants as they minister throughout the world. Meet their needs, whether physically, financially, mentally, or spiritually, and shield them from all harm. Deliver us all from the enemy's oppression and persecution, and empower us with supernatural wisdom and strength to take the love of Jesus to a lost and dying world. For this, we give You praise, glory, and all honor. In Jesus' name, Amen.

SPAGHETTI SAUCE

1–2 pounds lean ground beef and/or sausage
3–5 tablespoons olive oil
1 large onion, diced
1 carrot, peeled and grated
3–6 cloves garlic, minced
1 (28-ounce) can diced tomatoes
1 (28-ounce) can tomato sauce or puree
1 (12-ounce) can tomato paste + 1 can water
1 tablespoon Italian spices (oregano, basil, parsley)
1 tablespoon sugar
1 teaspoon salt
1 teaspoon pepper
1 pack fresh mushrooms, sliced (optional)

Brown meat; drain. Add olive oil, onion, carrot, and garlic; cook until tender, about 5 minutes. Add rest of ingredients; cover pan and cook on low 30–45 minutes or put in crockpot on low for 8 hours or high for 4 hours. Serve with 1 pound cooked spaghetti noodles.

July 27

Now the God of peace be with you all. Amen.

—Romans 15:33, kjv

G od of peace was one of the apostle Paul's favorite names for God. Even when he was being persecuted and tortured for being a Christian, Paul encouraged and blessed his fellow believers with these words. In life, we become engrossed with our busy schedules; there's just so much to do and not enough time and money to do it. We have stress at work, at school, at home, and even in our recreation. Where is that place of peaceful rest, and how do we find it? God's peace brings a sense of well-being, even in adversity. His peace brings rest and security. Even during the busy times of our lives, we can know the peace of God that passes all understanding. It's there and God will bring peace into our lives if we look to Him for it.

Father: You are the God of peace, and there is none other like You. At times life is overwhelming, but You bring an inner peace that only comes from knowing You. Forgive me and cleanse my life from all sin and clutter. Help me to focus on You so I might find true peace in my life. In Jesus' name, Amen.

BLACK BEAN AND CORN SALSA

1 (14.5-ounce) can whole kernel corn, drained
1 (14.5-ounce) can black beans, rinsed and drained
6 plum or Roma tomatoes, seeded and chopped
1–2 jalapeno peppers, seeded and chopped (optional)
½ medium red onion, finely chopped
2–3 cloves garlic, finely minced
1 small red bell pepper, diced
¼ cup fresh cilantro, finely diced
¼ cup lime juice (from 1 lime)
1 teaspoon sugar
1 teaspoon cumin or chili powder
¼ teaspoon salt

In large bowl, combine all ingredients. Cover and refrigerate until serving time. Serve with tortilla chips.

July 28

For the message of the cross is foolishness to those who are perishing, but to us who are being saved it is the power of God.

—1 Corinthians 1:18

IN HURRICANE SEASON, many homes will experience a loss of electrical power. Just about everything we do involves some type of electricity, though we may not really think much about it until it is gone. Heating, cooling, cooking, hair care, television, radio, electrical appliances, computers, and so much more are affected when the power source is lost. But there is One who brings us the power we need to be saved from eternal death and hell. To those who do not know and serve Him, the story of Christ and His resurrection is foolish and makes no sense. Without the power of God in our lives, we too would perish. We have the ability to be recharged and powered up, but we must plug into the Almighty power source to do that. This comes by daily reading the Bible, praying, and living a holy life of obedience to God's Word. A lamp will only give light if it is plugged in, and the same goes for our lives. To shine with the light of Jesus, we must first plug in to God.

Powerful God: Thank you for being my source of strength when I am weak and in need of more of You. When I let my light get low or become a flicker, You are there ready to recharge me and give me the power I need to press on. Help me to be a powerful witness and servant to my family, friends, and especially those who are lost. In Jesus' name, Amen.

CABBAGE SOUP

4 slices of bacon, cooked and crumbled
2 potatoes, diced
2 medium onions, chopped
1 stalk celery, chopped
3 carrots, chopped
3 cloves garlic
1 or 2 (14 ½-ounce) cans tomatoes pieces
3 cups water + 3 bouillon cubes
1 teaspoon salt
1 teaspoon pepper
1 small head of cabbage, chopped
½–1 teaspoon dill weed (optional)
Other favorite seasonings, as desired
1 package onion soup mix (optional)

Put everything in crockpot and cook on high for 3–4 hours or until all vegetables done. May cook on stove on low heat for 2–3 hours. If meat desired, add Polish sausage, ground pork, or beef.

July 29

No eye has seen, no ear has heard, no mind has conceived what God has prepared for those who love Him—but God has revealed it to us by His Spirit.

—1 CORINTHIANS 2:9–10

As WE THINK about what our future holds and what lies beyond our life on earth, we sometimes focus on the here and now and the road that is often rocky and filled with trials. But Paul tells us to focus on the great hope of eternity and blessings to come if we love God. Our fleshly human nature wants to focus on the present trials and hardships we may endure, but when we do, we lose out on the joy of our Christianity because we have lost sight of heaven. It's hard to imagine what heaven will be like, but we know it will be wonderful. There is nothing we can imagine, nothing we have seen, nothing we have heard, and nothing we can even conceive that will compare with what our Father has planned for us. Surely the hope we have in God will give us courage to carry on in this troublesome world. Our Father loves us and has our best interest in mind. No matter what tomorrow brings, our hope lies in the Lord and the glory that is to come. May we keep our focus on the future and this glorious promise Paul gave us. Indeed, the best is yet to come.

Dear Lord: Thank You for Your Word and how it speaks to our hearts! Thank You for the plans You have made for us—plans beyond what our minds can comprehend. We are so blessed to have You for our Father and to be able to rest in the assurance of Your love and care. We look forward to going home and seeing the glories you have prepared for us. In Jesus' name, Amen.

POTATO SHRIMP SOUP

¼ cup (½ stick) butter
1 small onion, diced
2 medium carrots, diced
2 tablespoons all-purpose flour
8 medium potatoes, peeled and cubed
4 cups milk
2 chicken bouillons dissolved in ½ cup hot milk
1 pound medium shrimp, cooked, peeled, diced
1 cup half-and-half or whole milk
1 teaspoon salt
¼ teaspoon pepper
Bacon bits
Sharp grated cheddar cheese

Melt butter in saucepan; sauté onion and carrots until both slightly tender, about 5 minutes. Whisk in flour and cook 1 minute. Add potatoes, milk, and milk with dissolved bouillon. Cook over medium heat 15 minutes, until potatoes very soft and some have begun to turn mushy. Add shrimp, half-and-half, salt, and pepper. Serve in bowls and top with bacon bits and cheese.

July 30

The man without the Spirit does not accept the things that come from the Spirit of God, for they are foolishness to him, and he cannot understand them, because they are spiritually discerned.

—1 Corinthians 2:14

SOMETIMES WE GET upset when those without Christ don't see God's Word as we do. Sin, in our weak and depraved moral system, clouds our minds and wills so that we miss and resist the validity of Scripture. Unless we have the Spirit of the living Christ in our hearts and are living a holy life, we will not see the gospel message as it is meant to be. The apostle Paul is saying that only through the Holy Spirit are we able to evaluate the things that come from the Spirit of God. Whenever a person without the Spirit evaluates spiritual things, though he may mentally understand what they mean, he will disregard or not accept them. In his own judgment, they are foolish or stupid. We must pray for those who are without the Spirit, that they all might know Christ and that we will all do our part to make Him known to a sick, lonely, and hurting world.

Holy God: Thank You for saving my soul. Forgive me for the sins in my life of which I have not yet repented. Help me to see Your Word as a roadmap for my life and share it with others as I live before them. With Your Holy Spirit, draw those without Christ to make a decision to accept You as Savior and Lord. In Jesus' name, Amen.

SWEET AND SOUR MEATBALLS

2 pounds ground meat
1 package dry onion soup mix
½ cup cracker crumbs
2 eggs

Mix all ingredients; shape into small balls. Place on cookie sheet; bake at 350 degrees for 20 minutes; then place in baking dish or crockpot.

Sauce:

½ cup brown sugar
1 tablespoon cornstarch
1 (14-ounce) can pineapple chunks
⅓ cup cider vinegar
1 tablespoon soy sauce
1 small green pepper, cut in strips

Mix brown sugar, cornstarch, pineapple juice (drained from can of pineapple), vinegar, and soy sauce in pan; bring to boil over medium heat. Pour over meatballs; cook on low in crockpot 4–6 hours, or in 325-degree oven for 1 hour. Add pineapple chunks and green pepper during last 30 minutes of cooking.

July 31

But now I [Paul] am writing you that you must not associate with anyone who calls himself a brother but is sexually immoral or greedy, an idolater or a slanderer, a drunkard or a swindler. With such a man do not even eat.

—1 Corinthians 5:11

THESE ARE PRETTY harsh words that the apostle Paul is commanding us as Christians to not do. Though many may not accept them very well, they are the guidelines found in God's Word. However, without any communication or contact with non-believers, we could not carry out Christ's command to tell them about salvation (Matthew 28:19–20).

Paul tells us to not associate with those who claim to be Christians but are not. They might also be known as hypocrites. A believer should not accept their sinful behavior, and association with them should only be to encourage repentance. If they are unwilling to change, Paul gives us distinct instructions to disassociate with them personally and even have them removed from the church if attempts to correct them fail.

Those outside of Christ who do not profess to be Christians are the ones we are to target with our evangelistic efforts. While it is true that Christ died for all and wills that none should perish, there are those who will never submit to His authority. Throughout the Bible are warnings that no one can live for immoral gratifications and still inherit the kingdom of God (Romans 6:16; James 1:15; 1 John 2:4). The permissiveness of today's society is no reason to ignore God's truth and justify immoral behavior. It's up to each and every Christian to stand up for righteousness and not be ashamed to confront sin, even when it may mean the loss of friendship or relationship.

Dear Lord: Help me live humbly to the call You have placed on my life to win the lost for Christ. Give me strength to confront those who call themselves Christians yet live immorally so they might repent and turn to You for salvation. May I be led by Your Holy Spirit to choose friends and associates that also want to glorify You in their lives and live a holy lifestyle. In Jesus' name, Amen.

CHILI CHEESE PIE

3 cups corn chips
1 cup chopped onion
1 cup grated mild cheddar cheese
1 ½ cups chili (homemade or canned)

Put 2 cups corn chips in greased baking dish; top with half the onion and cheese. Add chili; top with remaining corn chips, onion, and cheese. Bake at 350 degrees for 15–20 minutes, or until cheese bubbles.

August

School
Days

August 1

Do you not know that the wicked will not inherit the kingdom of God? Do not be deceived: Neither the sexually immoral nor idolaters nor adulterers nor male prostitutes nor homosexual offenders nor thieves nor the greedy nor drunkards nor slanders or swindlers will inherit the kingdom of God. And that is what some of you were. But you were washed, you were sanctified, you were justified in the name of the Lord Jesus Christ and by the Spirit of our God.

—1 CORINTHIANS 6:9–11

THE PEOPLE OF Corinth believed they could live any way they desired and still reap God's blessings and inheritance. Just as they were deceived with this thinking, so are many of us today. Following Christ is a serious matter; in fact, it's a matter of life or death. Jesus is either Savior and Lord and we obey the biblical principles He has given us, or we choose eternal punishment that was meant for Satan and his fallen angels. When we choose Christ, repent of all our sin, abandon immorality, and live according to God's Word, our inheritance in God's kingdom is secure. If we choose to abandon the way of the Cross, disobey God's Word, and break fellowship with the Savior, Paul tells us we have no rights to God's kingdom and will spiritually die (Romans 8:13; James 1:15; Galatians 5:21; Ephesians 5:5–6). Salvation is for everyone, but not everyone will be saved. Without the ongoing, regenerating, sanctifying power of the Holy Spirit working in our lives, as we daily strive for the righteousness of God, it is impossible to acquire a place in His kingdom. But with His love, compassion, power, mercy, and grace, we are washed, sanctified, and justified in the name of the Lord Jesus Christ and by the Spirit of our God.

Father: Without You, I would be foolish, disobedient, deceived, and enslaved by all sorts of passions and pleasures. With You, I am a victor and an heir of Your glorious kingdom. Your mercy and grace have overwhelmed me, and I am eternally grateful for the continuous work You are doing in my life. Help me to be strong in every area of my life. In Jesus' name, Amen.

SAUCY CHICKEN

5–6 boneless, skinless, chicken breasts
2 cups salsa
⅓ cup brown sugar
2 tablespoons honey Dijon mustard

Combine all ingredients; put in greased 9x13-inch baking dish. Bake at 350 degrees for 45 minutes until chicken thoroughly cooked. Serve with rice.

August 2

Flee from sexual immorality. All other sins a man commits are outside his body, but he who sins sexually sins against his own body. Do you not know that your body is a temple of the Holy Spirit, who is in you, whom you have received from God? You are not your own; you were bought at a price. Therefore honor God with your body.

—1 CORINTHIANS 6:18–20

GOD IS NOT pleased with sin of any type, but He abhors sexual sin. In our sensual society, sexual immorality has become acceptable, even by many who call themselves Christians. Blatant disregard for biblical principles is not only devastating and desecrating to the one committing the sin, it breaks fellowship with God. Man was created to have an intimate relationship with God, but when sexual sins are committed, the relationship is broken. Intimacy is getting to know someone emotionally on the deepest level; it does not necessarily have anything to do with physical touch. It is impossible to have intimacy and sexual immorality at the same time. Sex was created for pleasure and procreation under God's guidelines. Even though God gave us natural needs and desires, we are to control and subdue them until the proper time. A believer must exercise self-control in all areas of sexuality, according to God's Word. Because our body is the temple of the Holy Spirit, we are not to defile it with impurities of evil. God wants us to refrain from evil thoughts, passionate desires or actions, films, magazines, books, music, Internet, music, or any other avenue of sexual immorality. God's standards are high because He wants the very best for us. He owns us; we are not our own. God paid the price for us with His very own Son; therefore, we *must* honor God with our bodies.

Father: Forgive me for my immoral thoughts and actions, and the lack of self-control in these areas. Your Word says in Proverbs 25:28 that a person who lacks self-control is like a city whose walls are broken down. Help me to be strong in my weak areas to flee all areas that might lead to immorality and sin. In Jesus' name, Amen.

LAWRY'S CHIP AND VEGGIE DIP

⅔ cup mayonnaise
⅔ cup sour cream
1 tablespoon onion flakes
1 teaspoon Lawry's Seasoned Salt
1 teaspoon dill weed
3–4 drops Tabasco or hot sauce

Mix together all ingredients; refrigerate until ready to use. Serve with veggies, crackers, or chips.

August 3

No temptation has seized you except what is common to man. And God is faithful; He will not let you be tempted beyond what you can bear. But when you are tempted, He will also provide a way out so that you can stand up under it.

—1 Corinthians 10:13

EVERYONE IS TEMPTED. If we're alive and have our being, we are tempted. Even Jesus was tempted when He was led into the desert by the Spirit of God. He had fasted forty days and was hungry. The tempter (Satan) came to tempt Jesus by urging Him to turn stones into bread (Matthew 4:1–3). Jesus was again tempted when Satan encouraged Him to bow down and worship him.

As Christians, we are subject to temptation, some more than others, but temptation alone is not a sin. However, sin takes offense if we yield to the temptation and commit an action contrary to God's Word. We are not responsible for thoughts that grieve or tempt us, but we are on a slippery slope if we entertain those thoughts. Before they even have a chance to last a moment, we must do as Jesus did and come against them with the Word of God. Jesus told Satan to flee in Matthew 4:10, and he fled. If it worked for Jesus, it will work for us. Though Jesus knew He was soon going to die a horrible death on Calvary, He was willing to do it for us. He made a choice that day to honor God and stay true to His Word. In Matthew 4:11, Jesus tells us to worship the Lord and Him only. We cannot save ourselves from the entrapment of sin and its eternal consequences, but God can. He has provided a way of escape through His Son, Jesus, who gave His life to pay sin's penalty. The choice is ours. Let's choose God's way the moment temptation strikes.

Father: Oh, but for Your mercy and grace would I be caught up in a world of sin and shame. Because of Your love for me, I have been given the opportunity to choose Your plan of salvation in Jesus. Forgive me for all my sin and help me to be strong when temptation comes. Show me how to come against the enemy's attack by the power of Your Word. In Jesus' name, Amen.

TERIYAKI MARINADE FOR STEAK OR CHICKEN

3 tablespoons teriyaki sauce
1 teaspoon garlic powder
1 tablespoon brown sugar
1 teaspoon ground ginger
1 tablespoon wine vinegar
⅓ cup pineapple juice
1–3 tablespoons soy sauce

Mix ingredients in large ziplock bag. Add meat; refrigerate 4–12 hours. Grill or cook as desired.

August 4

So whether you eat or drink or whatever you do, do it all for the glory of God.

—1 CORINTHIANS 10:31

MAN WAS CREATED for two reasons—one, to worship and give glory to God, and two, to witness His love to others so that they might also know Him as Savior and Lord. With that in mind, everything we do should be done in honor and obedience to God's Word. Obedience honors God, while disobedience always dishonors God. Jesus said that others would see our good works and glorify God (Matthew 5:16). Our lifestyle, behavior, attitude, and treatment to others is a testimony of our relationship with Christ. The apostle Paul urged the Corinthian people to follow his example as he followed the example of Christ and humbly lived as a disciple to others. Discipleship means we have committed ourselves to follow Christ and intend to follow Him in everything we do and say. If that is our heartbeat, then we should boldly invite people to follow our example as we follow the example of Jesus Christ. Furthermore, if we are living for Jesus Christ, we are bringing glory to God.

Glorious Lord: You are at work, carrying out the mission of showing Your love, mercy, and grace to the world You made, and I want to be a part of it. Forgive me for my foolishness and pride; help me to not get so worked up over meaningless things and for not focusing on matters that are important to You. Give me strength to sow seeds that will be fruitful in Your mission. May all I do be done as a conscious decision to honor and bring You respect. In Jesus' name, Amen.

CHICKEN RICE SOUP

3–4 boneless, skinless chicken breasts
2 quarts water + 6 chicken bouillon cubes
⅔ teaspoon salt
1 large onion, chopped in food processor
½ pound carrots, chopped in food processor
1 stick butter
1 cup uncooked rice
1 teaspoon pepper
1 can evaporated milk or 12 ounces milk
2 cups (16 ounces) sour cream

Boil chicken in water with bouillon until done (about 20 minutes). Remove chicken; dice and return to boiling water. Add onions, carrots, butter, salt, rice, and pepper; boil until vegetables and rice tender (about 30 minutes). Blend in milk and sour cream; add water if soup too thick. Heat without lid if too thin. Keep warm until ready to serve.

August 5

For whenever you eat this bread and drink this cup, you proclaim the Lord's death until He comes.

—1 Corinthians 11:26

UNLIKE BAPTISM, WHICH is a one-time event, communion is meant to be observed over and over throughout the life of a Christian. It is a time of corporate worship when we come together as one body to remember and celebrate what Christ did for us. The bread of communion symbolizes the body of Jesus that was broken for us through His sufferings. The grape juice represents the blood He sacrificially shed while being beaten and hung on the cross. Partaking of communion means to accept and proclaim redemption from sin and condemnation through Christ's sacrificial death. It is our ultimate motivation against falling into sin and for abstaining from all appearance of evil. The Lord's Supper comes from a part of the Passover meal that was celebrated only once a year; however, the early Christian church took Communion weekly and sometimes daily. There is no specific frequency of the Lord's Supper prescribed in Scripture. Partaking of communion is a profession of our faith; therefore, there are serious consequences for those who do so unworthily. Before taking communion, we each must examine ourselves to see whether or not our hearts are pure and ready to receive (2 Corinthians 13:5), for it is when we eat the bread and drink the cup that we solemnly accept the covenant of God's grace with all its promises and obligations while uniting with others to "proclaim the Lord's death until He comes."

Father: Thank You for sending Your Son to Calvary so we wouldn't have to go. I am eternally grateful for all You have done in my life. Cleanse my soul of all unrighteousness so I may receive and remember You during communion. In Jesus' name, Amen.

BEEF STEW (crockpot)

1–2 pounds stew meat in 1-inch cubes
¼ cup flour
1 teaspoon salt
1 teaspoon pepper
1 (14-ounce) can beef broth
1–2 teaspoons Worcestershire sauce
2–3 cloves minced garlic
½ teaspoon paprika
3–5 carrots, diced
3–5 potatoes, diced
1–2 onions, chopped
1–2 stalks celery

Put all ingredients in crockpot. Cook on low for 10 hours or high for 5 hours.

August 6

Now you are the body of Christ, and each one of you is a part of it.
—1 Corinthians 12:27

Each and every one of us who knows Jesus Christ as Savior and Lord is an integral part of the body of Christ. When we become a believer, the Holy Spirit supernaturally transforms us and makes us one with the body of Christ as we are united in purpose and love. Each person is a separate unit, just as a brick is one part of a building. Put all the bricks together, and they form the foundation and become the building. Though we each have our own being, together we are the body or church. No one is greater than the other, and all are created equal in the Lord's eyes. If even one small brick is removed from a building, it weakens the structure; so it is with the church. God equips each of us with strengths and abilities to be used to glorify Him and if we don't use them, the structure of the body of Christ weakens. That's why it is so important that we find out what our gifts or strengths are and then put them to work in the kingdom. It is up to each one of us to do our part to show the grace, power, and love of the Lord to one another. It is then that the body of Christ is strengthened and God is glorified.

Father: You said if anyone loves You, he will obey Your teachings. Forgive me for those times I did not obey and acted foolishly concerning Your Word. Holy Spirit, reveal to me what You would have me to do with my strengths and abilities. Help me to use them in my church, my home, my work place, and everywhere I go so You will be lifted up and glorified. Give me new revelation of how to make Your Word come alive as I strive to make You known in the mission field where You have placed me. In Jesus' name, Amen.

CHILI MAC (quick and easy)

1 pound ground beef
1 tablespoon vegetable oil
1 onion, chopped
2 (14.5-ounce) cans diced tomatoes
1 (6-ounce) can tomato paste
1 envelope chili seasoning
1 (15-ounce) can mild chili beans
2 teaspoons cumin
1 (7-ounce) package macaroni
Cheddar cheese, grated

Brown meat in large skillet; drain. Add oil and onion; cook until tender. Add all other ingredients, except cheese. Cover and cook on medium-low heat for 20–30 minutes, until macaroni done. Serve on plates and top with cheese.

August 7

And now these three remain: faith, hope and love. But the greatest of these is love.

—1 Corinthians 13:13

THERE ARE THREE essential elements that make up our Christian character: *faith, hope and love.* Hebrews 11:1 (KJV) says, "Now faith is the substance of things hoped for, the evidence of things not seen." *Faith* means firmly and wholly believing and trusting in the crucified and risen Christ as our personal Savior and Lord, thus allowing Him to have full control of our lives. Without faith, we could not come to Christ, and without faith, we could not walk in obedience to Him. Faith often motivates us to move forward, even when the odds are against us.

The second element of Christian character is hope. Christ is the actual object of the believer's hope because it is in His second coming that the hope of glory will be fulfilled. Hope keeps us going when the situation we face seems impossible. Hope is the expectation that we will obtain something specific we desire. Hope encourages us that victory is imminent.

The third element of Christian character is love. Because there are various types of love, there are many ways to describe love; however, they all provoke emotions and/or actions that are very similar. Love might be a feeling of warm personal attachment or deep affection, as for a parent, child, or friend. It may involve attraction, enthusiasm, devotion, or affection, based on admiration, benevolence, or common interests. Love should always portray an unselfish, loyal and benevolent concern for the good of another. As Christians, we are to emphasize character that is patient, kind, unselfish, and honest.

God's Word says that love is greater than faith or hope, for it is what motivated God to send His only Son to die for us. Without love, there would have been no redemption for mankind. Not only would we be without love, but without the redemption that was precipitated by love, there would also be no faith and no hope. Nothing really matters without love; it is the foundation for every good thing in our lives.

Dear Lord: Thank You for Your extravagant love, so great that You sacrificed Your only Son. You are the giver of life and have created us to love one another as we show our love for You. Help me to always demonstrate my faith, hope, and, most of all, love, to a world that is lost and looking for answers to circumstances and problems. May I be found faithful to living in obedience to Your Word as I strive to love You more. In Jesus' name, Amen.

Today's recipe found on page 384 GUMBO RECIPE

August 8

Behold, I shew you a mystery; We shall not all sleep, but we shall all be changed, In a moment, in the twinkling of an eye, at the last trump: for the trumpet shall sound, and the dead shall be raised incorruptible, and we shall be changed.

—1 Corinthians 15:51–52, kjv

As Paul was teaching on the resurrection of Christ, he stopped to get everyone's attention. He wanted no one to miss the details he was about to proclaim. A *mystery*, he called it. Surely this captured their thoughts. Paul went on to explain the rapture, or taking up of the church (those who have received and believed on the Lord Jesus Christ), and the assurance that both the dead and alive will be transformed when Jesus returns. Not only will the graves open and the souls of the believers who have already died ascend and receive their imperishable bodies, but those who are still alive on earth also will immediately be changed. This will happen as soon as the trumpet sounds and Jesus emerges in the clouds. The transformation of our bodies from mortality (death) to immortality (life) will take place in the *twinkling of an eye*. This has been equated to be about one billionth of a second, a time unfathomable to our minds. There will be no time to repent, so our eternal destination is predetermined. Thanks be to God for the hope we have in Him that one day soon He will send His Son to take us home. We must be ready to go!

Wonderful Father: I was created to worship You, and knowing I will be able to do that forever brings joy to my heart. Remove from my life all those things that cloud my vision of serving You and being prepared for Your return. In Jesus' name, Amen.

STEAK DINNER IN A PACKAGE

2 pounds chuck steak, 1 inch thick
1 can cream of mushroom soup
1 envelope dry onion soup mix
3 carrots, quartered
2 stalks celery, cut into 2-inch pieces (optional)
3 potatoes, pared and quartered
2 tablespoons water

Place a 24x18-inch piece of heavy-duty aluminum foil in baking pan; place meat on foil. Stir together mushroom soup and onion soup mix; spread over meat. Top with vegetables; sprinkle with water. Fold foil over and seal securely. Cook in 325-degree oven for 2 hours or until meat and vegetables tender.

August 9

Be on your guard; stand firm in the faith; be men of courage; be strong.

—1 Corinthians 16:13

P AUL WAS CONCLUDING his letter-writing to the people of Corinth, providing them with counsel and instruction on various issues. He addressed the types of problems that churches experience when members continue to delve into sin and don't separate themselves from the things of the world. Paul emphasizes the real possibility of falling away from the faith by those who continue to live unrighteous lives and don't hold firmly to the teachings of Christ. Just as Paul urged the Corinthians to be on their guard and courageously stand firm in their faith, we too must not exempt ourselves from this warning. Even then, Paul knew the conditions of the world were corrupt and yet enticing to believers. For this reason, he felt compelled to provide counsel and instruction so Christians would remain strong and pure. The tolerance of sin in our churches today has gone epidemic, and God's judgment is upon them. We must each one determine in our hearts to be on our guard, stand firm in our faith, and be courageous and strong.

Father: You made the heavens and the earth, and You are the great and glorious One. Today and forever I give You praise and thank You for the wonderful Lord You are. Help me remain strong in my faith, even when trials come and try to pull me away. Thank You for the witness Paul was to the people of Corinth; may I be the same for You in my world today. In Jesus' name, Amen.

PORK CHOPS WITH MUSHROOM GRAVY

4–6 pork chops
½ cup bread crumbs, cracker crumbs, or flour
2 tablespoons Parmesan cheese, grated
½ teaspoon salt
½ teaspoon pepper
1–2 tablespoons vegetable oil
1 can mushroom soup
1 can sliced mushrooms, drained
½ cup milk

Combine crumbs or flour with Parmesan cheese, salt, and pepper. Heat oil in large skillet on medium-high heat. Coat pork chops with crumb mixture and cook on both sides until brown. Remove chops; add soup, mushrooms, and milk to skillet; bring to gentle boil. Stir, scraping bottom of pan to loosen crust. Add pork chops, cover, and cook on low heat for about 20 minutes. Serve with rice or mashed potatoes. (Add more milk if gravy too thick.)

August 10

Praise be to the God and Father of our Lord Jesus Christ, the Father of compassion and the God of all comfort, who comforts us in all our troubles, so that we can comfort those in any trouble with the comfort we ourselves have received from God.

—2 CORINTHIANS 1:3–4

To COMFORT MEANS to soothe, console, reassure, bring cheer to, support, stand by, or encourage someone in need or trouble. The apostle Paul wanted those in and around Corinth who remained faithful to him as their spiritual father to know God would bring them comfort for the persecution they endured. There were many false apostles who continued to come against Paul's message of the gospel; therefore, they also treated those who were loyal to him badly. Paul's compassion for the people is evident in his writings, yet he too suffered terribly for the sake of Christ. In fact, he most likely was in prison at the time of writing this letter for merely preaching the gospel. How ironic that the imprisoned Paul was encouraging others, while he could have used some support and consolation. Paul relied on the comfort of his heavenly Father in his times of trouble yet never complained about his circumstances. God knows we all will go through trials and afflictions in our lives and yet permits it so we might rely on Him to be comforted. In turn, we are to comfort others in need. This is what Paul did, and he wants us to do the same. There is no suffering or hardship, no matter how severe, that can separate us from the care and compassion of our heavenly Father (Romans 8:35–39).

Dear Lord: I ask You to bring comfort and restoration to the weary and downtrodden. Wrap Your loving arms around them and shelter them under Your wings of strength and mercy. Teach me Your ways and comfort me in my times of need, so in turn I might be compassionate and comforting to others. In Jesus' name, Amen.

CHICKEN POT PIE

2 ready-made pie shells
3 boneless, skinless chicken breasts
1 (10-ounce) package frozen mixed vegetables
1 cup milk
2 tablespoons butter
1 can cream of chicken soup

Cook chicken breasts in pan with small amount water until done; dice. In saucepan, heat vegetables, milk, butter, soup, and chicken. Put pie shell in deep dish pie plate and pour mixture into it. Cover with second pie shell; cut slits in top. Bake at 350 degrees for 1 hour.

August 11

Now the Lord is the Spirit, and where the Spirit of the Lord is, there is freedom.

—2 Corinthians 3:17

THE MOMENT WE accept Christ as our personal Savior and repent of our unrighteousness, a freedom comes that liberates us from the condemnation and slavery of sin. This is known as a new birth because we are spiritually born again. Jesus tells us in John 3:3 (KJV), "Except a man be born again, he cannot see the kingdom of God." Christ no longer sees us as sinners but as redeemed, regenerated children of God. We are no longer to be conformed to the ways of the world; we are to live like God in holiness and righteousness. This doesn't mean we are free to live any way we want, but it does mean we are free to live how we should. Spiritual freedom does not justify sinful living; it is by the presence of God's Holy Spirit we are given freedom. The fruit of the Spirit is love, joy, peace, patience, kindness, goodness, faithfulness, gentleness, and self-control. The Spirit sets us free from every bondage, sin, temptation, bad emotion, and evil desire. It is then we are free to experience the presence of God, which is love, joy, and peace. Spiritual freedom is conditional on our faith in Christ throughout our earthly existence and is demonstrated by sincere love and obedience to God's Word.

Father: Thank You for the freedom I have been given through redemption in Your Son, Jesus. Because I have turned to You for forgiveness and repented of my sin, I am born again and have new life. No longer do I desire the things of this world, but it is You I long to know and serve. Help me in my weaknesses and cause my faith to grow stronger each day. In Jesus' name, Amen.

BAKED BEANS (crockpot)

1 pound small dry white beans
1 onion, chopped
½ pound bacon, chopped
¼ cup light (mild) molasses
½ cup packed brown sugar
1 teaspoon dry mustard
¼ cup ketchup
½ teaspoon ground black pepper
1 tablespoon Worcestershire sauce
1 teaspoons garlic salt
¼ cup barbecue sauce (optional)

Rinse, sort, and simmer beans in 6 cups water for 30 minutes. Let stand, covered, several hours or over night until softened; drain. Put all ingredients in crockpot. Add 1 cup water; stir. Cover and cook on low 10–12 hours or high 5–6 hours, stirring occasionally.

August 12

The god of this age has blinded the minds of unbelievers, so that they cannot see the light of the gospel of the glory of Christ, who is the image of God.

—2 Corinthians 4:4

THE "GOD OF this age" is Satan, the author of evil, lies, and deception. He uses many counterfeits to deceive the world and does everything possible to blind our eyes from the true message of Jesus Christ. Satan roams about the earth, seeking whom he may devour, and unless we are grounded in our faith in Christ, we are under his control. Even as Christians, we face the trials and temptations that are in the world; but we have the authority to have victory over them. When Jesus was tempted by Satan, He used the authority of the Scriptures as His weapon to rebuke the evil one. After each of Satan's attempts to deceive Him, Jesus responded with, "It is written" (Matthew 4:4, 7, 10). Jesus tells us in John 8:31–32, "If you hold to my teaching, you are really my disciples. Then you will know the truth, and the truth will set you free." The devil does not want anyone to be saved and therefore blinds the eyes of unbelievers to the only truth that will save them. We must pray against Satan with the power we have from the Almighty God in Jesus' name. Every believer has a responsibility to pray for the lost and continue to share God's Word so they might have their minds opened and choose to follow Christ.

Dear God: Today and forever I honor You as Savior and Redeemer. I pray for the lost that the blinders would be removed from their minds and Satan would have no power over them. Cause them to see their true spiritual condition and have a genuine sorrow over their sin. May they come to repentance through the power of Jesus Christ and be saved. In Jesus' name, Amen.

BROWN SUGAR MEATLOAF

½ cup brown sugar
½ cup ketchup
1 ½ pounds lean ground beef
½ cup milk
2 eggs
1 teaspoon salt
½ teaspoon pepper
1 small onion, chopped
¼ teaspoon ground ginger
¾ cup crushed saltine crackers

Press brown sugar on bottom of meatloaf dish; cover with ketchup. Mix together remaining ingredients; shape into loaf; put in pan over ketchup. Bake 1 hour at 350 degrees. When done, remove from pan; spoon juices over top.

August 13

We are troubled on every side, yet not distressed; we are perplexed, but not in despair;
Persecuted, but not forsaken; cast down, but not destroyed.

—2 CORINTHIANS 4:8–9, KJV

UNHAPPINESS PLAGUES THE world! A mood of depression has settled upon people of every color, race, ethnicity, gender, and marital status. There is conflict between nations and among one another. People are unhappy today not only because of the conditions in the world but because they are dissatisfied within themselves. We search daily to find contentment and joy, but oftentimes in the wrong places.

The apostle Paul obviously knew what it meant to live in perilous times, yet found his joy complete while imprisoned and chained in a deplorable underground prison. He found that happiness is not escape from reality but joy amid ugly reality. It is not immunity from tragedy or tranquilization against pain, but it is the joy and hope we find when we have a relationship with the King of kings and the Lord of lords, Jesus Christ. If we walk with Him and talk with Him, there is no trouble, sickness, or tragedy that will cause us spiritual defeat. When the weight of the world and the circumstances that daily cross our paths come upon us, we can remain hopeful and encouraged that God's strength and mercy will carry us to victory.

Dear Lord: I need You more than I ever have and trust You to carry me on eagle's wings through the storm I am in. Come now and pour Your oil into my wounds and those of all the brokenhearted; bring healing and peace to our souls. Even though all signs point to destruction, despair, and persecution, Your awesome power, strength, mercy, and love will guide us to victory. In Jesus' name, Amen.

COMPANY CHICKEN BREASTS

1 package dried beef
6 boneless, skinless chicken breast halves
6 bacon slices
1 can chicken or mushroom soup
8 ounces sour cream
2–3 tablespoons milk

Arrange dried beef on bottom of 9x13-inch baking dish. Halve each chicken breast and wrap with 1 slice bacon; put over dried beef. Bake uncovered 35 minutes. Combine soup, sour cream, and milk; pour over chicken. Bake additional 25 minutes or until chicken thoroughly cooked. May add 8 ounces sliced fresh mushrooms to chicken before pouring sauce over, if desired.

August 14

Therefore we do not lose heart. Though outwardly we are wasting away, yet inwardly we are being renewed day by day. For our light and momentary troubles are achieving for us an eternal glory that far outweighs them all.

—2 CORINTHIANS 4:16–17

I'M NOT SURE about you, but I don't think if I were shipwrecked, starved without food for days on end, beaten for no reason other than preaching God's Word, or put into stocks in a dark rat-and-roach-infested cold dungeon that I would call these things light and momentary troubles; but the apostle Paul did. He had been through some tremendous sufferings and hardships, yet he remained faithful to his Lord without complaining or throwing in the towel as most of us would do. Though our bodies began to age and waste away, once we were born, we, who have been reborn of the Spirit, experience ongoing renewal through the constant indwelling of Christ's presence and power. Paul so strongly believed that no matter what we endure here on earth, it is nothing compared to the abundant glory we have in Christ. There are no horrendous trials or tribulations that measure to any degree on life's Richter scale that could compare with our heavenly inheritance. To God be the glory!

Father in heaven: How awesome is Your mercy, grace, and power; I cannot even fathom the magnitude. Though my body is wasting away, my spirit remains encouraged and hopeful because of Your vast love for me. No matter what I endure here on earth, my hope is in You and I praise Your holy name. In Jesus' name, Amen.

PECAN CHICKEN

½ cup flour
½ cup ground pecans
2 tablespoons sesame seeds
½ teaspoon paprika
¾ teaspoon salt
¼ teaspoon pepper
1 egg, beaten
½ cup buttermilk (milk okay)
4 boneless, skinless chicken breasts
¼ cup butter
¼ cup coarsely chopped pecans

Combine first 6 ingredients. Mix together egg and buttermilk; dip chicken in it, then coat in flour mixture. Melt butter in baking dish; place chicken in dish, turning once to coat with butter. Sprinkle with pecans. Bake at 350 degrees for 30 minutes, or until chicken done.

August 15

So we fix our eyes not on what is seen, but what is unseen. For what is seen is temporary, but what is unseen is eternal.

—2 Corinthians 4:18

IT'S EASY TO believe that the things we see or touch are real, but it's more difficult believing in the things we don't see with our eyes. Some may say they don't believe in God because they don't see Him; but what about the air we breathe? We don't see it either, yet we keep on taking one breath after another. We can't see gravity, but we depend on it to keep our feet on the ground. As Christians, we don't put our trust only in the seen, but our hope is in much more than that. The material things here on earth will one day be gone, even though we work so hard to get them. Think about this: Do we spend as much time working on our relationship with Christ and spiritual blessings as we do our jobs and material things in life? One day the material will all be gone and only what we have done for Christ will remain. Are we to quit our jobs, sit back, and only worship God? No, but if we are focused on Christ in all that we do, every decision we make will be uplifting to His name and God will be glorified.

Father: Thank You for the air we breathe and for all Your many blessings. Sometimes we take You for granted and don't praise You enough. Help me to focus on the eternal and not the temporary, and put in proper prospective those things I need in my life. In Jesus' name, Amen.

CHICKEN ENCHILADA SOUP

1 small onion, chopped
1 garlic clove, chopped
2 tablespoons olive oil
1 tablespoon Worcestershire sauce
1 ½ cups water
1 teaspoon ground cumin
1 (14-ounce) can beef broth
1 teaspoon chili powder
1 (14-ounce) can chicken broth
½ teaspoon pepper
1 can cream of chicken soup
1 (4-ounce) can chopped green chiles
2 cups cooked chicken breast, diced
6 flour tortillas
3 cups grated cheddar cheese
Sour cream (optional)

Sauté onion and garlic in olive oil until soft. Add remaining ingredients except for tortillas, cheddar cheese, and sour cream; bring to a boil. Cover; turn to low heat and simmer one hour. Cut tortillas into ½-inch strips; add with cheese to soup. Simmer uncovered 10 minutes. Serve with a dollop of sour cream.

August 16

For we must all appear before the judgment seat of Christ, that every one may receive the things done in his body, according to that he hath done, whether it be good or bad.

—2 CORINTHIANS 5:10, KJV

GOD'S WORD SAYS that one day we all will give account of everything we have done, whether good or bad. This includes our secret actions (Mark 4:22), our character (Romans 2:5–11), our words (Matthew 12:36–37), our good deeds (Ephesians 6:8), our attitudes (Matthew 5:22), our motives (1 Corinthians 4:5), our lack of love (Colossians 3:18–4:1), our work and ministry (1 Corinthians 3:13), and our faithfulness or unfaithfulness to God (Matthew 25:21–23), (1 Corinthians 4:2–5). This day of judgment, known as the judgment seat of Christ, refers specifically to God's judgment and rewarding of the saints. The judgment seat (*bema* in Greek) was an elevated chair or platform resembling a throne that an official judge would sit upon in the Roman courts of law. In the Grecian world, the *bema* was the official seat of a judge who would observe the competitions in the theaters and award honor to those who competed well. This is different than the White Throne Judgment, which refers to the punishment of all sinners (Revelation 20:11–15). Between these two events, all mankind will be judged; then we will be rewarded or punished accordingly (Revelation 20:11–12). We should pray as David did: "Search me, O God, and know my heart" (Ps. 139:23, kjv). We are to use our God-given gifts to accomplish the work He has set before us. To glorify God and enjoy Him forever is the goal.

Dear Lord: You have revealed to us that one day we will stand before the judgment seat of Christ and give an account of our lives while on earth. Because I have accepted Christ as Savior, my sins have been forgiven and I will receive the rewards You have planned for me. I pray for my family and friends who don't know You personally that they will acknowledge You as their Savior and not have to face the White Throne Judgment. Help me to be a better witness of Your mercy and grace so others might come to a saving knowledge of You. In Jesus' name, Amen.

BARBECUED BEEF SHORT RIBS (crockpot)

3 pounds beef short ribs
1 cup grape or apple juice
1 tablespoon Worcestershire sauce
½ cup barbecue sauce

Place ribs standing in crockpot. Pour in rest of ingredients; cook on low 8 hours.

August 17

Be ye not unequally yoked together with unbelievers.

—2 Corinthians 6:14, KJV

A YOKE IS A wooden bar or frame by which two draft animals like oxen are joined at the heads or necks for working together. The Bible uses beasts of burden as an example. If a donkey and an ox were yoked together (which God forbid the people of Israel to do in Deuteronomy 22:10), the yoke would weigh heavily on one animal while choking the other. Or, as the animal with the longer stride moved ahead, it would painfully drag the other along by the neck. They would not be able to pull smoothly or painlessly together and little work would get done. But when two animals of closely related size and weight are yoked together, they pull the plow smoothly, helping each other and accomplishing work.

Becoming attached to a person who does not share like faith in Jesus Christ as Savior can be just as painful and counterproductive as the illustration of the unequally yoked animals. Christians are not to yoke together with unbelievers, whether it be in friendships, business partnerships, or in marriage. That doesn't mean we are supposed to shut everyone out of our lives that isn't a Christian, but it does mean that our association with an unbeliever should only be as necessary, such as for socioeconomic purposes or to show others the way of salvation. Whether it be in the social circle, the matrimonial circle, the business circle, or in the worship and service of God, the Lord will preserve the feet of His saints and enable us to yield our heartfelt, unhesitant obedience to His Word.

Father: According to Your Word, You have a wonderful plan for my life. When I am obedient and follow Your ways, my life is blessed. Help me to be strong as I form bonds of friendship with those of like faith. As I walk with You and talk with You, may my life display the power and mercy You have given me. Grant me wisdom to not become yoked with unbelievers in all areas of my life, and in doing so, may You receive all the glory. In Jesus' name, Amen.

BAKED BEANS AND WIENERS

1 (28-ounce) can pork and beans
⅓ cup ketchup or barbecue sauce
⅓ cup brown sugar
1 pound wieners, sliced
1 package dry onion soup mix
¼ cup water
1 tablespoon prepared mustard

Mix everything together; pour into greased baking dish. Bake uncovered 1 hour at 350 degrees.

August 18

Since we have these promises, dear friends, let us purify ourselves from everything that contaminates body and spirit, perfecting holiness out of reverence for God.

—2 Corinthians 7:1

ABANDONMENT FROM SIN is essential to everyone who calls himself a believer and child of God. Once we come to Christ, a separation from evil should result as we strive to live according to God's Word. This only happens when we make a deliberate choice to follow His righteous ways and draw near to Him in a daily, close, and intimate fellowship. The purification Paul talks about is an ongoing requirement for God's people. We must strive for holiness, even though it means standing up for what is right in a world that approves of wickedness and perverse living. Unholy compromise to the ways of the world is irreverence toward God and separates us from His presence and promises. Our attitude toward separation from "everything that contaminates body and spirit" should be from a genuine love for God and a hatred of sin. It is the pursuit of every believer to be found holy in the sight of God, making the very nature of Christ our highest goal and longing. We must seek to perfect holiness in our lives by putting off the flesh and putting on the qualities of God. It is then that He is glorified.

Thank You, God, for teaching me how to live according to Your holy and righteous ways. May I daily come to You with a repentant heart, desiring to flee from every evil thing that could contaminate my body and spirit. Your promises and Your presence are mine to hold, as long as I remain in fellowship with You. Forgive me for my sin and help me to always live for You. In Jesus' name, Amen.

LEMONADE CHICKEN (crockpot)

6 boneless, skinless chicken breast halves
1 (6-ounce) can frozen lemonade concentrate
2 tablespoons brown sugar
¼ cup soy sauce
2 tablespoons ketchup
1 teaspoon garlic powder
1 tablespoon cider vinegar
1 tablespoon cornstarch
2 tablespoons cold water

Place chicken in crockpot. Combine remaining ingredients in a bowl; whisk until cornstarch dissolved; pour over chicken. Cook on high for 4 hours, until chicken done. Serve with rice.

August 19

Godly sorrow brings repentance that leads to salvation and leaves no regret, but worldly sorrow brings death.

—2 Corinthians 7:10

THERE ARE TWO kinds of sorrow that Paul identifies in his letter to the believers at Corinth: godly sorrow and worldly sorrow. Godly sorrow is genuine *remorse* and leads to repentance, joy, and life, while worldly sorrow is *regret* and results in guilt, sadness, and death. Sorrow is distress or pain in the mind or spirit caused by a loss, affliction, or disappointment. Salvation results when one experiences sorrow and is drawn by the Holy Spirit to repentance and abandonment of sin. Regret, on the other hand, is usually disappointment that a sin has been found out, thus causing embarrassment, penalty, and death. The word *death* here refers to complete alienation from God that leaves one without hope for future fellowship with Him. It is the opposite of salvation. Confrontations in truth over one's evildoing (sin) may even produce worldly hurt to the point of physical death. The disciple Peter sinned, then repented and was forgiven. But when Judas Iscariot sinned, he just regretted and took his own life. Worldly sorrow is all about self. Godly sorrow is all about God. Worldly sorrow focuses on me and what I want, what I need, what I deserve, where I have been shortchanged, and where things did not go the way I wanted. Godly sorrow focuses on what God wants, what God deserves, and how God wants things to go. Faith in Christ and repentance from sin are both components of salvation. Jesus warned, "Unless you repent you will all likewise perish" (Luke 13:3, 5). Not only does God not want any man to undergo eternal judgment, He also wants every man to repent. That is, God desires harmony and fellowship with all and He desires that none perish.

Father: I believe that Jesus died for me and rose again on the third day. I confess that I am a sinner and need Your forgiveness. Come into my life, forgive me of my sins, and give me eternal life. I surrender every part of my life to You. In Jesus' name, Amen.

GRILLED TUNA MELT (sandwich)

1 can tuna, drained
3 tablespoons mayonnaise
2 tablespoons chopped green onion
2 slices American cheese
Bread
Butter

Mix tuna, mayo, and onion; spread on favorite bread; add cheese; top with bread. Spread outsides of bread with butter; grill both sides in pan over medium heat.

August 20

Remember this: Whoever sows sparingly will also reap sparingly, and whoever sows generously will also reap generously.

—2 Corinthians 9:6

This law applies to every aspect in the life of a Christian. We store up treasures in heaven by honoring God when we invest the time, talents, and resources of which He has made us a steward to supporting Christ's kingdom work here on earth. God promises He will pour out even more abundant grace into our lives to the degree we commit to Him. We have a choice to make—whether to give generously or whether to give sparingly—and God rewards accordingly. To the apostle Paul, giving is a form of saving because of the substantial benefits for those who give. The amount we give is not what is measured; it is the portion of what we have that we give and the condition and motives of our heart that is the determining factor.

A perfect example of this is the poor widow in Luke 21:1–4, who gave all she had: two very small coins. She gave sacrificially, having nothing left on which to live. Jesus was pleased because He values our service to Him by our sincere dedication, sacrifice, faith, and love, and not by our influence, success, or wealth. When God calls us out of our comfort zone to give beyond what we think we can, it's not because He wants us to have less; it's because He wants to give us more. If we hold back, we limit the harvest that comes from our sowing. When we take God at His Word, we sow generously and reap abundantly.

Father God: You are my Provider and everything I have belongs to You. Help me to release more readily and joyfully the resources You have given to me so others might be blessed and have their needs met. As I generously give, I will reap generously. Thank You for this wonderful plan You have established for Your children. In Jesus' name, Amen.

BUFFALO HOT WINGS

2–3 pounds chicken wings or legs
½ cup Frank's hot sauce
½ cup butter
Blue cheese salad dressing
Ranch salad dressing
Celery sticks (optional)

Fry or bake chicken wings until meat thoroughly cooked. In a small pan, heat hot sauce and butter until very warm. When chicken done, drain grease and coat with sauce. Serve with ranch or blue cheese dressing and celery sticks.

August 21

We demolish arguments and every pretension that sets itself up against the knowledge of God, and we take captive every thought to make it obedient to Christ.

—2 Corinthians 10:5

WHEN PAUL WROTE these words, he was in a battle for the hearts and minds of the people of Corinth. A portion of the Corinthians had submitted to some false teachings, and Paul knew their salvation was at risk. Paul taught that many of our sins begin with a thought. One thought leads to another and then to acts that are contrary to the Word of God. Our thoughts should not be lustful, greedy, covetous, hateful, envious, or idolatrous. If we choose to think these thoughts, knowing they are wrong, we are saying in essence that we don't care what God wants, nor do we care what the consequences are for our sin. As a result, we grieve the Holy Spirit and are separated from God (Ephesians 4:30). Remember that Jesus gave us the power to be victorious and He waits to add His victory to every thought, every feeling, every situation, and every need or desire that we surrender to Him in obedience. Since for many of us, our thought life is the area in which we sin most, we must have control of it. God has instructed us to occlude sinful thoughts and to take them captive for Christ. As soon as a wrong thought comes to mind, we should ask God to remove it and think on Him and His Word. It is good to memorize scriptures and hide them in our hearts for our times of need. We can live in victory with the strength and power of our Lord Jesus when we call on His name and follow His directions for godly living.

Merciful Father: I choose to believe that Your Word is true and my only hope for survival in a world that is corrupt and evil. I want to live for Jesus in the power and fullness of Your Spirit. Help me to take captive every thought that could lead me down the wrong pathway and into further sinful thoughts or actions. Forgive me for my past sins and help me to live for You. In Jesus' name, Amen.

SAUSAGE BALLS

1 pound ground pork sausage
2 cups biscuit baking mix (Bisquick)
1 pound sharp cheddar cheese, shredded
Favorite dipping sauce

Combine sausage, biscuit mix, and cheese. Form into walnut size balls and place on baking sheet. Bake at 350 degrees for 10 minutes, or until golden brown. Serve with favorite dipping sauce (barbecue, honey mustard, sweet and sour) as an appetizer or as a meat dish.

August 22

To keep me from becoming conceited because of these surpassingly great revelations, there was given me a thorn in my flesh, a messenger of Satan, to torment me. Three times I pleaded with the Lord to take it away from me. But he said to me, "My grace is sufficient for you, for my power is made perfect in weakness." Therefore I will boast all the more gladly about my weaknesses, so that Christ's power may rest on me. That is why, for Christ's sake, I delight in weaknesses in insults, in hardships, in persecutions, in difficulties. For when I am weak, then I am strong.

—2 Corinthians 12:7–10

PAUL RECEIVED VISIONS and revelations from the Lord so profound he could not share them with anyone. He was a very humble man and would not boast or brag about his experiences. He didn't want to be looked at as special or greater than anyone else. Paul believed God allowed him to be afflicted with a thorn in his flesh so he would remain humble. This thorn was not defined as a particular type of illness, disease, mental or spiritual anguish, pain, temptation, or demonic oppression because it was to represent to us whatever our particular affliction might be. Paul also believed that his thorn kept him humble and dependent on the Lord for grace to withstand the suffering it caused. Our ways are not always God's ways, just as the answers to our prayers are not always what we think they should be. We cannot see in the spiritual realm as God sees; and when we pray, believing, and according to His Word, we should trust Him to answer our prayers as He chooses. The grace of God is a gift He gives His faithful believers and is always sufficient, no matter how severe the situation or suffering may be. When we draw near to Christ in our time of need, He is always faithful to give us strength and comfort. For it is when we are weak that we are made strong.

Dear Lord: You are my strength when I am weak and tormented by the thorns and afflictions that the enemy tries to use against me, but I find power to overcome when I seek You. I believe You provided healing and redemption on the cross as You gave Your life on my account. Keep me focused on You even when I may not think You are hearing and answering my prayers as I want. As I strive to live for You no matter what may come my way, I know Your grace will always be sufficient to carry me to victory. In Jesus' name, Amen.

Today's recipe found on page 384 JAMBALAYA

August 23

Examine yourselves to see whether you are in the faith; test yourselves. Do you not realize that Christ Jesus is in you—unless, of course, you fail the test?

—2 CORINTHIANS 13:5

L IFE IS A test! It's a test of our faith and endurance to either achieve eternal life with Christ (salvation) or reject His wonderful plan and end up in a place designed for Satan and his followers (lostness). Salvation not only involves forgiveness of sins and a guarantee of heaven, it also results in a complete change of who we are (2 Corinthians 5). When we decide to believe on the Lord Jesus Christ, we are saved (Acts 16:31) and are never the same again. The New Testament describes a person's conversion as a death of the old man and a birth of the new one in Christ (Romans 6). That's why Jesus described it as being *born again* (John 3). This change in our lives is a result of the Holy Spirit who is sent to live in us (Romans 8:11). God wants us to examine ourselves to make sure our faith is real, because if it is, we will live according to His Word. The only thing worse than going to hell is ending up there after *thinking* we were a Christian and on our way to heaven. Faith in Jesus Christ is the only way to be saved (John 3:16), but being saved always produces the evidence of a new, changed life. In this short text, the apostle Paul wanted to know if the preaching of the Cross had just reached the minds of the Corinthians or if it had truly pierced their hearts. Not only did he want Christ to apprehend the Corinthians, he wanted them to apprehend Christ. In other words, Paul wants God's sovereignty to infect every believer and he wants God to be Lord of everyone's life.

Dear Lord: Thank You for the gift of salvation that You have allowed me to receive by faith. Help me fight the good fight of faith so I might be a good witness for You. That You will forever be glorified in my life is my earnest prayer. In Jesus' name, Amen.

BACON CHEESE AND TOMATO CRESCENTS

1 (8-ounce) can refrigerated crescent dinner rolls
4 ounces (½ of 8-ounce package) cream cheese, softened
4 slices bacon, crisply cooked, drained, and chopped
¼ cup finely chopped red peppers (optional)
¼ cup finely chopped tomatoes

Separate dough into 8 triangles; spread with cream cheese; top with remaining ingredients. Roll starting at shortest side of triangle. Place point-sides down on baking sheet; bake 12–15 minutes at 375 degrees, until brown.

August 24

I am astonished that you are so quickly deserting the one who called you by the grace of Christ and are turning to a different gospel—which is really no gospel at all.

—GALATIANS 1:6–7

THIS VERSE IS from the letter Paul had written to the churches in Galatia. He and Barnabas previously evangelized there, but he heard that some of the new converts were following some Jewish teachers that came and taught doctrine other than the true gospel. They were teaching that certain Mosaic or Jewish laws had to be followed for one to be saved and that grace alone was not enough. Paul was astonished that the Galatians accepted these teachings and deserted the true gospel he had taught them. He knew God's Word was true, inspired by the Holy Spirit, and the only way to salvation. Paul was passionate in defending the gospel of Jesus Christ as the only way to be saved. Any other teachings, doctrines, or ideas added by man to pervert the true and original content should not be expressed or implied. Paul went on to say in verse 9 that if anyone is guilty of this, they are eternally condemned. Today, there are many false teachings and we must study and know what the fundamental truth is and then defend it in love.

Father: Thank You for the gospel that teaches us how to live according to Your will. Forgive me for the times I deserted what was truth and followed in ways that were not of Your Word. It is only by the wonderful grace of Jesus Christ that I am saved. Thank You for this gift. In Jesus' name, Amen.

AMISH CHICKEN CASSEROLE

½ cup butter
⅓ cup flour
1 cup milk
2 cups chicken broth
1 teaspoon salt
½ teaspoon pepper
1 can mushrooms
2 cups cooked chicken, diced
8 ounces noodles, cooked according to package
⅓ cup Parmesan cheese

Melt butter in pan over low heat; add flour; stir until smooth. Gradually add milk, broth, seasonings, and mushrooms. Combine chicken, cooked noodles, and sauce. Place in greased 9x13-inch baking dish. Top with Parmesan cheese. Bake at 350 degrees for 35–45 minutes, until heated through and top slightly browned.

August 25

As we have therefore opportunity, let us do good unto all men, especially unto them who are of the household of faith.

—Galatians 6:10, KJV

As followers of Christ, we are called to do good deeds! When God gives us the opportunity, we should take advantage of it. Unlike those in the world looking to get ahead, get even with someone, or trying to get out of difficult situations, we should look for opportunities to do good. The apostle Paul not only encourages us to do good to all people, whether they are neighbors, strangers, good, evil, friends, or enemies, but he tells us to be especially good to those who belong to the family of believers. This includes all who know Jesus as Savior, without regard to denominations or divisions. Though our kindness is not to be limited to believers, it is to be shown to them in a special way. When we see a brother or a sister in need, we should help them. As we do, we show obedience to God's Word and receive both heavenly rewards and eternal life.

Father: You are the only good and perfect One. I pray that some of Your goodness may be seen in me as I serve You today and until that time when the Savior returns for me in glory. Help me to be aware of and look for opportunities to do good to and for others. In Jesus' name, Amen.

CORNED BEEF HASH CASSEROLE

1 (26-ounce) package frozen hash browns
1 medium onion, finely chopped
2 cups cooked corned beef (canned okay) or leftover roast beef, diced
½ teaspoon salt
½ teaspoon pepper
12 ounces shredded American or cheddar cheese
1 can cream of celery soup
¾ cup evaporated milk (whole milk or 2% okay)

Grease a baking dish with butter; put in ¼ of potatoes, ⅓ of onion, and ⅓ of corned beef. Sprinkle with salt and pepper. Repeat two more times, ending with remaining potato, cheese, and another sprinkling of salt and pepper. Mix soup and milk together and pour over mixture. Cover; bake at 350 degrees for 45 minutes. Remove cover; bake for 10 more minutes.

August 26

But God forbid that I should glory, save in the cross of our Lord Jesus Christ, by whom the world is crucified unto me, and I unto the world.

—GALATIANS 6:14, KJV

THROUGHOUT THE BOOK of Galatians, Paul emphatically defends the essentials of mere Christianity and the characteristics we all should have as born-again believers. He stresses the need for us to know God's Word so well that we are not confused with counterfeit teachings. Paul's love for the Lord is evident in all he says and does. Though he maintains there is freedom in the true gospel of Christ from rituals and laws, he vigorously emphasizes that this freedom involves being set free from sin and the sinful nature. This only happens when we surrender ourselves totally and completely to Jesus Christ and ask Him to forgive us for all the sins we have committed. Paul desired to give God all glory, honor, and praise for what He did on the cross for the sake of us all. He wanted no recognition or esteem for the persecution he endured while preaching the gospel in a world opposed to God, His kingdom, and His righteousness. We are all faced with a decision: Will we choose to follow the world and live according to its accepted standards, values, and lifestyles, or to be crucified with Christ (Galatians 2:20) as the apostle Paul did, and cherish the old rugged cross on which Jesus gave His life?

Lord Jesus: My heart rejoices to think of the price You paid so I might have freedom and eternal life. Thank You for the example that Paul was in the Bible and how he lived according to Your Word yet was persecuted all along the way. Give me strength to go forward and follow after the freedom and grace You so willing provided on the cross. In Jesus' name, Amen.

BACON CORN CHOWDER

6 bacon strips
¾ cup diced celery
1 cup diced potato
1 small diced onion
1 large carrot, finely diced
1 cup water
1 can cream-style corn
1 cup milk
½ teaspoon seasoned salt
½ teaspoon salt
¼ teaspoon garlic powder
⅛ teaspoon pepper

In saucepan, cook bacon until crisp; remove; discard all but 2–3 tablespoons grease. Add celery, onion, potato, and carrot to pan; sauté 10 to 15 minutes. Add water; cover and simmer 20 minutes until vegetables tender. Stir in creamed corn, milk, and seasonings. Heat; do not boil.

August 27

As for you, you were dead in your transgressions and sins, in which you used to live when you followed the ways of this world and of the ruler of the kingdom of the air, the spirit who is now at work in those who are disobedient.

—EPHESIANS 2:1–2

I T'S HARD TO imagine, but every baby that comes into the world is a sinner and has a sin nature. They never have to be taught how to sin or be disobedient; it comes naturally. While a child is still young, they are covered under God's grace until an age of which they can reason and decide for themselves whether or not to be disobedient or accept God's plan of salvation in Jesus Christ. This age may vary and is only known for sure by God.

So, if we are all born sinners, we are all dead spiritually and controlled by "the ruler of the kingdom of the air," Satan. He blinds our minds from the real truth of God and causes us to be enslaved to the cravings of our sinful nature. Unless we experience the new birth that comes when we believe and receive Christ into our hearts by repentance and faith, we are responsible for the wages of our sin (Romans 6:23). Choosing to follow the ways of the world means choosing to be enslaved by the wicked one whose spirit controls every unbeliever. How much greater it is to be transformed from death unto life when we yield ourselves over to the One who brings us abundant living. God loves us, even when we sin and disobey His Word. He offers us hope, joy, peace, and eternal life with Him in glory. Jesus paid the price for our transgressions when He died on the cross. Because of this, we are no longer dead in our sins but have life in Him.

Father: Thank You for my new life in Jesus Christ. I was once lost and disobedient, but now I am set free and desire righteousness and sanctification for my life. Give me a passion for the lost who are still under the control of the enemy's snare so they might also reap the blessings of Your mercy and grace. Thank You for saving my soul. In Jesus' name, Amen.

HEAVENLY CHICKEN

4 boneless, skinless chicken breasts
1 can cream of chicken soup
8 ounces sour cream
40 Ritz crackers, crushed
1 stick butter

Cook chicken in greased pan with lid until done. Dice and put in greased baking dish. Mix soup and sour cream; pour over chicken. Sprinkle cracker crumbs on top; pour melted butter over crumbs. Bake 30 minutes at 350 degrees until bubbly.

August 28

Now to him who is able to do immeasurably more than all we ask or imagine, according to his power that is at work within us, to him be glory in the church and in Christ Jesus throughout all generations for ever and ever! Amen.

—EPHESIANS 3:20–21

D O YOU EVER wonder if your prayers are really being heard because you don't see answers for many of the things you ask? Perhaps you are grieving deep in your heart about some matter. It may be a child who's gone astray, or there may be a deep wound in your soul because you've lost a loved one and know you will never ever see them this side of glory. Maybe you have been betrayed by a friend or family member or have failed relentlessly to conquer a sin.

We all experience these feelings of frustration and hopelessness at times, but the apostle Paul wants us to know that God's power is not in question as to His ability to answer our prayers and requests. He encourages us to praise God for His power and focus on His unlimited ability to meet our every need. The same power that raised Christ from the dead will accomplish everything we need in our lives. We must meditate on God's great power as the Creator of all things and His authority over everything He has created. He knows our temptations, our hurts, our pains, and our struggles, and He sees every tear that falls from our face. He is the One we can turn to for help for He has promised to never leave us or forsake us. He is the God who cares and has demonstrated His love for us by sending His only Son to be our Savior. Our Lord bids us to come to Him with our burdens and leave them with Him. He is the God who provides and we can trust Him to meet our every need.

Father: You are all-powerful and can do anything and everything You desire. Thank You for the desire You have to meet my every need and to do even more than what I could ever ask for or imagine. Help me to take the focus off myself and my problems and put it on You. In Jesus' name, Amen.

CHEESEBURGER AND FRIES CASSEROLE

2 pounds lean ground beef
1 can cream of mushroom soup
1 can cheddar cheese soup
20-ounce bag crinkle-cut French fries

Brown meat; drain. Add soups; mix and pour into greased dish. Arrange French fries on top. Bake, uncovered, at 350 degrees for 45–55 minutes, until fries are golden.

August 29

Be completely humble and gentle; be patient, bearing with one another in love. Make every effort to keep the unity of the Spirit through the bond of peace.

—Ephesians 4:2–3

THE CALL FOR unity is something that God speaks about throughout the Bible. When sinners come to Christ and are redeemed by His shed blood, it is no longer an option whether or not to love one another. In spite of all our differences in background, nationality, lifestyle, personality, opinions, strengths, interests, and so on, God is honored and glorified when He sees His children humbly love one another. Jesus commands us to love one another as He loved us (John 13:34), but how much more pleased He must be when we willingly show love because we truly want to, and not because we have to. It is only the Holy Spirit who brings unity into our hearts, minds, and souls, and that results when we strive to be obedient to the truth of God's Word. The church cannot effectively manifest the glory of Christ to a lost and dying world unless it is unified in Spirit and in truth. For this to happen, Paul instructs us to have humility (Christ is everything and outside of Him, I am nothing), gentleness (Christ is my strength), patience (maturity in the Spirit), forbearance (God's grace), love (*agape* mercy), and diligence (zeal). "Unity of the Spirit in the bond of peace" is a result of our focus on the only thing that belongs in the center of our will—the Lord Jesus Christ and the gospel of His grace.

Dear Lord: Your Word shows me how to live in unity of the Spirit and what I must do to produce it. Help me to be humble, gentle, patient, forbearing, loving, and zealous so I might do my part to bring unity of the Spirit through the bond of peace to this world. Show me how to love not only the lovely, but the unlovely as well, just as You so willingly do. In Jesus' name, Amen.

BAKED POTATO SOUP

8–10 slices bacon, fried crisp and diced
1 stick butter
⅓ cup flour
4 cups milk
3–4 potatoes, baked, peeled, and cubed
4 green onions, chopped
1 cup shredded cheddar cheese
1 cup sour cream
1 teaspoon salt
1 teaspoon pepper

In large deep pan, melt butter on low heat. Whisk in flour until smooth. Gradually add milk, whisking constantly until well blended. Add potatoes and onions; bring to boil. Reduce heat; simmer 10 minutes. Add bacon, cheese, sour cream, salt, and pepper. Stir until cheese is melted.

August 30

In your anger do not sin. Do not let the sun go down while you are still angry, and do not give the devil a foothold.

—EPHESIANS 4:26–27

ANGER IS A God-given emotion that warns a person that something is wrong. We cannot stop it from arising, but we can control our anger so it is not inappropriate and does not become a sin. Our anger rises up when our personal worth has been attacked, our legitimate and essential needs have not been met, or our basic convictions of right and wrong have been violated. Everyone gets angry at times. In fact, the Bible records Jesus getting angry a few times. Anger becomes a problem when it is uncontrolled and we react in the wrong way. God's Word says anger is to be dealt with every day; it's that important to our spiritual, mental, and physical well-being. When angry emotions accumulate, they eventually explode in ways that hurt others and ourselves. When anger is turned inward, it may cause depression, resentment, bitterness and hard-heartedness (Hebrews 12:14–15). Anger gives Satan a foothold into our soul. The Holy Spirit can teach us how to express our anger appropriately if we admit we are angry, try to determine why we are angry, ask ourselves if this is the best way to express our emotions, spend time praying for the difficulty that we have in handling this emotion, ask for God's help, and forgive those we feel have wronged us is some way. As we give ourselves over to the Holy Spirit, He will help us to grow in self-control. It is then that God is glorified!

Wonderful Father and my Creator: Forgive me for the times when I have become angry and hurt others. Help me to control my exasperations and inappropriate behavior. I give myself completely over to You and praise You now for the strength You will supply for me to live victoriously and according to Your will. In Jesus' name, Amen.

HAMBURGER CASSEROLE

1 pound ground beef
1 small onion, chopped
2 cups elbow macaroni
1 can cream of mushroom soup
1 can corn, peas, or green beans, drained
1 cup Velveeta, cubed
⅔ cup milk
30 Ritz crackers, crumbled, divided

Cook ground beef in pan until done; drain. Add chopped onion; cook until tender. Boil macaroni according to box; drain. Mix together all ingredients except half the crackers. Pour into greased baking dish; sprinkle remaining cracker crumbs on top. Bake at 350 degrees for 30 minutes.

August 31

Do not let any unwholesome talk come out of your mouths, but only what is helpful for building others up according to their needs, that it may benefit those who listen. And do not grieve the Holy Spirit of God, with whom you were sealed for the day of redemption. Get rid of all bitterness, rage and anger, brawling and slander, along with every form of malice. Be kind and compassionate to one another, forgiving each other, just as in Christ God forgave you.

—Ephesians 4:29–32

GOD HAS GIVEN us the power through his Holy Spirit to renew our minds and become transformed by the mind of Christ. Therefore, we have the power to control our tongue. If there is trash coming out of our mouth, that means there's trash inside our mind. When we see the shortfallings of others, we must speak things to edify and build them up, not tear them down. The life of a Christian is to be totally different from that of an unbeliever. This is because we have been crucified with Christ and have put off once and for all our former manner of life. We have put on the new man, created to be like God in righteousness and holiness of the truth. This knowledge of Christ affects all of the believer's life and ethics. We are made alive and given a new nature because the Holy Spirit dwells in us. Because we are new creations, we now have the freedom and ability to live righteously, doing all things for the glory of God. If we continue to live unholy lives, we grieve the Holy Spirit and bring destruction on ourselves. It's time to repent of our sins, take off the graveclothes of our old life, and put on the garments of proper behavior of the new life so the Holy Spirit may rejoice in our lives.

Holy God: How glorious to know I am created anew and no longer have to live in sin and shame. Because of Christ, I am able to live in victory over things that once pulled me into bondage to Satan. With my renewed mind, I am able to think, speak, and behave in ways that are glorifying to You. Thank You for sending Your Holy Spirit to live in me. In Jesus' name, Amen.

CHICKEN BAKE

8 boneless, skinless chicken breast halves
8 slices Swiss cheese
1 can cream of chicken soup
1 (8-ounce) box chicken stuffing mix

Flatten chicken breasts with rolling pin; put in large greased baking dish. Place cheese slices over top. Mix soup with ½ cup water and pour over chicken. Prepare stuffing mix according to package directions; sprinkle over chicken. Bake uncovered at 325 degrees for 1 hour.

Fall~ing Forward

September

September 1

But among you there must not be even a hint of sexual immorality, or of any kind of impurity, or of greed, because these are improper for God's holy people. Nor should there be obscenity, foolish talk or coarse joking, which are out of place, but rather thanksgiving. For of this you can be sure: No immoral, impure or greedy person—such a man is an idolater—has any inheritance in the kingdom of Christ and of God.

—EPHESIANS 5:3–5

How can we know for sure we are saved and on our way to heaven? If our lives do not line up with the Word of God, we probably don't have a true personal relationship with Jesus. Though we aren't perfect after becoming believers, God's Word says we will not continue a lifestyle of sin. If we do, Paul says we will not have "any inheritance in the kingdom of Christ and of God." When we come to a real saving knowledge of the Lord Jesus Christ, it is impossible to continue life as usual. After coming face to face with the risen Lord, we see ourselves as we are—dirty and unclean. If we truly give ourselves to God, His Holy Spirit will convict us of sin and we will repent and turn from it. To ignore the Spirit's conviction and continue living contrary to what the Word of God says puts us in danger of judgment and the lake of fire (Revelation 19:20). Paul reminds us very plainly that one cannot continue in the acts of the sinful nature and have any inheritance with Christ and God. Where is our inheritance? We must examine ourselves and be certain that it is in the kingdom of Christ and of God.

Dear God: I praise You for the blood of Christ that washes away my sin. Forgive me for even the hint of immorality of which I am guilty. Convict my heart when I am near a dangerous situation, and protect my mind from evil thoughts. Strengthen me so I am able to resist everything Satan throws at me. Fill my spirit with Yours and keep me pure. In Jesus' name, Amen.

EASY CHEESY CHICKEN SKILLET

2 teaspoons vegetable oil
4 boneless, skinless chicken breast halves
2 cups frozen broccoli florets, thawed
1 can cream of chicken soup
¼ pound Velveeta cheese, in chunks
2 cups cooked rice

Heat oil in large skillet on medium-high heat. Add chicken; cover. Cook until done. Add broccoli, soup and Velveeta; mix well. Reduce heat to medium; cover; simmer until broccoli tender. If too thick, add a little milk; serve with rice.

September 2

Wives, submit to your husbands as to the Lord. For the husband is the head of the wife as Christ is the head of the church, his body, of which he is the Savior. Now as the church submits to Christ, so also wives should submit to their husbands in everything.

—EPHESIANS 5:22–24

THE APOSTLE PAUL had just stated in Ephesians 5:21 that we must submit ourselves to one another out of reverence for Christ. He enforces this teaching by speaking about wives and their need to not only submit to one another and Christ, but also their husbands. To submit to another means to yield to their authority or will. If we are going to follow Paul's counsel and be submissive to one another as unto Christ, we must humbly and freely do so in a sacrificial mode. The church's submission to Christ has nothing to do with external control or coercion because the life and ministry of Jesus does not demand our respect, but rather offers an invitation for us to willingly serve Him. Wives are to submit to their husbands because God created the family and in His Word established husbands to be responsible for their households. Out of gratitude to the Lord for all that He has done for us, we choose to submit to His Word. It is not because men are superior to women but because we trust God to know what is best for the family He created. A wife's submission to her husband is as to the Lord, Paul tells us. Out of reverence and respect, we must be willing to do whatever it is God tells us to do.

Father: With Your infinite wisdom You created the family. You knew there needed to be a leader so You assigned that position to the husband. Help us all to trust Your judgment and do our best to put this plan into action in our world today. Give me the right thoughts, words and actions to teach others about Your perfect will for our lives. In Jesus' name, Amen.

GARLIC CHICKEN ALFREDO (crockpot)

1 (16-ounce) jar creamy garlic Alfredo sauce or homemade sauce (see recipe index for page #)
4 boneless, skinless chicken breasts
1 (4.5-ounce) can or 8 ounces fresh sliced mushrooms (optional)
8 ounces spaghetti, cooked and hot
Grated Parmesan cheese

Pour ⅓ of sauce in crockpot. Add chicken breasts; top with mushrooms and remaining sauce. Cook on low 6–8 hours. Serve with hot spaghetti noodles and sprinkle Parmesan cheese over top.

September 3

Husbands, love your wives, even as Christ also loved the church, and gave himself for it; That he might sanctify and cleanse it with the washing of water by the word, That he might present it to himself a glorious church, not having spot, or wrinkle, or any such thing; but that it should be holy and without blemish. So ought men to love their wives as their own bodies. He that loveth his wife loveth himself.

—Ephesians 5:25–28, kjv

It would be fitting to say that Paul's teachings would be offensive to the majority of the world because he doesn't agree with modern ideas of political correctness and feminism. Though he says wives should submit to their husbands as to the Lord, Paul's exhortation to husbands as their role as head of the wife (Ephesians 5:22) is much more intense. Husbands are not only told to love their wives as Christ loved the church, but they must love their wives as much as they love themselves. When marriage takes place, there is a union of the man and the woman. No longer are they two, but they have become one. When the husband is told to love his wife, he is actually being told to love himself because the two are really one. Our culture does not accept this truth, and marriages are suffering for it. Each partner's rights, freedoms, and self-identity have been over-emphasized and a couple's unity and oneness underemphasized. Married couples no longer function the way God designed them to in oneness and unity. Oneness respects our individual functions and gifts as we work for the good of the whole body. A husband and wife are truly one flesh and ultimately are called to submit to one another. But there are leadership roles within the home that God established. To submit to them is to reflect the role of Christ and His bride in our marriage.

Father: We have fallen so short of Your plan for Christian marriages. Forgive us as a nation for our failures and help us develop a heart for Your Word. Teach us to submit ourselves sacrificially to one another. You created this world not for chaos or confusion, but for order and purpose. Help me to do my part to bring love and respect back to You. In Jesus' name, Amen.

SAVORY BEEF DISH (crockpot)

3 pounds lean beef, cubed
2 cans cream of mushroom soup
2 cans water

1 envelope dry onion soup mix
1 cup sour cream

Put everything, except sour cream, in a crockpot and cook on low 8–10 hours. When done, mix in sour cream and serve over noodles, potatoes, or rice.

September 4

Children, obey your parents in the Lord: for this is right. Honour thy father and mother; which is the first commandment with promise; That it may be well with thee, and thou mayest live long on the earth.

—Ephesians 6:1–3, kjv

It does not go over well when someone who has never had children tries to advise others how to raise theirs. As far as we know, the apostle Paul was not married and did not have any children, but he is exempt from this rule because he was an apostle of the Lord Jesus Christ. In Ephesians 5, Paul spoke about order in the Christian home concerning wives and husbands. Now he addresses the relationship of children and their parents. The Bible says children are created in the likeness and image of God and are a heritage from the Lord. Jesus was once a child, and He also loved children. Children are to obey their parents until the parents die or the children marry. When a couple marries, they establish a new unit where the husband is the head. *Children* can mean infants to adults who are not married. A single woman still has the covering or headship of her earthly father, if he is still living. Paul instructs children to obey, which is different than how he told wives to submit. Obedience isn't an option, but a command. The only time children should not obey is if the parents prohibit them from worshiping God or specifically command them to sin. Otherwise, God requires every child to obey his or her parents in the Lord at all times. When a child obeys his parents, he is obeying the Lord, the one who invested His authority into those parents.

Dear Lord: You have blessed this world with children and it needs Your knowledge and strength to teach and train them in Your ways. I pray that every child would be filled with a desire to know You personally and become a disciple of Your Word. As this happens, may they have the will to obey their parents and behave according to Your plan. In Jesus' name, Amen.

BUFFALO CHICKEN TORTILLA PIZZA

4 (10-inch) flour tortillas
1 tablespoon oil
4 cups diced cooked chicken breast
¼ cup Frank's hot sauce
4 cups grated smoked mozzarella cheese
½ cup blue cheese crumbles

Lay tortillas on 2 cookie sheets. Brush each with oil. In bowl, toss chicken with hot sauce; spread over tortillas. Sprinkle on the cheeses. Bake at 375 degrees for 3–5 minutes or until cheese melted, bubbly and golden brown. Cut into quarters.

September 5

Serve wholeheartedly, as if you were serving the Lord, not men, because you know that the Lord will reward everyone for whatever good he does, whether he is slave or free.

—Ephesians 6:7–8

THOUGH PAUL IS addressing slaves in the Roman Empire who were enduring the hardships of slavery, there is a great truth for us to learn here as well. The slaves wanted their freedom and a change in their status and living conditions. Paul felt compassion for them, but he knew God would reward them for their good work if they respected their masters and served them well. Paul was not as interested in the legal aspects of slavery as much as he was interested in the spiritual ramifications of being a slave for Christ. But even so, Paul made it quite clear that slaves must approach their duties to their masters with respect and sincerity.

This powerful principle is so important to the Christian faith. If a believer works at his job as though he is doing it for the Lord, his enthusiasm spreads to those around him. It invites the presence of God into a workplace and ignites other employees to also work well. Working as for the Lord is the opposite of how the world operates. The world works out of selfishness, greed, and pride, and rarely out of love and obedience to God. We are to accomplish our work in a way that we are not seen as unproductive or lazy. Paul is trying to convey that we need to look beyond our earthly masters (employers) to our heavenly Master. This must be done in a way to not only please Christ because we love Him, but also in a way that shows the world our true master is a God who loves us and is worthy of our obedience and loyalty.

Master and Lord of all: I choose to serve with respect and sincerity because I love You. Help me to prove this by my attitude and job performance in all I do. Forgive me for the times I was slothful and negligent in my duties and workmanship. May I be found faithful as I serve wholeheartedly knowing that You will reward me for all the good I do. In Jesus' name, Amen.

DRIED BEEF WRAPS (low-carb)

1–2 packages or small jars dried beef
1 (8-ounce) package cream cheese
4 green onions, diced, *or* ½ small onion
½ small pepper, minced (optional)
1 teaspoon Worcestershire sauce (optional)
1 teaspoon horseradish (optional)

Soften cream cheese; blend in all ingredients, except beef. Spread mixture on beef slices; roll up tightly. Refrigerate at least 1 hour. Cut into small slices and arrange on platter with toothpicks.

September 6

Being confident of this, that he who began a good work in you will carry it on to completion until the day of Christ Jesus.

—PHILIPPIANS 1:6

WHILE IMPRISONED IN Rome, Paul wrote to the believers in Philippi, a fellowship he visited at least three times during his missionary journeys. The church was a small-town congregation that Paul founded with his team, Silas, Timothy, and Luke, and he still had a strong bond of friendship with many of the people. There were some strong personality conflicts going on in the church, and Paul wrote to encourage them. He wanted them to know that because of God's love for them and their desire to know and love God, they would be victorious until the end.

God has begun a good work in all of us, and He will continue to develop and perfect that work, bringing His purpose for our lives to completion until the day Jesus returns. The fruit of the labors of loved ones gone on before is still at work in the world today and the same will be for us when we are gone. Only when we arrive at our final destination will we know the impact each of us had while on earth. We are all a work-in-progress and still under construction! As we stay in close fellowship with God and live according to His Word, the Holy Spirit will continue His work within us according to His good pleasure.

Father: I praise and thank You for the work You are doing in my life. When I stumble and fall, You pick me up and continue to form me into the person of Your wonderful design. With Your help I want to become everything You desire...nothing more and nothing less. May I be found faithful in everything You have required of me until that day of completion when You return. In Jesus' name, Amen.

CAESAR SALAD

1 bunch romaine lettuce, washed
2 eggs, coddled (boiled 1–2 minutes)
3–4 cloves garlic, minced
½ cup olive or canola oil
⅓ cup lemon juice
½ teaspoon salt
½ teaspoon pepper
2 cups croutons (homemade or packaged)
½ cup grated Parmesan cheese
1 small can anchovies, diced (optional)

Tear lettuce in bite-sized pieces; put in bowl. Mix coddled eggs, garlic, oil, lemon juice, salt, and pepper in a glass jar; shake to blend; refrigerate until ready to use. To serve: pour cold dressing over lettuce; add croutons, cheese, and anchovies. Toss and serve.

September 7

For to me to live is Christ, and to die is gain.

—Philippians 1:21, KJV

WHAT COMES TO mind when you think of the future—a job, children, grandchildren, retirement, life insurance, or health? Are spiritual aspirations a part of your plans? The apostle Paul was in prison when he wrote this, but he remained hopeful and focused. He knew that as long as he was alive, he would serve Christ and glorify His name. This was his testimony, and he lived it in prison and out of prison. In prison, in chains, in a cold, dark, damp, rat-infested prison cell, Paul proclaimed that Jesus was his very life. When his life on earth would end, he would graduate to a greater place. What a wonderful way this is to look at life and death. Could we also be like the apostle Paul and give praise to God, no matter what circumstance we may be in, and then look forward to one day dying and being with Christ? It isn't the norm, but we can ask God to help us focus on Him for now and for eternity.

Loving Father: Thank You for the life You have given to me and for the abundance of blessings You have poured out upon my life. I am thankful for the place I am and for the call You have given me to take Your message to the world. You are the reason I live, and because of You I have purpose and meaning. In Jesus' name, Amen.

LETTUCE WRAPS

1–2 pounds boneless, skinless chicken breasts
1 tablespoon oil
1 (8-ounce) can water chestnuts, diced
1 teaspoon ginger
2 tablespoons vinegar
2 tablespoons teriyaki sauce
1 tablespoon soy sauce
½ teaspoon garlic powder
Dash of crushed red pepper flakes
1 teaspoon oil (preferably peanut oil)
1 cup shredded carrots
4 green onions, finely diced
¼ cup sliced almonds, toasted
Lettuce leaves

Dice chicken; cook in large skillet with oil on medium-high heat until almost done. Add water chestnuts and ginger; cook until chicken totally done; set aside. In small bowl whisk vinegar, teriyaki sauce, soy sauce, garlic powder, red pepper flakes, and 1 teaspoon oil. Stir in carrots, onions, and chicken. Spoon onto lettuce leaves; sprinkle with almonds. Fold side of lettuce over filling and snugly roll.

September 8

Whatever happens, conduct yourselves in a manner worthy of the gospel of Christ.

—PHILIPPIANS 1:27

THE APOSTLE PAUL was suffering in prison when he wrote these words to the church in Philippi, yet he continued to support a pure and positive attitude. It would have been very easy for him to become discouraged and angry, but he held strong to his faith and remained humble and joyful. Paul knew many people depended on his strength and support. To show negative reactions to the suffering he endured would have been destructive to the church, and that was the last thing Paul wanted to see happen. Some of the members were causing problems for those who wanted to stand firm to the truth of God's Word. If Paul were to react negatively, the faithful brethren might be more apt to harden their hearts and become bitter toward those who were causing them problems. This too would hurt the church, and Paul knew the manner in which the good brethren at Philippi handled themselves would be critical to the ongoing of the work there.

How we conduct ourselves in the midst of trouble is very important to God. There are times when we may feel justified to be angry and show hatred toward others or even God for the circumstances in which we find ourselves. We can choose to fight back against those who have hurt or robbed us of what we believed was ours, or we can take on the mind of Christ and respond as He would. If Jesus' mind were reflected as ours, our testimonies of Him would be more effective. If we, as the church universal, took on the mind of Christ and conducted ourselves in a manner worthy of the gospel of Christ, what a wonderful world this would be.

Father: There are times when my actions aren't worthy of the gospel of Christ. Forgive me and help me to have better control over my emotions and attitudes. Before I react, may I be slow to speak so not to offend others and jeopardize my testimony. Help me to live in a manner worthy of the gospel of Christ. In Jesus' name, Amen.

OVEN-CRISPY CHICKEN

6–8 boneless, skinless chicken breast halves
½–¾ cup mayonnaise
2 cups crushed corn flakes
½ cup grated Parmesan cheese

Sprinkle chicken with salt and pepper. Coat chicken with mayonnaise. Combine corn flake crumbs and cheese in bowl; dip chicken in crumbs coating completely. Place chicken in greased 9x13-inch baking dish; bake uncovered at 325 degrees for 1 hour.

September 9

Do nothing out of selfish ambition or vain conceit, but in humility consider others better than yourselves.

—PHILIPPIANS 2:3

SELFISHNESS IS ONE of the most tragic results of the fall of man through sin. We are born self-centered and egotistical and must be taught how to become humble and lowly. God says we are to esteem others better than ourselves and look to their interests above ours. Paul suffered many things in obeying these commands, but he continued to serve Christ in spite of his pain and circumstance. The Spirit of Christ should lead His followers to be concerned not only for their success and advantage, but equally interested for the success and advantage of their brethren. This means to love our neighbor as ourselves. None of us are perfect and we all err at times by acting in ways that are not Christlike, but we all need to examine our hearts daily and see if our actions and words are consistent with Christ's teachings. If they aren't, Jesus tells us to repent, which means to turn from our sin and turn to Him. Jesus promises to forgive us and cleanse our hearts. His Spirit will help us to follow Him when we ask for His help.

Forgiving Father: You know my heart, my faults, when I do things to benefit only myself, and when my intentions are right. I repent of any selfish and egotistical attitudes I may have and ask for Your Holy Spirit to guide me as I strive to esteem others. May I have the mind of Christ as I make decisions each day. Help me to always glorify You in all I say and do. In Jesus' name, Amen.

CASHEW CHICKEN CASSEROLE

3–4 boneless, skinless, chicken breasts
1 ½ cups water
1 cup reserved chicken broth
1 can cream of mushroom soup
1 can cream of chicken soup
2 tablespoons soy sauce
6 green onions, chopped (optional)
4 cups cooked rice
1 cup cashew nuts

Cook chicken in water in pan with lid until tender. Reserve 1 cup broth. Remove chicken and dice into bite-sized pieces. Add both soups and soy sauce to skillet with reserved liquid; bring to boil. Add green onions, cooked rice, chicken, and ¾ cup cashew nuts. Mix well and pour into casserole dish. Top with remaining cashews. Bake uncovered at 350 degrees for 20 minutes.

September 10

Therefore God exalted him to the highest place and gave him the name that is above every name, that at the name of Jesus every knee should bow, in heaven and on earth and under the earth, and every tongue confess that Jesus Christ is Lord, to the glory of God the Father.

—PHILIPPIANS 2:9–11

GOD THE SON has always existed, and He will always exist. In the beginning, He existed only as God, but when He came to earth through the Holy Spirit and Mary, He became truly human and yet truly divine. Jesus is fully God and also fully human. His name was given by God before His birth and means Savior: "You are to call Him the name Jesus, because he will save his people from their sins" (Matt. 1:21). Jesus, the Lord of glory, the Creator of the universe, came down from the very heart of God to identify Himself in love and grace with mankind, but He was spurned and refused.

Because of who Christ is and what He suffered for God's glory and the salvation of man, God is going to cause every creature to honor and extol the name of Jesus. Everyone will confess that Jesus is Lord; some will do it gladly and others will do it sadly. Some will voluntarily confess while others will be forced to acknowledge His lordship. Each one of us will stand before Him one day and make that confession. Whether or not we have chosen to honor Jesus as our Savior and Lord, we will still all bow before Him and recognize that He is the King of kings and Lord of lords. The choice is ours; will we make this confession willingly and acknowledge Him as Savior and Lord, or will we be forced to acknowledge Him with shame just before being banished forever from His presence?

Glorious Lord: Today I confess You as my Savior and Lord. For the times I disrespected Your holy name and used it in a way that was defaming and shameful, I ask for Your forgiveness. There have been times when I neglected Your Holy Spirit nudging me to turn from my sin; for this I repent. I love You and willingly acknowledge You as Lord of all. In Jesus' name, Amen.

APPLESAUCE 7-UP JELL-O SALAD

2 cups applesauce
1 large box lime Jell-O (regular or diet)
2 cups lemon-lime soda (regular or diet)
Cool Whip

In saucepan, heat applesauce. Add Jell-O; stir until dissolved. Add lemon-lime soda. Mix well and pour into a dish; refrigerate until set. Serve with dollop of Cool Whip.

September 11

Do everything without complaining or arguing, so that you may become blameless and pure, children of God without fault in a crooked and depraved generation, in which you shine like stars in the universe.

—PHILIPPIANS 2:14–15

THE APOSTLE PAUL tells us to live godly lifestyles, pure and blameless. To do so means holding different views and values from those who follow the immoral ways of the world. Following God's ways not only proves our love for Him, but it points people in the direction of a saving knowledge of our Lord and Savior. While it's true we'll never reach sinless perfection, we do have an obligation to strive for purity and holiness in our motives and actions. As the world around us continues on a downward spiral, Christians need to be examples of how it's possible to have positive attitudes regardless of the exterior circumstances. Jesus and His apostles knew that the world is an unbelieving and perverse generation (Matthew 17:17; 12:39; Acts 2:40), yet we are told that if we remain pure, we will shine like stars in the universe. We all know the brilliance of the stars at night and how they illuminate the sky though millions of miles away. Similarly, Christians stand out in the darkness when vibrant, sold out, and on fire for Jesus. A shining white light dramatically contrasts the black of perverseness and depravity. Our generation is no different than Paul's was, and we are to follow his exhortations today just as he instructed the Philippians believers. John Wesley once said, "Give me a hundred men who love nothing but God and hate nothing but sin, and I will shake the whole world for Christ."

Father God: I praise You today for the strength You give me to proclaim Christ's glorious redemption to the lost world where I live. Forgive me when I have a bad attitude, argue, or complain about life and the circumstances in which I find myself. Help me to shine like the stars in the universe so those in darkness might be saved from their sin and find Your mercy and grace. In Jesus' name, Amen.

HASH BROWN TUNA CASSEROLE

1 (16-ounce) package cubed hash brown potatoes
2 cans tuna, drained
1 can cream of chicken soup
½ cup milk
1 ½ cups grated cheddar cheese

Place potatoes in greased 2-quart baking dish. Combine tuna, soup, and milk. Pour over potatoes and sprinkle with cheese. Cover and bake at 350 degrees for 1 hour. Makes 6 servings.

September 12

But whatever was to my profit I now consider loss for the sake of Christ. What is more, I consider everything a loss compared to the surpassing greatness of knowing Christ Jesus my Lord, for whose sake I have lost all things. I consider them rubbish, that I may gain Christ and be found in him, not having a righteousness of my own that comes from the law, but that which is through faith in Christ—the righteousness that comes from God and is by faith.

—PHILIPPIANS 3:7–9

THIS IS THE true heart of Paul and the essence of mere Christianity. It's obvious that Paul is sold out, on fire, a lover of righteousness, a faithful warrior, concerned for the lost, an exhorter of His fellow Christians, and in love with the Lord. He is an awesome example of what it means to be a true follower of Christ.

Where do we all stand in this scenario? How much is Jesus really worth to us? Do we treasure our time and fellowship with Him like nothing else? Do we take time each day to read His Word, pray, and have fellowship with Him? In this beautiful testimony of Paul's, it becomes clear that there is nothing we should consider profitable and great in our lives except for knowing Christ and making Him known. If we become distracted by the things of this world such as money, work, studies, recreation, and even our families and put them before Christ, we have lost the whole meaning of what Paul is saying in these scriptures. This is not to say those things are bad; but compared to Christ's worth nothing else has any value. As Paul puts it, they are as rubbish. Nothing else can fill our hearts with the same satisfaction, peace, and love that Jesus Christ can, and His worth is immeasurable to us if He is our Lord.

Father: I honor You and give You praise for Your greatness and power. You are everything I need just for believing and receiving. May the testimony of my life in You be an example to the lost so they might consider the value of Your love and be saved. In Jesus' name, Amen.

CUCUMBER SANDWICHES

1 (8-ounce) package cream cheese, softened
⅓ cup Miracle Whip
1 package ranch salad dressing mix
1 cucumber, sliced ¼ inch
Dill weed
Hearty rye or part rye bread

Mix first 3 ingredients; spread thin layer on bread. Place cucumber slice on top; sprinkle with dill. Top with bread or eat open-faced.

September 13

Forgetting those things which are behind, and reaching forth unto those things which are before, I press toward the mark for the prize of the high calling of God in Christ Jesus.

—Philippians 3:13–14, KJV

Have you ever failed at anything? Did you give up or try again? God's Word tells us to forget the past and go forward. Life is like a race; we are lined up facing the mark (goal) and must run as though we want to be the winner. Do we get tired and weary? Yes! Does the thought of quitting ever enter our minds when we feel worn out and unable to press on? Yes! It takes commitment, perseverance, and hard work to run the Christian race. Along the way we encounter trials, tribulations, and circumstances that bring discouragement. Life is about choices. How will we react when the storms of life come? Is reaching the goal and winning the prize important enough for us? Jesus is the prize at the end of the race. He's waiting there to take us to our heavenly home. We cannot give up no matter the cost and must press on to receive the prize.

Heavenly Father: Thank You for all You have done for me. Pardon me when I am selfish, take my eyes off the goal, and leave the race of life. Today, I focus on You and with Your strength I will run and be a winner even when weariness comes. You are my goal and my prize. I choose You no matter the cost. In Jesus' name, Amen.

MEATBALL SANDWICHES

2 eggs
1 tablespoon tomato paste
1 small onion, diced small
¼ cup Parmesan cheese
2 teaspoons parsley
1 clove garlic, minced
1 pound ground beef
1 ½ slices crumbled bread
2 teaspoons salt
1 (12-ounce) can tomato paste
2 ½ cups water
2 teaspoons sugar
1 teaspoon oregano
1 teaspoon basil
¼ teaspoon pepper
Hoagie buns

Combine the first 8 ingredients and ½ the salt, and form into balls; cook in large pan until done. To pan with meatballs add remaining tomato paste, water, sugar, oregano, basil, salt, and pepper; cover and simmer 15 minutes. Remove lid and simmer 10 more minutes. Serve on buns.

September 14

But our citizenship is in heaven. And we eagerly await a Savior from there, the Lord Jesus Christ, who, by the power that enables him to bring everything under his control, will transform our lowly bodies so that they will be like his glorious body.

—PHILIPPIANS 3:20–21

NEARLY EVERYONE WANTS to go to heaven when they die. Rarely will anyone say they would rather go to hell, but merely wanting to go to heaven is not enough. Paul is speaking to true Christians who realized they were saved by grace and willingly chose to live according to God's Word. When we make a decision to come to Christ, repent of our sins, and then turn from them, we are given a spiritual passport that will allow us to pass from this life into heaven when we die. No longer are we citizens of Planet Earth, but our true citizenship is in heaven. We must ask ourselves if we are pioneers or homesteaders. Pioneers are never settled and always moving on. They believe that wherever they are is not their home; they are just passing through. This should be the mind-set of all Christians. We are not to become homesteaders with our roots and investments sunk into this world. This is not our true home, and as believers we eagerly await the return of the Lord. That is when we will be taken to our eternal home where our temporary physical bodies will be transformed forever, to be like that of our Savior.

Wonderful Savior: Thank You for preparing a wonderful place for us as we pass through this world as sojourners. By Your grace, those who have accepted Your plan of salvation will inherit eternal life in heaven with You. May we be reminded and encouraged that this world is not our home, but the one we look forward to is where You are. In Jesus' name, Amen.

PLANTATION SUPPER

8 ounces wide egg noodles
1 ½ pounds ground beef
1 medium onion, chopped
1 (15-ounce) can corn, drained
1 can cream of mushroom soup
8 ounces cream cheese, cubed
1 cup milk
1 teaspoon beef bouillon granules
½ teaspoon garlic or seasoned salt
¼ teaspoon pepper

Cook noodles according to package; drain. In large skillet brown beef; drain. Add onion; cook until tender. Add corn, soup, cream cheese, milk, bouillon, and pepper; cook until bubbly. Simmer about 10 minutes. Add noodles and thoroughly heat.

September 15

Rejoice in the Lord always: and again I will say, Rejoice.

—PHILIPPIANS 4:4, KJV

JOY IS ONE of the outward signs of an inward peace and delight. As Christians, this results when we come to know Jesus Christ as Savior and Lord. The apostle Paul amazingly wrote this text while he was suffering in prison, yet one would never know that by his uplifting attitude. He doesn't tell us we have to be happy in our circumstances and situations, but simply to *rejoice in the Lord*. Paul had inner joy, even when his external circumstances were oppressing and painful. Joy is an attitude and it is a *choice*. We may not feel happy because of the place in life in which we find ourselves, but if we *choose* to obey God's inspired words and Paul's example, we will rejoice in the Lord no matter what pain, misery, burdens, or concerns we may have. Our hope and joy is in Jesus Christ because He saved us, filled us with His Holy Spirit, and has taken permanent residence in us. He is our Savior, Comforter, Deliver, Companion, Friend, Healer, and the One who promises to be with us 24/7, never forsaking us even for a moment. We must rejoice because of the Lord's covenant of grace, His redeeming blood, His divine sovereignty, justification and sanctification, and because He commands us to. That gives us every reason to "rejoice in the Lord always: and again I will say, rejoice."

Wonderful Lord: You are my joy, my strength, and the Redeemer of my soul. I praise You for the hope You give me, especially in the rough times of life. You know the circumstances I face, and You are the answer for every situation and crisis I face. Forgive me for complaining, grumbling, and for not rejoicing in You at all times. I choose this day to not only have joy, but to speak it and display it in my life. In Jesus' name, Amen.

SAVORY POT ROAST (crockpot)

3 pounds boneless beef chuck roast
1 tablespoon olive oil
8 small potatoes, cut in half
3 cups baby carrots
1 onion, chopped
3 cloves garlic, minced
3–5 tablespoons horseradish
½ teaspoon salt
¼ teaspoon pepper
1 cup water

Heat oil in large pan; brown roast on all sides. Place vegetables in crockpot; place beef on top. Mix together horseradish, salt and pepper; spread over beef. Add water; cook on low 8–10 hours.

September 16

Let your gentleness be evident to all. The Lord is near. Do not be anxious about anything, but in everything, by prayer and petition, with thanksgiving, present your requests to God. And the peace of God, which transcends all understanding, will guard your hearts and your minds in Christ Jesus.

—PHILIPPIANS 4:5–7

GENTLENESS IS A fruit of the Spirit and a requirement of God for Christians. It can be a great witness to the lost if we remain gentle or meek in our attitudes and responses to life. The Lord is coming back soon, and we must live as though we believe it could happen at any moment. Through prayer and communication with God, our faith in Him becomes strengthened. It is then that we are able to release our worries and cares to the One who has all the answers. As we have fellowship with God and praise and thank Him for who we are in Him and who He is in us, a peace that is incomprehensible by the world comes upon us and we have the reassurance that all is well with our soul. When we come to Jesus Christ, the Prince of Peace, He is able to bring us wholeness, soundness, and a sense of composure in a world of unrest and confusion. If we unite ourselves with God and take our petitions and cares to Him, He promises to guard our hearts and minds in Jesus Christ. He is such a wonderful Lord.

Dear Lord: In a world of unrest and turmoil, I sometimes become anxious and fearful, wondering which way to turn. Thank You for the encouragement I find in Your Word, reassuring me that peace is mine just for the asking. Forgive me for the times I tried to solve my own problems when all along I could have gone to You with my petitions and requests. Bring peace to my anxious soul and allow me to be overcome with tranquility beyond all understanding. In Jesus' name, Amen.

BEANS, BEEF, AND DOGS

4 slices bacon cut into 1-inch pieces
1 pound ground beef
½ cup chopped onion
6–8 hot dogs cut into ½-inch pieces
1 (28-ounce) can Bush's Baked Beans
2–3 tablespoons favorite barbecue sauce
⅓ cup brown sugar

Brown bacon until crisp; drain; remove for later use. Brown ground meat; drain. Add onions and cook until tender. Add hot dogs; simmer 3–4 minutes. Add beans, bacon, barbecue sauce, and brown sugar; heat.

September 17

Finally, brethren, whatsoever things are true, whatsoever things are honest, whatsoever things are just, whatsoever things are pure, whatsoever things are lovely, whatsoever things are of good report; if there be any virtue, and if there be any praise, think on these things.

—PHILIPPIANS 4:8, KJV

In PAUL'S FINAL exhortation to the Philippians, he tells us to put into practice his teachings that cover all aspects of life: the internal, the external, what we think, and what we do. Our minds are never idle and always occupied with something. It requires effort on our part to make sure we feed them wholesome food. Though this might be difficult because of the sensuous world in which we live, it *is* possible and required of us by God. The things we put into our minds should be true (line up with God's Word), honest (of moral and worthy character), just (according to God's law), pure (wholesome and clean), lovely (reflecting God's creation), of good report (reputable and respectful), and virtuous (moral and decent). This covers all the things we look at, listen to, become involved with, the places we go, our friends, hobbies, recreation, and so forth. If we call ourselves Christians and want to experience God's will, joy, nearness, peace, and freedom, then we must do as we're told. Romans 12:2 (KJV) says it so well, "And be not conformed to this world: but be ye transformed by the renewing of your mind, that ye may prove what is that good, and acceptable, and perfect, will of God."

Dear Lord: I praise You for Your peace and presence in my life. Thank You for teaching us how to live. Help me to follow this good word so I might learn to fill my mind with wholesome thoughts and all that is good, right, and praiseworthy. May these thoughts then overflow into my life as I put the teaching of Your Word into practice. In Jesus' name, Amen.

CHICKEN SALAD WRAP

2–3 boneless, skinless chicken breasts
Lawry's Seasoned Salt
1–3 stalks celery, diced
Craisins or raisins
Pecans
Mayonnaise
Spinach tortilla wraps
Romaine lettuce

Sauté chicken in pan with lid until fully cooked; dice. Sprinkle with seasoned salt. In bowl, mix chicken, celery, handful of craisins, and handful of chopped pecans. Add enough mayonnaise to wet all ingredients. Line spinach wraps with romaine lettuce; add scoop of chicken salad. Roll; cut in half to serve. If making ahead of time, cover with plastic wrap and refrigerate.

September 18

I know what it is to be in need, and I know what it is to have plenty. I have learned the secret of being content in any and every situation, whether well fed or hungry, whether living in plenty or in want.

—Philippians 4:12

PAUL WAS VERY aware of his needs and the intense suffering he endured for the Lord. Yet he remained fruitful and satisfied, even when he was imprisoned, such as he was when he wrote this letter. Paul was not naïve, nor was he a masochist, but his focus was on the Lord and evangelizing the world, no matter the circumstances and trials he had to endure. Paul wanted to impress upon us the need to live our lives totally surrendered to the Lord Jesus Christ and be content or satisfied in all we do no matter the situation or circumstance that arises. Unless we focus on our goal (living eternally with Christ and pleasing Him now) we will be too fearful to go beyond our comfort zones to do anything of significance. In our humanness, we tend to be selfish, superficial, and sometimes give greater value to our possessions than we give to faith, hope, and love. We should cherish every precious thing God gives to us: His saving grace, mercy, strength, forgiveness, daily bread, shelter, and even the air we breathe. If we pray to God for strength to work through all our difficult situations, we will be astounded to look back at the ease with which we went through them.

Dear God: Thank You for the bountiful blessings with which my life is filled. You have been the giver of all that I have, both big and small. When I go through the storms and valleys of life, may I not be found complaining and grumbling, but with Your strength and power be content until the storm is over and the circumstances change. Help me to appreciate the wonderful plan You have for me and may I have divine strength to always walk in it. In Jesus' name, Amen.

EGG SALAD (even the kids will love this)

4–6 eggs
¼ cup Miracle Whip or mayonnaise
1 teaspoon sweet relish (optional)
2 teaspoons sugar
½–1 teaspoon mustard (optional)
¼ teaspoon onion salt or seasoned salt
Paprika, dash (optional)
Salt and pepper to taste

Boil eggs 5 minutes; cool and remove shells. Dice eggs and add all ingredients; gently mix. Refrigerate until ready to eat. Spread on crackers, toast, or bread.

September 19

I can do all things through Christ which strengtheneth me.

—PHILIPPIANS 4:13, KJV

PAUL WAS IN prison when he wrote that he could be content no matter what his circumstances were. His inner peace and joy remained the same whether he was in need or had plenty, or was hungry or full (Philippians 4:12). Calvin Johnson also experienced the truth of this often-quoted statement. He was sentenced to life in prison after being wrongly convicted of rape. In the courtroom he said, "God is my witness, I have been falsely accused…I just pray in the name of Jesus Christ that the truth will eventually be brought out." Sixteen years later in 1999, DNA tests proved him innocent and he was freed. Amazingly, he holds no bitter feelings toward the woman who falsely accused him, the jury that found him guilty, or the judge who sentenced him. Upon his release he said, "Bitterness will destroy you. Now I just need a job." How true that is. Jesus our Savior is always with us enabling us to be content no matter what our circumstances are. Because of Him, we can be kind, even toward those who mistreat us. As we love Christ, trust Him, and depend on Him, He will give us strength to do those things we believe to be impossible. What a wonderful Father we have!

Heavenly Father: Thank You for the strength I find only in knowing and serving You. Without You I am nothing, and with You I am everything You have called me to be. When I am weak, You make me strong. Forgive me when I mistrust You and give up too soon, often before I have completed a task You have called me to do. Help me to put my anchor in You so that when storms come, I will be strong. In Jesus' name, Amen.

TWICE-BAKED SWEET POTATOES

2 large sweet potatoes
4 ounces cream cheese
2 tablespoons milk
1 tablespoons brown sugar
¼ teaspoon cinnamon
¼ cup pecan pieces

Cut potatoes lengthwise in half; place cut sides down in foil-lined baking pan.

Bake 30 minutes or until tender. Scoop out centers of potatoes into bowl, leaving ¼ inch thick shells. Add cream cheese, milk, sugar and cinnamon to potatoes; mash until blended. Spoon potato mixture into shells; top with nuts. Bake 8 minutes or until potatoes heated through and nuts toasted.

September 20

But my God shall supply all your need according to his riches in glory by Christ Jesus.

—Philippians 4:19, KJV

C HRIST IS THE abundant life! In a materialistic society, when we see the word *prosperity*, we immediately think of financial wealth. However, to a true Christian who knows God's Word, prosperity has nothing to do with money. It does, however, have everything to do with the spiritual blessings that Christ abundantly gives to His children. Paul was still imprisoned when he wrote these words to the Philippian believers who had sacrificially supported his ministry. Though Paul experienced more hardships in his lifetime than we could ever imagine, he knew God's purpose was being accomplished in his life and that his every need would be met. His joy did not come from his physical situation but from his spiritual standing in Christ.

We can all learn from Paul's attitude because most of us believe happiness comes from material possessions. We think that with just a little more money all of our problems would be solved. Could we consider ourselves having had our needs met if we were in prison (especially if our only crime were telling others about Christ), or if we were homeless, owned no personal possessions, nor had any money in the bank? Paul did! He felt blessed and praised God because he truly believed the Lord has the ability to meet all our needs (not desires, wants, or lusts), *according to his riches in glory by Christ Jesus.*

Dear God: You are my life! You are the abundance in my life! It is You that I base my joy and prosperity on, not that of the world. When I am weak and begin to focus on material things, come and strengthen me with your power and remind me that nothing outside of you is able to bring me contentment. Thank You for meeting all my needs according to Your Word. In Jesus' name, Amen.

SAUSAGE BARLEY SOUP (crockpot)

½ pound sweet Italian sausage, cut into ¼-inch slices
1 sweet red, orange or yellow pepper, chopped
4 cups water + 4 beef bouillon cubes dissolved
1 large sweet onion, chopped
½ cup barley
3 stalks of celery, chopped
16 ounces stewed tomatoes

Place all ingredients in crockpot and cook on high for 6–8 hours.

September 21

And whatsoever ye do in word or deed, do all in the name of the Lord Jesus, giving thanks to God and the Father by Him.

—Colossians 3:17, KJV

EVERYTHING WE DO either honors or dishonors our Lord. The things we say and do represent our respect of God's authority. Some days are harder than others to worship Him with our actions and things we say. Life can be stressful and there are so many demands on us. But God knows our schedules and our stresses and yet He expects us to still live with a thankful and obedient heart. To do so is a living testament of thankfulness for what the Lord has done for us.

Father God: You are the Magnificent One and I praise Your holy name. I choose to follow after Your will in everything I do. Forgive me when I speak unkindly to my family members or people who cross my path each day. I want them to see You in me and the only way that will happen is if I react as You would in every circumstance. Help me in my weak areas so I don't live as a hypocrite saying I am a Christian, yet speaking and acting otherwise. In Jesus' name, Amen.

ROASTED CHICKEN CAPRESE

Marinade:

¼ cup olive oil
2 tablespoons lemon juice
1 clove minced garlic
¾ teaspoon salt
½ teaspoon pepper
4–6 boneless, skinless chicken breast halves

Whisk together first 5 ingredients; put in a resealable bag with chicken. Refrigerate 1 hour.

1 teaspoon sugar
1 teaspoon salt
¼ cup olive oil
6 Roma tomatoes, quartered
8 ounces fresh mozzarella cheese, cut into ¼ -inch slices
¼ cup basil leaves, cut up (or 2 tablespoons dried basil)
½ teaspoon pepper

Mix first 4 ingredients together; place on rimmed cookie sheet so tomatoes don't touch. Bake at 375 degrees for 30 minutes; when done pour into small bowl. Add cheese, basil, and pepper; gently toss. Let sit at room temperature while chicken cooks. Remove chicken from refrigerator; discard marinade. Place chicken on same cookie sheet as vegetables were roasted. Cook chicken 30 minutes, turn once. Serve with pasta or rice. Put 1 chicken breast half on each plate. Spoon tomato mixture over top.

September 22

Devote yourselves to prayer, being watchful and thankful.

—Colossians 4:2

To DEVOTE ONESELF to something means to give or apply one's time, attention, or self entirely to a particular activity, pursuit, cause, or person. Prayer is the communication, communion, and fellowship we have with God through His Son Jesus for purposes of supplication, thanksgiving, adoration, or confession. Being watchful is a state of continually remaining vigilant, alert, and closely observant. To show appreciation, gratitude, or kindness for something received is to be thankful. So, to devote oneself to prayer, according to Paul's instructions here, simply implies pursuing a strong, continual persistence and fervor for prayer while being cautious and on the alert for the enemy's schemes to deter. All the while, we must be thankful to the Lord for everything He has given and done.

The reason Paul put such an emphasis on prayer was the fact that he knew prayer was vital for victory. Prayer is the key that unlocks the resources of God's power. God is our light source, and we are continually dependent upon Him. It is only through prayer and expressing our needs to Him that He can supply us with the guidance and strength needed to see us through every situation and circumstance we face. Just because we devote ourselves to prayer does not mean God will remove every trial we face, but it does mean He will be with us every step of the way. As we devote ourselves to prayer, our faith is strengthened, and we find the grace needed to face each new day. If we are watchful, we will recognize God's hand moving. If we are thankful, His grace and compassion will carry us through any situation. Let us all resolve this day to devote ourselves to prayer and be watchful and thankful in doing so.

Merciful Father: I praise You this day for the power of prayer and for allowing me to communicate and have fellowship with You, the King of kings and Lord of lords. With Your help, may I become devoted, watchful, and thankful for the privilege You have given to me to become a person devoted to prayer. In Jesus' name, Amen.

ONE-STEP CHICKEN AND POTATO BAKE

4 bone-in chicken pieces
4 large potatoes, cut into wedges
¼ cup Zesty Italian dressing
¼ cup grated Parmesan cheese
Fresh parsley, chopped (optional)

Put chicken and potatoes in 13x9-inch baking dish. Pour dressing over top; sprinkle with cheese. Bake 1 hour at 350 degrees until chicken thoroughly cooked. Sprinkle with parsley.

September 23

I, Paul, write this greeting in my own hand. Remember my chains. Grace be with you.

—COLOSSIANS 4:18

THE APOSTLE PAUL was an amazing man, full of God's character and grace. Though he was unjustly imprisoned during the time of most of his writings, Paul remained joyful, thankful, and uplifting. He was without a doubt one of the most humble men of the Bible. Paul wanted no attention brought to himself for his achievements, hardships, or persecution; nor did he in any way want to take the focus off the Lord and onto him. All he did proved this to be true; however, at the end of this great letter to the Colossians, Paul briefly mentioned that He was still in chains. This is the only place where he deliberately mentioned his circumstance and need for prayer. He asked for prayer for the further advancement of the gospel and even mentioned he was imprisoned. But the thought of seeking support in his chains didn't occur to him until he was about to close the letter. Due to poor eyesight and deplorable prison conditions, it was very difficult for Paul to write his letters. He did not sit down in a comfortable chair at a computer, but he dictated to a slave and then painfully with his hands in chains wrote his name at the close to prove they were from him. Down through the ages this letter, along with others, has transformed the history of the world. It is good for us to remember the cost Paul had to pay to put these scriptures in our hands. May we all be moved as Paul was to serve God wholeheartedly in our own form of chains under our own set of difficult circumstances.

Holy Lord: Thank You for reminding me to be humble, joyful, and thankful, no matter in what circumstance I find myself. You are with me everywhere I am; never am I alone. Help me to live as the apostle Paul did and trust You in the good times and in the bad. In Jesus' name, Amen.

MIXED GREENS AND PEAR SALAD

⅓ cup pecan halves
¼ teaspoon cinnamon
1 teaspoon sugar
1 large pear, thinly sliced
1 (5-ounce) package mixed salad greens
½ cup cheddar cheese, shredded
⅓ cup dried cranberries (or cranraisins)
⅓ cup Italian dressing + 2 teaspoons sugar

Combine nuts, cinnamon, and sugar. Spread on greased pie dish; microwave on high 1–1 ½ minutes, until nuts toasted; stir every 30 seconds. In large bowl, toss greens with pear, cheese, cranberries, nuts, and dressing. Serve immediately.

September 24

May the Lord make your love increase and overflow for each other and for everyone else, just as ours does for you. May he strengthen your hearts so that you will be blameless and holy in the presence of our God and Father when our Lord Jesus comes with all his holy ones.

—1 Thessalonians 3:12–13

This was Paul's prayer for the church at Thessalonica, and it should be our prayer for everyone we know. Paul loved people and wanted them in turn to love others. He believed we needed one another for encouragement and accountability to keep our faith strong. Paul always had the Lord's return on his mind. He knew it would be a tragedy for those who once walked with the Lord to be found in sin or in a state of lukewarmness (Revelation 3:14–19) at the time of the Lord's return and not inherit eternal life. Jesus showed the same concern (Matthew 24:42–51; 25:1–13) and warns us all to be ready and watching for the time of His coming. God's Word is clear about the kind of life we are to be living in preparation for Jesus' return. Though many of us want to do our own thing and live according to the fleshly desires we have, we must choose to separate ourselves from anything that might offend our Lord. Is this always easy? No! But as we pray for one another, like the apostle Paul did, our hearts will be strengthened and God will help us. It is then that we are found "blameless and holy in the presence of our God and Father when our Lord Jesus comes with all his holy ones" to take us to our heavenly home.

Dear Lord: Thank You for Your love and for using Paul to emulate how we should love others. Help me to live a godly life so others would be encouraged to do the same. Strengthen my heart that I might not fall into sin and away from Your perfect will for my life. In Jesus' name, Amen.

DORITOS CHICKEN CASSEROLE

2–3 cups diced cooked chicken
1 cup sour cream
1 can cream of chicken soup
¼ cup finely minced onion
1 teaspoon chili powder
½ teaspoon pepper
½ teaspoon garlic salt
½ cup grated cheddar cheese
½ cup grated mozzarella cheese
1 medium size bag of Doritos, crushed

Spread half the crushed Doritos on bottom of greased baking dish. Mix all other ingredients, except cheese; place on Doritos. Add on remaining Doritos and cheese. Bake at 350 degrees for 40 minutes.

September 25

It is God's will that you should be sanctified: that you should avoid sexual immorality.

—1 Thessalonians 4:3

ANY SEXUAL ACTIVITY, mental or physical (Matthew 5:28), outside of marriage between a man and woman is sexual immorality. This includes premarital sex, homosexual acts, viewing pornography, incest, and any other form of mental or physical sexual activity (outside of marriage) that stimulates arousal or lust. From the beginning of time (after Adam and Eve sinned), sexual immorality has been a problem.

The apostle Paul says Christians must be different than the world in the area of sexuality. He explains in Ephesians 5:5–7 that no unrepentant sexually immoral person has the blessings, rewards, treasures, or inheritance of the kingdom of God in Christ. In other words, Paul says those who choose to go against the commandments of God in the area of sexual immorality have not experienced the saving, transforming, and forgiving, gracious power of the living God. Paul points out that sexual sin is especially deadly because it delves deep into the hearts of men and women. Where there should be love for God, receiving fulfillment, satisfaction, and pleasure from Him, instead fulfillment is sought and obtained in areas of immorality. To continue in sexual sin requires a decision to ignore God's appeal for us to repent and receive His grace and forgiveness. As Christians, we are required to not compromise our pure and moral standards to follow those of the impure and immoral society in which we live. It is God's will that we separate ourselves from all thoughts and actions that are unholy or dishonorable to the Lord and attach ourselves to what is righteous.

Holy God: Your Word says I should be sanctified and avoid sexual immorality. This is what I desire; but because of the enemy's desire to see me fail I need your strength and power. Without You I would be enslaved by all sorts of passions and pleasures. With You I have Your strength to help me resist the temptations of this world and avoid sexual sin. Forgive me for all of my sin; give me courage and strength to do only those things that honor You. In Jesus' name, Amen.

ASIAN PORK ROAST (crockpot)

1 (3–4 pounds) pork roast
¼ cup soy sauce
2 cloves crushed garlic
¼ cup orange marmalade
1 tablespoon ketchup

Put all ingredients in a crockpot. Cook on low for 8–10 hours.

September 26

For the Lord himself shall descend from heaven with a shout, with the voice of the arch-angel, and with the trump of God: and the dead in Christ shall rise first: Then we which are alive and remain shall be caught up together with them in the clouds, to meet the Lord in the air: and so shall we ever be with the Lord.

—1 Thessalonians 4:16–17, KJV

THIS GLORIOUS EVENT, commonly known as the Rapture, is derived from the Latin word *raptu,* which means "caught away or caught up." Though the word *rapture* is not found in the Bible, it represents what God's Word says will happen to the church of Jesus Christ and those who have been faithful. Just about everyone would say they'd prefer going to heaven rather than going to hell when they die. Heaven is known as a glorious place where there is peace and the presence of Jesus. Hell is known as a wicked place of fire and torment where bad people go to be with the devil. God's desire is that we all accept His Son as Savior and live eternally with Him. In Jesus' wonderful prayer to the Father, just before going to the cross, He expressed these words, "Father, I want those you have given me to be with me where I am, and to see my glory, the glory you have given me because you loved me before the creation of the world" (John 17:24). Jesus said this knowing He would soon suffer a horrible death as He allowed the consequences of our sin to fall on Him.

The apostle Paul instructs us about the coming of Christ and how things will happen. As the Lord comes, the sleeping saints (Christians who have previously died) will hear His call and come out of their graves. Christians alive all over the world will be taken upward to meet the Lord in the air. This is the hope of every believer and used by the Holy Spirit to bring comfort to the godly and warning to the ungodly. For the redeemed this is our heavenly hope and the reason we live for God. *And so shall we ever be with the Lord.*

Dear Lord: With anticipation and expectation I await Your coming. What a joy it will be to hear the voice of the archangel and Your trumpet sound as Jesus approaches through the clouds. Cleanse me and find me redeemed when that glorious day approaches. In Jesus' name, Amen.

SWEET AND SPICY KIELBASA (crockpot)

1 cup brown sugar
3 tablespoons ketchup
3 tablespoons spicy mustard
2 pounds smoked, fully cooked kielbasa, cut into 1-inch pieces

Combine brown sugar, ketchup, and mustard in crockpot; add kielbasa and stir to coat. Cook on low 3–4 hours. Stir occasionally. Serve with or without buns.

September 27

Now, brothers, about times and dates we do not need to write to you, for you know very well that the day of the Lord will come like a thief in the night. While people are saying, "Peace and safety," destruction will come on them suddenly, as labor pains on a pregnant woman, and they will not escape.

—1 Thessalonians 5:1–3

The "day of the Lord" is when the Lord Jesus will come to judge the world. Only God the Father knows when this day will be. Paul compares this day to a thief in the night because of its unexpectedness and imminence. He comments that his Thessalonian brothers already know about this spectacular event, but he believes it is crucial enough to be repeated. Throughout history, just as it was in the days of Noah, unbelievers talk about peace and security, giving no thought to their spiritual condition. Just as a thief quietly sneaks in to do his destruction when no one is looking, so will it be when the Lord returns. When a pregnant lady begins to have labor pains, there is no stopping the baby from being born. So it will be for those who have refused to live according to God's Word. At this point, there is no return and the opportunity to come to Christ and repent is not possible. Faithful believers will escape this wrath, but for the unbeliever, there is no hope. The day of the Lord is not something to be feared. If we have trusted our souls to the Christ and have repented of our sin, this day will be an exciting one. No longer will there be any heartache or pain in our lives, but we will be united with Christ and taken to His Father's house in heaven. There, our loved ones who have gone on before will welcome us home.

Father: Thank You for the day of the Lord when You will come to judge the world. Though everyone talks about peace and how to find it, Your Word says it's only found in You. Help me to live my life worthy of Your mercy and grace. In Jesus' name, Amen.

PINEAPPLE GLAZED CHICKEN

4 boneless, skinless chicken breasts
Dash garlic salt and pepper
2 tablespoons butter
1 (15-ounce) can chunk pineapple
2 tablespoons vinegar
1 tablespoons soy sauce
2 tablespoons cornstarch
¼ cup packed brown sugar

Season chicken breasts with salt, or garlic salt, and pepper; brown in butter over medium heat. Mix together entire can of pineapple, vinegar, cornstarch, soy sauce, and brown sugar. Add to pan with chicken. Continue cooking until liquid is thickened and forms a sauce. Serve over rice.

September 28

And we urge you, brothers, warn those who are idle, encourage the timid, help the weak, be patient with everyone. Make sure that nobody pays back wrong for wrong, but always try to be kind to each other and to everyone else.

—1 Thessalonians 5:14–15

As Christians, we have certain responsibilities concerning those God has entrusted to our care. The apostle Paul urges us to be watchmen and protect others from harm's way. We must constantly be on guard that the enemy doesn't get a foothold in our own lives as well as others. He will try every way possible to discourage God's people and tempt them to fall. If we become slack, lose focus, become idle, or fall asleep on the job, it gives an opportunity for the enemy to move in and do his damage. Those who are timid or weak need encouragement and support. A timid person is one who is faced with a great task and doesn't feel they have the resources or strength to accomplish it. Most all of us hit periods in life when we get weary and feel like quitting. We become tired and worn, maybe even in our Christian walk, and feel like we aren't accomplishing anything. This is when we need someone to encourage us. A phone call, prayer, card, written note, visit, hug, gentle pat on the back, or an invitation for fellowship, perhaps over a meal or cup of coffee, would bring more encouragement and strength to someone than words could ever express. This is what Paul tells the Thessalonian church to do, and this is what God's Word says we should do. Being patient, kind, and showing brotherly love, even though we may not be able to fix the problem, will help others find God's plan and purposes for their lives. In turn, we are living out the attitude of Christ while reaping eternal rewards.

Father: Thank You for the honor of caring for Your children and showing them Your patience, love, forgiveness, kindness, and encouragement. May others come to know You as their Savior and Lord by the life I lead before them. In Jesus' name, Amen.

BAKED FRENCH ONION PORK CHOPS

2 cups original or cheddar French fried onions
2 tablespoons all-purpose flour
4 (½-inch thick) bone-in or boneless pork chops
1 egg, beaten

Place onions and flour in plastic bag; lightly crush with hands or rolling pin. Transfer to plate or waxed paper. Dip chops in beaten egg; then coat with onion crumbs, pressing firmly to adhere. Place on greased baking sheet; bake at 400 degrees for 30 minutes, or until center no longer pink.

September 29

Rejoice evermore. Pray without ceasing. In every thing give thanks: for this is the will of God in Christ Jesus concerning you.

—I Thessalonians 5:16–18, KJV

THE APOSTLE PAUL encouraged the church at Thessalonica with these words. He knew that serving Christ also meant suffering. The believers were persecuted for their faith and yet were willing to endure for the cause. We are reminded to be joyful no matter what the circumstances are and to have thankful hearts. Knowing Christ and walking with Him should be our ultimate goal. If our lives are centered on Him, then we are in a state of continuous prayer. *Everything* we do should be pleasing, uplifting, and glorifying to God; this is His will for us in Christ Jesus. What gift could we give to God today to thank Him for sending His Son to be slaughtered for us? A thankful heart, speaking words of joy, giving praise to His name, and thanking Him for the privilege of being His child are all ways of showing our appreciation and thankfulness to God. These are gifts that cost us nothing but are treasures when offered to our Lord.

Father: I praise and thank You for the privilege of knowing and serving You. What an honor it is and I am forever grateful to be Your child. At times, I grumble and complain about circumstances; please forgive me. Help me to be more cautious of the things I say and do. May my life reflect a deeper appreciation and a more profound awareness of Your presence in my life. In Jesus' name, Amen.

CHICKEN AND STUFFING CASSEROLE

4 cups prepared herb-seasoned stuffing (such as Pepperidge Farm)
1 ¼ cups boiling water
½ stick butter
4–6 skinless boneless chicken breasts
Paprika
1 can cream of mushroom soup
⅓ cup milk

Mix stuffing with boiling water and butter; spread in baking dish. Lay chicken over top; sprinkle with paprika. Mix soup and milk together; pour over chicken. Cover with lid or foil. Bake at 350 degrees for 45 minutes, until chicken done.

September 30

Abstain from all appearance of evil.

—1 Thessalonians 5:22, KJV

EVIL IS ANYTHING morally bad or wrong according to God's Word. All that is in agreement or conformance with God's exposed will is good and all that is contrary to God's will is evil. John 3:18–21 describes the wicked as those who love evil and darkness and find pleasure in sin and immorality. Contrary to this are those who hate wickedness and love righteousness. They have put their faith in Jesus Christ and grieve when the darkness of sin is expressed. There is an evil nature within every human being. Jeremiah 17:9 (KJV) says, "The heart is deceitful above all things, and desperately wicked." Even though we are drawn to evil, God commands us to avoid it. His Holy Spirit graciously allows us to see evil, but hate it and ultimately avoid it. The apostle Paul instructed the Thessalonians to live a holy lifestyle and avoid things that were contrary to God's Word. As Christians, we must be set apart and live an exemplary life as a man or woman of holiness. We are to live beyond reproach, embrace the truth, and put into practice what God's Word teaches. To avoid every kind of evil means to eliminate even the smallest sin from our lives. Just as a little bit of poison added everyday to our food would eventually kill us, so does sin do that to our soul. Our lives must be transparent and show integrity in everything we do. We are representatives of Jesus, portraying God's holiness and righteousness in an immoral world.

Holy Father: You know so well the struggles I have with temptation and sin, yet Your Holy Spirit gives me strength and power to turn from it and have victory. Forgive me for the times I yielded and did evil. Cleanse me from all righteousness and help me to make moral choices in the immoral world in which I live. In Jesus' name, Amen.

TUNA NOODLE BAKE

6 ounces medium noodles
1 (7-ounce) can of tuna, drained
½ cup mayonnaise
½ cup chopped onion
1 can cream of mushroom or chicken soup
¾ cup milk
1 cup American cheese, shredded
Salt and pepper to taste (pinch of each)

Cook noodles to package directions; mix with tuna, mayonnaise and onion. Heat soup and milk together in pan, until blended. Combine all ingredients; pour into baking dish. Bake 30 minutes at 375 degrees.

October

Reaping the Harvest

October 1

He will punish those who do not know God and do not obey the gospel of our Lord Jesus. They will be punished with everlasting destruction and shut out from the presence of the Lord and from the majesty of his power on the day he comes to be glorified in his holy people and to be marveled at among all those who have believed.

—2 THESSALONIANS 1:8–10

To a Christian, this is probably the most distressing statement the apostle Paul could ever make. In one way, it assures believers of their security in knowing Christ and reaping the benefits of eternal life with Him. But our hearts are grieved when we recognize the dreadful eternal destiny of unsaved loved ones or those who say they are Christians but do not obey the gospel. If a soul transformation has really occurred when someone claims to have come to know Christ, the desires of their heart will change. First Corinthians 5:17 tells us the old is gone and the new has come. The Scriptures are plain concerning our thoughts and behavior, and God is serious about His Word. Contrary to what we want to believe, God does not turn His head and ignore our sin. Throughout the Bible, He gives us not just His advice, but His commands. God's Word is not pro-choice; we cannot pick and choose which of His words we desire to obey. It will be a joyful day when Jesus returns for those who believed and obeyed, but the mere thought of being shut out from the presence of the Lord is incomprehensible. God's power will be shown throughout the universe as Christians receive their reward and justice is shown to the disobedient. Many church leaders neglect the judgment of God while exaggerating His mercy because they are afraid it will scare people away. The church is marketed to make it attractive to the flesh so the world will come in and an increase in numbers will result. The gospel calls us to repent and turn from our ways to God's ways so we may be saved by His grace. There is no other way.

Dear God: You are the Maker of the heavens and the earth; there is none like You. Help me to arrange my time so it includes studying the Scriptures because I want to know what You require of me. I pray earnestly for my family and friends who are without Christ. Draw them with Your Holy Spirit to know You as Savior. In Jesus' name, Amen.

SWEET AND SPICY CHICKEN

6–8 chicken legs
½ cup orange marmalade
1–2 teaspoons chili powder

Mix chili powder and marmalade; rub on chicken. Put in greased baking dish. Bake at 350 degrees for 30 minutes, or until done.

October 2

Don't let anyone deceive you in any way, for that day will not come until the rebellion occurs and the man of lawlessness is revealed, the man doomed to destruction.

—2 Thessalonians 2:3

I N THIS, PAUL'S second letter to the Thessalonians, he again gave instructions about the return of Christ and the Day of the Lord (Zephaniah 1:14–15; 1 Thessalonians 5:1–10). In both letters Paul reiterated what he had previously taught but wanted to make sure the people understood how crucial these End Time events were. Some believed the tribulation and Day of the Lord had already begun and Paul wanted to set them straight. The Day of the Lord will not come until two things occur: the rebellion (apostasy) and the revealing of the man of lawlessness (those deceived by the spirit of the Antichrist and disobedient to the laws of God). The rebellion or apostasy is a falling away from the faith and will take place in magnitude before Jesus returns to gather the church. Those who once served Christ will abandon their faith and return to a state of lostness (Matthew 24:10). Many believe there will be a great revival before the Lord returns, but the biggest revival will occur during the post-church period known as the Great Tribulation. Because of the rapture of the church (those who have kept God's laws), a huge number of unbelievers left behind will remember the warnings of family, friends, and church leaders who disappeared. Many will be converted because of the fulfillment of prophecy right before their eyes. The result will be the largest increase of believers in all of history. But the consequences and persecution will be extreme and almost impossible for new believers. This is another reason why Christians must be about the Father's will to fulfill the purpose for which we are born: (1) to worship and be obedient to God through faith is Jesus Christ and (2) to lead and disciple others in the ways of God so they too might be saved and do the same for others.

Heavenly Father: You are my hope and the only reason I exist. To fulfill Your purpose is what I desire. Help me worship, work, and serve You passionately while I have the opportunity. I pray for my family and friends who don't yet serve You that they would be drawn by Your Holy Spirit to repentance and salvation. In Jesus' name, Amen.

SASSY CHICKEN

8 pieces chicken
1 (8-ounce) bottle Italian dressing

Put chicken in baking dish; cover with dressing. Bake at 350 degrees for 60 minutes. Turn once.

October 3

But the Lord is faithful, and he will strengthen and protect you from the evil one.

—2 Thessalonians 3:3

The apostle Paul was faithful to encourage new believers as well as the old to stand firm in their faith and live a disciplined life. At times he had to be a little firm, just as a father exhorts his children to be obedient to what is required of them. Paul not only used this letter to the Thessalonians to clear up some misunderstandings regarding the second coming of Christ, he also wanted to warn them to be ready and watching for the approaching Day of the Lord. We all have a choice to make in our lifetime: (1) to accept Christ as our Savior and live obedient to God's Word or (2) to reject Christ as Savior and live in disobedience to God's Word. Of course, the decision we make will determine our eternal destination. When we put our trust in the Lord and choose to live according to His Word, He will be faithful to protect us from the evil one, Satan, and give us the strength we need to face any temptation.

Faithful Lord: Your faithfulness is all around me, and I see Your mighty hand at work in my life; I praise You for the strength You give me. When I am weak and weary, You help me to continue to press on. Thank You for protecting me against all harm and evil. Help me to become more disciplined and obedient to Your holy Word. In Jesus' name, Amen.

LEMON-PEPPER CHICKEN PASTA

1 tablespoon cooking oil + 3 tablespoons butter
3 boneless, skinless chicken breasts (cut into small pieces)
8 ounces uncooked pasta (spaghetti, linguine—your choice)
1 tablespoon lemon juice
1–2 teaspoons dried basil
½ teaspoon garlic powder
½ teaspoon lemon pepper seasoning
¼ cup grated Parmesan cheese

Heat oil and butter in pan; sauté chicken pieces until done. Cook pasta according to package directions. Add lemon juice, basil, garlic powder, and lemon pepper to pan with cooked chicken; cook about 2 minutes. Drain pasta; add to chicken mixture. Add Parmesan cheese; toss.

October 4

In the name of the Lord Jesus Christ, we command you, brothers, to keep away from every brother who is idle and does not live according to the teaching you received from us.

—2 THESSALONIANS 3:6

For even when we were with you, we gave you this rule: "If a man will not work, he shall not eat."

—2 THESSALONIANS 3:10

THESE ARE PRETTY harsh words, but the apostle Paul had good reason why he said them. Among the Thessalonians were those who so strongly believed in Christ's imminent return that they quit working. They no longer provided for their families but had become idle and negligent in living according to Paul's teachings. These men were convinced by false teachers that Christ would return any moment, and if that be the case, why work? Paul was adamant in his letter to them concerning this issue because many of them were taking advantage of the church and others' generosity who continued to work, expecting them to meet their needs. God encourages us to help those in need and share our resources with them, but those who are able to work and yet do not are not considered as ones in need. Paul even emphasizes that not only are we not to help those who are lazy and won't work, but we are to not even be around them. Perhaps he believed that their slothfulness and lack of regard for living according to God's Word would weaken the faith of fellow believers who were obedient. There are some who are physically or mentally unable to work; this does not apply to them. Nor does it apply to widows, single moms, or those at home caring for children. These are the ones we are instructed to help. Man was created to work, and the Bible says much about this. God's Word is true and hopeful and He knows what is best for us. If we follow His rules, we will live in victory and reap eternal rewards.

Father: Forgive me for the times I was lazy, slothful, and disregarded doing what I knew to be right. Help me to do the work You have called me to do so I might provide for my family and also share with those in need. In Jesus' name, Amen.

FRIED CORN

2 pounds frozen whole kernel corn
1 stick butter
1 cup whipping cream
1 tablespoon sugar

Put everything in pan on medium heat. Stir constantly until most of liquid absorbed, about 15 minutes.

October 5

For this is good and acceptable in the sight of God our Saviour; Who will have all men to be saved, and to come unto the knowledge of the truth.

—1 TIMOTHY 2:3-4, KJV

THERE IS SOME controversy regarding God's will for all mankind concerning predestination and whether God desires for everyone to go to heaven or just a select number that only He knows. There is ample proof throughout the Scriptures that God truly does wants everyone to be saved. The most common verse known is John 3:16 (KJV): "For God so loved the world, that he gave his only begotten Son, that whosoever believeth in him should not perish, but have everlasting life." The key word here is whosoever. Knowing that God is no respecter of persons and accepts men equally (Acts 10:34–35), whosoever means anyone and everyone. Romans 10:13 (KJV) says: "For whosoever shall call upon the name of the Lord shall be saved." We see that God's perfect will is that everyone be saved by believing on the Lord Jesus Christ (Acts 16:31). But God also has a permissive will, and this allows us to refuse His plan of salvation and not accept Christ as Savior. Though it isn't God's desire that anyone perish, He forces His will on no one. It is our decision to either refuse His wonderful plan for our lives and pay the penalty in an eternal place of punishment or accept His plan and live eternally with Him. God's Word is our hope and our salvation. It is the good news that reveals the love God has for each of us. If we believe and receive His wonderful plan that reveals Christ's righteousness alone as that which saves sinners and keeps them saved, we will enter into heaven with nothing to fear.

God and Savior: Thank You for the perfect plan You made for my life. Thank You for sacrificing Your Son so I might find redemption and forgiveness and spend eternity with You. Teach me Your ways and draw me with Your Holy Spirit to hunger after the righteousness of Christ. In Jesus' name, Amen.

GARLIC CHEESE BISCUITS (like Red Lobster's)

2 cups biscuit baking mix (such as Bisquick)
½ teaspoon garlic powder
1 cup shredded cheddar cheese
⅔ cup milk
2 tablespoons melted butter

Combine biscuit mix, garlic powder, and cheese; make a well in center. Add milk; stir until well mixed. Drop by tablespoonfuls onto greased baking sheet; bake at 450 degrees for 10–12 minutes. Brush with butter; serve while warm. Makes 8–10.

October 6

I also want women to dress modestly, with decency and propriety, not with braided hair or gold or pearls or expensive clothes, but with good deeds, appropriate for women who profess to worship God.

—1 TIMOTHY 2:9–10

PAUL IS SPEAKING to the young pastor Timothy regarding what God expects of women who profess to be Christians. Dressing modestly needs to be something both Christian women and men practice, but here Paul specifically addresses women. If we profess to be children of God, we must please the Lord in every area of our lives. To dress modestly means to wear clothing this is proper and decent, never extreme or drawing attention to oneself. What we wear should reflect godliness, the character of which our Lord is pleased. Was it not God who designed the first clothing? When He created Adam and Eve, they were naked and unashamed because sin had not yet entered their lives. But after their disobedience to God, they were embarrassed and tried to hide their bodies. This was the first effect of sin, so God designed clothing to cover their bodies. Our intentions should be the same as God's were—to cover our bodies and do so in a way that would not draw attention to body parts, but would take attention away from our body. Our beauty should not come from outward adornment with fine jewelry and expensive clothes. Instead, it should be that of our inner self, the beauty of a gentle and quiet spirit that is of great worth in God's sight (1 Peter 3:3–4). We are to dress modestly and act appropriately to draw others to Christ and not ourselves. Many women play with fire by the way they dress. Dressing immodestly is a way of advertising one's body, something that should be saved only for a spouse. Dressing modestly is an act of worship to our heavenly Father. It is not a fashion suggestion but a command of the Lord for every woman.

Father: Thank You for teaching me how to dress and present myself as a godly person. Forgive me for the times I dressed immodest, drawing attention to my body and causing the opposite sex to look at me in a sensual way. Help me to always dress with decency and propriety so others will see You in my life. In Jesus' name, Amen.

CREAMY PORK TENDERLOIN (crockpot)

1 ½ pounds pork tenderloin
1 can cream of celery soup
1 can water

Place pork in crockpot. Add soup and water. Cook on high for 3–4 hours.

October 7

But godliness with contentment is great gain. For we brought nothing into this world, and it is certain we can carry nothing out.

—1 TIMOTHY 6:6–7, KJV

EVERYONE DEALS WITH attitudes of envy and covetousness at some time or another in their lives; but as Christians, we are given instructions regarding this sin. In the tenth commandment God tells us not to covet (desire) what others have. This is probably one of the hardest commandments to follow because the world sees the one who drives the older, least expensive car or lives in a plain, smaller home or wears cheaper brands of clothing, and so on, as someone of less importance. The media and advertisements contribute to that way of thinking, but God says it's the opposite. If we are content with little, then it is considered as great gain. It is more important that we understand the truth of Paul's statement in this verse then to actually have material wealth. We do not lose when we choose to forsake covetousness; we gain. Living for Jesus with a contented heart brings fulfillment and freedom.

Dear Lord: You are all I need. If I seek You, everything I need will come. Thank You for taking such good care of me and for all the many blessings You pour into my life. Help me to be content with what I have and not be envious of what others have. Guide me with Your Spirit to make right decisions in all I do. May I live my life so others will see You in me and be saved. In Jesus' name, Amen.

SWEDISH MEATBALLS

1 pound lean ground beef
1 cup soft bread crumbs
1 medium onion, finely chopped
1 cup milk
1 egg
1 teaspoon salt
½ teaspoon pepper
⅛ teaspoon nutmeg
4 tablespoons flour
1 cup water with 1 dissolved beef bouillon cube
8 ounces fresh sliced mushrooms (optional)
1 cup half-and-half or whole milk

Combine ground beef, bread crumbs, onion, milk, egg, salt, pepper, and nutmeg. Form into small balls; brown in greased pan. When done, whisk in flour until dissolved. Add water with bouillon, mushrooms, and milk or cream. Cover and simmer 10–15 minutes; stirring occasionally. Serve with cooked noodles, mashed potatoes, or rice.

October 8

For the love of money is the root of all evil: which while some coveted after, they have erred from the faith, and pierced themselves through with many sorrows.

—1 TIMOTHY 6:10, KJV

WE OFTEN HEAR it said that money is the root of all evil; but that isn't true. It is the love of money that is the root of all evil. While money often gets the blame, this verse is really talking about our heart toward money. Many of us believe that money brings happiness and if we just had more of it, all our problems would be solved. It's true; we need money to survive; but it's our level of desire for it that can turn great intentions into evil. We cannot serve both Christ and cash; the service of one cancels out the service of the other. Paul describes the opposite of the love of money as contentment. First Timothy 6:6–7, 9 (KJV) says, "But godliness with contentment is great gain. For we brought nothing into this world, and it is certain we can carry nothing out. But if we have food and clothing, we will be content with that." In Philippians 4:11–12, Paul makes a similar statement and emphasizes the importance of being content in any and every situation. We live in a society that doesn't want us to be content. There's always something else we've got to have. Proverbs 3:9–10 (KJV) says, "Honour the Lord with thy substance, and with the firstfruits of all thine increase: So shall thy barns be filled with plenty, and thy presses shall burst out with new wine." God wants us to be successful and prosperous, but He doesn't want us to love money more than Him. When we honor God by giving Him the first of whatever we get, it breaks the power of the love of money off our life. When we put God above our desire for money, He is honored and our lives are blessed.

Father: Everything I have belongs to You, not only 10 percent (tithe), but also the other 90. Thank You for the ability You have given me to earn money to pay my bills. Show me how to use it more wisely so I might give more to further Your kingdom. Forgive me for focusing on things that attract my flesh. Help me to find contentment in only You. In Jesus' name, Amen.

GARLIC-BUTTER SPAGHETTI

1 pound package thin spaghetti
4 garlic cloves, minced
¼ cup olive oil
¼ cup butter
Salt
Pepper

Cook spaghetti according to package; drain. In large skillet, lightly brown garlic in olive oil and butter. Add spaghetti; season and toss.

October 9

But you, man of God, flee from all this, and pursue righteousness, godliness, faith, love, endurance and gentleness. Fight the good fight of the faith.

—1 TIMOTHY 6:11–12

THE APOSTLE PAUL had been speaking to the young pastor Timothy about money and how many fall away from the Lord and into a life of destruction because of their bondage to it. Paul encourages Timothy to run from this sort of lifestyle and instead seek "righteousness, godliness, faith, love, endurance, and gentleness." This is what God desires for each of us, and He uses Paul's teaching to pierce our hearts. The Christian life is not to be taken lightly, and it isn't for the coward. In fact, Paul speaks about it as being a fight, a word derived from the Greek word agonize. In other words, we are to strive or put forth great effort, even if it causes us pain or agony, to live for Christ. Paul knew what he was talking about because he lived most of his Christian life in prison, not because he was bad but because he was strong, forthright, and unshakeable in his defense of the gospel of Jesus Christ. He eventually was martyred for the sake of his call. We all are called to defend the gospel and pursue a life of righteousness and godliness, no matter what circumstances we face. If we love the Lord and long for His presence in our lives, that alone should be the motivation we need to "fight the good fight of the faith" until the day God calls us home.

Dear God: Thank You for this day. Thank You for using the apostle Paul to teach us about life. Help me to flee from the strongholds of the enemy and pursue only after those things that are righteous and good. Give me boldness to stand up for what I believe, even when it seems as though everyone else is following the ways of the evil one. May I be found faithful when the fight is over and I am standing in the presence of You, my Savior and King. In Jesus' name, Amen.

BAKED FISH WITH ROSEMARY LEMON BUTTER

2 large fish fillets or several small ones
1 tablespoon soft butter
¼ teaspoon salt
¼ teaspoon pepper
2 cloves garlic, finely chopped
2 tablespoon lemon juice
2 teaspoons dried rosemary
2 teaspoons olive oil

Clean and pat dry fish; lay skin side down in greased baking dish. Mix rest of ingredients together; spread on fish. Bake in 425 degree oven for 8–10 minutes, until fish is flakey and done.

October 10

For God did not give us a spirit of timidity, but a spirit of power, of love and of self-discipline. So do not be ashamed to testify about our Lord.

—2 Timothy 1:7–8

God is the giver of life and all that is good. He loves us with an everlasting and unconditional love and wants only what is best for our lives. It seems ironic that the apostle Paul would write this message from death row in prison, being punished for the very thing he is telling us to do. Before he was converted to Christianity, Paul hated Christians and had them persecuted and put to death. But after his dramatic conversion experience on the road to Damascus, he was a changed man. From then until his death, Paul poured his life into teaching and training pastors, leaders, and others about what is required of them to inherit eternal life with Christ.

In this scripture, Paul encourages shy Pastor Timothy to trust the Holy Spirit to give him the power, love, and self-discipline needed to testify on behalf of the Lord. We all need that same advice because intimidation often takes over and prevents us from being fruitful and effective for the kingdom. When that happens, we must confess our weakness to the Lord and ask for His Holy Spirit to come, empower, and equip us with boldness to accomplish the tasks He has given us. As Paul encourages us to "not be ashamed to testify about our Lord," he invites us to suffer with him for the gospel, finding strength in our prayer, faith, obedience, and diligence to God.

Precious Father: I am so grateful for how You continually take care of me. Thank You for giving to me a spirit of power, love, and self-discipline so I might do all You have called me to do. Forgive me when I am timid about sharing my faith, and help me to always be eager and willing to testify to others about Your mercy, goodness, grace, and power. In Jesus' name, Amen.

BAKED SPAGHETTI

1 pound spaghetti noodles (cooked)
3 eggs, beaten
1 stick butter, soft
1 cup Parmesan cheese (grated)
2 (26-ounce) jars spaghetti sauce
2 cups shredded mozzarella cheese

Mix noodles, eggs, butter, Parmesan cheese, and spaghetti sauce together; pour into greased 9x13-inch pan. Cover with foil; bake at 350 for 25 minutes. Remove foil and top with mozzarella cheese; bake 10 more minutes or until cheese is melted.

October 11

That is why I am suffering as I am. Yet I am not ashamed, because I know whom I have believed, and am convinced that He is able to guard what I have entrusted to Him for that day.

—2 TIMOTHY 1:12

PAUL WROTE THIS letter to Timothy, his spiritual son, to let him know that he was proud of his heritage and that though he was persecuted because of his faith in Christ, he was still totally committed to serving His Lord. Paul knew what it was to be beaten, starved, tortured, and imprisoned. In spite of it, he had no less trust in His Lord. He wasn't embarrassed for the suffering he endured, nor was he ashamed. He proclaimed that he not only knew God, but knew He was in control of his life. Shouldn't we be the same way? We are too easily discouraged and ready to give up when things don't go as we think they should. We blame God or question Him for allowing something to happen. It is in these times that we need to stop and think about our heritage and what it really means to be a born-again child of God. Let's praise and thank our Lord for who we are in Him. If Paul did it with all He endured, we too can trust God to guard our lives no matter the cost.

Trusting Father: I praise and thank You for the privilege of serving You. I believe in Your Son and look forward to seeing Him face to face one day. My life is in Your hands, and I trust You to guard it until that day when You call me home. Forgive me for the times when I was too embarrassed to tell of Your love and what You have done in my life. Give me strength to be a witness for You, no matter what sufferings I must endure. In Jesus' name, Amen.

CHEESY SPINACH AND BACON DIP

1 (10-ounce) package frozen chopped spinach, thawed and drained well
1 pound (16 ounces) Velveeta, cut into ½-inch cubes
4 ounces Philadelphia cream cheese, cubed
1 (10-ounce) can Rotel diced tomatoes and green chiles, undrained
8 slices bacon, crisply cooked and crumbled

Combine all ingredients in microwaveable bowl. Microwave on high 5 minutes or until Velveeta is completely melted and mixture is well blended, stirring after 2 minutes. Serve with tortilla chips or cut-up vegetables.

October 12

Flee the evil desires of youth, and pursue righteousness, faith, love and peace, along with those who call on the Lord out of a pure heart.

—2 TIMOTHY 2:22

To FLEE MEANS to make a run for it. Desires are those things we have a passion for or really want. The teen or adolescent years are usually referred to as youth. The apostle Paul is urging young Pastor Timothy to abandon those things that are evil or sinful and instead pursue a life of purity. Paul was once young and understood the temptations of youth. Though we all have sinned and fallen short of the glory of God (Romans 3:23), it is obvious that young people seem to have a natural desire to rebel and do their own thing. Paul makes it clear that sin springs from uncontrolled desires. Our challenge, then, is to manage our desires. Paul give us one way to do that—flee or run from those things that tempt us. It is never wise to put ourselves in a place where temptation is strong and defeat is inevitable. We all have succumbed to the temptation of sin, even after we have surrendered our wills to God and accepted Christ as Savior, but we should do everything possible to avoid sinning. Our hope for victory is the help and strength we receive through Jesus Christ. God made Him to be like us in order that He might understand the struggles of temptation and help us (Hebrews 2:17–18). We actually don't have another choice but to flee while calling on Jesus for strength and help to do so. In this way, we humble ourselves before God and follow His plan of action.

Father: Thank You for always being with me to help me flee from the evil desires that come each day. Thank You for always providing a way out for me when I'm tempted. Help me to control my desires so my actions line up with Your Word. Convict me with Your Holy Spirit and give me strength to always pursue righteousness, faith, love, peace, and a pure heart. In Jesus' name, Amen.

RANCH CHICKEN

½ cup grated Parmesan cheese
1 ½ cups corn flakes
1 (1-ounce) packet ranch salad dressing mix
2 pounds chicken legs or thighs
1 stick butter, melted

Combine cheese, corn flakes, and dressing mix in bowl. Dip washed and dried chicken in melted butter and dredge in corn flake mixture. Put single layer in baking dish; drizzle remaining butter overtop. Bake at 350 degrees for 50 minutes or until golden brown.

October 13

But mark this: There will be terrible times in the last days. People will be lovers of themselves, lovers of money, boastful, proud, abusive, disobedient to their parents, ungrateful, unholy, without love, unforgiving, slanderous, without self-control, brutal, not lovers of the good, treacherous, rash, conceited, lovers of pleasure rather than lovers of God—having a form of godliness but denying its power. Have nothing to do with them.

—2 TIMOTHY 3:1–5

THESE ARE THE moral conditions the apostle Paul says will be characteristic of society in the last days. The word terrible means perilous, hard to take or bear, troublesome, dangerous, harsh, fierce, or savage. These words could have been taken right out of today's newspaper. People everywhere are anxious and concerned, and many live in fear of what terrible things might happen next. There is just so much uncertainty in the world. Daily we hear of wars, natural disasters, poverty, sickness, crime, and the list goes on and on. But Paul's portrayal of terrible times has nothing to do with terrorism, disease, or earthquakes. It does, however, have everything to do with our attitudes and behavior. We have all been guilty of being ungrateful, unforgiving, without self-control, boastful, and conceited, but the worst of all would be having a form of godliness by saying we are Christians but living in blatant disobedience to God's Word. Let us not simply do the Christian thing by talking the lingo or doing the duties, but instead allow the power of Jesus' resurrection to transform our lives. These are challenging and terrible times in which we live, but when we surrender our will to God, the power of His love and grace changes us. When God's truth is alive in us, we become a light in this dark world.

Loving Father: Thank You for taking such wonderful care of me. You know my thoughts and every deed. Forgive me when my attitude and behavior are not what they should be. Help me to always look to You for the strength and ability I need to walk in victory. In Jesus' name, Amen.

SOUTHWEST CHICKEN (crockpot)

2 chicken breasts
1 can black beans, drained and rinsed
1 cup salsa
Tortillas
Grated cheese
Sour cream, sliced black olives, onions, etc.

Add first 3 ingredients to crockpot. Cook on low 8 hours or on high 4 hours. Shred or dice chicken. Serve on tortillas with favorite cheese and toppings.

October 14

In fact, everyone who wants to live a godly life in Christ Jesus will be persecuted, while evil men and impostors will go from bad to worse, deceiving and being deceived.

—2 TIMOTHY 3:12–13

JUST LIKE THE song "I Never Promised You a Rose Garden" says, God's Word does not promise us an easy life when we become Christians. In fact, it says if we live for God in this world, we will be persecuted. Believers are persecuted because they belong to a new Master and their lives intimidate others. Luke 6:22–23 says, "Blessed are you when men hate you, when they exclude you and insult you and reject your name as evil, because of the Son of Man. Rejoice in that day and leap for joy, because great is your reward in heaven."

Men of the Bible were persecuted because of their strong faith in Christ. Stephen was the first Christian to be murdered because of his commitment to Jesus Christ. James and most of the apostles were murdered in some way. Peter was crucified upside down. Paul was beheaded, and many were fed to the lions. Jesus was spat upon, beaten, and mocked on His way to be crucified. Around the world such persecution continues, though not so much in this country. Faithfulness to Christ may cause others to taunt and insult us, but it will be worth it all one day when we reach our final destiny and are rewarded with eternal life.

Dear Lord: Thank You for this wonderful day You have so graciously allowed me to have my being. Thank You for allowing Your body to be beaten and crucified for me. Forgive me for the times I became one of the crowd and didn't stand up for what I knew was right. Guide me with Your Holy Spirit and help me to walk in the ways of righteousness even if I am persecuted or mocked. In Jesus' name, Amen.

SLOPPY JOES

1 pound lean ground beef
¼ cup finely diced onion
2 teaspoons vinegar
⅓ cup ketchup
2 tablespoons brown sugar
1 teaspoon prepared mustard
1 tablespoon Worcestershire sauce

Brown ground beef; drain. Add onion; cook until tender (about 5 minutes). Add rest of ingredients; simmer 20–30 minutes. Serve on buns.

October 15

All scripture is given by inspiration of God, and is profitable for doctrine, for reproof, for correction, for instruction in righteousness: That the man of God may be perfect, thoroughly furnished unto all good works.

—2 Timothy 3:16–17, KJV

HAVE YOU EVER purchased an item that comes in many different parts and has to be assembled at home? The directions are included, but for some reason we will try to put that thing together without reading them. Finally, when all attempts fail, we refer to the instructions to see how it really should be done. The same is true with our life; we want to do it our way without reading God's instructions. The Bible is our training manual, road map, and set of directions for living here on earth. Its purpose is to teach, rebuke, correct, and train us; but we must pick it up, read it, and then obey it to have God's blessings on our life. We wouldn't want to ride in a car that was put together by someone who didn't follow the instructions; nor should we want to live our life without reading God's Word and training manual.

Dear God: Forgive me for not reading Your instructions before I make decisions for my family and me. I want to make wise choices, and I need Your help and guidance. Quicken my heart if I begin to do something that doesn't line up with Your Word. Give me the courage and character I need to put Your will into practice so I might honor You more. In Jesus' name, Amen.

REUBEN SOUP

½ cup chopped onion
½ cup diced celery
2 tablespoons butter
1 cup chicken broth
½ teaspoon baking soda
2 tablespoons cornstarch
2 tablespoons water
¾ cup sauerkraut, rinsed and drained
2 cups half-and-half
2 cups chopped cooked corned beef
1 cup (4 ounces) shredded Swiss cheese
¼ teaspoon salt
¼ teaspoon pepper
Rye croutons

In large saucepan, sauté onion and celery in butter until tender. Add broth and baking soda. Combine cornstarch and water until smooth; gradually add to pan. Bring to boil; cook and stir for 2 minutes or until thickened. Reduce heat. Add sauerkraut, cream, and corned beef; simmer and stir for 15 minutes. Add cheese; heat until melted. Add salt and pepper. Serve in bowls with croutons on top.

October 16

Preach the word; be prepared in season and out of season; correct, rebuke and encourage—with great patience and careful instruction. For the time will come when men will not put up with sound doctrine. Instead, to suit their own desires, they will gather around them a great number of teachers to say what their itching ears want to hear.

—2 TIMOTHY 4:2–3

ALTHOUGH THESE SCRIPTURES are especially applicable for pastors and Bible teachers, they are also for every believer. Seeker-sensitive churches are emerging everywhere to attract those who want just enough religion to make them feel as though they are doing their Christian duty by attending church. The inspired apostle Paul instructs us to preach the Word and not our opinions about God's Word. The critical importance of this is seen in verse 1: "In the presence of God and of Christ Jesus, who will judge the living and the dead, and in view of his appearing and his kingdom, I give you this charge."

We are all ministers of God if we have experienced a new birth by accepting Christ as Savior and living in obedience to His Word. Therefore, we are commanded to preach the Word by knowing what the Scriptures say and then correcting, rebuking, and encouraging others carefully and patiently. This can only be done if we are students of the Bible, hungry to know God's inspired Word, and daily prepared to face an unsaved world. The end is drawing near, and time is running out to teach others what God's Word really says. It must not be watered down to not offend the listening audience, but be taught with boldness and clarity. Our job is to present the real truth of the gospel to the lost so they have an opportunity to avoid spending eternity in hell. There is no middle ground in the spiritual war for the souls of men. We have two choices: heaven or hell. Which will it be?

Gracious Lord: Thank You for Your Holy Spirit who gives us direction for righteous living. Help me to not put my trust in manmade theories or experiences but to believe and follow only after Your truth. May I have wisdom to know when unsound doctrine is presented so I am not deceived and follow the ways of Satan. I choose this day to become a student of Your Word. Open my heart and my mind to receive all you desire me to have. In Jesus' name, Amen.

COCA-COLA CHICKEN

1 chicken, cut up (or the equivalent)
½ cup ketchup
1 tablespoon Worcestershire sauce
1 can Coca-Cola

Put everything in a slow-cooker; cook on high 6–8 hours or until chicken is done.

October 17

I have fought a good fight, I have finished my course, I have kept the faith: Henceforth there is laid up for me a crown of righteousness, which the Lord, the righteous judge, shall give to me at that day: and not to me only, but unto all them also that love his appearing.

—2 TIMOTHY 4:7–8, KJV

AUL USES AN athletic metaphor to describe the grandest, noblest contest in all of history: living the Christian life. In spite of all his adversities, Paul remained faithful to the Lord once he turned his life over completely to Him. Paul fought against Satan, Jews, pagans, false teachers, immorality in the church, worldliness, and sin, all because he believed the "crown of righteousness" was worth anything and everything he had to endure. Though he had every reason to pull out of the race, he continued with faithfulness, passion, and courage. Paul's use of this metaphor continues with an athletic theme. The crown here is not the one a king wears but the laurel or olive wreath that was placed on the heads of winners at ancient Olympic games. The crown of righteousness is the crown that consists of the righteousness that was purchased at great cost by the blood of Jesus. This crown is being saved for those who continue in the race of life and will be awarded to it on that wonderful day when the righteous Judge returns for His followers. Paul encourages us to fight the good fight, remain in the race, keep the faith, and one day along with him receive this reward.

Righteous Judge: I look forward to that day when You will come with the crown of righteousness and place it on my life. Grant me strength to run the race of life and finish in victory. When I begin to slow down and waver in my path, pour out Your anointing on my life. Cause me to press on, no matter what hardships or adversities may come. With You, I will make it to the end where I will receive my crown. In Jesus' name, Amen.

GREEN BEANS WITH BACON

5 slices bacon
½ stick butter
1 large sweet onion, diced
2–3 (16-ounce) cans of green beans, drained
¼ teaspoon garlic salt
¼ teaspoon pepper

Cook bacon until crisp; remove to paper towel and crumble. Discard half the grease. Add butter to pan with remaining grease; add onions and cook until tender. Drain cans of green beans; add beans, bacon, garlic salt and pepper to pan; heat and serve.

October 18

For the grace of God that brings salvation has appeared to all men. It teaches us to say "No" to ungodliness and worthy passions, and to live self-controlled, upright and godly lives in this present age, while we await for the blessed hope—the glorious appearing of our great God and savior, Jesus Christ, who gave himself for us to redeem us from all wickedness and to purify for himself a people that are his very own, eager to do what is good.

—Titus 2:11–13

THE BASIS FOR these verses describes God's character and purpose—His grace. According to Paul, God's grace provides the power and ability for us to reject the ungodly passions of the world and live righteous lives. This means if we are saved by God's grace, in that we have accepted Jesus as our Savior and are living according to God's Word, we are able say no to sin, whether it is rebellion against God or pursuit of sinful desires. God's grace enables us to live "self-controlled, upright, and godly lives." We have no excuse to continue dabbling in sinful lusts and habits because the price of victory has already been paid for us to quit. God's grace also holds a future perspective for those who know Christ and eagerly "do what is good." The glorious appearing of the blessed hope, the One who was ransomed on our behalf, the Lord Jesus Christ, is soon to arrive on the scene. This is the One who redeemed us from all our sin and impurities so we might live victoriously on earth and eternally be with Him forever.

Gracious Lord: All signs point to Your imminent return. Although You have poured out Your grace on this world, most do not even know who You are. Forgive me for not sharing Your Word with the lost. You have equipped me with Your Holy Spirit and power to be a witness, and today I commit myself in a greater way to labor for You. In Jesus' name, Amen.

HALUSHKI (BACON CABBAGE AND NOODLES) (Polish)

¾ pound bacon (about 8 slices)
4 tablespoons butter
1 head cabbage, thinly sliced pieces
1 sweet onion, thinly sliced
¼ teaspoon salt
Dash pepper
8 ounces wide egg noodles

In large pan, cook bacon until crisp. Remove to paper towels; crumble. Drain all but 3 tablespoons bacon grease. Add butter, cabbage, and onions to pan. Cover and cook on low for 20 minutes or until cabbage tender, stirring occasionally. Stir in salt, pepper, noodles, and bacon. Thoroughly heat.

October 19

Remind the people to be subject to rulers and authorities, to be obedient, to be ready to do whatever is good, to slander no one, to be peaceable and considerate, and to show true humility toward all men.

—TITUS 3:1–2

Ⓞ NE OF PAUL'S purposes for writing this letter to Titus was to encourage him to teach the people on the island of Crete how to live godly lives. Paul wanted the church there to grow in faith and knowledge of the truth so their character as Christian leaders would be genuine and represent sound doctrine. For the good of society, God established the government and its laws and we are to respect them, except when they contradict His Word. The Lord is saying to us, through Paul, that as Christians we must uphold and live out the guidelines mentioned in these verses. We are to be people of peace, submission, obedience, consideration, humility, thoughtful words, and ready to do good in every situation. The Christian life is only possible as we allow the Lord Jesus to live in and through us. The Christian life is not really our life at all; it is Christ's life lived out in us in the person of His Holy Spirit.

Heavenly Father: Your Holy Spirit has given me the desire and strength to live a disciplined, godly life; for this I praise and thank You. Help me to make right choices and live as though Jesus Christ is really Lord of my life. Guide me with Your Spirit to be obedient to those You have placed over me in authority. Keep me humble, and may I never be found guilty of slander or injustice to anyone. Live through me and be glorified in my life. In Jesus' name, Amen.

TACO SOUP (crockpot)

1 pound ground beef
1 onion, chopped
1 (14.5-ounce) can diced tomatoes (undrained)
1 (16-ounce can) chili beans (undrained)
1 (4-ounce) can green chili peppers (undrained)
1 (15-ounce) can kidney beans (undrained)
1 package taco seasoning mix
1 (8-ounce) can tomato sauce
2 cups water
1 bag corn chips
Sour cream (optional)
Shredded cheese (optional)

Brown ground beef; drain. Add chopped onion; cook two minutes. Put meat and all other ingredients (except chips, sour cream, and cheese) in crockpot. Cook on high 4 hours or low 8 hours. To serve: put corn chips in bowl; pour soup overtop. Garnish with sour cream and cheese.

October 20

I appeal to you for my son Onesimus, who became my son while I was in chains. Formerly he was useless to you, but now he has become useful both to you and to me.

—PHILEMON 10–11

ONESIMUS WAS A runaway slave who belonged to Philemon, a Christian in the church at Colosse. At the time of this letter, Paul was imprisoned in Rome. Philemon had become a believer under the ministry of Paul, and now Onesimus had come into Paul's life and was also converted to Christ. Paul loved both of these men and knew it was only right that Onesimus be returned to his owner. With Paul's heart of compassion and love, he pleaded for Philemon to accept Onesimus back not as a slave but as a brother in the Lord. Paul went on to explain to Philemon that though once this slave was useless to him, now being converted to Christ, he is useful. Paul encouraged Philemon to welcome Onesimus back with kindness, love, forgiveness, and of his own volition. Just as Onesimus was previously useless, probably having had a bad attitude and poor work ethics before coming to Christ, many of us are the same way. We all are born slaves to Satan, but once our lives are turned completely over to Jesus, we are set free and no longer bound to sin. Therefore, our character and actions should line up with God's Word. If they do not, it is imperative that we stop this moment and ask for God's forgiveness and help. Just as Onesimus became useful, the same will happen to us.

Father: Just like Onesimus, I was once lost, useless, and bound to sin. Because I asked You to forgive me and come into my heart to reign forever, I am now a redeemed child and useful. Thank You for accepting me, just as I was, and turning my life around. I choose to follow Your ways by reading my Bible and learning what You require of my life. In Jesus' name, Amen.

POTATO PANCAKES

2 pounds potatoes (about 6 medium)
1 egg
⅓ cup finely chopped onion
3 tablespoons flour
1 teaspoon salt
¼ cup butter

Pare potatoes; shred to make 4 cups (food processor works great); drain any liquid. In small bowl, beat egg until thick and lemon colored. Mix in potatoes, onion, flour, and salt. Melt butter in large pan over low heat. Shape potato mixture into 8 patties; cook over medium heat, turning once, about 5 minutes, until golden brown. Serve with applesauce on the side.

October 21

You have loved righteousness and hated wickedness; therefore God, your God, has set you above your companions by anointing you with the oil of joy.

—HEBREWS 1:9

IN A WORLD full of deceptions, illusions, and lies, it is sometimes hard to tell what is good and what is evil. One thing we know for sure is God loves righteousness and hates wickedness. How do we really know if something is good or bad? As we become more like Christ in our growth and spiritual maturity, the better we become at discerning right from wrong or good from bad. If we have truly experienced the new birth or new life in Christ, the Holy Spirit dwells within our hearts and helps us recognize what is evil (contrary to God's Word). It then is our decision how we respond to the conviction and whether or not we choose God's way or the way of the wicked one. If we are living in blatant opposition to God's Word, we are still lost in our sin. It's not enough to merely love what is good and right; we must abhor evil and how it hurts, maims, and destroys all it touches. Our love of righteousness and hatred of evil will increase as we identify with our Lord's love and compassion for those whose lives are being destroyed by sin. There may be times when doing the right thing comes at great personal cost, but God will anoint us with the oil of joy, peace, and an outpouring of His love and grace if we stay true to His Word.

Dear God: Every moment of the day, many are stricken and tormented by the wicked ways of man. Come quickly and remove Your children from the pain and anguish brought on in their innocence, possibly even by those who pretend to love them. Jesus, You wept over Jerusalem as You saw the sin and state of lostness of the people; surely You must now bear great sadness over the deplorable spiritual condition of the world today. Anoint me with the oil of joy as I proclaim Your glory. In Jesus' name, Amen.

BROCCOLI SLAW

2 packages Ramen noodles (chicken flavor)
1 package broccoli slaw
1 small package sunflower seeds
1 small package slivered almonds
1 small bunch green onions, chopped

Dressing:

1 cup canola oil
½ cup sugar
⅓ cup vinegar

Break up noodles; sprinkle with flavor packets. Toss everything together. Mix dressing ingredients together and pour over salad mixture. Refrigerate 2–3 hours.

October 22

We must pay more careful attention, therefore, to what we have heard, so that we do not drift away.

—Hebrews 2:1

THE AUTHOR (POSSIBLY LUKE) strongly encourages those who serve Christ to take their salvation with intense seriousness and sincerity. Our relationship with the Lord should always hold utmost priority; nothing or no one should take precedence over God. Romans 10:17 tells us that "faith (our belief in God) comes from hearing the message, and the message is heard through the word of Christ." Therefore, our spiritual understanding of what we believe is founded on what God's Word says and is fed into our souls by reading and hearing it with our spiritual ears, or by audibly hearing it read or told by others. God's Word is perfect, sure, right, pure, and true, and the only way we might be converted and transformed to the likeness of the Master (Ps. 19). God wants us to be attentive and vigilant to His message of salvation and not aimlessly be carried away from the faith because of complacency or negligence. The opposite of drift away is anchor down. Hebrews 7:19 says, "We have this hope as an anchor for the soul, firm and secure." We must make a conscious decision to be anchored in our faith in Christ by reading the Bible and being obedient to what it says. Just as the prophet Jeremiah could not hold back the divine message within him, saying the Word was in his heart like a fire shut up in his bones (Jeremiah 20:9), so should we be ignited by the fire of the Holy Spirit to proclaim the good news of Jesus to a world that has drifted away from the truth of God's Word.

Father: Your Word is a lamp to our feet and a light for our path; without it we would walk in darkness and remain lost. I want to be attentive to Your Word and instruction so not to drift from my faith in You. You are my hope and the anchor for my soul. Please help me to stay focused and heed Your plan for my life. In Jesus' name, Amen.

GARLIC CAESAR CHICKEN

4 boneless, skinless chicken breasts
8 cloves of garlic, peeled and left whole
¾ cup water and 1 chicken bouillon cube
¼ cup classic Caesar dressing
¼ cup grated Parmesan cheese

Cook chicken and garlic in pan over medium-high heat for 4 minutes, turning after 2 minutes. Stir in water, bouillon, and dressing; cover with lid. Cook chicken until thoroughly done. Sprinkle with Parmesan cheese. Remove from heat; let stand, covered, 1 minute.

October 23

Because he himself suffered when he was tempted, he is able to help those who are being tempted.

—HEBREWS 2:18

For we do not have a high priest who is unable to sympathize with our weaknesses, but we have one who has been tempted in every way, just as we are—yet was without sin.

—HEBREWS 4:15

THE BOOK OF Matthew tells us how Jesus was led by the Spirit into the desert to be tempted by the devil. James 1:13 says God tempts no one. So why would He not only allow this to happen, but do it on purpose? The author of Hebrews explains it so well. Jesus had to suffer temptation so He would be able to feel our temptations and weaknesses and help us in our times of need.

Jesus is the righteous Judge. The only way He is able to issue judgment upon mankind is if He Himself had proven that there is no temptation, under any circumstance, that cannot be endured. Jesus had to make sure there would never come a time when anyone who had given in to a temptation could say to Him, "You just don't understand!"

Jesus was temped by the devil when He was extremely physically fatigued after fasting forty days. Satan hoped Jesus would ruin His perfect sinless life and fall from God's grace, but it didn't happen. Jesus continued to be tempted by the devil during that time, and yet each time He submitted His will to the authority of God's Word. With each temptation Jesus told Satan, "It is written…" No temptation could move Him to disobey the will of His Father, so finally the devil left Him.

Jesus wants us to realize that we, too, have the power to resist any temptation or sin. Just as Jesus knew the Scriptures to come against Satan, we too must study and memorize them. With the help of the Holy Spirit we can be overcomers and definitely more than conquerors in the world in which we live.

Father: Thank You for suffering while facing temptations put on You by the enemy. You could have called ten thousand angels to come to Your aid, but You chose to suffer, knowing it would benefit Your children. Help me in my times of temptation to be strong and come against the devil with the powerful Scriptures You provided for me to learn. In Jesus' name, Amen.

TORTILLA CHIP DIP

1 ½ cups Miracle Whip or mayonnaise
1 ½ cups sour cream
1 package taco seasoning mix

Mix all together; refrigerate. Dip in your favorite chip, cracker, or veggie.

October 24

See to it, brothers, that none of you has a sinful, unbelieving heart that turns away from the living God.

—Hebrews 3:12

THE GREEK TERM apostasy refers to a falling or turning away, abandoning, withdrawing, or rebelling from something formerly done or known. In Christianity, apostasy represents the severing of one's saving relationship with Christ and turning away from faith in the living God. One cannot turn away from someone he has not once known or from something he has not done. To turn away from God means that someone once served Him and then the relationship was lost. One way this happens is if we make a deliberate and conscious choice to abandon our faith in God. The other way is if we reject the teachings of God by living immoral lifestyles of sin and disobedience. This happens when a believer begins to dabble in sin by becoming more tolerant to the ways of the world.

Giving in to temptations and fleshly desires puts us on a slippery slope and gradually draws us further and further away from Christ. When the Holy Spirit's nudge on our hearts (conviction of sin) is ignored, our heart begins to harden and we increasingly grow more and more immune to the deceitfulness of sin. This grieves the Holy Spirit, and without repentance and turning from sin, we may be eternally lost and reap the consequences of an eternal hell. There are many who may call themselves Christians, but their indifference to God and His warnings throughout the Scriptures reveals otherwise. Paul urges us in 2 Corinthians 13:5 to examine or test ourselves to see if we are in the faith. God does not want anyone to perish, but we must follow *His* plan for salvation and not our own.

Dear Lord: You are the living hope of my salvation. Thank You for continually loving me even when I begin to wander from my faith. Help me to stay focused on You and what You require of me. Keep my heart soft and yielded to the guidance and direction of Your Holy Spirit so I don't stray from a life of purity and righteousness. In Jesus' name, Amen.

CRESCENT DOGS

8 hot dogs, split ⅔ down middle
4 slices cheese, each cut into 6 strips
1 can refrigerated crescent dinner rolls
Dipping sauce (ketchup, mustard, etc.)

Insert 3 strips cheese in slit of each hot dog; separate dough into 8 triangles. Wrap dough triangle around each hot dog; place on cookie sheet, cheese side up. Bake at 375 degrees for 12–15 minutes, until golden brown.

October 25

For the word of God is quick, and powerful, and sharper than any two-edged sword, piercing even to the dividing asunder of soul and spirit, and of the joints and marrow, and is a discerner of the thoughts and intents of the heart.

—HEBREWS 4:12, KJV

THE WORD OF God may be referred to as the Bible, Truth, Scriptures, Word, Law, Teachings of God, Good Book, or God's Word; it is anything that God has spoken. In the Old Testament, God spoke directly to Adam and Eve in the Garden of Eden. He also spoke directly to Moses when he recited the Ten Commandments. God spoke through prophets and apostles throughout the entire Bible, but in the New Testament it was Jesus who did most of the speaking.

The Word of God is the written record of what the prophets, apostles, and Jesus have been inspired to speak. God's Word is Jesus in the flesh. John 1:1 (KJV) says, "In the beginning was the Word, and the Word was with God, and the Word was God." God's Word is dynamic, powerful, creative, and determines who will be saved or lost. John 8:51 (KJV) says, "Verily, verily, I say unto you, If a man keeps my saying (word), he shall never see death."

God gave us the gift of His Word, and we determine whether or not we accept or refuse it. God's Word reflects His nature; it is His revelation to man. It is always right, pure, sure, perfect, and true. Only God's Word is able to convert the soul of a sinful man and save him by His grace and mercy. The living Word of God discerns our thoughts and motives and with its sharpness cuts into our innermost being to judge the good and the evil. The Word that is perfect and pure, sure and true is the most powerful instrument of God working in the lives of His children so we might be saved and transformed to the likeness of the Master.

Dear God: Thank You for speaking to me through Your inspired Word as You breathed it into the hearts and souls of prophets, apostles, and Your Son. It is my source of power to live a godly life. May I never be found guilty of dishonoring it by my disobedience. In Jesus' name, Amen.

MASHED POTATOES (best ever)

4 pounds potatoes
1 cup sour cream
½ teaspoon pepper
1 teaspoon onion or garlic salt
4 ounces Philadelphia cream cheese, softened
2–3 tablespoons milk (if needed)

Pare, dice, and cook potatoes in salted water until tender (10–15 minutes); drain. Add next 4 ingredients and mash until creamy. Add milk as needed. Serves 8.

October 26

Nothing in all creation is hidden from God's sight. Everything is uncovered and laid bare before the eyes of him to whom we must give account.

—HEBREWS 4:13

LIFE IS PLAGUED with mysteries. There are so many things we don't know or understand, but that's okay because it's not God's will that we know. He alone knows all things, understands all things, and sees all things. The eyes of God rove over the whole earth piercing our innermost thoughts; nothing is hidden from Him, not even the future. God knows all the stars by name and even the number of hairs on our heads. God knows everything!

Some of us are very private and share very little about ourselves with anyone. Sometimes we even try to hide our secret sins and weaknesses from ourselves by ignoring the Holy Spirit's conviction while doing them. After our sinful deed, we repress the fact that we did anything wrong; but God sees and knows all. He knows us; He knows us better than we know ourselves. We have no secrets from Him. "Everything is uncovered and laid bare before His eyes." God knows what we do out in the open, and He knows what we do under the cover of darkness. Yet because of His love, we can approach His throne of grace with confidence. God invites us to come to Him in prayer and repent of our sins. If we ask, He will give us the strength we need to live a holy life unashamedly before the Lord.

Father: I have sinned! You already know what I have done, and yet You welcome me to come into Your holy presence. Forgive me! It is my desire to turn my life completely over to You and no longer live in shame. Help me to study Your Word and learn how to follow after the ways of righteousness and holiness. Grant me the strength I need to live in victory every day. In Jesus' name, Amen.

CHILI-CHEESE-DOG PIE

2 cups biscuit baking mix
⅔ cup water
3 cups chili with beans
½ pound hot dogs, sliced
2 cups shredded cheddar cheese

In medium bowl, mix together baking mix and water to form smooth dough; set aside. Spread half of chili into bottom of a greased casserole dish; make layer of hot dogs over chili. Cover hot dog layer with cheese; then top with rest of chili. On lightly floured surface, roll out biscuit dough to ¼ -inch thickness. Lay dough over contents of dish and poke few slits to vent steam. Bake at 350 degrees for 15 to 25 minutes or until top crust is golden.

October 27

During the days of Jesus' life on earth, he offered up prayers and petitions with loud cries and tears to the one who could save him from death, and he was heard because of his reverent submission.

—HEBREWS 5:7

PRAYER IS COMMUNION with God, usually in the form of petition, adoration, praise, confession, and thanksgiving. The Bible tells us that while on earth Jesus prayed, even though He was the Son of God. If the Son of God needed to pray, how much more do we stand in need of prayer? Much of what Jesus prayed was an expression of His thankfulness and honor to God, yet there were times when His prayers were intense and expressed with loud cries and tears. When Jesus prayed in the Garden of Gethsemane, overwhelmed with sorrow at the thought of being separated from God during the time of death on the cross, His sweat turned to blood. He prayed, "My Father, if it is possible, may this cup be taken from me. Yet not as I will, but as you will" (Matt. 26:39).

No prayer pleases God any more than when we pray according to His will. To avoid distraction and showiness, Jesus often went to a quiet place to pray, at times in the early morning and at times late at night. The main thing is, He prayed. He did so with great reverence, submission, obedience, compassion, and love for God. Jesus prayed that God would be glorified and His will done in the outcome of His prayers. We are to follow Jesus' example by designating a quiet place and time where we are less apt to be bothered by family, friends, and other distractions. Our heavenly Father yearns to hear us cry out to Him in prayer. We have the assurance that our prayers are heard if we are reverent and submissive to Him.

Our Father in heaven: Holy is Your name. May Your kingdom come soon and Your will be done on earth as it is in heaven. Provide for us today the food we need and forgive our sins as we also forgive those who sin against us. Don't let us yield to temptation, but rescue us from the evil one. For Yours is the kingdom and the power and the glory forever. Just as Jesus taught His disciples to pray this prayer, I also pray this in His name, Amen.

SMOTHERED STEAK

2 pounds round steak
1 can cream of mushroom soup
1 packet onion soup mix
⅔ cup milk

Cut steak into serving-size pieces; place in greased baking dish. Mix together soups and milk; pour over steak. Cover and bake at 325 degrees for 60–90 minutes, until tender.

October 28

Although he was a son, he learned obedience from what he suffered and, once made perfect, he became the source of eternal salvation for all who obey him.

—HEBREWS 5:8–9

MUCH IS SAID concerning God's mercy and grace, but little is said about His wrath. It just doesn't sound as enticing to the ears, so many churches avoid the subject. But there is a real place called hell where unbelievers will spend eternity. Jesus, who represents purity, perfection, salvation, and eternal life, came to rescue our sin-sick souls from this place if we obey Him. Even though Jesus was God's Son, He had to learn obedience. But He loved the Father so much, nothing else mattered except being in His perfect will. Jesus knew that to say He believed in the Father meant obeying Him, so that is what He did all the way to the Cross.

We may think we can believe in Jesus and not obey Him, but this is not the message of the Bible. Instead, it is a dangerous, deadly, spiritual misunderstanding and snare. To not obey God is the same as to not believe in Him and His Word. Jesus said in John 14:15, "If you love me, you will obey what I command." Second Thessalonians 1:8–9 says, "He will punish those who do not know God and do not obey the gospel of our Lord Jesus. They will be punished with everlasting destruction and shut out from the presence of the Lord and from the majesty of his power." Jesus suffered in His obedience to the Father, and we too may suffer. The cost of our obedience to God now will one day be known when we claim our eternal rewards. Paul said in 2 Corinthians 4:17, "For our light and momentary troubles are achieving for us an eternal glory that far outweighs them all." Jesus believed in His Father; therefore, He was made perfect in His obedience to Him. Christ is our deliverer and the source of eternal salvation for all who obey Him.

Dear God: Thank You for sending the Spirit of Christ to dwell in my heart. Help me to be obedient to You, therefore reaping heavenly eternal rewards. Thank You for saving me and writing my name in the Book of Life. In Jesus' name, Amen.

CARROT CASSEROLE

2 pounds fresh carrots, cut in circles
¼ cup butter
½ pound Velveeta cheese
½ cup Ritz crackers, crushed

Boil carrots about 5 minutes, until semi-tender; drain. Put in a greased baking dish. In a pan over low heat or in a dish in microwave, melt butter and cheese; mix and pour over carrots. Top with crackers; bake at 350 degrees for 30–45 minutes, until carrots tender.

October 29

God is not unjust; he will not forget your work and the love you have shown him as you have helped his people and continue to help them.

—HEBREWS 6:10

GOD KNOWS EVERYTHING we do and our purpose for doing it. He knows our minds, our hearts, and our souls. Jesus tells us in Matthew 25:40 that what we do for others is the same as if we were doing it to Him. Romans 12:1–2 encourages us to be living sacrifices for the Lord. This is accomplished when we live for the Lord and do what He wills us to do.

One way of showing our love for Him is by serving others. Jesus was a humble, compassionate servant, and He took advantage of every opportunity to instill these same traits in His disciples. He wanted them to understand that they must learn to think little of serving self and much of serving others. There are endless opportunities for us to demonstrate our love this way. Speaking kind words, visiting shut-ins, sending cards, preparing meals, doing household chores, babysitting, providing financial assistance, praying with someone, or extending a helpful hand for whatever the need may be are just a few. Each of us will be used in different ways according to our abilities and availabilities. The important thing is that we offer ourselves to those in need so God's love might be shown. He will not forget what we do and will recognize our labors of love on Judgment Day. "For we must all appear before the judgment seat of Christ, that each one may receive what is due him for the things done while in the body, whether good or bad" (2 Cor. 5:10).

Dear God: You are just and always fair. You never forget the good deeds of Your children. Thank You for Your Son and the wonderful example of a real servant He is. Help me to see my world with the same compassion and love as You. Forgive me for not using my abilities and resources to help others when I knew they had needs. As I strive to change, grant me wisdom to adjust my time, talents, and abilities to suit the needs of my family and others, and most of all, glorify You. In Jesus' name, Amen.

BEEF STROGANOFF (crockpot)

2 cans cream of mushroom soup
2 cans water + 3 beef bouillon cubes
1 cup sour cream
1 (1-ounce) package dry onion soup mix
2 pounds beef stew meat, cut in smaller pieces
2 tablespoons ketchup

Put everything in crockpot; cook on low for 8 hours. Serve over hot cooked rice or noodles.

October 30

In fact, the law requires that nearly everything be cleansed with blood, and without the shedding of blood there is no forgiveness.

—Hebrews 9:22

W<small>E DON'T HEAR</small> enough today about the precious blood of Jesus, but the truth is, if it weren't for the blood He shed, we all would be held accountable for our own sin. Instead, God elected us to become His children and made a way of escape for us by sending Jesus to the cross in our place. We must accept this plan by being obedient to it or reject it and suffer the consequences. In the Old Testament, the continual sacrifices of unblemished animals were required to satisfy God's wrath and judgment. However, Jesus Christ, the Son of God, purchased God's forgiveness on our behalf when He became the Lamb of God and died on the cross. Our sin had to be paid for with Jesus' blood. The blood Jesus shed for the sins of mankind is an extravagant expression of God's love for us, as mentioned by Jesus in John 3:16. We know our righteousness was not good enough through the works of either the law or of ourselves to save us from the penalty of sin. And of course God, knowing this was so, sent His Son to die for us and cleanse us of our sins. When Jesus' blood spilled from His pierced wounds, His spotless life was poured out at the foot of the cross and the price of our redemption was paid in full.

Father: Words cannot express my gratitude for allowing Your Son to shed His blood for me. Even though Jesus was pure and spotless, He paid the penalty of my sin. Surely, this is the greatest act of mercy, grace and love. Thank You! To prove my love for You, I give You my heart and life. Use me to touch others so they may find forgiveness and be cleansed by Your blood. In Jesus' name, Amen.

ORIENTAL SEAFOOD SALAD

2 tablespoons butter
1 package Oriental-flavored Ramen noodles
½ cup sliced almonds
⅔ cup vegetable oil
3 tablespoons vinegar
2 tablespoons sugar
Ramen noodle seasoning packet
6–8 ounces precooked shrimp
2 (10-ounce) bags salad greens
6 green onions, diced

Melt butter in skillet; add crushed noodles and almonds; cook on low until noodles are golden. Remove from pan and cool. Mix well the oil, vinegar, sugar, and seasoning packet (best in blender). Mix everything together in bowl and immediately serve.

October 31

Let us not give up meeting together, as some are in the habit of doing, but let us encourage one another—and all the more as you see the Day approaching.

—Hebrews 10:25

In New Testament days, Christians met together to worship God, partake of communion, break bread, teach and train, pursue missions and evangelization, deal with issues and situations at hand, meet one another's needs, and pray. As a result, their faith and unity were strengthened and they grew in size and power. Today, our churches meet for the very same reasons. We need one another to fulfill God's purpose. He tells us to meet together until the day Christ returns to earth to redeem His faithful believers and send unbelievers to an eternal perdition. There are hundreds of excuses to not attend church or Christian fellowships, but most of them are just that—excuses that really have no validity. A survey showed the following to be the most popular: too busy, too tired, would rather do housework, shop, sleep, entertain guests, travel, have family time, do yard work, wash the car, play or watch sports, or just do nothing. One of the basic benefits of plugging into a local church is to give and receive encouragement, comfort, and strength. This happens when we use the spiritual gifts God gave us. Since each person's gift is different, meeting as a group provides a wonderful way to meet the needs of the fellowship. Like a beautiful painting, the assembled church with their gifts reflects the very glory of God.

Heavenly Father: Thank You for giving me the body of Christ for encouragement and strengthening of my faith. Teach me how to use my spiritual gifts to help and encourage others and grant me humility to receive help and training from others so my needs are also met. Thank You for my church family and Christian friends. Because of Your plan for my life, I don't have to walk the Christian life alone. In Jesus' name, Amen.

LEMON GARLIC CHICKEN AND POTATOES (Greek)

3–4 pounds chicken parts, cleaned
3–4 pounds potatoes, peeled and quartered
Dash salt and pepper
1 heaping tablespoon oregano
8 cloves garlic, finely chopped
⅓ cup olive oil
Juice from 2–3 medium lemons
1 ½ cups water

Season chicken and potatoes with salt and pepper. Put chicken skin-side down in pan; place potatoes around it. Add oregano, garlic, olive oil, and lemon juice; distribute evenly in pan. Add water; place uncovered in 350 degree oven for 90 minutes. After 45 minutes, turn chicken.

November

In
Everything Give
Thanks

November 1

If we deliberately keep on sinning after we have received the knowledge of the truth, no sacrifice for sins is left, but only a fearful expectation of judgment and of raging fire that will consume the enemies of God.

—Hebrews 10:26–27

T HE BIBLE IS clear about the chains of sin that dwell in our flesh in the form of lusts and passions that so easily overtake and deceive us. This is different than deliberate, premeditated sin. Though God is ready and able through the Lord Jesus to forgive and completely deliver us from every sin, willful disobedience to God's commands is a critical matter. Deliberate sin is willful disobedience to God and rebellion against His Word, even though we know it's wrong. The Hebrew's writer is speaking here to Christians about the seriousness of deliberate sin and the result of it. Just as becoming a Christian is a choice each one of us has to make, so is the choice to sin or not to sin. God is not pleased when we deliberately keep on sinning—when we know it is evil and contrary to the truth. To do so is to take advantage of God's mercy and grace, and at one point—and only God knows at what point that is—our faith and trust in the Lord is lost. God doesn't remove our salvation from us; we remove ourselves from Him. God is a gentle God and will never push Himself on anyone. It is a choice to receive God's way or to keep on sinning and face eternal judgment and raging fire. Throughout the Word we are told how to live. In 2 Corinthians 13:5, the apostle Paul urges us all to examine ourselves to see whether or not we are in the faith. Let's each one do that today to avoid the consequences of our sin.

Lord God: Your Word is truth and the way of life. I have gone against what I knew to be right and I am sorry. Holy Spirit, dwell in me and help me to not give in to lusts and passions of my flesh. Show me paths I should take to become the person of God You have called me to be. In Jesus' name, Amen.

MASHED POTATOES SUPREME

1 (8-ounce) package cream cheese, softened
1 (1-ounce) packet ranch-style salad dressing
2 tablespoons butter, softened
½ cup sour cream
6–8 cups warm real or instant mashed potatoes
½ cup grated cheddar cheese

Combine cream cheese, ranch dressing mix, butter, and sour cream in bowl; beat well. Add potatoes and mix. Pour into baking dish; top with cheddar cheese. Bake at 350 degrees for 25 minutes or until cheese is melted.

November 2

Now faith is the substance of things hoped for, the evidence of things not seen.

—HEBREWS 11:1, KJV

ACCORDING TO HEBREWS 11, faith is the complete trust or confidence we have that something is true or real and will come to pass, even though it may not be visible to our eyes at the time. Faith is knowing and believing all God's promises will be fulfilled. Faith is assurance that if God's Word says it, it's true. Paul says in 2 Corinthians 5:7 (KJV), "For we walk by faith, not by sight." Matthew Henry says, "Faith demonstrates to the eye of the mind the reality of those things which cannot be discerned by the eye of the body."

Throughout the eleventh chapter of Hebrews, the author uses the examples of several pillars of faith such as Noah, Abraham, Sarah, Joseph, and Moses and how they proved their faith to be real. In each one's particular case, their faith was manifested by obedience to God. Faith is belief. To be saved, we must believe on the Lord Jesus Christ. In the Old Testament, the Israelites perished in the wilderness because they did not believe the gospel. They did not mix the Word of God with faith (Hebrews 4:2) and were unbelieving (Hebrews 3:12, 19) and disobedient (Hebrews 3:18); therefore, they did not enter into God's rest.

All around us we see people who are restless because of their unbelief in God. By faith we know there is going to be a final judgment, where every believer will receive his heavenly reward and every unbeliever will face eternal punishment. May God help us to be obedient to His Word and faithfully witness His love to the world, while there is still yet time.

Faithful Father: You are the Creator of faith and the One for whom I have reason and purpose. Rid my mind of any negative thoughts and doubts concerning Your Word and replace them with hope and trust in You, the Almighty God. Help me to see with my spirit those things You desire for my life and give me wisdom to understand the truth of the gospel. In Jesus' name, Amen.

GREEN RICE CASSEROLE

1 (10-ounce) package frozen chopped broccoli
2 cups cooked rice
1 can cream of mushroom soup
½ cup (1 stick) butter, room temperature
1 (8-ounce) jar Cheez Whiz

Cook broccoli according to package; drain well. Mix well the broccoli, rice, soup, butter, and Cheez Whiz, reserving small amount cheese for top. Transfer to greased baking dish; top with remaining Cheez Whiz. Bake at 325 degrees for 30 minutes, or until top starts to bubble.

November 3

Therefore, since we are surrounded by such a great cloud of witnesses, let us throw off everything that hinders and the sin that so easily entangles, and let us run with perseverance the race marked out for us.

—HEBREWS 12:1

DURING THE OLYMPICS, numerous athletes compete in their prospective competitions. Surrounded by fans and media, each one perseveres to win the gold. These men and women don't just show up for the race randomly or impulsively, but they train for years to get to that point. In the training, they learn to eat, sleep, and exercise properly. They know that everything they do either has a positive or negative impact on their ability to perform.

Life is like a race. Our goal is to reach heaven, and though we know how to get there, we get easily tangled along the way in hindrances. Little by little they creep in, and pretty soon we aren't running or even walking with God. This verse tells us how we need to throw off or get rid of everything that gets in our way of serving God. It may mean taking some drastic measures in our lives, but it will be worth it to win God's inheritance. We each need to take a look into our own life and throw off everything that hinders our passion for serving God.

Dear Lord: Thank You for giving me a purpose and reason to persevere in life's race. Forgive me for all my sin, the big and the small. Forgive me for even thinking about doing something that wouldn't be holy in Your sight and for exposing myself to Satan's world. Give me strength to say no to the things that distract me from You and to embrace with passion those things that make me more like You. Help me to live my life and run as though I want to win the gold, which is You. In Jesus' name, Amen.

CORN CASSEROLE

1 can regular corn, drained
1 can creamed corn, undrained
2 eggs
1 cup sour cream
1 stick butter, softened
1 box Jiffy cornbread mix
1 tablespoon sugar
¼ cup minced or grated onion (optional)
1 (4-ounce) can diced green chiles, drained
8 ounces grated cheddar cheese

Mix all ingredients together; pour into greased baking dish. Bake 1 hour at 350 degrees, until inserted knife comes out clean and top slightly brown. Let stand 5 minutes before cutting.

November 4

Endure hardship as discipline; God is treating you as sons.

—HEBREWS 12:7

WHEN WE HEAR the word *discipline,* our minds immediately think punishment. But the two are totally different in God's eyes. Discipline is the training and instruction required to bring about obedience to the rules of the road, which in this case is God's Word. Punishment is the penalty one pays for a crime he or she has committed. Discipline is administered with the good of the individual being disciplined in mind, while punishment is normally delivered with a payback attitude. Discipline is necessary for everyone, and yet it appears as though it becomes weaker and weaker in every generation.

In the beginning God said to Adam, "You are free to eat from any fruit in the garden, but you must not eat from the tree of the knowledge of good and evil, for when you eat of it you will surely die" (Gen. 2:16–17). Adam and Eve chose to break God's law that day, and because of God's discipline every one of us will die a physical death. The Bible makes it clear—God disciplines us because He loves us. His loving hand is at work just as much through life's stressful times as it is in times of joy and pleasure. God disciplines us by allowing us to experience uncomfortable circumstances in our lives because of situations we have brought on ourselves. He did not send them, but He uses them to encourage us to do things His way the next time we have a choice to make.

When doing things contrary to God's will, we can expect to suffer the consequences of our decisions. Jesus paid for the punishment of our sin when He went to the cross. It's up to us to accept His redemption plan and live accordingly. "Blessed is the man who perseveres under trial, because when he has stood the test, he will receive the crown of life that God has promised to those who love him" (James 1:12).

Father: You always have my best interest in mind. Even when I make bad choices, You are willing to forgive and discipline me with Your gentle hand. Help me to learn from my mistakes and endure hardship as discipline. In Jesus' name, Amen.

LEMON GARLIC BAKED FISH

2 tablespoons olive oil
1 pound fresh or frozen fish fillets (your choice)
Garlic salt and pepper
3 tablespoons lemon juice
Fresh dill

Arrange fish in baking dish greased with olive oil. Season with little garlic salt and pepper. Pour lemon juice over fish and sprinkle dill on top. Bake at 350 degrees for 20 to 30 minutes.

November 5

Make every effort to live in peace with all men and to be holy; without holiness no one will see the Lord.

—Hebrews 12:14

Spiritual growth is imperative—something that happens only by yielding to the power and unction of the Holy Spirit. The process begins the moment we admit we are sinners and place our trust in Jesus Christ as our personal Savior and Lord. From that point, until death or the return of Jesus, our purpose in life is to grow in Christlikeness. Leviticus 11:44 says, "I am the Lord your God; consecrate yourselves and be holy, because I am holy."

Spiritual growth and holiness go hand in hand. One cannot grow spiritually without becoming holy. Holiness involves being separated from sin and set apart for God. It is being like Jesus and taking on His attributes and personality. To be holy, we must first repent of all sin and rely on the Holy Spirit to guide our every step. It involves a conscious desire to please or love God with all our heart, mind, soul, and strength (Matthew 22:37). This is done by praying and daily meditating on the Word so God's thoughts and truths can control our thinking and govern our actions. As we separate ourselves from sin and strive to live in peace and holiness, the Holy Spirit will enable us to live holy and victorious lives of dedication to God.

Father: Thank You for giving us Your Son to save us from our sin. Your ways are pure and holy and I desire to become like You in all my ways. Show me the ways of holiness and guide me with Your Holy Spirit to live only in peace and righteousness. In Jesus' name, Amen.

CHICKEN QUESADILLAS

½ cup salsa
2 tablespoons Miracle Whip salad dressing
½ teaspoon chili powder
8 (6-inch) flour tortillas
3 small boneless, skinless chicken breasts (cooked and chopped)
1 cup Mexican-style shredded cheese

Combine salsa, Miracle Whip, and chili powder; spread evenly onto bottom halves of tortillas. Top with chicken and cheese. Fold tortillas in half to enclose filling. Cook in greased skillet on medium heat for 4 to 5 minutes on each side or until both sides golden brown and cheese melted. Cut each quesadilla into 3 wedges to serve. Serve with sour cream and salsa, if desired.

November 6

Keep on loving each other as brothers. Do not forget to entertain strangers, for by so doing some people have entertained angels without knowing it. Remember those in prison as if you were their fellow prisoners, and those who are mistreated as if you yourselves were suffering.

—Hebrews 13:1–3

I N ANCIENT TIMES, during the days of the apostles, most of the people that traveled did so for business purposes; others traveled for the specific purpose of spreading the gospel. Travel was much more difficult then than it is now. Inns were expensive and hard to find; they were often filthy, of questionable character, and dangerous for the Christian. If innkeepers found their guests to be Christians, they reported them to the authorities. This is why Christians were encouraged to show hospitality to travelers, especially fellow believers, so these strangers did not have to stay in inns.

Today in America, the need is not as great because of the freedom we have to spread the gospel without fear of being imprisoned or openly persecuted. There are other ways, though, to carry out this command to love one another and show hospitality. We have material possessions and finances to share with those in need. We can also pray and visit shut-ins, nursing homes, and prisons. When we practice hospitality, we do so because we are Christians, out of love for God, and not expecting anything in return. If we remember to always treat others how we would want to be treated, God will help us demonstrate His love, especially on behalf of the household of faith. As we do, perhaps that stranger we helped was really an angel sent by God.

Dear God: Thank You for reminding us over and over in Your Word to love one another, especially those who are needy, mistreated, and unloved. Help me to use my resources to show hospitality to others even when they are strangers and have nothing to give in return. May many come to know You as Savior as I do my part to show God's love to a lost and hurting world. In Jesus' name, Amen.

BARBECUE JACK CHICKEN

4 boneless, skinless chicken breast halves
4 slices pepper jack cheese
Vegetable oil for pan
½–1 cup barbecue sauce

Carefully cut a pocket in each chicken breast half. Fill with cheese; secure with metal or soaked wooden toothpicks. Place in greased pan, covered, over medium heat for 6–8 minutes on each side or until done (170 degrees on meat thermometer). Baste frequently with barbecue sauce.

November 7

Marriage should be honored by all, and the marriage bed kept pure, for God will judge the adulterer and all the sexually immoral.

—HEBREWS 13:4

GOD HAS HIGH standards for us not because He wants to ruin our fun but because He cares about every aspect of our lives. A marriage is the legal, formal union between a man and woman by which they become husband and wife. It is God's will that we *all* respect His requirements for marriage and the right to have a sexual relationship with someone. The world has blatantly disregarded God's rules, causing an increase in divorce, abortion, sexually transmitted diseases, child abuse, pornography, alcohol and drug abuse, broken homes, and the heartache and pain that culminates with sexual perversion or any sin.

God says we are to refrain from all sexual acts and enticing thoughts outside of marriage. A single person is not to engage in or entertain thoughts that would lead to sexual actions or excitements, and a married person is to refrain from acts or thoughts that would involve anyone except his or her spouse. This is honoring and keeping the marriage bed pure. Sexual intimacy is to be reserved for those who are legally married and is only permitted and blessed by God in those conditions.

First Corinthians 6:18, says, "Flee from sexual immorality. All other sins a man commits are outside his body, but he who sins sexually sins against his own body." Paul was inspired by the Holy Spirit to express that sexual sin is different from other sins. Because the sin is against the human body, Christians commit the sin against the dwelling place of the Holy Spirit. All sin deserves God's judgment, but not all sins receive the same judgment. Every sin will lead us to hell if we don't have the grace and forgiveness of Jesus. That is why God offers salvation to even the most wicked. First John 1:7 says, "The blood of Jesus purifies us from every sin." God is willing to forgive all, just for the asking!

Father: Thank You for caring about my life and for the high standards You require of all. Thank You for the blood of Jesus that purifies us from every sin when we repent and turn from them. Help me to honor You in everything I do. Forgive me of the sins I have committed and, as I am tempted, may the choices I make be in direct submission to Your will. In Jesus' name, Amen.

CHICKEN MOZZARELLA

4 boneless chicken breasts
1 (16-ounce) jar spaghetti sauce
8 slices mozzarella cheese

Put chicken and spaghetti sauce in greased dish. Bake at 350 degrees for 40–50 minutes, until chicken done. Cover with cheese; bake just until cheese melted.

November 8

Keep your lives free from the love of money and be content with what you have, because God has said, "Never will I leave you; never will I forsake you."

—HEBREWS 13:5

GREED IS A sin that man has dealt with from the beginning of time. Adam and Eve had everything they could possibly need or want in the Garden of Eden, yet once temptation came along, they yielded and ate a forbidden fruit. They defiled the will of God that day and removed themselves from His blessing of living forever without illness or death. From that day on, man's feelings of dissatisfaction have run rampant, thus continually generating an insatiable desire to have more than what is needed or deserved. Scripture clearly condemns discontentment, envy, and covetousness because they can lead us down a destructive path of self-centered, self-absorbing, and self-gratifying pursuits. God wants us to be free from things centered around money so we can place our love and trust in Him and be about His business. We are to love Christ with all our heart, soul, mind, and strength, and love our neighbor as ourselves. When we give this kind of love, God showers us with His blessings. We are free from the burden of dependency on money by placing our total trust in the One who owns it all. God has already promised us that He will never leave us or forsake us. Now He wants us to respond to Him with our commitment to never forsake following after Him.

Lord God: You are the Giver of life and have blessed us with health, talents, and opportunities for service. Everything we have is a gift from You. Forgive me for my selfishness and envy and cause me to be content with what I have. When I see others in need, grant me compassion so I might share my resources with them. In Jesus' name, Amen.

TACO MAC AND CHEESE

1 pound ground beef
2 ¾ cups water
⅓ cup thick and chunky salsa
1 ½ teaspoon chili powder
2 cups elbow macaroni, uncooked
½ pound Velveeta cheese, cut in chunks
½ cup tortilla chips, crushed
¼ cup tomato, chopped
2 tablespoons green onion, chopped

Brown meat in large skillet; drain. Add water, salsa, chili powder, and macaroni; cover and bring to boil. Turn to medium-low; simmer 8–10 minutes until most of water is absorbed. Add Velveeta; cook until melted, stirring often. Garnish with chips, tomato, and green onion, as desired.

November 9

So that we may boldly say, The Lord is my helper, and I will not fear what man shall do unto me.

—Hebrews 13:6, KJV

THESE ARE THE same words the psalmist spoke in Psalm 118:6–7. They were written as a praise offering to God for the great and marvelous things He had done. Hundreds of years later, the author of Hebrews uses them to encourage us as believers to trust God to help us in every situation we face.

A helper is someone who comes to the aid of another to make his or her job easier. If we are obedient Christians and walking in the truth of God's Word, we have the assurance or confidence that God will be with us at all times and will meet our every need. Confidence comes when we have a firm foundation in the Lord. This results in a peace that passes all understanding (Philippians 4:7). Even when man comes against us in all sorts of ways, we are encouraged if we remember who we are in the Lord. The enemy will try to steal, kill, and destroy us, but the Lord promises to come to our aid and be our helper. So the next time Satan comes knocking at our doors, we need to ask Jesus if He would please get that for us. We have confidence that He will.

Dear Lord: Thank You for coming to be my Aid and Helper. Your promises are true, and as long as I am walking in the truth, You are there to bring me peace and joy and meet my every need. When I walk through the valleys of fear and evil, Your Word says You are there with me. No man can harm me or remove my confidence that You are my Savior, Lord, and Helper. In Jesus' name, Amen.

POTATO SAUSAGE CASSEROLE

1 pound bulk pork sausage
1 can cream of mushroom soup
¾ cup milk
½ cup chopped onion
½ teaspoon salt
1 teaspoon black pepper
3 cups sliced potatoes
1 tablespoon butter, divided
1 ½ cups (8 ounces) grated cheddar cheese

Cook sausage over medium-high heat until done; drain. Stir together soup, milk, onion, salt, and pepper in a medium bowl. Place half the potatoes in greased baking dish. Top with half of soup mixture, then with half of sausage. Repeat layers, ending with sausage. Dot with butter. Cover pan with foil. Bake 60–90 minutes until potatoes tender. Uncover; sprinkle with cheese and return to oven; bake until cheese melted.

November 10

Remember your leaders, who spoke the word of God to you. Consider the outcome of their way of life and imitate their faith. Jesus Christ is the same yesterday and today and forever.
—Hebrews 13:7–8

W E ALL KNOW people who have influenced us throughout our lives to follow Christ. Like the Jewish Christians the author of Hebrews is speaking to here, it is good to remember these ones and give serious thought to how they persevered through the tribulations and circumstances they had to face. Peer pressure and popularity says to follow the trends of the day by emulating the ways of movie stars, sports heroes, and those held in high esteem in our schools, jobs, media, and even churches. But these are not necessarily the people after whom God wants us to follow and pattern our lives. Unless their character lines up with the Word of God, they should merely remain a figure or representative of their trade or walk in life. Instead, we should recall those who were passionate about the gospel and the things of God. They may have come from our families, friends, teachers, pastors, bosses, employees, employers, political leaders, biblical characters, and the list goes on. They may have spoken a word, taught a lesson, preached a sermon, or performed an act that the Holy Spirit used to make a lasting impression on our lives. As we remember those who have enriched our lives for Christ, let's keep in mind that there is only one hero who is perfect and unchangeable: *Jesus Christ is the same yesterday, today, and forever,* and He is the ultimate Hero whose ways we need to imitate.

Heavenly Father: Thank You for the people You have placed in my life to bring me to a personal relationship with You. Thank You for Jesus, who is my ultimate Leader and Hero. Bring to my memory all those who You would have me imitate, and help me follow their example. In turn, may I be a witness and example to those with whom I come in contact, so they too might copy my ways and follow after You. In Jesus' name, Amen.

SOUTHWEST CHICKEN AND RICE

3 cups cooked diced chicken
2 cups cooked rice
1 can fiesta nacho cheese soup
1 (10-ounce) can diced tomatoes and green chiles

Combine chicken, rice, soup, and tomatoes and green chiles in bowl and mix well. Spoon mixture into sprayed 3-quart baking dish. Cover and bake at 350 degrees for 45 minutes.

November 11

Let us, then, go to him outside the camp, bearing the disgrace he bore. For here we do not have an enduring city, but we are looking for the city that is to come.

—Hebrews 13:13–14

In the Bible, *outside the camp* (sometimes meaning the city) was a place of defilement, uncleanness, corruption, filthiness, pollution, contamination, condemnation, punishment, rejection, and reproach. It was a place where animals were sacrificed, slaughtered, and buried. Lepers were sent outside the city to live. Those found guilty of breaking certain laws were stoned or put to death there. Animal and human excrement was taken outside the city and buried. It was a place of disease, dung, and death. Anyone who was deported outside the camp was excluded, isolated, and ostracized—yet the most important event in history happened there.

Our Lord and Savior chose, on His own accord, to go "outside the camp" and become unclean (and indeed He was, as He bore the sins of the world) to be crucified so we might have eternal life. Therefore, Jesus was nailed to the cross outside the camp so His cleansing blood would fall on the most unclean place. The world and all its sinful pleasures and ungodliness represent a place outside the camp where we as Christians are aliens, yet Christ calls us to "go to him outside the camp, bearing the disgrace he bore." To do so means to accept Jesus as Savior and follow Him in obedience, no matter what humiliation, embarrassment, or discomfort it brings. This life will soon be over, and God has an eternal city prepared to receive those who have trusted Jesus as Savior. If we follow Jesus today outside the camp, He will wash us in His pure blood to grant us access into the gates of the city that is forever without shame.

Father: Thank You for the Holy Scriptures, where I am able to come into Your presence and walk with You in spirit and in truth. Forgive me of my uncleanness and purify me in Your cleansing blood. Equip me with boldness and strength to follow after You and be welcomed into Your eternal city that is without shame. In Jesus' name, Amen.

PINEAPPLE CASSEROLE

1 cup sugar
6 tablespoons flour
2 cups grated sharp cheddar cheese
2 (20-ounce) cans pineapple chunks, drained, and 6 tablespoons pineapple juice reserved
1 cup Ritz cracker crumbs
1 stick butter, melted

In large bowl, stir together sugar and flour; gradually stir in cheese. Add drained pineapple chunks; stir until ingredients well combined. Pour mixture into greased casserole dish. In another bowl, combine cracker crumbs, melted butter, and reserved pineapple juice; stir with rubber spatula until evenly blended. Spread crumb mixture on top of pineapple mixture. Bake at 350 degrees for 25–30 minutes, or until golden brown.

November 12

Obey them that have the rule over you, and submit yourselves: for they watch for your souls, as they that must give account.

—HEBREWS 13:17, KJV

LOYALTY IN THE way of obedience and submission to our Christian leaders, pastors, and teachers is another way of letting God know we love and respect Him as our foremost Commander in Chief. If we have surrendered our lives to Jesus Christ, we must trust God's plan for our lives and live according to His will. God has placed an entire network of people in this world into positions of authority not only in the government, but also in the workplace, in our families, and in the church. They, in turn, are accountable to their leaders and God.

Coming under the authority of others and showing them respect isn't always easy. We don't really like being told what to do or how to do it, and oftentimes we criticize, rebel, and complain about those who make decisions we don't like. When this happens, the protection and favor God has over us as His children is lifted. God expects us to respect Him and the people He's placed in authority over us. This doesn't mean we have to agree with every decision made, but it does mean we should be respectful. Submitting to authority is right, unless the counsel or teaching does not line up with God's Word. When we make the conscious effort to do what God says, regardless of how we feel, God is honored and our lives are blessed. The challenge is before us. May we be found worthy of being obedient to all God's commands when He returns one day as our righteous Judge.

Heavenly Father: Forgive me for grumbling and complaining about those in authority over me. Help me to see that You are the One who put them there so my life would be fruitful, productive, and honorable to You. I praise You for the protection and shelter You have placed over my life by orchestrating the authority of every leader called to serve on my behalf. Thank You for Your wonderful plan; may I forever be found faithful to it. In Jesus' name, Amen.

OVEN-BAKED FRIED CHICKEN

½ cup butter
6–12 pieces of chicken
Garlic or seasoning salt and pepper
1 egg, beaten
2 tablespoons water
Potato flakes

Melt butter in baking dish. Sprinkle chicken with garlic salt and pepper. Mix egg and water in bowl; coat chicken in egg, then roll in potato flakes. Place in baking dish; bake 1 hour at 325 degrees. Turn once during baking. Baste once or twice.

November 13

Consider it pure joy, my brothers, whenever you face trials of many kinds, because you know that the testing of your faith develops perseverance. Perseverance must finish its work so that you may be mature and complete, not lacking anything.

—JAMES 1:2–4

JAMES WAS THE half-brother of Jesus and the leader of the Jerusalem church. He wrote this letter to encourage scattered Jewish believers who were persecuted because of their belief in Christ so that they might persevere in spite of their circumstances. Not only did James tell them to have joy, but to have pure or undiluted joy. He wanted them to know that no matter what degree of persecution they had endured, nothing should mar the perfect gift of joy they had received from knowing and serving the resurrected Christ.

Today, we who are believers are also scattered across this world, facing the trials of everyday life. They may be struggles with finances, health, family, friends, jobs, marriage, or any number of things, but God wants us to know that as we persevere and finish our work here on earth, He is with us every step of the way. God knows every trial, hurt, pain, mistreatment, abuse, and circumstance we face; He has not left us alone to face them by ourselves. As we press on through every test and hardship, our faith becomes mature and gives us hope, assurance, and most of all, pure joy to the end.

Gracious Father and soon-coming King: You alone are the joy of my life and the hope that gives me strength to do all things. Cleanse me from all my impurities and create a desire within me to be more like You. As I endure pain and hardships, Your Word says I will develop perseverance to finish the work You have called me to do. Help me to remain in Your truth and to consider all my trials pure joy as I stand the test of faith and do Your will. In Jesus' name, Amen.

SEVEN-LAYER TOSSED SALAD

2 cups torn iceberg lettuce
1 cup fresh cauliflowerets
1 cup fresh broccoli florets
1 cup shredded carrots
⅓ cup red onion
6 bacon strips, cooked and crumbled
1 cup (4 ounces) shredded cheese

Dressing—mix together:

¾ cup mayonnaise
3 tablespoons sugar
3 tablespoons lemon juice

Combine salad ingredients in bowl; pour dressing over; toss to coat. Serve immediately.

November 14

If any of you lacks wisdom, he should ask God, who gives generously to all without finding fault, and it will be given to him.

—JAMES 1:5

WISDOM IS THE knowledge it takes to make good or sound judgment when action is needed. The wisdom spoken about by James in this passage refers to spiritual wisdom, which is the insight or knowledge required to make decisions that honor God. While the world's wisdom comes from common sense, experience, and learning from others, God's wisdom comes by meditating on His Word, praying, and receiving understanding and discernment from the Holy Spirit.

As Christians, we have access to God every moment of every day; He loves when we call on His name for help. He is our heavenly Father, and He adores us. God isn't bothered by our pleas and requests but is more than willing to provide us with the knowledge we need to make decisions that are upright and noble. Oftentimes we may feel confused or troubled about a certain situation or circumstance, but it is probably because we have not tapped into God's supply source by reading His Word and seeking His counsel and direction in prayer. God wants us to live triumphantly and victoriously. He is interested in every detail of our lives, whether big or small. If we lack wisdom concerning a situation or decision, we should pause and seek God's guidance, asking Him to give us direction and clarity, and it will be given to us.

Dear God: Thank You for always being available, no matter when I need You. Not only do you offer Your blessings to Your children, but You generously give them to us just for asking. Just as saints of the Bible called on You when they needed help, I call on You today to give me direction for some areas that are rather troubling. Guide me with Your Holy Spirit and fill my mind with wisdom to make the right choices. In Jesus' name, Amen.

BUFFALO FRIED CHICKEN

Cut-up chicken pieces (any amount)
Frank's hot sauce
Equal amounts vegetable oil and butter
¼–½ teaspoon black pepper
½–1 teaspoon garlic salt
½–1 cup flour

Soak chicken in salted water in refrigerator 4–6 hours or overnight (about 1 teaspoon salt for every 2 cups water). Drain and discard water; dry chicken with paper towels. Drizzle Frank's hot sauce all over chicken. Heat just enough oil and butter to cover bottom of large skillet. Put flour, garlic salt, and pepper in a bowl or ziplock bag. Coat chicken; fry in pan until thoroughly done.

November 15

Blessed is the man who perseveres under trial, because when he has stood the test, he will receive the crown of life that God has promised to those who love Him.

—James 1:12

JAMES, A BROTHER of Jesus, had endured trials and tests of his faith and wants us to know we can also. Though he was referring to being persecuted for the cause of Christ, we are also encouraged to not give up in any test we may experience. There are all sorts of trials we encounter, and the decisions we make regarding them will determine where we spend eternity. Will we stay true to God and not give in to peer pressure and attend the party that we know will not honor godly living? Will we join in the gossip at work, school, or even church when another person is the topic of conversation? The pressures of living a Christian life in the world today are very great, but the reward we will receive one day will be greater. The choice is up to us; the crown of life is promised to all who love God.

Father: Thank You for all the times You gave me strength when I was about to give up. Help me to persevere and not become weak when facing tests and trials. I want to endure, no matter the cost and severity. I look forward to receiving the crown of life that awaits me. In Jesus' name, Amen.

HAWAIIAN MEATBALLS

1 ½ pounds ground beef
2/3 cups cracker crumbs
½ cup minced onion
1 egg
1 teaspoon salt
1 teaspoon ginger
¼ cup milk
1 tablespoon oil

Sauce:

2 tablespoons cornstarch
½ cup brown sugar
1 (14-ounce) can pineapple tidbits
½ cup vinegar
1 tablespoon soy sauce
½ cup water
½ cup chopped green pepper

Mix meat, crumbs, onion, egg, salt, ginger, and milk; shape into balls. Heat oil in skillet; brown meatballs until done. In separate pan, mix cornstarch and sugar; add juice from pineapple, vinegar, soy sauce, and water; stir until smooth. On medium heat, cook mixture until it comes to boil and thickens. Add meatballs, pineapple tidbits, and green peppers. Heat and serve over rice.

November 16

Let no man say when he is tempted, I am tempted of God: for God cannot be tempted with evil, neither tempteth he any man: But every man is tempted, when he is drawn away of his own lust, and enticed.

—JAMES 1:13–15, KJV

TEMPTATION IS A part of our lives; it was even something Jesus faced. Temptation is the urge or inclination to react to something or someone because of an attraction or fascination with him, her, or it. The temptation is not the sin; it's how we react to the temptation that determines whether or not we sin. In every situation we face, a choice has to be made. Each of us is tempted differently. For one, it may be with sexual issues; for another, to overeat; and yet for others, temptation may be to gossip, lie, cheat, steal, or gamble.

James says God doesn't tempt us; but it is our evil or fleshly desire that does. When temptation comes, we can react by entertaining it in our minds or by acting it out physically. Both these reactions give birth to sin (Matthew 5:27–28; Mark 7:20–23). There is a third choice and the one that honors our Lord. If the temptation is evil and contrary to the Word of God, James says to submit to God, resist the devil, and he will flee (James 4:7). Jesus resisted temptation by quoting scripture to Satan, "It is written…" (Matt. 4:4; Luke 4:4). Yes, temptation is everywhere, but we can overcome by knowing the Word and applying it to the situation at hand. May we do as Jesus did and be victorious Christians, ready and willing be pure and holy so our souls live forever and not die. With Christ, we can and will do it!

Father: With You all things are possible and I choose today to live a holy lifestyle. When temptation comes, help me to be strong. Thank You for Jesus who paid a price on Calvary so I could overcome and not yield to fleshly desires. Forgive me for the times I did; give me strength to be strong from this day forward. In Jesus' name, Amen.

BLUE CHEESE–ITALIAN SALAD DRESSING

2 cups canola oil
⅔ cup apple cider vinegar
1 teaspoon parsley flakes
1 teaspoon garlic salt
1 teaspoon black pepper
4 packets artificial sweetener or 8 teaspoons sugar
1 teaspoon salt
6 ounces blue cheese

Mix oil and vinegar in blender on low speed. Add parsley, garlic salt, pepper, sweetener, and salt; blend 10 seconds. Add blue cheese; mix just until cheese broken into small pieces. Refrigerate until ready to use.

November 17

Every good and perfect gift is from above, coming down from the Father of the heavenly lights, who does not change like shifting shadows.

—JAMES 1:17

FROM THE BEGINNING of time, many have looked to the stars, sun, and moon to try and figure out their life's destiny. James says God is the "Father of the heavenly lights" and has our destiny already planned. God is our Creator and He created all things well and for a purpose. "Shifting shadows" are the illusions made from objects on the earth in the sunlight. As the world turns, the shadows change, appearing and disappearing in the sun's rays. James says God's light is not like that. Even though our situations change in life, God's light remains constant, steady, and bright. In the midst of our difficulties, tragedies, and seeming unfairness of life, God's love is shining. The sorrows and struggles of this world are not caused by God, but by the sin of mankind. Adam and Eve rebelled against God's authority, and sin and death entered the world. But Jesus came to overcome the sinful nature of man when He took our sin to the cross and was crucified in our stead. This made it possible for each of us to experience salvation by repenting of our sin and accepting Christ as Savior and Lord. After that, we are to become shadows in God's light, spreading His good and perfect news to those still in darkness.

Lord God: You are good and perfect and the giver of all that is right and pure. Forgive me for complaining and blaming You for the circumstances and situations that arise in my life that seem unfair and frustrating. I know in my heart You love me and have good plans for my life. In times of struggle, may I draw on You for my source of strength and light. In Jesus' name, Amen!

STOVE TOP ONE-DISH CHICKEN SKILLET

1 ½ cups hot water
1 stick butter, melted
1 (6-ounce) package Stove Top stuffing mix for chicken
4–6 small boneless, skinless chicken breast halves (1 ½ pounds)
1 can cream of mushroom soup
⅓ cup sour cream

Mix hot water, butter, and stuffing mix. Cook chicken in nonstick skillet on medium-high 5–8 minutes on each side or until browned. Mix soup and sour cream; pour over chicken. Top with stuffing; cover. Cook on low 10–15 minutes or until chicken is done.

November 18

My dear brothers, take note of this: Everyone should be quick to listen, slow to speak and slow to become angry, for man's anger does not bring about the righteous life that God desires.

—James 1:19–20

THERE'S A LOT of meaning to the cliché that we should count to ten to slow our anger and prevent blowing our top. Broken marriages, severed friendships, family feuds, lost jobs, damaged walls, thrown objects, physical and verbal abuse, and even ended lives have all resulted over words that were said in the heat of anger. The Bible has much to say about our tongues and how we need to control them. James tells us to be quick to listen and slow to speak. If we do these two things, our anger will also decrease and be controlled. A true sign of wisdom and Christian maturity is seen when we listen to others speak before we do. Remember this: God gave us two ears and one mouth, so we should listen twice as much as we speak. If only we would take more time to filter our words before we say them, our conversations would be much more uplifting and peaceful. Life is too short to be angry with everyone who crosses our path or pulls out in front of us in a car. James gives us the perfect reason why we "should be quick to listen, slow to speak and slow to become angry, for man's anger does not bring about the righteous life that God desires."

Father: I surrender my whole self to You, including my emotions and attitude. All that I am and ever hope to be, I submit to You. Help me cope with the trials and circumstances that enter my life. I want to do right in Your eyes and honor You in my thoughts and actions. Place in me the qualities I need to bring about the righteous life You desire. In Jesus' name, Amen.

TURKEY CASSEROLE

3 cups cubed bread
3 eggs, beaten
¾ cup milk
¼ cup chopped onion
¼ cup celery
¼ teaspoon pepper
¼ teaspoon salt
1 can cream of mushroom or chicken soup
½ teaspoon poultry seasoning
¼ teaspoon paprika
3–4 cups cooked diced chicken or turkey
3 tablespoons butter, melted

In large bowl, combine bread cubes with eggs and milk. Add all remaining ingredients in order given; mix well. Pour into baking dish; brush with melted butter. Bake at 350 degrees 1 hour, until browned.

November 19

Therefore, get rid of all moral filth and the evil that is so prevalent and humbly accept the word planted in you, which can save you.

—JAMES 1:21

JAMES IS A tell-it-like-it-is kind of person. He is God-inspired and definitely an exhorter of the truth. He is speaking here from the heart of a true Christian, encouraging other believers to be cautious about their lifestyles. James is aware of the fleshly desires of man (and woman) and knows how easy it is to get caught up in worldly pleasures and entertainment. If we have made a profession of faith in the Lord Jesus Christ and call ourselves Christians, we will not dabble in the immoral "filth and evil" the world has to offer. We either are saved from the consequences of sin or we are not; there is no middle ground or compromise. If we have chosen salvation by repenting of our sins and are living for Christ, the old lifestyle that honored Satan (evil and filth) is gone and the new one that honors God has come (2 Corinthians 5:17).

What are filth and evil? They are anything and everything that grieve the Holy Spirit and violate God's holy standards. It may come through movies, films, Internet, magazines, music, correspondence, material items, or others' or our own language, thoughts, or actions. To allow these things in our homes or our own personal temples (1 Corinthians 6:19) leads to spiritual death (Romans 6:23). As believers, we are commanded to take righteousness and holiness seriously. Our homes and temples must be swept clean of any questionable sign of evil and filled with the holiness of Christ illustrated in God's Word.

Precious Savior: Your Word lights my path so I might know where it is You want me to go. When I seek You in the holy Scriptures, I find You there guiding me to the way of righteousness. Forgive me for the evil and moral filth I've allowed to come into my life all because of selfish desires. As I remove them all from my home and personal life, help me to be strong and never again allow them to come back. In Jesus' name, Amen.

BREAKFAST CASSEROLE

1 can crescent rolls
1 pound sausage, browned and drained
4 eggs beaten with ¼ cup water added
2–3 cups shredded cheese

In greased 13x9-inch dish place rolls on bottom to form crust. Add meat to egg mixture; pour over crust. Top with cheese. Bake at 350 degrees for 30–35 minutes.

November 20

Do not merely listen to the word, and so deceive yourselves. Do what it says.

—JAMES 1:22

JAMES, JESUS' HALF brother and leader of the Jerusalem church, is speaking to his brothers and sisters in the Lord about their lifestyles and behavior. As a disciple of Christ, he wants to make sure they all not only know what God's Word (also called law or truth) says, but are also living it. James tells us that the law (will of God for each of us) brings freedom in the Holy Spirit to obey God's truth. If we heard a sermon every day of the week and Jesus were the preacher, and yet we merely listened and took no part in acting on what He said, we would be as deceived and lost as the vilest sinner on earth.

God longs for us to live His Word, but in order to do so we have to know what it says. Most all of us own Bibles, but they sit on a shelf rarely opened. Just as one cannot be nourished by a can of unopened soup sitting on a shelf, the same is true for the gospel. Through faith in Christ we receive not only God's mercy and forgiveness of our sins, but also the freedom and power to choose God's will to live a holy and righteous life. We are set free from the bondages of sin and evil and no longer are slaves of Satan. The chains that held us captive were broken when Christ went to the cross. Now we must choose to accept that freedom and be doers of the Word and no longer just hearers.

Father: Remove from my life the junk that holds me down. As I read Your Word and meditate on it, show me exactly what You want me to do because I want to live for You and You alone. Help me to discern what is right and holy and do those things that only bring You glory. In Jesus' name, Amen.

BLT PIZZA

1 (8-ounce) tube crescent rolls
1 cup mayonnaise
1 tablespoon Dijon mustard
3 cups shredded lettuce
12 bacon strips, cooked and crumbled
1 medium tomato, chopped
2 green onions, sliced
1 ½ cups shredded cheddar cheese

Separate crescent dough into eight triangles; place on lightly greased 14-inch pizza pan with points toward center. Press dough onto bottom and up sides of pan, forming a crust; seal perforations. Bake at 375 for 12–15 minutes, until golden brown; cool completely. In bowl, combine mayonnaise and mustard; spread over crust. Sprinkle with lettuce, bacon, tomato, onions, and cheese.

November 21

You see that a person is justified by what he does and not by faith alone.

—JAMES 2:24

As the body without the spirit is dead, so faith without deeds is dead.

—JAMES 2:26

AMES WANTS US to know that both faith and works are integral parts of God's plan for every Christian. Faith to accept Jesus as Savior and Lord is definitely foremost, but true saving faith will inevitably produce the desire to do good deeds. If it doesn't, perhaps there really hasn't been a transformation of a soul. Faith without deeds would be the same as someone inheriting a million dollars but never spending or sharing it with anyone. He would still be a millionaire, but no one would ever know nor would anyone receive any blessings from it.

When we come to Christ, our desires are different from what they used to be. Where we once were selfish and wanted to do our own thing, seeing ourselves blessed, now we are thinking of others and how we might bless them. As believers, we have certain obligations God wants us to meet and they all focus on obedience to His Word. Faith and deeds are totally different yet cannot be separated; the latter always follows the former (Galatians 5:6). For faith to be real, it must demonstrate itself in service. Faith not only moves mountains; it moves believers to act in ways that honor God and bless others, portraying their thankfulness for God's incredible grace.

Faithful Father: At times I have been lazy in my spiritual walk. Help me to see the many opportunities available for service and equip and empower me to do my part in seeing that the work is done and needs are met. I choose today to put my love in action and follow Your prompting and leading while serving others. In Jesus' name, Amen.

TURKEY OR CHICKEN CRESCENT AMANDINE

1 can cream of chicken soup
⅔ cup mayonnaise
½ cup sour cream
2 tablespoons minced onion
3 cups cooked chicken or turkey, diced
1 can water chestnuts
1 can crescent rolls
⅔ cup shredded cheese
½ cup silvered almonds
2 tablespoons melted butter

Combine soup, mayonnaise, sour cream, onion, cooked chicken, and water chestnuts in a large skillet. Cook over medium heat until mixture bubbles. Pour into 9x13-inch baking dish. Separate crescent rolls into triangles and put over top chicken mixture. Combine cheese and almonds; sprinkle over dough. Drizzle with melted butter. Bake at 375 degrees for 25 minutes.

November 22

You adulterous people, don't you know that friendship with the world is hatred toward God? Anyone who chooses to be a friend of the world becomes an enemy of God.

—James 4:4

JAMES IS QUITE outspoken and adamant here as he questions the sinful behavior of his fellow believers who were dabbling in the pleasures of the world. Did they not know the seriousness of the spiritual adultery they were committing? Why is it so easy for us to abandon what we know to be right and holy and embrace the sins of the world? Are we too embarrassed to let others know we won't be joining them in certain types of entertainment or gatherings? Those who oppose Christianity have no problem proclaiming their antagonistic views while many of us remain silent. Jesus was ridiculed, scorned, hated, called every name, attacked, even tortured and then crucified for taking His stand for God; so why shouldn't we? Were we not the reason Christ did what He did?

In this life, we have choices to make, and those choices determine our destiny. If we choose to love God by accepting Christ as our Savior and following His commands, we have chosen to be a friend of God's. If we give in to our fleshly desires and follow the ways of the world that are in opposition to God's ways, we have made a proclamation with our lifestyle to be God's enemy. We cannot be both. It is contrary to the Word of God to go to church one day a week and worship Him and then live for the world the rest of the time. We choose to be a friend or enemy of God by the choices we make each and every day. God chose to be our friend as He watched His Son lay down His life so that ours might be spared. Christ has asked us to be His friend; now the choice is ours to accept or reject this wonderful offer.

Father: I want friendship with You, not the world or anything in it. As I take this stand, grant me strength to resist the temptations of the world. Give me a spirit of boldness so I am able to witness the truth of Your Word to others. May the way I live my life be a proclamation that I have chosen to live for You. In Jesus' name, Amen.

WILTED LETTUCE SALAD

4 slices bacon
2 tablespoons sugar
⅓ cup apple-cider vinegar
Couple dashes of pepper
1 bunch leaf lettuce, torn
1 small sweet onion, sliced thin

Fry bacon until crisp; remove and crumble. To pan drippings, add sugar, vinegar and pepper; heat to almost boiling. Mix and pour over lettuce and onion; toss. Add bacon; serve immediately.

November 23

Submit yourselves therefore to God. Resist the devil, and he will flee from you.

—James 4:7, KJV

MOST OF US would like our spiritual growth to be easy. We think our ability to withstand temptation should require little effort. Thankfully, God does empower us through His Holy Spirit to live holy in an unholy world. However, He reminds us that for the Spirit to work powerfully in our lives, we must intentionally *submit* our wills to His and *resist the devil.* Easier said than done? Submitting to God means surrendering completely to His authority. It's throwing up our hands and admitting we can no longer fight the battle on our own. Once that is done, James tells us to resist or fight against the devil, something that requires boldness and God's strength. Temptation is all around, but we don't have to give in to it. Satan even tempted Jesus on several occasions and in each instance Jesus' response to the devil was, "It is written!" (Luke 4:1–13). If we incorporate God's Word into every facet of our lives—every thought, word, and action—the devil will flee and the battle will be won.

Dear God: Thank You for your presence and power of Your Holy Spirit in me. I intentionally submit my will to Yours. Please use Your Spirit to motivate and inspire me to resist the devil and recognize his attempts to derail my commitment to You. In Jesus' name, Amen.

SWEET POTATO CASSEROLE

4 large sweet potatoes/yams
4 cups water
1 stick butter
½ teaspoon cinnamon
1 cup brown sugar
½ teaspoon vanilla
2 eggs, slightly beaten
Marshmallows (regular or mini)

Peel potatoes; cut into chunks. Put in large pan; add water and bring to boil. Cook until potatoes soft and easy to mash (about 20 minutes). Drain off excess water (if any); mash with potato masher. Add butter, cinnamon, brown sugar, vanilla, and eggs; mix well and pour into large greased baking dish. Bake 30 minutes at 375 degrees. Remove from oven; cover top with marshmallows. Return to oven until marshmallows browned on top. Note: 2 (40-ounce) cans of sweet potatoes/yams may be used instead of fresh whole yams. Drain off liquid and mash. Add rest of ingredients (melt butter before adding) and continue as above.

November 24

Brothers, do not slander one another. Anyone who speaks against his brother or judges him speaks against the law and judges it.

—JAMES 4:11

JAMES IS SPEAKING openly to his brothers in Christ about their tongues. He wants them and us to know how wrong it is to slander, criticize, gossip, judge, or use harsh words when speaking about another believer. If our words will help another person, they probably are okay to speak. If our words will harm the other person or make a situation worse, we should not speak them. When we do slander and speak against others, it's because we want everyone to realize how great we are in comparison to them. There is a right manner in which God has given us the authority to make moral evaluations and condemn sin (John 7:24), but we must be very careful not to speak evil of our brethren. God is the Judge and we are not. We are to build our brothers and sisters up in the Lord for the edifying of the body instead of griping and complaining about them. God wants us to use our tongues to share His love with a world that is lost and very much in need of a Savior. God sent His Son Jesus to this world, not to condemn it but to save it from condemnation (John 3:17). God is patient with us because He desires that all men accept His free gift of salvation. We are all in desperate need of God's mercy and grace; therefore, we should not be judgmental of others. Instead, we must examine ourselves before God, repent of our sin, embrace others, and support them in prayer. God is glorified as we respect His law and allow Him to be the righteous Judge.

Father: Forgive me for judging my brothers and sisters and for saying unkind things about them. Help me to hold my tongue when I am tempted even if others have spoken evil against me. You are the righteous Judge; I am not. Give me strength to live before others as one who speaks only things that glorify You. In Jesus' name, Amen.

SWEET-AND-SOUR HAM OVER RICE

½ cup brown sugar
2 tablespoons cornstarch
1 (15-ounce) can pineapple chunks
1 cup water
2 tablespoons vinegar
1 green pepper, cut into strips
1 ½–2 cups cubed ham
3 cups cooked hot rice

Put brown sugar, cornstarch, drained pineapple juice, water, and vinegar in a pan. Stir constantly over medium heat until thick. Add pineapple, green pepper, and ham. Heat and serve over rice.

November 25

My brothers, if one of you should wander from the truth and someone should bring him back, remember this: Whoever turns a sinner from the error of his way will save him from death and cover over a multitude of sins.

—James 5:19–20

JAMES IS QUITE aware of the wandering process that plagues every believer. Life is not always a bed of roses, and there are times when we get discouraged or distracted and take our eyes off the truth of God's Word. When once we were thriving Christians, teaching, serving, and worshiping God with our gifts and talents, someone hurt our feelings or our priorities have changed and sports and recreation have slid into first base; no longer are we in fellowship as we once were. It usually isn't an immediate response but a slow process. This is why James uses the word *wander,* because we are usually carefree and unaware that it is even happening.

God inspires James to encourage every Christian to be motivated in bringing back into fellowship those who have wandered from the truth. It is not just the pastor's or church leader's responsibility to turn a sinner from his or her error, but every believer's. Whatever the reason for a person straying from God and the Christian community, their only hope in avoiding an eternal spiritual death and separation from God is to repent and come back to a saving relationship with Jesus Christ. It may cause friction and resentment when we confront another regarding his wandering state, but if that person returns to the Lord, any pain experienced will be small in comparison to the joy that will be felt when the sinner repents. Second Corinthians 7:10 says, "Godly sorrow brings repentance that leads to salvation and leaves no regret, but worldly sorrow brings death." May we each do our part in bringing back souls for Christ.

Father: I repent and come back to You with remorse for taking my eyes off You and onto the world of sin and ruin. Bring me back to the place where I knew You the greatest and keep me sheltered beneath Your strong covering. May I forever remain in the truth of Your Word and be ready to rescue other souls who are perishing before it is too late. In Jesus' name, Amen.

BAKED APPLES

4 Rome apples
1 (12-ounce) can regular or diet black cherry soda
Cinnamon

Core apples; put in small baking dish. Pour soda over; sprinkle with cinnamon. Bake at 375 degrees for 45 minutes, or until tender.

November 26

In this you greatly rejoice, though now for a little while you may have had to suffer grief in all kinds of trials. These have come so that your faith—of great worth than gold, which perishes even though refined by fire—may be proved genuine and may result in praise, glory and honor when Jesus Christ is revealed.

—1 PETER 1:6–7

THERE ARE MANY reasons why Christians suffer today, but the early Christians suffered because they were living godly lives in a pagan society. The persecution and trials they endured were a result of the world's hostile view of Jesus. Peter wrote to encourage them to remain hopeful and continue to persevere through all their times of grief and pain.

Although suffering is a normal part of life, salvation results in more suffering and persecution because it's an opposite lifestyle from the world's. At the same time, though, knowledge of our salvation enables us to hold on to our faith, joy, and hope in the midst of our sufferings. Peter also says our suffering is short term and will not last long. All of this doesn't mean that trials will make our faith genuine, but rather it proves or confirms whether our faith is genuine in the first place. If our faith is not genuine, we will not remain faithful to God's Word when trials come. But if our faith is genuine, it will manifest itself when undergoing trials. In other words, trials do not change our faith, but rather reveal what kind of faith we truly have. We must hold on to the fact that at the end of our time on earth, when Jesus is revealed, our salvation will result in an everlasting life free from any kind of hardship or suffering.

Heavenly Father: In You alone do I put my trust. In times of grief and suffering, You are my comfort and strength. Help me to remain hopeful and not take my eyes off You and onto my woes when trials come. Thank You for Your mercy and grace. In Jesus' name, Amen.

RITZY CHICKEN CASSEROLE

4 boneless, skinless chicken breasts
1 can cream of chicken soup
1 cup sour cream
1 stick butter, melted
1 tube Ritz crackers

Sauté chicken in ½ cup water until done. Cut into bite-sized pieces; place on bottom of baking dish, with any juice left after cooking. Mix soup and sour cream together and spread over chicken. Mash crackers and add to melted butter. Sprinkle over top. Bake uncovered at 350 degrees for 25–30 minutes.

November 27

Though you have not seen him, you love him; and even though you do not see him now, you believe in him and are filled with an inexpressible and glorious joy, for you are receiving the goal of your faith, the salvation of your souls.

—1 Peter 1:8–9

For the believer, living the Christian life should be as consequential as breathing. Just as air is invisible, we trust it to be there each time we inhale. The same is true with our faith in God. We don't see Him with the natural eye, but we trust God to be there every moment of every day. When Christ walked this earth, it was easy for the early followers to believe in Him because He manifested a tangible body where they could physically converse with and touch Him. But Peter says how much more profound it is that even though we are not yet privileged to see Christ's fleshly body, we who love Him are "filled with an inexpressible and glorious joy." Why? Just as the Israelites traveled through the rugged wilderness to reach their inheritance in the Promised Land, so do we as Christians joyfully journey through this life, with all its obstacles, knowing one day we will receive the goal of our faith— our eternal inheritance in the kingdom of God.

Father God: My heart is filled with the inexpressible joy that only comes by putting my trust in You. Though I don't see You with my physical eyes, my spirit knows You are there. I praise You for instilling within me a desire to know You personally and receive the goal of my faith—eternal inheritance in Your kingdom. Thank You for this marvelous gift! In Jesus' name, Amen.

CHICKEN DIANE

2 tablespoons butter
4 boneless, skinless chicken breasts
½ teaspoon seasoning salt
¼ teaspoon pepper
1 teaspoon dried parsley
1 clove garlic, minced
1 (16-ounce) package sliced mushrooms
⅓ cup onion, sliced
1 can cream of mushroom soup
⅓ cup milk
1 teaspoon dried chives (optional)

Melt butter in pan over medium heat; add chicken. Sprinkle with seasoning salt, pepper, and parsley; cook until golden, turning once. Add garlic, mushrooms, and onion; cook until chicken thoroughly cooked. Remove chicken from skillet. Add soup and milk to skillet, stirring briskly until sauce well blended. Return chicken to pan; heat through. Garnish with chives.

November 28

Therefore, prepare your minds for action; be self-controlled; set your hope fully on the grace to be given you when Jesus Christ is revealed. As obedient children, do not conform to the evil desires you had when you lived in ignorance. But just as he who called you is holy, so be holy in all you do; for it is written: "Be holy, because I am holy."

—1 PETER 1:13–16

HOLINESS IS A state of submission, consecration, and obedience to God's Word. One doesn't just happen to fall into holiness; it is a result of watchfulness, prayer, and perseverance to follow and be like Christ. Peter refers to it as a form of mind control that helps us strive for holiness. Being holy is often thought of as impossible to achieve, since we are imperfect humans, but God would not have commanded us to be holy if He thought it impossible. It essentially involves taking authority over our minds and making Christ Lord over our thoughts. When we were slaves to sin, we allowed sin to be lord over our thoughts. We used them to serve sinful passions and found ourselves further enslaved. As redeemed children of God, we have authority in Christ to rule over our thoughts and bring them into obedience to God's Word. This is done by resisting temptation, by taking our thoughts captive, and by setting our hope fully on the grace extended to us from Jesus Christ. No longer are we to conform to our evil desires, but we must take control of our thoughts and bring them into alignment with God's. Because all sin starts in our thoughts, it takes a daily commitment of the will to keep our minds holy. God will not make us holy against our will. When God calls us to be holy, He imparts to us the power to obey.

Father: Thank You for the gift of Your Holy Spirit. I confess that at times wrong thoughts have taken me into sin; I repent and ask for forgiveness. Provide me strength to conform no longer to the evil desires of my flesh, but instead take every evil or wrong thought captive in Jesus' name. With You as my guide, I am able to live according to Your Word. In Jesus' name, Amen!

HAWAIIAN PORK CHOPS

6 lean pork chops
1 (20-ounce) can pineapple slices, in own juice
⅓ cup brown sugar or honey
2 tablespoons soy sauce
¼ teaspoon ground ginger
¼ teaspoon garlic powder

Arrange pork chops in greased baking dish; put pineapple slices on top. Mix rest of ingredients together and pour over chops. Cover; bake 30 minutes at 350 degrees. Uncover and bake an additional 20 minutes, until pork is done. Serve with rice.

November 29

But ye are a chosen generation, a royal priesthood, an holy nation, a peculiar people; that ye should shew forth the praises of him who hath called you out of darkness into his marvelous light.

—1 PETER 2:9, KJV

HAVE YOU OR a loved one ever been one of the last ones picked to be on a team where the captain was choosing his or her players? You waited, wondering if either side were ever going to call your name. Well, there is a team where everyone who wants to play will be chosen. God has called each of us to be on His team. He has given us the privilege and opportunity to say good-bye to the darkness of sin and shame and walk with Him in the light of His love. It is our choice; if we want to play on His team, He has already chosen us.

Heavenly Father: Thank You for choosing me to be on your team. Forgive me for my sin and help me to live as though I have chosen to walk in the light with You, and not in darkness. You are the captain of my team, and I praise and thank You with all my heart for choosing me. In Jesus' name, Amen.

CHICKEN AND DUMPLINGS SOUP

1 whole chicken or (about 3 pounds pieces)
2 quarts water
2 teaspoons salt
2 cans cream of chicken soup
2 bouillon cubes
1 can evaporated milk
1 teaspoon pepper

Dumplings:

1 ½ cups sifted flour
2 teaspoons baking powder
¾ teaspoon salt
¾ cup milk
3 tablespoons vegetable shortening

Boil chicken in salted water for 30 minutes; turn off heat. Remove chicken and discard skin and bones. Skim off excess fat. Cut chicken into bite-sized pieces and return to stock. Add cans of soup, bouillon, milk, and pepper; bring to boil and simmer while preparing dumplings.

Dumplings: Sift flour into bowl and add baking powder and salt. Cut in shortening until it looks like meal. Stir in milk. Drop dough by spoonfuls into simmering chicken soup. Cook uncovered for 10 minutes or until dumplings done.

November 30

Slaves, submit yourselves to your masters with all respect, not only those who are good and considerate, but also to those that are harsh.

—1 PETER 2:18

TREATMENT AT WORK, school, or among family and friends can sometimes be unfair. Peter instructs us to be submissive to our boss, employer, or that person in our life who is over us in some way. Perhaps we are not being paid fairly or have been cheated out of a raise. Maybe we've been accused of something we didn't do or have been loaded down with more than our fair share of work. As Christians, we are instructed to be obedient and humble, even if treated unfairly. There are times when injustice should be confronted, especially if the employer is grossly unjust or causes a compromise to be made in what we believe is morally right. This should be done not with a cowardly or unwilling attitude but with a compliant spirit so that Christ is honored. Verses 19–21 explain it so well: "For this is commendable, if because of conscience toward God one endures grief, suffering wrongfully. For what credit is it if, when you are beaten for your faults, you take it patiently? But when you do good and suffer, if you take it patiently, this is commendable before God. For to this you were called, because Christ also suffered for us, leaving us an example, that you should follow His steps."

Father: Thank You for the wonderful example You are and for showing us how to act toward our employers and those in authority, even when they are harsh. You received the ultimate harsh treatment yet did not give up and quit before the job was done. Thank You! Help me to not give up and quit my job prematurely unless it would be honorable to You. May I have wisdom and strength to endure any hardship. Help me to be a submissive, hard-working, faithful employee. In Jesus' name, Amen.

POTATO AND CORN CHOWDER (crockpot)

1 (16-ounce) bag frozen hash brown potatoes, thawed
1 (15.25-ounce) can whole kernel corn, undrained
1 (14.75-ounce) can cream-style corn
1 (12-ounce) can evaporated milk
1 medium onion, chopped (about ½ cup)
8 slices bacon, cooked and crumbled
½ teaspoon salt
½ teaspoon Worcestershire sauce
¼ teaspoon pepper

Put all ingredients in crockpot. Cook on low 7–8 hours or on high 4 hours.

December

The *Savior* *is* *Born*

December 1

He himself bore our sins in his body on the tree, so that we might die to sins and live for righteousness; by his wounds you have been healed. For you were like sheep going astray, but now you have returned to the Shepherd and Overseer of your souls.

—1 Peter 2:24–25

How is it that one must die to live? Some might call this an oxymoron, but God calls it the plan of salvation (Luke 9:24). In 1 Corinthians 15:31, the apostle Paul says, "I die daily." So not only are we to die, but we are to die every day. This doesn't mean we have to die a literal death, but we are to dedicate ourselves anew to God each and every day. This constant, daily dedication is essential in keeping focused on our goal (living eternally with Jesus Christ). How, then, do we accept this death and life plan about which God inspired Peter to write? When the purpose of the Cross pierces our hearts by the power of God's Spirit and we accept the fact that God loves us so much that He took the life of His own Son in order to bring us under His care, protection, provision, and guidance, it is at that moment we die to the bondage of sin and are saved from the enemy's schemes. The key word is *accept*. God did everything He needed to do to provide salvation in Jesus for us, but He cannot force us to receive this free gift. It is our choice. If we choose God's way, we die to the deceitfulness of Satan and we live for righteousness under the care of the Shepherd and Overseer of our souls.

Wonderful Shepherd and Overseer: You bore my sin, and I am so grateful. Though I was guilty, You paid the price in my place so I might reap the blessings of eternal life with You. My heart is overwhelmed with joy as I once again die to my fleshly desires and choose to live a righteous life. I accept this marvelous plan of salvation and Your mercy and grace. In Jesus' name, Amen.

SHEPHERD'S PIE II

1 pound ground beef
1 small onion chopped
½ teaspoon salt
¼ teaspoon pepper
1 can tomato soup
1 can corn or green beans, drained
6 potatoes, cooked, mashed with butter, milk, salt, and pepper
8 ounces grated cheddar cheese

Brown meat and drain; add onions and cook until tender. Add salt, pepper, and tomato soup; mix well. Pour into baking dish; top with corn or beans and then mashed potatoes (may use prepared instant mashed potatoes, if desired). Sprinkle cheese on top; bake 30 minutes at 350 degrees.

December 2

For the eyes of the Lord are over the righteous, and his ears are open unto their prayers: but the face of the Lord is against them who do evil.

—1 Peter 3:12, KJV

PETER WAS ONCE a rugged fisherman, but he became a devout follower and disciple of Christ. Over time, he wanted others to serve God with the same zeal for holiness and righteousness as he did. Here, he quotes Psalms 34:15–16, a warning and appeal to all the earth. Peter reminds us that not only does God see everything we do, He also hears us; but he says it is conditional. To have the assurance that God is watching over us and hearing our prayers, we must keep our tongues from evil and our lips from speaking guile (lies and deceit). We must also turn from evil and do good and seek peace and pursue it (Psalm 34:13–14). These six conditions represent both the attitudes of our hearts as well as the actions of our lives.

Some might think this is too hard and a hopeless cause, but it really isn't. God will provide the strength we need to meet these conditions, if our hearts are true, repentant, and eager to receive His grace. Sometimes we may feel as though God is not answering our prayers; it's then that we need to do a soul inventory and see what it is we are keeping onboard that needs to go. Are we holding unforgiveness or using our tongues to gossip or speak evil of others? Are our lips speaking peace and kind and gentle words? Perhaps we've refused to turn from evil and do good? Let's all stop this moment and ask our heavenly Father to forgive us of any unconfessed sin. If we do as Peter implores in this verse, we have the assurance that the eyes of the Lord are on us and His ears attentive to our prayers.

Omnipotent Father: You are everywhere, but Your Word says You turn Your face from us if we are doing evil things. I have not always followed Your righteous ways and I need Your forgiveness. Help me to turn away from speaking, listening, and doing things contrary to Your Word. May I always live my life to honor You. In Jesus' name, Amen.

SAUSAGE BEANS AND RICE CHOWDER (crockpot)

1 (8-ounce) box of rice and black or red bean mix
1 pound ground sausage
2 (14.5-ounce) cans zesty diced tomatoes with mild green chiles

Brown sausage; drain. Put all ingredients in crockpot; cook on low 6–8 hours. Serve on rice; top with sour cream and diced green onions, as desired.

December 3

The end of all things is near. Therefore be clear minded and self-controlled so that you can pray. Above all, love each other deeply, because love covers over a multitude of sins. Offer hospitality to one another without grumbling. Each one should use whatever gift he has received to serve others, faithfully administering God's grace in its various forms.

—1 PETER 4:7–10

CHRIST'S RETURN IS imminent. Even though Peter preached this many years ago, the end is near. This is great news for all who are in Christ and should affect the way we conduct our lives. Each of us is on this earth for a limited amount of time; for some the time is short, while others live to be very old. Whatever the case, we are to live as though Christ could come at any moment or that our own lives could be taken from us. Peter instructs us to pray fervently, love each other deeply, show hospitality and kindness to others, use our spiritual gifts in serving, witness for Christ, and remain loyal to God, even in our trials. Peter's warning to us should be like a two-minute warning at a football game. If the score is tied or close, the players on both teams realize the end is near and something inside each of them happens. They press in and begin to play with urgency, all the while focusing on their goal of winning. This is what God expects of all of us as we live our short time on earth. Everything we do should be done to the best of our God-given ability and strength with our minds set on the goal—winning the prize of eternal life with Jesus.

Soon-Coming King: The two-minute warning has sounded and the end is near! That is good news because You have covered us with the righteousness of Christ. Keep me focused on You by loving others and using my gifts to serve them. In Jesus' name, Amen.

LEMON-BUTTER LINGUINE

8 ounces uncooked linguine
3 tablespoon butter
1 tablespoon lemon juice
1 ½ teaspoon dried basil
½ teaspoon garlic powder
½ teaspoon lemon pepper seasoning
¼ cup grated Parmesan cheese

Cook linguine according to package. In another saucepan combine butter, lemon juice, basil, garlic powder, and lemon pepper; cook and stir until butter melted. Drain linguine; add to butter mixture and toss. Add Parmesan cheese; toss.

December 4

Be self-controlled and alert. Your enemy the devil prowls around like a roaring lion looking for someone to devour. Resist him, standing firm in the faith, because you know that your brothers throughout the world are undergoing the same kind of sufferings.

—1 Peter 5:8–9

P ROBABLY MOST OF us could agree that life can be tough, rough, and even sometimes ruthless and brutal. It seems fair enough that the wicked should endure hard times, but why those who are living sold-out lives for Christ? We have a tendency in life to drop our guard and think the enemy will leave us alone if we're serving as Christ's ambassadors and soldiers. The truth is, when we represent Christ, it carries with it the reality that we are in a constant war. Satan, along with a third of the heavenly hosts, were cast into this world as punishment from God for their rebellion, and that rebellion hasn't ceased. Satan is still at war with God, venting his anger on God's people and trying to scheme ways to discourage and cause us to give up and fall back into complacency and sin. Peter gives us five things we need to do to ensure victory. First, he says to *be self-controlled* (sober) and *alert* (vigilant). Second, we are to *resist* Satan. Third, Peter says to stand *firm in the faith*. Fourth, we are to *keep the faith*. And fifth, we are to be willing to *suffer and endure hardships*. If we have made a profession of faith in Jesus Christ, then with Peter's instructions, we Christians can and will experience spiritual victory over our enemy.

Powerful and all-knowing God: I praise and thank You for blessing me with a plan of attack to use against the enemy and his schemes. You know what the situations are in my life and as I put my trust in You and stand firm in my faith. I acknowledge that You are Lord over every problem and crisis and I believe that You will bring me to victory. In Jesus' name, Amen.

ZUPPA TOSCANA SOUP

1 pound ground Italian sausage
1 ½ teaspoons crushed red pepper flakes
1 large white onion, diced
4 tablespoons bacon pieces
2 teaspoons garlic, minced
10 cups water
10 chicken bouillon cubes
1 pound or 3 large potatoes, sliced
¼ bunch of kale
1 cup heavy cream

Sauté Italian sausage and pepper flakes until done; drain excess grease. Add onion, bacon, and garlic; sauté for 15 minutes or until onions tender. Add water and bouillon and bring to a boil. Add potatoes and cook until done, about 20 minutes. Add kale and cream; thoroughly heat.

December 5

His divine power has given us everything we need for life and godliness through our knowledge of him who called us by his own glory and goodness. Through these he has given us his very great and precious promises, so that through them you may participate in the divine nature and escape the corruption in the world caused by evil desires.

—2 PETER 1:3–4

IT'S THROUGH GOD'S "great and precious promises" that we are able to "participate in the divine nature" and live as transformed people for His sake. That is a wonderful, powerful promise in itself, yet Peter goes on to say we also are able to "escape the corruption in the world caused by evil desires." This is great news for anyone who is struggling to be free of addictions and bondages, knowing they can stand on God's promises and walk in freedom. Everything we need to know and do to experience perfect salvation in Jesus Christ is given to us by the power of God. The Holy Spirit enters our lives at the moment we accept Christ as our Savior. If the believer submits himself to obeying God's Word then the powerful and holy attributes of God will be manifested in his life. A regeneration takes place and we take on the very nature of God. We no longer are to pattern our lives after the corrupt ways of the world caused by evil desires, but we are to conform to the holiness and righteousness of our Lord. In doing so we become spiritually victorious and fruitful.

Heavenly Father: Thank You for Your precious promises that bring me power to live a holy and righteous life. Guide me with Your Holy Spirit to have the mind of Christ in all I say and do. As You lead, I will follow; this is how I prove my love and honor to You. In Jesus' name, Amen.

HAM LOAF

1 pound ground ham
1 ½ pounds ground pork or beef
1 egg
1 cup milk
1 cup bread crumbs
¼ teaspoon salt
½ teaspoon pepper
½ cup packed brown sugar
½ cup water
1 teaspoon mustard
¼ cup white vinegar

Combine ham, pork, egg, milk, breadcrumbs, salt, and pepper; form into loaf; place in baking dish. Put brown sugar, water, mustard, and vinegar in small saucepan on medium high heat; boil 10 minutes; pour over loaf. Bake at 350 degrees until done, about 1 hour, basting occasionally.

December 6

It would have been better for them not to have known the way of righteousness, than to have known it and then to turn their backs on the sacred command that was passed on to them. Of them the proverbs are true: "A dog returns to its vomit," and, "A sow that is washed goes back to her wallowing in the mud."

—2 PETER 2:21–22

THERE ARE TWO important aspects of being saved. The first is salvation, as it relates to the sinner. A sinner experiences new birth by repenting of sin and accepting Christ as Savior. There is nothing a sinner can do to earn the new birth; it is a free gift. The second aspect of salvation relates to the born-again Christian maintaining his salvation. He does so through holiness and bearing good fruit. Although God freely gives us salvation by the sacrifice Jesus paid on the cross, once we receive it we must take care of it. God tells us in Ezekiel 18:24 that none of the righteous things a righteous man does will be remembered if he returns to his sin. "Because of the unfaithfulness he is guilty of and because of the sins he has committed, he will die." Peter tells us that Christians who have lost their salvation are worse off than unbelievers who have never been saved. This should be an alarm clock for sleeping or lukewarm Christians. God definitely promises to do His part to keep us saved to the end, but this does not mean we don't need to do our part. Nearly all God's promises are conditional; they are dependent in part on us for their fulfillment. Certainly, if God does a good work in us (redemption), He will continue that good work forever. The eternality of our redemption is in Him and not in us. Our side of the equation is to remain steadfast in the faith once we receive the free gift of Jesus Christ.

Righteous Father: Thank You for this wake-up call. I no longer want to cruise along in life or take for granted the precious commands I have been taught. I ask You to forgive my sins and renew my relationship with You in Christ Jesus. I am guilty of returning to my previous sins, but no longer want to do that. Help me to make choices that are honorable to Your Word. In Jesus' name, Amen.

TWO-STEP PORK CHOPS

4 boneless pork chops
1 tablespoon oil
1 can cream of mushroom soup
½ can water

In a large skillet, brown pork chops in hot oil on medium-low heat. Add soup and water; cover and simmer until pork no longer pink, about 30 minutes.

December 7

The day of the Lord will come like a thief. The heavens will disappear with a roar; the elements will be destroyed by fire, and the earth and everything in it will be laid bare. Since everything will be destroyed this way, what kind of people ought you to be? You ought to live holy and godly lives.

—2 PETER 3:10–11

NONE OF US like having unexpected company show up at our doors when the house is a mess or if we are not properly groomed. If only we had known they were coming, we would have been ready. The house would have been clean and tidy, and we would have been dressed, ready to entertain. If only we had known! The Bible tells us that is how the Lord will come—unexpected and unannounced. It could be today. What house cleaning do we need to do so we won't be embarrassed and ashamed? What do we have in our homes that might be unholy and ungodly that needs to go? Material possessions will no longer have meaning; they can't be taken on the heavenly trip. And more so, what do we have in our hearts that needs removed? Perhaps we have unforgiveness or unrepentance of sins that have taken up occupancy there. Let's all do some spiritual house-cleaning and have our hearts and homes ready, if the Lord should come today.

Dear Lord: I want to live a holy life that pleases You; please help me when I begin to falter and dabble into all sorts of sinful pleasures and situations. I repent of all my evil ways and desire to clean up my life once and for all. I want my heart and my home to be clean and holy when You come. In Jesus' name, Amen.

TACO CASSEROLE

1 pound ground beef
1 small onion, chopped
1 package taco seasoning mix
1 (8-ounce) can tomato sauce
1 cup water
1 can kidney beans
2 cups small corn chips
10 sliced pitted black olives (optional)
1–2 cups cheddar cheese, grated
Toppings: onions, tomatoes, lettuce, salsa, sour cream

Brown meat in skillet; drain. Add onion; sauté 2 minutes. Add seasoning mix, tomato sauce, and water; bring to boil. Turn to low; simmer 15 minutes, stirring occasionally. Remove from heat; add beans. Pour into baking dish; top with corn chips, black olives, and cheese. Bake uncovered at 350 degrees for 30 minutes. Serve with chopped onions, diced tomatoes, shredded lettuce, salsa, and sour cream, as desired.

December 8

So then, dear friends, since you are looking forward to this, make every effort to be found spotless, blameless and at peace with him.

—2 PETER 3:14

PETER WAS WRITING his second letter to the believers throughout Asia when he reiterated the fact that they must make every effort to live a life of holiness. Knowing his time was short before being martyred for his beliefs, Peter wanted to make sure his fellow Christians were aware that the earth would be destroyed by fire that would consume everyone not living a holy lifestyle. He wanted them to focus more than ever on this because of the imminent return of Christ. Surely, we in the twenty-first century are closer to the Second Coming than in Peter's time (approximately A.D. 65), and yet his message seemed urgent and critical. We too need to be more serious about the message we are proclaiming, not only with our words, but also with our attitudes and actions. Would the things we do and say imitate the characteristics of Jesus or do our lifestyles require quite a bit of change for us to be considered "spotless, blameless, and at peace with him"? Only those who are clothed with the righteousness of Christ and sanctified by the Holy Ghost will be accepted into heaven. There, we who have had our sins pardoned and have made peace with God will dwell forever with Christ.

Heavenly Father: Cleanse me now and purify my sin-sick soul. For my family and friends I pray for Your Holy Spirit to also draw them to seek this same cleansing and forgiveness. Thank You for the wonderful hope of eternal life with Jesus when You come to take us to our heavenly home. May I live spotless, blameless, and at peace until that day. In Jesus' name, Amen.

CREAMY ITALIAN CHICKEN (crockpot)

4 boneless, skinless chicken breast halves
1 envelope Italian salad dressing mix
⅓ cup water
1 (8-ounce) package cream cheese, softened
1 can cream of chicken soup, undiluted
1 (4-ounce) can mushroom pieces, drained
Hot cooked rice or noodles

Place chicken breast halves in crockpot. Combine salad dressing mix and water; pour over chicken. Cover and cook on low for 3 hours. In small mixing bowl, whisk together cream cheese and soup until blended; stir in mushrooms. Pour cream cheese mixture over chicken. Cook 1–3 hours longer or until chicken juices run clear. Serve with rice or hot cooked noodles.

December 9

Ye therefore, beloved, seeing ye know these things before, beware lest ye also, being led away with the error of the wicked, fall from your own steadfastness. But grow in grace, and knowledge of our Lord and Savior Jesus Christ. To him be glory both now and for ever.

—2 PETER 3:17–18, KJV

THROUGHOUT PETER'S TWO letters to the Christians in all of Asia, he encouraged them to live in purity and godliness. One day our Lord will come suddenly and remove the righteous who have surrendered themselves to God and take them to their heavenly home. This was Peter's one final warning to us about the distorted things "unlearned and unstable" people (verse 16) teach about God's Word. If we fail to learn the true ways of God, we will be unstable in our Christian lives and always chase one fad after another—the opposite of growing and maturing in the grace and knowledge of our Lord. This is the same thing Paul said in Ephesians 4:14, where he instructs us to grow into maturity in our Christian lives so we will "no longer be infants, tossed back and forth by the waves, and blown here and there by every wind of teaching and by the cunning and craftiness of men in their deceitful scheming."

To be on guard means to be careful, watchful, shielding, secure, testing, and vigilant. Peter is alerting us to be cautious and on guard so not to lose the security we have with our salvation in Jesus Christ. This is done by nurturing our spirits in the study of God's Word, praying, and obeying the Scriptures. This was the last appeal of Peter before he was put to death. May we all do as he did and live godly lives while encouraging others to do the same. We must be diligent as we watch daily for the return of Christ.

Most Holy Lord: I must be on guard and take more seriously my Christian walk. Though a free gift, it costs me time if I want my position in Jesus to be secure. It is a joy to read Your Word and nurture on what is good for my soul. In Jesus' name, Amen.

COUNTRY STYLE STEAK AND GRAVY

1–2 pounds round or top sirloin steak
1 stick butter
8 ounces fresh sliced mushrooms
1 large sweet onion
1–2 cloves garlic, minced
½ teaspoon pepper
½–1 teaspoon seasoning salt
1 can cream of mushroom soup + 1 can milk

Brown steak in butter over med-high heat. Add remaining ingredients; cover and simmer on medium-low until meat tender, about 1 hour. Serve with mashed potatoes, noodles, or rice.

December 10

This then is the message which we have heard of him, and declare unto you, that God is light, and in him is no darkness at all. If we say that we have fellowship with him, and walk in darkness, we lie, and do not the truth. But if we walk in the light, as he is in the light, we have fellowship one with another, and the blood of Jesus Christ his Son cleanseth us from all sin.

—1 JOHN 1:5–7, KJV

THE BLOOD OF Jesus is one of the most important elements of our Christian doctrine, yet the thought of it to an unbeliever may be offensive. How is something like blood able to purify a soul from sin? When the Holy Spirit draws us to repentance and we yield our hearts to accept Christ as Lord and Savior, it is by faith that we accept the shed blood of Jesus to cleanse us and wash away the dirt and pollution of our sin. When this happens, God sees us as pure and clean, no longer tainted by evil, and we are able to have fellowship with Him. If we claim to have done this and call ourselves Christians and yet continue to disobey God's Word, John says we are living a lie. God is light, and one cannot walk in both darkness (sin) and light (purity). We know light not only reveals that which is hidden in darkness, it also provides energy needed for giving and sustaining life. When the earth was dark and void (Genesis 1), God created light. This light provides physical energy for the development of all life and spiritual direction for our obedience to God's Word. The message Jesus brings to this world will bring light to the darkness of any heart. It is the good news about God's love that is capable of overcoming any obstacle no matter how dark. God is not touched by sin, but He endured the sin of all mankind by allowing His Son to die. From this, we know God has overcome sin, though He is not corrupted by sin. God's light is shed upon the darkness of all sin, allowing all men the opportunity to escape the dark grip of sin for the light of God. This is why and how the blood of Jesus, His Son, purifies us from all sin.

Father: You are the Light of this world. In You, I find the brilliance and luster of Your living Word, Jesus Christ, whom You sent to overcome the darkness of this evil world. Thank You for this marvelous gift. Help me to be a light so others will be drawn to You. In Jesus' name, Amen.

ORANGE CHICKEN (crockpot)

6 chicken breasts (boneless, skinless okay)
½ cup soy sauce
1 can orange soda
1 can mandarin oranges

Put everything in crockpot; cook on low 7–8 hours. Serve with rice.

December 11

And hereby we do know that we know him, if we keep his commandments. He that saith, I know him, and keepeth not his commandments, is a liar, and the truth is not in him. But whoso keepeth his word, in him verily is the love of God perfected: hereby know we that we are in him. He that saith he abideth in him ought himself also so to walk, even as he walked.

—1 JOHN 2:3–6, KJV

THERE IT IS plain and clear for the one who asks, "What and who is a Christian?" God's commands are His instructions, requirements, and divine schedule for our lives. They are not recommendations, ideas, suggestions, proposals, motions, or thoughts! God's commands are who He is coming forth to us in the form of written words from men and women inspired by the Holy Spirit. God's commands are truth and have no errors or inaccuracies. They will never mislead or cause us to stumble in any way. If God said it, then it is the truth and law by which we should base every decision we make. If it is so imperative that we follow God's commands (if we say we know Him and want to avoid the eternal hell after death), how do we know exactly what they are and how to follow them? John, inspired by the Holy Spirit, says we must "walk as Jesus did," if we claim to know God. In John's Gospel, we are told that Jesus is God and was so from the very beginning. John also says the Word is God (John 1:1). So we know that God, Jesus, and the Word are all the same. Therefore, to know what God requires of us and to find out how to walk as Jesus walked, we have to read the Word. The four Gospels, Matthew, Mark, Luke, and John, are great places to study the life of Jesus. When we know and obey God's Word, God's love is truly made complete in us. This is what and who a Christian truly is.

Holy God: Thank You for inspiring great men and women to write the holy Scriptures and commands for my life. Forgive me when I ignore Your instructions and instead do what my flesh desires. Help me to live a sinless life and walk as Jesus did. In Jesus' name, Amen.

BARBECUE BEANS (crockpot)

2 (15-ounce) cans great northern beans
2 (15-ounce) cans black beans
1 (15-ounce) cans butter beans
½–1 cup barbecue sauce
1 cup salsa
½ cup brown sugar
Couple dashes hot sauce (optional)

Combine all ingredients in crockpot. Cook on low 4–6 hours or high 2–3 hours.

December 12

Love not the world, neither the things that are in the world. If any man love the world, the love of the Father is not in him. For all that is in the world, the lust of the flesh, and the lust of the eyes, and the pride of life, is not of the Father, but is of the world.

—1 John 2:15–16, KJV

THE MEDIA HAS warped our minds into thinking that the more material things we have, the happier we'll be. We live in an age of information, videos, commercials, programming, magazines, advertisements, and the like that revolves around materialism and money. This has infiltrated the twenty-first century church in a way that has caused real stewardship to be all but lost. Christians are spending too much time being entertained on their fleshly, lustful cravings than on biblical stewardship. There is a great need for revival in the hearts and souls of all men, something that happens only by fasting and prayer. Without a drastic change in the world's view on this particular issue, things will only get worse. Since we know that nothing is too hard for God, we must all begin to pray that the Holy Spirit will move upon us all, Christians and non-Christians, like never before. Let us each one repent of our own sin and love of the world, change our ways, and follow the ways of the Father before it is too late.

Father: Forgive me for taking my eyes off You and putting them onto the world. Give me wisdom to invest in biblical stewardship and things that matter. I confess to You that my eyes and heart are often distracted by the glitzy stuff that is temporary. Stir my heart to yearn for only You. In Jesus' name, Amen.

THYME FOR A CHICKEN POT ROAST

8 pieces of chicken
1 pound white or red potatoes, halved
1 large red onion, cut into eighths
6–8 cloves garlic, diced
6 sprigs thyme
1 lemon, quartered
¼ cup olive oil
2 tablespoons balsamic vinegar
Salt and pepper to taste

Put chicken, potatoes, onion, garlic, thyme, and lemon in roasting pan. Mix oil and vinegar; pour over chicken and vegetables; toss. Season with salt and pepper. Roast skin side up in 350-degree oven for 1 hour, until chicken thoroughly cooked.

December 13

How great is the love the Father has lavished on us, that we should be called children of God! And that is what we are!

—1 JOHN 3:1

THE DECLINE OF fatherhood has gone rampant throughout the world. Statistics show one out of every two children in America is growing up without a father in his or her home. For some, it's because they have lost their fathers to death. For others, it is because of a divorce or separation, while others may not have even ever known their fathers. Whatever the case, it is a major force behind many of the disturbing problems that plague our society: crime, premature sexuality, out-of-wedlock births, deteriorating educational achievement, suicide, depression, substance abuse, gang activity, bullying, and the list goes on. The biblical earthly father that God created has become a member of the endangered species, as many fathers are often remote, indifferent, unapproachable, and unavailable. But there is hope! God, in His infinite wisdom, knew what the stats would be and orchestrated His divine job description to include being *a Father to the fatherless* (Psalm 68:5; Hosea 14:3). God is our Father and we are His children; there is no greater privilege offered to man as this. From the moment we surrender our hearts to Jesus Christ and believe and receive Him as Savior and Lord, we become God's children. We are heirs of God and joint-heirs with Christ. All God has, He wants to lavish or generously give to us—the ultimate goal being eternal life. *Children of God! And that is what we are!*

Father God: Thank You for the extravagant love You lavish on me. Being Your child is the very center and foundation of my life. Help me remember that I am Your child first; then I am Your servant. I pray for an increased capacity to not only receive Your love, but to show my love for You in return by being obedient to Your Word. May Your love penetrate deep into my heart causing it to fill up, overflow, and spill into every person I meet. In Jesus' name, Amen.

BROCCOLI WITH WALNUT-GARLIC BUTTER

1 (14-ounce) package Green Giant Select frozen 100% broccoli florets
1 tablespoon butter
1 garlic clove, minced
¼ cup walnut pieces

Cook broccoli according to package directions; drain. Cook garlic in butter in saucepan over low heat for 2 minutes. Stir in walnuts; heat through. Pour over broccoli; toss.

December 14

We love him because he first loved us. If a man say, I love God, and hateth his brother, he is a liar: for he that loveth not his brother whom he hath seen, how can he love God whom he hath not seen? And this commandment have we from him, That he who loveth God love his brother also.

—1 John 4:19–21, kjv

WHAT THE WORLD needs now is love, sweet love." Everyone needs love; it permeates and lies at the heart of our biblical message. Love was invented by God. He is the original designer and His name is on the patent. The world has its own view of what love is, but the real meaning can only be found in God's Word. Most of us think about love as an emotion or affectionate feeling, but God's love is so much more. John 3:16 says, "For God so loved the world, that he gave his one and only Son, that whoever believes in him should not perish but have eternal life." That is the depth of God's love and because of it, He allowed His Son to be mercilessly beaten, mocked, and finally crucified in the most mortifying manner imaginable. In spite of the hostility shown to Jesus, God allowed it because of His love for mankind. This is called *agape,* or God's love. First Corinthians 13 is known as the love chapter because here Paul describes what love does rather than what love is. When we love (*agape*) others, we show concern for them, their welfare, and meeting their needs (1 John 3:17). Love is primarily giving and serving. Jesus commands us to love one another as He loved us (John 13:35). If we do not show love and continue to hold unforgiveness and hatred toward those on earth (our Christian brothers) whom we visibly see and withhold our personal resources from them when we know they have needs, God says we cannot love Him whom we cannot see. We must love (*agape*) because God first loved us and prove our love to Him by loving (serving and giving to) others.

Dear God: Thank You for sending Your Son to die on my behalf. Thank You for loving us, Your children, even when we are unlovely. May I do the same toward others and be willing to share my resources and time, helping to meet their needs. Forgive me for withholding agape love from my brother. Change me from within to love as You love. In Jesus' name, Amen.

ORANGE COTTAGE CHEESE SALAD

1 pint cottage cheese, small curd
1 (8-ounce) carton Cool Whip
1 (3-ounce) package orange gelatin
1 small can mandarin oranges, undrained

Mix all ingredients together. Chill and serve.

December 15

This is love for God: to obey his commands. And his commands are not burdensome, for everyone born of God overcomes the world.

—1 John 5:3–4

WHEN JESUS WAS asked which of the commandments was most important, He replied, "Love the Lord your God with all your heart and with all your soul and with all your mind and with all your strength" (Matt. 22:37). This was the same thing Moses told the Israelites in Deuteronomy 6:5. He instructed them to impress God's commandments upon their hearts and on their children's hearts by talking about them when they sit at home, walk along the road, lie down, get up, and to tie them as symbols on their hands, bind them on their foreheads, and write them on the doorframes of their houses and on their gates. This is how important Moses believed God's commandments to be, not only for the Israelites, but for all the world then and now.

We are living in perilous times and if ever the world needed evangelized, it is now. All around us, the Lord and His Word are being dishonored by society. If God's people don't rise up from a bed of sleepy complacency and reflect the holiness of Christ Jesus, our children are in graver danger than we can fathom. God's commands should not be a burden to embrace but a blessing and joyful expression of our love and appreciation for being saved from an eternal place of fire and torment (Mark 9:43). This doesn't mean God's commands are not hard, but it does mean that with Christ they are not only possible but attainable and achievable.

Father God: Thank You for Your commandments that teach me how to live to prove my love for You. Your will for my life is good and not burdensome. It is a privilege and honor to obey the instructions You placed in Your Word. Help me to follow after You all the days of my life. In Jesus' name, Amen.

HAM AND POTATO CASSEROLE

2 pounds hash brown potatoes
1 can cream of mushroom soup
1 stick melted butter
1 ½ cups shredded cheddar cheese
⅓ cup chopped green onions (optional)
2 cups cooked cubed ham
½ teaspoon pepper
2 cups sour cream

Combine all ingredients; mix well. Pour into 9x13-inch casserole dish and bake at 350 degrees for 1 hour.

For crunchy topping: mix 2 cups crushed corn flakes with ½ stick butter and sprinkle over top casserole before baking.

December 16

If anyone comes to you and does not bring this teaching, do not take him into your house or welcome him. Anyone who welcomes him shares in his wicked work.

—2 JOHN 10–11

JOHN WROTE THIS letter to caution us about extending hospitality and friendship to those outside the body of Christ and even to those who call themselves Christians, but continue to commit certain sins (1 Corinthians 5:11). They may have once known the truth and departed from it or distorted it, or it may be those who never knew Christ at all. This warning from John is out of his love for God and those of us who know Christ and want to make Him known. John's message about God's love for us and our love for Him is the basis of our Christianity. As the Holy Spirit helps us to discern right from wrong, we have a choice to accept or reject it. If we love God, we will follow His ways; if we don't follow God, we don't love Him. How then should we as Christians witness to unbelievers if we don't have fellowship with them? There should be a definite difference in our times of Christian fellowship and that of time spent with unbelievers. Fellowship and friendship with non-Christians should only be for the purpose of winning them to Christ, but we must be very careful and pray to not fall into temptation during the process (Matthew 26:41). The newer Christian must be exceptionally cautious when spending time with former friends because it is so easy to be pulled back into old lifestyles and sinful pleasures. The more mature Christian may find it easier to be with those outside of Christ and not yield when tempted. Oftentimes, we don't want to offend the unbeliever so will compromise our own Christian values to not hurt feelings. As Christians, we must continually seek God's counsel and trust His Holy Spirit to guide our evangelistic efforts to win the lost, whether they are friends, neighbors, or those outside our communities (1 Corinthians 5:9–13; James 4:4).

Father: I worship You and exalt You as my Lord and King. Help me to be faithful and strong in my efforts to reach others for Your sake. Guide me with Your Holy Spirit as I separate myself from the world so not to be unequally yoked with unbelievers and yet be able to lead them to a personal relationship with Christ Jesus. In Jesus' name, Amen.

BEANS AND WIENERS (crockpot)

1 package hot dogs, diced
2 cans pork and beans
3 tablespoons barbecue sauce
4 tablespoons brown sugar

Put all ingredients in a crockpot. Cook 6–8 hours on low or 3–4 hours on high.

December 17

I have no greater joy than to hear that my children walk in truth.

—3 John 4, KJV

INNATELY, EVERY PARENT wants the best for their children. We want them to be healthy, happy, and prosper in everything they do. More than this though, as Christian parents, we want our children to know Christ and walk in truth, which is to be obedient to the Word of God. Our child's salvation should bring us more joy than anything else in this world. If a child should sway from the truth and not live according to the Scriptures, our spirits are troubled and we grieve for their souls. Though we want our children to be happy, have good jobs, and enjoy good health, we want even more to see them in love with Jesus and serving Him wholeheartedly. Each day, as we bring our loved ones to God in prayer, our hope and joy is in knowing that they know Christ as their Savior and walk every step with Him.

Father: Thank You for the children and family members You have given me. Thank You for saving their souls and for giving them spiritual prosperity. Today I lift my loved ones to You who don't walk according to Your Word. I pray that the hearts of _____, _____, and _____, would be softened, convicted of their sinful lives, and hunger and thirst after You. May they come to know You personally and walk in the truth of Your Word. Thank You for giving Your life so we might all have our sins forgiven and live eternally with You. In Jesus' name, Amen.

CRANBERRY FRENCH TOAST

1 loaf French bread, cut into 1 ½ inch slices
1 (8-ounce) package cream cheese
¾ cup sugar
¼ cup butter
2 teaspoons vanilla
4 eggs
2 ½ cups milk
1 cup cranberries, crushed

Syrup:

1 cup maple syrup
2 cups cranberries
2 tablespoons sugar

Put bread in buttered 9x13-inch baking dish. Beat together cream cheese, sugar, butter, and vanilla. Add eggs, one at a time, alternating with milk. Pour ½ of mixture over bread. Put 1 cup cranberries over top; pour rest of egg mixture over and refrigerate 6–8 hours or overnight. Bake at 350 degrees for 40–45 minutes. Serve with syrup.

For syrup: boil maple syrup, cranberries, and sugar for 10 minutes.

December 18

Beloved, follow not that which is evil, but that which is good. He that doeth good is of God: but he that doeth evil hath not seen God.

—3 JOHN 11, KJV

THE BELOVED APOSTLE John, in this, his last letter, closes with some of the same exhortations he had in his previous letters. Hospitality, kindness, imitators of good, and love are qualities every believer should have, and God uses John to remind us again of our responsibilities if we call ourselves Christians. In fact, if we don't do these things, John says we have not seen God. Seeing God means to know Him and love Him with a sincere reverence, respect, and desire to obey His divine Word. Though no man has seen God with the visible eye, except for Jesus (John 1:18), once we have come to know Christ as our personal Savior, we see or perceive God in the supernatural and witness His power, attributes, character, glory, and holiness. To see God is to understand the principles of mere Christianity and then accept them by faith. After that, we must nurture our souls and become more familiar with this One whom we have seen with our spiritual eyes and entrusted our lives. This happens by reading God's Word and consuming it into our hearts and souls. Matthew 5:8 says, "Blessed are the pure in heart, for they will see God." To be pure in heart means to have an undivided heart, a heart that is uncontaminated and clean, and a heart that seeks one thing above all else. If we are pure in heart and see or know God, we will prepare ourselves for the day when our one desire will be granted—entering the presence of the King of kings. May the Lord grant us an undivided heart, a heart that longs to see Him this and every day, until that day when we shall see Him face to face.

Dear God: Purify my heart and cleanse me from within so I might be ready to see You in all Your glory. Help me to imitate what is good and turn from the evil of this world. My desire is to know You more and one day see You face to face. In Jesus' name, Amen.

CHRISTMAS ANYTIME FRUIT SALAD

1 (11-ounce) can mandarin oranges, drained
1 small jar maraschino cherries, drained and halved
1 cup flaked coconut (optional)
6 ounces sour cream
1 (8-ounce) can crushed pineapple, drained
2 cups miniature marshmallows
½ cup chopped nuts (optional)

Combine all ingredients; mix well. Refrigerate.

December 19

For certain men whose condemnation was written about long ago have secretly slipped in among you. They are godless men, who change the grace of our God into a license for immorality and deny Jesus Christ our only Sovereign and Lord.

—JUDE 4

CONTRARY TO WHAT many think, there's only one kind of Christian. A person is either saved (John 3:3) and living a Christian life, or he is lost and facing a place of eternal punishment called hell (Matthew 5:29). There's no such thing as a carnal (follower of fleshly or sensual desires) Christian. It is impossible to accept Christ as Savior while simultaneously continuing a lifestyle of rebellion, sin, and unwillingness to walk in obedience to God. Passages such as 1 Corinthians 2:14–3:3 are sometimes mistaken as Paul saying there are two classes of Christians. He is not referring to two classes but is comparing those who are truly born again and those who have a false assurance of salvation. God doesn't give us a two-step salvation where we first accept Him as Savior and then somewhere down the road begin to obey Him. Those who are drawn by the Holy Spirit and truly saved by faith will submit their will to Christ's will when first saved (Acts 2:35). God's grace is often mistaken for permission to sin, as Jude speaks here. A saved individual, if truly saved, will make lifestyle changes and abandon his old ways for a new life in Christ (2 Corinthians 5:17). If there is no change, salvation has not taken place. God does not blink when we sin and ignore our immorality. Many teachers and preachers today speak more of grace and pardon than they do about how to be accepted by God's grace. This is very dangerous both for the teacher and the receiver because the gospel is very clear about the dangers of living the unrepentant sin-filled life. Jude calls these men godless and deniers of Christ's sovereignty and lordship. Let's clean up our lives, abandon the old, and celebrate new life in Christ.

Sovereign Lord: Forgive me for taking Your mercy and grace for granted and following my own carnal desires. I want to walk in true obedience to Your holy Word. Be my strength when I am tempted and weak. When teachers change Your message of grace, help me to discern right from wrong so You are glorified in my words, actions, thoughts, and deeds. In Jesus' name, Amen.

BACON QUESADILLAS

4 (6-inch) flour tortillas
1 cup shredded cheese (your choice)
¼ cup real bacon bits
¼ cup diced thin green onions

Top each tortilla with the 3 ingredients. Fold in half; bake at 400 degrees 8–10 minutes.

December 20

Snatch others from the fire and save them.

—Jude 23

U RGENCY IS THE tone of Jude's letter to fellow Christians about the seriousness of rising up and contending for the faith (Jude 3). The gospel message is the same for us today as it was for those back in Jude's time: Every one of us has sinned and fallen short of the glory of God (Romans 3:23). God sent His Son to save us from going to hell, if we choose His way. There is a real heaven and a real hell where the choices we make determine our destination.

One thing has changed throughout the ages, though—our receptivity of the gospel. The fundamental tenets of our faith concerning heaven, hell, sin, the need for a Savior, and repentance are no longer familiar concepts to our culture. The world does not want to hear what we have to say about these issues because popular philosophy teaches there are no absolutes (nothing is right or wrong and everyone is entitled to believe whatever they desire since there really is nothing that is really true). What are we to do in this no-sin, no-truth world that has removed Jesus as the way and the truth and the life (John 14:6)? It would be easy to give up and say it's gone too far; there is no hope. This attitude would be tragic for those who need to hear the good news that could save them from going to hell. Jude, inspired by God, tells us to snatch, or quickly take hold of those without Christ and rescue them from the fire (eternal judgment). In spite of the conditions of the world, we must continue our purpose for being on earth: worshiping the Lord and witnessing His saving grace to others. There is no other option; the message must go forth. We who are alive in Christ must continue to snatch as many as possible from the fire, while there is still time.

Saving Lord: Remove the blinders from those who don't yet know You and are on the road to an eternal place of torment and fire. Draw them with Your Holy Spirit and soften their hard hearts to receive the salvation message. Help me to effectively witness my faith with them in hope that they will give their hearts to You. In Jesus' name, Amen.

HOLIDAY CHICKEN

6 boneless, skinless chicken breast halves
1 (16-ounce) whole-berry cranberry sauce
1 cup dark French salad dressing
1 package dry onion soup mix

Mix all ingredients except chicken; pour half into greased baking dish. Add chicken; pour over remainder of sauce. Cover with foil; bake at 350 degrees for 20 minutes. Turn chicken and return to oven for 20 more minutes or until chicken done.

December 21

Look, he is coming with the clouds, and every eye will see him, even those who pierced him; and all the peoples of the earth will mourn because of him.

—REVELATION 1:7

THE SECOND COMING of Christ will occur in several stages. First, all Christians will be removed from the earth; this is what is known as the Rapture. It comes from the Latin word *raptare* and the Greek word *harpizo*, both meaning "to be caught up or snatched." Jesus will snatch us out of harm's way before the great persecutions by the Antichrist and seven years of tribulation (1 Thessalonians 4:16–17). John wants to capture our attention by saying, "Look," which means "behold or consider." This one word is a prelude to his announcement of the coming of our Lord, and he wants us to stand at attention and captivate the moment of Jesus' arrival. Not only will the eyes of the righteous and ready see Jesus come, but so will all those who did not prepare for Christ's coming by dying to self and submitting to God's will.

Each of us pierce the side, hands, and feet of Jesus when we sin; only those who have asked for pardon will stand ready to meet Christ when He comes. There will be no time to run and prepare for His coming, if not previously done. We will not be able nor have time to run to church and make things right with God. Nor will there be time to say a quick prayer of repentance. It will be too late; there will be no more time. Whatever state we are in is the state the Lord will find us when He arrives.

Hence, like the five wise virgins of Matthew 25, we must prepare ourselves to meet our Bridegroom, Christ, while it is yet day, lest we find ourselves like the five foolish virgins, unprepared to meet their bridegroom. Remember, the night cometh when it will all be over and "all the peoples of the earth will mourn because of him." May we each one at this very moment take time to search our hearts and call out to this One who will soon come in the clouds and snatch up those who are ready to live with Him for all eternity.

Soon-Coming King: Forgive me for all my sin and unrighteousness. Cleanse my heart and make me pure and ready to meet Jesus when He comes in the clouds. Help me to be looking for You to come with great expectation and excitement in my heart. In Jesus' name, Amen.

BROWN SUGAR HAM (crockpot)

2 cups brown sugar
6–8 pound ham
1 (20-ounce) can crushed pineapple

Spread 1 ½ cups brown sugar on bottom of crockpot. Put flat side of ham down; put rest of brown sugar on top of ham. Pour on pineapple. Cook on low 8 hours.

December 22

You have forgotten your first love. Remember the height from which you have fallen? Repent and do the things you did at first. If you do not repent, I will come to you and remove your lampstand from its place.

—REVELATION 2:4–5

NOTHING IS MORE valuable than our relationship with Christ (Romans 3:22–23). We were created by God to know Him, walk with Him, love Him, enjoy Him, serve Him, and work for Him, but it takes a conscious decision to do so. When we decide to follow Christ, regeneration takes place; the old life is abandoned for a new one (2 Corinthians 5:17). The burdens we carried from a sin-filled life are lifted and our hearts are filled with Jesus-joy. A fervency occurs to know this One who saved our souls from the wrath of sin.

Unfortunately, many lose this passion and begin to fall away from that first love by dabbling in sin. Salvation oftentimes is taken for granted, and God is served merely out of habit. That's what happened to the church of Ephesus, whom John is addressing in this letter. Their love had turned cold, and obedience to Christ had declined.

We too must examine our hearts, making sure we aren't in the same position as the Ephesians. Jesus says to repent and do the things we did at first. Pouring our hearts out to God in prayer, lifting our voices in worship, singing, and expressing our appreciation to Him with grateful hearts will all draw us closer to God. We must saturate our hearts and minds with God's Word, grow in knowledge and grace, and share the gospel with those who don't yet know Him. Jesus says to not repent will result in our lampstand being removed. This is symbolic of the glorious light of the Holy Spirit in a Christian's life. This means we would be removed from the kingdom of God and face eternal judgment. Repentance and obedience will bring victory to overcome and give us "the right to eat from the tree of life, which is in the paradise of God" (Rev. 2:7).

Wonderful Savior: I repent of all my sin and unrighteousness. Forgive me for falling out of love with You by disobeying Your Word and allowing sin to enter my life. I praise and thank You for the gift of life and for bringing me back to my first love. Help me to stay focused, disciplined, and in love with You always. In Jesus' name, Amen.

FIESTA CHICKEN (crockpot)

6 boneless, skinless chicken breasts
1 can fiesta cheese soup
1 can cream of chicken soup

Put everything in crockpot; cook on low 6–8 hours, until chicken done. Serve with noodles or rice.

December 23

I am coming soon. Hold on to what you have, so that no one will take your crown.

—REVELATION 3:11

THE LORD'S WORD to the church of Philadelphia is also a personal message to our own hearts. Christ promises a glorious reward to the victorious believer who fights the good fight to the end (Matthew 24:14). We are told that the end-result of our lives lies within our own hands. Life is a test and if we pass the test by holding firm until the end, we will receive the crown of life (Hebrews 3:14). Though the test is not an easy one, we take great comfort from Jesus' last message in the Bible: "Behold, I am coming soon! My reward is with me, and I will give to everyone according to what he has done" (Rev. 22:12). Faith in Jesus Christ and obedience to the Lord is required throughout our lives. James 1:12 says, "Blessed is the man who perseveres under trial, because when he has stood the test, he will receive the *crown of life* that God has promised to those that love him." This is important because we are required to be faithful even to the point of death to get our crown (Revelation 2:10–11). We must assess our spiritual lives and ask whether or not we voluntarily bear our crosses daily and carry the suffering in our own lives for the gospel's sake not because we have to, but because of our own volition. Are we being faithful and true to God's Word, making every effort to obey His commands? Can Jesus really count on us daily to be His faithful warriors? May the reality of our Lord's return give us strength and power to hold on to what we have in Christ Jesus, knowing our reward is coming soon.

Soon-Coming King: Thank You for the hope that one day we will receive the crown of life. Eternity with You is our reward for persevering, even to the point of suffering and death. Help me to be strong, courageous, and fight the good fight until You come. In Jesus' name, Amen.

HAM AND BEAN SOUP (crockpot)

8 ounces great northern beans
8 cups water
2 (8-ounce) cans tomato sauce
4 potatoes, peeled and diced
2 cloves garlic, finely chopped
1 large onion, diced
4 carrots, peeled and diced
2 cups ham, diced
1 teaspoon pepper
½ teaspoon salt

Soak beans 6–8 hours; drain. Put all ingredients in crockpot; cook on low 8–10 hours.

December 24

I know your deeds, that you are neither cold nor hot. I wish you were either one or the other! So, because you are lukewarm—neither hot nor cold—I am about to spit you out of my mouth.

—Revelation 3:15–16

THESE ARE OUR Lord's words to the church of Laodicea, a group of people who thought they were saved but were not. Like many of us today, they called themselves Christians yet used the precious grace of God as a license to sin. Many years have passed and not much has changed since the fall of man in Genesis. Without a true born-again experience and new life in Christ (2 Corinthians 5:17), man will continue to follow his fleshly desires. Jesus warns us in Matthew 7:21–23, "Not everyone who says to me, 'Lord, Lord,' will enter the kingdom of heaven, but only he who does the will of my Father who is in heaven." Those who choose to be indifferent to God's commands yet say they are Christians do so at their own peril. Many will base professing to be a Christian not on the fact that they have actually repented of their sins and been born again, but rather on such faulty logic as, "I go to church on Sundays" or "I'm a member of a church" or "I was raised in a Christian home" or "I was baptized as a child." Some may even say they once accepted Christ as Savior. It's very difficult to draw a distinction between the church and world. Paul warned Timothy that in the last days the church would be infected with people who "will be lovers of themselves, lovers of money, boastful, proud, abusive, disobedient to their parents, ungrateful, unholy, without love, unforgiving, slanderous, without self-control, brutal, not lovers of the good, treacherous, rash, conceited, lovers of pleasure rather than lovers of God—having a form of godliness but denying its power." Much of what passes for Christianity is nothing more than a whatever-feels-or-sounds-good religion. The fate of the lukewarm is indeed dreadful—that of being vomited out of the mouth of God. Some would caution against reading too much into phrases like this, but one thing to consider is this: how can one be spewed or spit out if they were never in, in the first place? We must repent of our lukewarm spiritual states and come to grips with the truth of God's Word.

Father: You know my deeds and actions; nothing is hidden from Your sight. Search my heart for any unrighteousness. I repent of all my sin and complacency toward serving You and ask for Your help and guidance in living a life that honors Your Word. May I never be found guilty of being lukewarm or complacent in my relationship with You. In Jesus' name, Amen.

Today's recipe found on page 385 PIZZA CASSEROLE

December 25

As many as I love, I rebuke and chasten: be zealous therefore, and repent. Behold, I stand at the door, and knock: if any man hear my voice, and open the door, I will come in to him, and will sup with him, and he with me.

—REVELATION 3:19–20, KJV

OUR HEAVENLY FATHER knows and understands our weaknesses and as a parent reprimands and corrects us out of love. Though Christ is speaking here to the church of Laodicea, He continues to speak to every church today about their lukewarmness, unrighteousness, complacency, and sin. Many churches carry on each week in their ritualistic religious approach to Christianity and have allowed the world and its influence to enter in while Jesus is ushered out. Our Lord continues to knock on the doors of our churches, practically pleading to be invited in.

Each one of us makes up the church and has our own private door on which Jesus knocks. Though the invitation is universal for all, not all will respond the way Christ desires. Some will hear the knock on the door and ignore it, acting like they didn't hear it. Others won't even hear the knock because the sounds of the world are so dominant. Sadly, another group will hear the knock, go to the door, open it, but refuse to let Jesus in.

Couldn't Jesus open the door Himself and enter? After all, He created the door and certainly has that right. God created man with a free will and will not force Himself on anyone; therefore, He will not open the door and enter our hearts without invitation. For those who hear the voice of the Savior and respond to the knock on the door of their hearts by repenting of sin and inviting Christ in, the treasures of glory await them. For it is written: "No eye has seen, no ear has heard, no mind has conceived what God has prepared for those who love him" (1 Cor. 2:9).

Merciful Savior: Stir within me a desire to know and serve You like never before. Come close to my heart and let me dine and fellowship with you. May I remain strong and faithful to Your Word until You return. Continue to knock at the door of my loved ones' hearts. May they be attentive to Your Holy Spirit and allow You to come inside. In Jesus' name, Amen.

MACARONI AND CHEESE (15 minutes)

1 cup uncooked macaroni
3 tablespoons butter
¼ cup milk
4 ounces Velveeta cheese, cubed

Boil noodles 6 minutes; drain. Add butter, milk and cheese; mix and heat until cheese melted.

December 26

Thou art worthy, O Lord, to receive glory and honour and power: for thou hast created all things, and for thy pleasure they are and were created.

—REVELATION 4:11, KJV

ONE DAY THESE words will flow out of the mouths of all creation (Philippians 2:9–11). Man was created to worship God, but when Adam fell into sin in the Garden of Eden, the special relationship between God and man was destroyed. Instead of God reigning in the hearts of man, sin moved in and set up residency. No longer was worshiping God the ultimate reason for man's being; the desires of the flesh took supremacy: "the cravings of sinful man, the lust of his eyes and the boasting of what he has and does - comes not from the Father but from the world" (1 John 2:16). The rest is history. With self on the throne, a place where God should be, the whole course of our existence is out of alignment with God's wonderful plan for our lives. All that we pursue in life to make ourselves happy or please the cravings of our flesh and worldly desires is for naught (Ecclesiastes 1:2–3). We experience a void that nothing nor anyone can fill. Until we make the decision to remove self from the throne of our hearts and replace our will with God's will, true joy will never come. When God is in His rightful place in our lives, there is cause for great rejoicing! Worthy is He to receive glory and honor and power! We will know this with confident assurance and worshiping our Lord will become of utmost importance.

Lord God: I praise You for Your glory, strength, and the splendor of Your holiness. You are the voice over the waters and the God of the thunders. Your voice is powerful and majestic (Psalm 29)! "Holy, holy, holy is the Lord God Almighty, who was, and is, and is to come" (Rev. 4:8). "You are worthy, our Lord and God, to receive glory and honor and power, for you created all things, and by your will they were created and have their being" (Rev. 4:11). I long for the day when I will worship You face to face. In Jesus' name, Amen.

GARLIC TORTELLINI (crockpot)

2 pounds cheese tortellini
2 sticks butter
½ pint whipping cream
1 pint half-and-half
1 small can mushrooms, drained
3 tablespoons minced garlic
¼–½ cup Parmesan cheese

Put everything but cheese in crockpot. Cook on high 2 hours; add cheese; mix and serve.

December 27

Then I heard what sounded like a great multitude, like the roar of rushing waters and like loud peals of thunder, shouting: "Hallelujah! For our Lord God Almighty reigns. Let us rejoice and be glad and give him glory! For the wedding of the Lamb has come, and his bride has made herself ready."

—REVELATION 19:6–7

THIS IS THE fourth and last time *hallelujah* is used in Scripture. John continues sharing his vision from the Lord and, with this *hallelujah,* announces the wedding of the Lamb and His bride. The contrast is clear as the wicked have been destroyed (when the first *hallelujah* was announced) and the bride (the church) is now ready to meet her Groom (the Lamb of God). She is dressed in the finest of linen (fine linen stands for the righteous acts of the saints). The saints have given their lives to this adornment and are prepared for the wedding. Not only have they made Christ their Savior and Lord by repenting of their sin and obeying God's Word, but the fine linen also represents the sufferings, hardships, and trials Christians endured throughout their lives while striving to live for God. It is the fine linen, or righteous acts of the saints (verse 8), that make the wedding of the Lamb of God possible.

The bride is also referred to as the Holy City or a New Jerusalem coming down out of heaven from God. Those who are living for Christ will be part of that Holy City when the Lord returns for His bride, the church. Just as a bride prepares for her wedding day with excitement and anticipation, so must we prepare our hearts and lives for our wedding day with the Lamb of God. We must remain clothed in our finest linen and not soil our garments with the sin and unrighteousness of the world's pleasures. Revelation 16:15 says Christ will "come like a thief! Blessed is he who stays awake and keeps his clothes with him, so that he may not go naked and be shamefully exposed." Our clothing represents our righteous deeds and the preparation we made to meet our Groom. Let's be adorned and ready when the Hallelujah Chorus sings the wedding song: "For the Lord God almighty reigns. Let us rejoice and be glad and give him glory! For the wedding of the Lamb has come, and his bride has made herself ready."

Hallelujah to the Lamb of God! I rejoice and praise You forever. You are the Almighty One, full of glory and grace. Cleanse me from all unrighteousness and help me to stay awake, clothed, and ready to meet my Groom. With joy and anticipation I look forward to that day when I will sing, Hallelujah to the Lamb of God! *In Jesus' name, Amen.*

Today's recipe found on page 385 SPINACH PIE RECIPE

December 28

I saw heaven standing open and there before me was a white horse, whose rider is called Faithful and True. With justice he judges and makes war. His eyes are like blazing fire, and on his head are many crowns. He has a name written on him that no one knows but he himself. He is dressed in a robe dipped in blood, and his name is the Word of God. The armies of heaven were following him, riding on white horses and dressed in fine linen, white and clean. Out of his mouth comes a sharp sword with which to strike down the nations. 'He will rule them with an iron scepter.' He treads the winepress of the fury of the wrath of God Almighty. On his robe and on his thigh he has this name written: KING OF KINGS AND LORD OF LORDS.

—REVELATION 19:11–16

JOHN IS DESCRIBING the glorious entry of the King of kings and Lord of lords. This is Jesus, the faithful and true rider of the white horse. The armies of heaven are saints who have followed Christ. They are in contrast to those in Revelation 13:3 who followed the beast (Satan). The saints also ride white horses and are mentioned because they (the church) share in the Lord's victory. They are mentioned again in verse 19 when the beast, kings of the earth, and their armies gather to make war against the rider on the horse and his army. Revelation 1:5 describes the rider as the ruler of the kings of the earth and this, His second coming, is the final victory for all the generations of faithful followers. His title is on His robe, visible to all. The kings of earth gather against the Lord, but He overpowers them because He is the great and mighty Warrior and Messiah. Out of His mouth is a sharp sword (the Word of God—Hebrews 4:12), and with it He strikes down the wicked nations who blasphemed His name. In the same way, Christ overthrows Satan (Antichrist) with the breath of His mouth and destroys him by the splendor of His coming (2 Thessalonians 2:8). We should not be surprised at Christ using the Word of God to fight His enemies because in actuality, the Word is God (John 1:1) and God is just in everything He does. "He will judge the world in righteousness; he will govern the peoples with justice" (Ps. 9:8). God hates sin, but loves the sinner. He has given us a Savior who has won our battle, but we must choose whether or not to join His army and with Him ride a white horse.

King of kings and Lord of lords: You are the righteous Judge and the ruler of my life. I choose to ride a white horse in Your army and be found in my fine linen when You come. In Jesus' name, Amen.

Today's recipe found on page 385 STRAWBERRY-BANANA CREPES

December 29

He said to me: "It is done. I am the Alpha and the Omega, the Beginning and the End. To him who is thirsty I will give to drink without cost from the spring of the water of life. He who overcomes will inherit all this, and I will be his God and he will be my son. But the cowardly, the unbelieving, the vile, the murderers, the sexually immoral, those who practice magic arts, the idolaters and all liars—their place will be in the fiery lake of burning sulfur. This is the second death."

—REVELATION 21:6–8

GOD SPOKE TO John about the effects sin played on those who faithfully persevered as Christ's overcomers, even while enduring pain, sorrow, and death. *Alpha* is the first letter of the Greek alphabet and *omega* the last. God used that as an example of who He is in our lives. Life begins and ends with God. He is our source of spiritual sustenance and freely gives drink to all who are thirsty and call on His name. God is the righteous Judge and determines who will inherit the blessings of eternal life. God hates sin! His wrath one day will be on all who lived immoral lives while on earth. Many of us, including ministers of the gospel, are timid about mentioning hell, the fiery lake that will be the forever home of the unrighteous. Hell is a real place and we must value the salvation of others enough to not be cowardly in warning them of this horrific site of doom. For the Christian, "to live is Christ, and to die is gain" (Phil. 1:21, KJV). But the cowardly, the unbelieving, the vile, the murderers, the sexually immoral, those who practice magic arts, the idolaters, and all liars—their place will be in the fiery lake of burning sulfur. What a glorious day it will be when we see Jesus. We must be about our Father's business and spread the life-saving news of the gospel to those outside of Christ while there is time.

You, O Lord, are the Alpha and the Omega, my Savior and Friend. I thirst for You and the water of Your spring. Help me to spread the message of salvation with the lost so they might escape the fiery lake of burning sulfur. May I be forever faithful to Your Word. In Jesus' name, Amen.

GLAZED SPIRAL HAM

1 fully cooked spiral ham
⅓ cup mustard
½ cup firmly packed brown sugar
1 (18-ounce) jar pineapple marmalade

Wrap ham in foil; put cut side down in pan. Cook 1 hour at 350 degrees. Combine rest of ingredients; remove foil and spread over ham. Return to oven uncovered; bake at 400 degrees for 10–15 minutes. Watch carefully not to burn.

December 30

Nothing impure will ever enter it, nor will anyone who does what is shameful or deceitful, but only those whose names are written in the Lamb's book of life.

—REVELATION 21:27

THE PLACE WHERE John is speaking is the Holy City, Jerusalem, better known to us as heaven. God created us to live in perfect harmony with Him and one another, but when sin entered the world through Satan's schemes in the Garden of Eden, all that changed. So God perfected His original plan and created a perfect place for all those who come to Him through Jesus. This is heaven and every person whose name is written in the Lamb's Book of Life will go there. They are those who have been born again (saved through the blood of the Lamb, the Lord Jesus Christ) (John 3:3–8). God keeps track of our names and all we have done while on earth, whether good or bad, in the Lamb's Book (Psalm 139:16). Some say it's not an actual book, but God's way of speaking in a language we can understand. Whether or not it is an actual book or just an expressive way to show how important each one of us is to our Lord, it would be fitting to say we are on God's mind all the time. He sees us when we are sleeping and He knows when we're awake. He even knows if we are bad or good. Our thoughts, actions, deeds, ambitions, physical and mental health, intentions, and, most importantly, our spiritual state (Psalm 139:1) are known by God because His eyes are everywhere (Proverbs 15:3). One day, all God's records are going to be revealed when He opens the books (Revelation 20:12) and gives account of what we have done. Only those who have overcome the shame and deceit of the enemy and whose faith in the Lord Jesus has remained pure will hear their names called out by the Lamb (Jesus) to enter this wonderful place called heaven.

Merciful Lord: I look forward to heaven and being with You for all eternity. Forgive me of my impure thoughts and actions. Help me to remain pure in an impure world. In Jesus' name, Amen.

LEMON TERIYAKI GLAZED CHICKEN

½ cup lemon juice
½ cup soy sauce
¼ cup sugar
3 tablespoons brown sugar
2 tablespoons water
4 cloves garlic, minced
¾ teaspoon ground ginger
4 boneless, skinless chicken breasts, cut in strips

Put all ingredients, except chicken, in skillet; Cook on medium heat 3–4 minutes. Add chicken; simmer 30 minutes or until thoroughly cooked. Serve with rice or angel hair pasta.

December 31

Behold, I am coming soon! Blessed is he who keeps the words of the prophecy in this book.

—Revelation 22:7

Behold, I am coming soon! My reward is with me, and I will give to everyone according to what he has done.

—Revelation 22:12

"Yes, I am coming soon." Amen. Come, Lord Jesus. The grace of the Lord Jesus be with God's people. Amen.

—Revelation 22:20b-21

I N THE BEGINNING, God..." That's when it all began, back in Genesis 1:1. Now at the end of His holy, inspired manuscript, God ascribes Jesus, the living flesh of Himself, to consummate His strategic plan of bringing an end to His marvelous creation. Throughout the book of Revelation, John gives a glimpse of what was revealed to him as the end unfolds and the new begins. The main thing God wants us to know in this last prophetic Book is that Jesus is coming soon and we are to be ready. Jesus asks us to behold, or stop, watch, and listen, to what He is saying. He warns that only if we keep the commands of His Book will we receive eternal blessings and enter heaven.

God inspired Revelation to reveal the glory of His Son and call us to live godly, obedient lives in light of His soon return. Three times in this last chapter, Jesus proclaims with exuberance that He is coming quickly. This is relevant to a mother who tells a child to hurry and clean his room because his father is coming home but the child ignores the warning. She tells him again with a little more firmness. The child has to decide whether to obey or again ignore his mother's command, thus risking the consequence. Soon the child hears his father say, "I'm home." John the Revelator was able to respond to Jesus with, "Amen. Come, Lord Jesus" because he had responded to warnings throughout God's Word and his heart was pure. We all have a serious decision to make—follow after God or ignore the warning and spend eternity in hell. Will we respond as John did and enthusiastically and joyfully welcome Christ as He comes, or will we be ashamed because of lifestyles and sinful choices we have made and not want to see Him? Behold! Jesus is coming soon! We must be ready!

Soon-Coming King: My heart rejoices, knowing You are on Your way. You are my reward, and I wait with anticipation for You to come. I pray for my friends and family and those who don't know You as Savior. May Your Holy Spirit draw them to repentance before it's too late. Come, Lord Jesus! Come! I ask this all in the wonderful and holy name of Jesus, Amen and Amen!

Today's recipe is found on page 386 CHICKEN OR TURKEY SALAD CROISSANTS

LASAGNA (with no-boil noodles)

1 pound ground beef or sausage (or mixture of both)
2 tablespoons olive oil (canola okay)
1 medium onion, chopped (optional)
3 cloves garlic, minced (optional)
2 (24-ounce) jars favorite spaghetti sauce
1 (9-ounce) box Barilla no-boil lasagna noodles
2 eggs
1 (15-ounce) container ricotta cheese
4 cups (16 ounces) shredded mozzarella cheese (divided)
½ cup Parmesan cheese

Brown meat in pan; drain. Add oil, onion, and garlic; sauté 5 minutes. Add spaghetti sauce; cover and simmer 30 minutes. In bowl, combine eggs, ricotta, 2 cups mozzarella, and Parmesan cheese. Spread 1 cup sauce on bottom of greased baking dish. Layer 4 uncooked lasagna sheets, ⅓ of ricotta mix, and ⅓ of sauce. Layer another 4 uncooked sheets, ½ of ricotta mix, and ½ of sauce. Repeat process. Layer 4 sheets, remaining sauce, and mozzarella. Cover with foil; bake 1 hour at 350 degrees. Uncover; return to oven until cheese melted. Let sit 15 minutes before cutting.

SEAFOOD ANGEL HAIR PASTA

12 ounces uncooked angel hair pasta
½ pound uncooked medium shrimp, peeled/deveined
2 garlic cloves, minced
2 tablespoons butter
2 tablespoons olive oil
8 Roma tomatoes, chopped
½ cup water + one chicken bouillon cube, dissolved
1 teaspoon sugar
½ teaspoon salt
⅛ teaspoon pepper
1 (8-ounce) package crabmeat, chopped

Cook pasta according to package; drain. In large pan with oil and butter, sauté shrimp until pink (about 5 minutes); remove and keep warm. In same pan, combine tomatoes, broth, sugar, salt, and pepper; bring to boil. Reduce heat; simmer 5 minutes. Mix in crabmeat, shrimp, and pasta.

SWEET AND SOUR CHICKEN

3–4 boneless, skinless chicken breasts, diced
3 tablespoons teriyaki sauce
1 tablespoon soy sauce
1 teaspoon ginger
1 teaspoon garlic powder
Dash salt and pepper
Vegetable oil
3 eggs
¾ cup flour

Sauce:

1 can pineapple tidbits
¾ cup sugar
½ cup vinegar
2 tablespoons soy sauce
3 tablespoons ketchup
2 tablespoons cornstarch in ¼ cup water
1 green pepper
Small tomatoes, quartered or halved

Marinate chicken in teriyaki, soy sauce, ginger, garlic powder, salt, and pepper for 1–3 hours. Mix together eggs and flour. Remove chicken from marinade; dip in flour mixture. Fry until brown over medium-high heat in pan with oil covering bottom. Remove to paper towels; keep warm.

Sauce: drain juice from pineapple; add water to make 1 cup. Put juice, sugar, vinegar, soy sauce, ketchup, and water with cornstarch in saucepan over medium heat. Bring to boil; simmer until thick, stirring often. Add peppers, tomatoes, and chicken just before serving; heat and serve.

FRIED RICE

2 cups long-grain rice (jasmine best)
8 strips bacon, diced
4 tablespoons canola oil
1 medium sweet onion, diced
1 (10-ounce) package frozen peas
1 small can sliced water chestnuts, diced
5 eggs, lightly beaten
4–6 green onions, diced
1 green pepper, diced
2–3 tablespoons soy sauce

Cook rice according to package. Cook bacon in large pan; drain half the grease. Add oil, onion, peas, and water chestnuts; cook until onions are tender. Move vegetables to side of pan; add eggs and cook until done. Add green onions, green pepper, rice, and soy sauce. Thoroughly heat.

ITALIAN CHICKEN (crockpot)

3 pounds boneless, skinless chicken breasts
1 (8-ounce) bottle Italian dressing
1 jar banana peppers or pepperoncinis, undrained
Barbecue sauce, rolls, rice (your choice)

Put all but barbecue sauce in crockpot; cook on low 6–8 hours. Shred; serve on rolls or with rice.

CORN AND SHRIMP CHOWDER

1 pound frozen corn
4 slices bacon, diced
8 scallions (green onions), diced (separate white from green pieces)
2 medium baking potatoes, peeled and diced into ½-inch cubes
2 tablespoons flour
3 cups milk
1 teaspoon seafood seasoning
½ teaspoon dried thyme leaves
2 cups water
1 pound large peeled and deveined shrimp
Coarse salt and ground pepper

In large saucepan, cook bacon until crisp; remove to paper towels. Add scallion whites and potatoes to pan; cook, stirring until scallions softened. Add flour and cook, stirring, about 1 minute. Add milk, seasonings, and water. Bring to boil; reduce to simmer and cook, stirring occasionally, until potatoes are tender. Add corn, shrimp, and scallion greens. Cook until shrimp opaque, 2–3 minutes. Season chowder with salt and pepper. Serve topped with bacon.

GUMBO

1 pound boneless, skinless chicken breasts, diced and/or
1 pound shrimp, peeled and deveined
1 pound andouille or smoked sausage, sliced thin
1 package Zatarain's gumbo base
1 (15-ounce) can diced tomatoes, with juice
½ cup chopped green bell pepper
½ cup chopped celery
½ cup chopped onion
9 cups water
Rice, prepared according to package directions

Put all ingredients (except rice) in large saucepan; bring to boil on high. Reduce to low; cover and simmer 1 hour, stirring occasionally. Serve in bowls over scoop of rice. Season as desired with salt, pepper, hot sauce, or File seasoning.

JAMBALAYA

4 tablespoons canola or vegetable oil
1 medium onion, diced
1 each medium green and yellow pepper, chopped

3 cups water
1 (14.5-ounce) can diced tomatoes, undrained
1 package Zatarain's original jambalaya mix
1 pound boneless, skinless chicken breasts, diced and/or
1 pound large shrimp, peeled and deveined
1 pound smoked sausage, sliced ¼-inch thick
½ cup sliced green onions (optional)

Put oil in large pan. Sauté onion and pepper just until soft. Stir in water, tomatoes, package of Zatarain's, chicken, shrimp, and sausage; bring to boil. Reduce heat to low; cover and simmer 25 minutes or until rice tender. Sprinkle with green onions before serving.

PIZZA CASSEROLE

1 pound ground beef
3 cups shredded mozzarella cheese
2 cups cooked elbow macaroni
1 (14-ounce) jar favorite spaghetti sauce
1 cup grated Parmesan cheese
4 ounces thin pepperoni, chopped

Brown meat; drain. Mix with one cup mozzarella cheese and rest of ingredients. Spread in lightly greased 13x9-inch baking dish; top with remaining cheese. Bake at 350 degrees for 30 minutes.

SPINACH PIE

1 pound frozen spinach
¼ cup chopped onion
4 eggs
1 teaspoon lemon juice
¼ teaspoon salt
¼ teaspoon pepper
1 (8-ounce) package cream cheese
¾ cup milk
8 ounces grated cheddar cheese
1 unbaked pie shell

Cook spinach until done; drain *very* well by squeezing out as much moisture as possible. Add all other ingredients and only half the cheddar cheese. Pour into pie shell. Bake at 375 degrees for 25 minutes. Sprinkle rest of cheese over top; bake until cheese melted, about 5 minutes.

STRAWBERRY-BANANA CREPES (for breakfast, brunch, or dessert)
Crepes:

3 large eggs, beaten
1 ½ cups milk
⅔ cup flour
Pinch of salt
4 tablespoons melted butter
Vegetable spray for pan

In blender, combine all ingredients and pulse 10 seconds. Heat a sprayed, 8–9-inch, nonstick pan over medium-high heat. When hot, add ¼ cup batter; swirl to spread evenly. Cook 30 seconds or until dry on top; flip and cook other side. Cool on racks; stack with waxed paper between crepes.

Filling:

8 ounces cream cheese, softened
¼ cup granulated sugar
1 teaspoon vanilla

Blend well cream cheese, sugar, and vanilla. Spread about 2 tablespoons onto each crepe; fold in thirds. Place in 13x9-inch baking dish. Bake at 350 degrees for 15–20 minutes, until thoroughly heated. May also individually heat filled crepe on plate in microwave for 10–15 seconds. Then add topping.

Topping:

1 (10-ounce) package frozen strawberries, thawed
1 tablespoon cornstarch
1 banana, sliced
Whipped cream

Drain strawberries, reserving liquid. Add enough water to liquid to measure 1 ½ cups; pour into small pan. Add cornstarch and bring to boil over medium heat, stirring constantly. Boil for 1 minute; stir in fruit. Serve over crepes. Top with whipped cream, as desired.

CHICKEN OR TURKEY SALAD CROISSANTS

2 cups cooked chicken or turkey, diced
⅔ cup mayonnaise
⅓ cup celery, diced
¼ cup cranraisins or diced grapes
¼ cup slivered almonds
1 tablespoon lemon juice
1 teaspoon mustard
⅛ teaspoon pepper
4–6 lettuce leaves
4–6 croissant rolls, split in half horizontally

Combine first 8 ingredients in bowl; mix well. Cover and refrigerate 2–3 hours. Place lettuce leaf on bottom half of each croissant; top with about ⅓ cup chicken mixture. Add top of croissant.

INDEX OF RECIPES

ABOUT THE AUTHOR

A NATIVE OF PITTSBURGH, Pennsylvania, Karen Doughty is the second of four daughters and one son, born to LeRoy and Kathryn Gordon. She is also the wife of Reverend Fred Doughty, mother of four wonderful daughters, Debbie, Tami, Cindy, and Tracy, and grandmother to eight precious grandchildren. Karen is a retired registered nurse, though she continues to delve into the medical arena as much as possible. Her passion and zeal to serve God by loving and serving His children is the wind beneath her wings. Writing poetry and short compositions since age eight, Karen gives all the glory to God for allowing her the privilege of writing for Him. She and her husband, Fred, have been in full-time ministry for thirty years, serving as Christian school administrators, program directors for Teen Challenge, and church pastors. They presently pastor Glad Tidings Assembly of God in East Peoria, Illinois.

ABOUT THE ARTIST

CAROL KAMP, BORN and raised in northern Illinois, is the third of four children born to Dennis and Patsy Schwanke. She met her husband, Michael Kamp, in Belgium, where they were both in full-time ministry. Their three incredible children, David, Kimberly, and Stephen, were very young when Michael went home to be with Jesus following a lengthy illness. As a single mom, Carol uses her bachelor of fine arts degree in art to help provide for her family. She praises her Lord for the many ways He has continued to supply the family's needs throughout the ensuing years. Carol and her children currently live in Grand Rapids, Michigan, where they faithfully serve in their church home, Grand Rapids First.

CONTACT THE AUTHOR

www.Foodforthehungrysoul.wordpress.com